Baseball's Great Experiment

BASEBALL'S
GREAT EXPERIMENT

Jackie Robinson
and His Legacy

JULES TYGIEL

OXFORD UNIVERSITY PRESS
New York   Oxford

Oxford University Press

Oxford   New York   Toronto
Delhi   Bombay   Calcutta   Madras   Karachi
Kuala Lumpur   Singapore   Hong Kong   Tokyo
Nairobi   Dar es Salaam   Cape Town
Melbourne   Auckland   Madrid

and associated companies in
Berlin   Ibadan

First published in 1983 by Oxford University Press, Inc.,
200 Madison Avenue, New York, New York 10016

First published as a paperback in 1984 by Vintage Books,
a Division of Random House, Inc.

First issued as an Oxford University Press paperback, 1993

Oxford is a registered trademark of Oxford University Press

Library of Congress Cataloging in Publication Data
Tygiel, Jules.
   Baseball's Great Experiment.
   Includes index.
   1. Robinson, Jackie, 1919-1972.   2. Baseball
players—United States—Biography.   3. Baseball—
United States—History.   4. United States—Race
relations.   I. Title.
GV865.R6T93 1993   796.357′092′4 [B]   83-4042
ISBN 0-19-503300-0
ISBN 0-19-507826-8 (PBK.)

10 9 8 7 6 5 4 3 2 1

Printed in the United States of America

For my parents,
Gustave and Rose Tygiel,
who gave me a love
of history, books, and baseball—
although not necessarily in that order.

Acknowledgments

This book had its origins in 1973 on the second floor of the University Research Library at the University of California, Los Angeles. I routinely retreated to the URL to study for my doctoral examinations in American history. One afternoon, an unknown individual fortuitously failed to reshelve the 1947 volume of *Time* magazine and left it at my workplace. Naturally, "1947" triggered thoughts of Jackie Robinson. That year Robinson had broken baseball's color barrier and although I was not born until 1949, I had been nurtured on his legend. My father, wanting his son to have a proper Brooklyn upbringing, introduced me to Ebbets Field when I was seven. The Dodgers had obliged with three home runs in the bottom of the ninth inning to beat the Phillies and I became an instant convert. The Dodger exodus in 1958 ranks among the traumatic events of my youth. My favorite player was Jackie Robinson, largely because he integrated baseball. I was not sure what this meant, but I knew it was wonderful. I thus learned my first lesson in politics and race relations.

Now, seventeen years later, I had followed the Dodgers to Los Angeles, where my past unexpectedly confronted me. Thoughts of my impending examinations dissolved as I thumbed through the hefty volume of *Time* searching for reports on Robinson. He finally appeared quite suddenly and dramatically on the cover of the September 22 issue—his bold, handsome, smiling face floating in a sea of white baseballs. A lengthy article depicted the struggles and successes of his rookie season. After savoring my discovery I turned to subsequent issues to see the response to the Robinson story. The letters from readers included a mixture of praise and opprobrium, reflecting the intense feelings aroused by baseball's "great experiment."

As I read the *Time* article and the letters that it had inspired, I realized that the Robinson story, easily the most familiar chapter of American sports history, had never really been told in its entirety. Most accounts, primarily biographies and autobiographies, had stressed events and personalities, but had failed to place them into a social or historical context. Robinson's entry into organized baseball had created a national drama, emotionally involving millions of Americans, both black and white. His triumph had ramifications that transcended the realm of sports, influencing public attitudes and facilitating the spread of the ideology of the civil rights movement. In addition, Robinson had only launched the integration process. Surely the heritage of decades of discrimination and ostracism had not disappeared overnight. What were the experiences of the scores of other black players who had entered baseball in the 1940s and 1950s? What had happened to the now forgotten Negro Leagues in the aftermath of desegregation? I also realized that numerous sources of information—black newspapers, personal papers and scrapbooks, and the recollections of many of the more obscure pioneers of baseball integration—had been largely ignored. Here, it seemed, lay a tale still worthy of re-examination and re-telling.

I dared not, however, mention my idea to too many people. Baseball is not the stuff upon which successful careers in history are normally made. I chose a more conventional topic (the nineteenth-century San Francisco working class) for my doctoral dissertation and spent the next four years compiling the "definitive" tome on that subject. But Jackie Robinson continued to haunt me. I read everything published about him and began to lay the groundwork for a future study. Occasionally, I even dared mention my project to a colleague. To my surprise, the typical reaction was not disdain, but enthusiasm and excitement. Everyone, it seemed, had his or her own particular memory of Robinson and the Brooklyn Dodgers. Finally, in 1978, my dissertation completed and a tenure-track job acquired, I emerged from the closet. Despite my affection for the San Francisco working class, my passion for the Brooklyn Dodgers was greater. I began work in earnest on a history of baseball integration.

Over the next five years I incurred numerous debts of gratitude in the course of preparing this manuscript. The first, naturally belongs to that unnamed soul who failed to reshelve the 1947 volume of *Time*. I also thank the National Endowment for the Humanities for a 1980 Summer Stipend which enabled me to travel throughout the country visiting archives and interviewing baseball figures. Without the support of the Endowment this volume would be far poorer. The Affirmative Action Faculty Development Fund at San Francisco State provided me with released time for work on this book. My colleagues in the history department at San Francisco State offered only encouragement for my somewhat unorthodox project.

I am indebted to several archives and collections and the people who run them. Bill Marshall of the University of Kentucky proved a gracious host and guide to the A. B. "Happy" Chandler Papers. Marshall's excellent interviews dealing with Chandler's baseball career are an invaluable resource. Clifford Kachline at the library of the Baseball Hall of Fame at Cooperstown, New York, was also helpful. Al Campanis, vice-president of the Los Angeles Dodgers, provided important assistance in locating former players. I would particularly like to thank Rachel Robinson for her cooperation and for allowing me to look through the Robinson family scrapbooks at the Jackie Robinson Foundation in Brooklyn. The interlibrary loan service at San Francisco State must have worked overtime to process my incessant requests.

The willingness of the following people to share their memories has greatly enriched this book: Walter Alston, Ernie Banks, Gene Benson, Joe Black, Joe Bostic, Stanley "Frenchy" Bordagaray, Bobby Bragan, Roy Campanella, Al Campanis, Lorenzo "Piper" Davis, Charles Feeney, Robert Fishel, Elijah "Pumpsie" Green, Chuck Harmon, Elston Howard, Monte Irvin, Sam Jethroe, Connie Johnson, John "Spider" Jorgenson, Sam Lacy, Brooks Lawrence, Lee MacPhail, Don Newcombe, Harold "Pee Wee" Reese, Rachel Robinson, Albert "Red" Schoendienst, Dick Sisler, Clyde Sukeforth, Tom Tatum, Bob Thurman, Quincy Trouppe, Bill Veeck, John Welaj, Artie Wilson, and Bill White.

I would also like to pay tribute to two reporters upon whose work I relied heavily. Wendell Smith of the Pittsburgh *Courier* and Sam Lacy of the Baltimore *Afro-American* are writers whose work remains largely unknown to the white sports fan. But they rank among the best sportswriters of their generation for their considerable reportorial talents as well as the major roles that they played in the integration of American sports. I am deeply in their debt. One other source proved invaluable to the completion of this study. At various times in the course of this manuscript I take issue with the editorial policies of the *Sporting News*. Its coverage of the integration story, however, was thorough and impartial. Indeed, if not for the extent and high quality of the *Sporting News* reporting, a book of this nature could not have been written.

Numerous people provided encouragement and assistance at various stages of this book's development. Al-Tony Gilmore, Dick Crepeau, and Stephan Thernstrom gave support and reassurance that this was a worthwhile undertaking. Marc Onigman was a welcome and helpful companion during my week at Cooperstown. Robert Barnett interviewed Artie Wilson for me and, with his wife Liz, provided free room and board during the 1980 Negro League Reunion. Judy Powers served at various times during the course of this project as morale booster, moral supporter, researcher, critic, and always, as a good friend. I would also like to thank my fellow owners in the Pacific Ghost League for adding a new dimension to my enjoyment of baseball during the past two seasons.

Many people assisted in the preparation of the manuscript. Martha Hjelle performed yeoman service as a typist. Eric Solomon, John Tricamo, and Glenn Becker critiqued an earlier draft. My father and sister, Gustave and Martha Tygiel, and my uncle, Sidney Rosen, all offered helpful suggestions. Kathy Antrim and Sheldon Meyer performed the editorial chores at Oxford University Press. I also would like to thank Susan Rabiner, the news editor of my high school newspaper. (I, of course, was the sports editor.) Steve Appel and Naomi Weinstein contributed the three section titles at a breakfast brainstorming session.

Above all, I express unending gratitude to four friends who lavished careful attention and harsh criticism on earlier drafts of this book. Peter Carroll, Michael Kazin, Mike Pincus, and Richard Zitrin devoted considerable time and energies to making this a better book. I only hope that I have fulfilled their expectations.

Finally, I wish to thank my wife, Luise Custer. She didn't type, critique, or edit. Luise has simply made my world a far better place to live in.

Writing this book has allowed me to combine my vocation as a historian and my avocation as a baseball fanatic. I spent joyous months poring over sports pages, reading microfilmed back issues of the *Sporting News*, and devouring baseball biographies. The high point of my research occurred in the summer of 1980 when I toured the nation, living the baseball fan's version of the American Dream. I traveled through thirty-three states, interviewing the heroes of my youth while stopping at different major league ball parks to attend games. I dined at press clubs and sat in a press box. I entered the sacred confines of locker rooms and dugouts. One incident summed up my feelings about the trip and the entire experience of writing and researching this book. At Shea Stadium, after conducting pre-game interviews, I found myself seated in the stands next to a nine- or ten-year-old boy, reminiscent of another boy at Ebbets Field more than two decades earlier. He noticed my tape recorder. "You gonna tape the game?" he asked. I explained that I had just been on the field speaking with some of the Met coaches. "You were down on the field?" he asked with envy. I nodded. "You talked to the coaches?" I nodded again. "Let me hear it," he implored. I turned on the tape of Dick Sisler reminiscing about the 1947 season, but after a few seconds the boy yelled, "Stop! That's enough!" He looked at me, his eyes filled with admiration. "Boy," he exclaimed, "you are *so* lucky." The little boy in me smiled; he was *so* right.

San Francisco, California   J.T.
February 1983

Contents

I
EARLY INNINGS

1

The Crucible
of White Hot Competition

*This is a particularly good year to cam-
paign against the evils of bigotry, prejudice, and race hatred because we have
witnessed the defeat of enemies who
tried to found a mastery of the world
upon such cruel and fallacious policy.*

New York Times editorial,
February 17, 1946

I

Opening Day of the baseball season was always a festive occasion in Jersey
City on the banks of the Passaic River. Each year Mayor Frank Hague
closed the schools and required all city employees to purchase tickets, guaranteeing a sellout for the hometown Giants of the International League.
The Giants sold 52,000 tickets to Roosevelt Stadium, double the ball park
capacity. For those who could not be squeezed into the arena, Mayor Hague
staged an annual pre-game jamboree. Jersey City students regaled the crowd
outside the stadium with exhibitions of running, jumping, and acrobatics,
while two bands provided musical entertainment.

On April 18, 1946, the air crackled with a special electricity. Hague's
extravaganza marked the start of the first minor league baseball season
since the end of the war. But this did not fully account for the added tension and excitement. Nor could it explain why people from nearby New
York City had burrowed through the Hudson Tubes for the event. Others
had arrived from Philadelphia, Baltimore, and even greater distances to
witness this contest. Most striking was the large number of blacks in the
crowd, many undoubtedly attending a minor league baseball game for the
first time. In the small area reserved for reporters chaotic conditions prevailed. "The press box was as crowded as the subway during rush hours,"
wrote one of its denizens in the Montreal *Gazette*. On the field photog-

raphers "seemed to be under everybody's feet."[1] The focus of their attention was a handsome, broad-shouldered athlete in the uniform of the visiting Montreal Royals. When he batted in the first inning, he would be the
first black man in the twentieth century to play in organized baseball.
Jackie Robinson was about to shatter the color barrier.

"This in a way is another Emancipation Day for the Negro race," wrote
sportswriter Baz O'Meara of Montreal's *Daily Star,* "a day that Abraham
Lincoln would like." Wendell Smith, the black sportswriter of the Pittsburgh
Courier who had recommended Robinson to Brooklyn Dodger President
Branch Rickey, reported, "Everyone sensed the significance of the occasion
as Robinson . . . marched with the Montreal team to deep centerfield for
the raising of the Stars and Stripes and the 'Star-Spangled Banner.' We sang
lustily and freely for this was a great day." And in the playing area, the
black ballplayer partook in the ceremonies "with a lump in my throat and
my heart beating rapidly, my stomach feeling as if it were full of feverish
fireflies with claws on their feet."[2]

Six months had passed since Rickey had surprised the nation by signing
Robinson to play for the Dodgers' top farm club. It had been a period of
intense speculation about the wisdom of Rickey's action. Many predicted
that the effort to integrate baseball would prove abortive, undermined by
opposition from players and fans, or by Robinson's own inadequacies as a
ballplayer. Renowned as a collegiate football and track star, Robinson had
played only one season in professional baseball with the Kansas City Monarchs of the Negro National League. Upon Robinson's husky, inexperienced
shoulders rested the fate of desegregation in baseball.

Robinson's experiences in spring training had dampened optimism. Compelled to endure the indignities of the Jim Crow South, barred by racism
from many ball parks, and plagued by a sore arm, Robinson had performed
poorly in exhibition games. One reporter suggested that had he been white,
the Royals would have dropped him immediately. Other experts also expressed grave doubts. Jim Semler, owner of the New York Black Yankees,
commented before the opener, "The pace in the IL is very fast. . . . I doubt
that Robinson will hit the kind of pitching they'll be dishing up to him."
And Negro League veteran Willie Wells predicted, "It's going to take him
a couple of months to get used to International League pitching."[3]

Robinson, the second Montreal batter, waited anxiously as "Boss" Hague
threw out the first ball and lead-off hitter Marvin Rackley advanced to the
plate. Rackley, a speedy center fielder from South Carolina, grounded out to
the shortstop. Robinson then strode to the batter's box, his pigeon-toed gait
enhancing the image of nervousness. His thick neck and tightly muscled

frame seemed more appropriate to his earlier gridiron exploits than to the baseball diamond.

Many had speculated about the crowd reaction. Smith watched anxiously from the press box to see "whether the fears which had been so often expressed were real or imagined." In the stands Jackie's wife, Rachel, wandered through the aisles, too nervous to remain in her seat. "You worry more when you are not participating than when you are participating," she later explained, "so I carried the anxiety for Jack." Standing at home plate, Jackie Robinson avoided looking at the spectators, "for fear I would see only Negroes applauding—that the white fans would be sitting stony-faced or yelling epithets." The capacity crowd responded with a polite, if unenthusiastic welcome.[4]

Robinson's knees felt rubbery; his palms, he recalled, seemed "too moist to grip the bat."[5] Warren Sandell, a promising young left-hander opposed him on the mound. For five pitches Robinson did not swing and the count ran to three and two. On the next pitch, Robinson hit a bouncing ball to the shortstop who easily retired him at first base. Robinson returned to the dugout accompanied by another round of applause. He had broken the ice.

Neither side scored in the first inning. In the second the Royals tallied twice on a prodigious home run by right fielder Red Durrett. Robinson returned to the plate in the third inning. Sandell had walked the first batter and surrendered a single to the second. With two men on base and nobody out, the Giants expected Robinson, already acknowledged as a master bunter, to sacrifice. Sandell threw a letter-high fastball, a difficult pitch to lay down. But Robinson did not bunt. The crowd heard "an explosive crack as bat and ball met and the ball glistened brilliantly in the afternoon sun as it went hurtling high and far over the left field fence," 330 feet away. In his second at-bat in the International League, Robinson had hit a three-run home run.[6]

Robinson trotted around the bases with a broad smile on his face. As he rounded third, Manager Clay Hopper, the Mississippian who reportedly had begged Rickey not to put Robinson on his team, gave him a pat on the back. "That's the way to hit 'em, Jackie," exclaimed Rackley in his southern drawl. All of the players in the dugout rose to greet him, and John Wright, a black pitcher recruited to room with Robinson, laughed in delight. In the crowded press box Wendell Smith turned to Joe Bostic of the *People's Voice* and the two black reporters "laughed and smiled. . . . Our hearts beat just a little faster and the thrill ran through us like champagne bubbles." Most of their white colleagues seemed equally pleased, though one swore softly, according to one account, and "there were some very long faces in the gathering" as well.[7]

The black second baseman's day had just begun. In the fifth inning, with the score 6-0, Robinson faced Giant relief pitcher Phil Oates. The "dark dasher," as Canadian sportswriters came to call Robinson, bunted expertly and outraced the throw "with something to spare." During spring training Rickey had urged the fleet-footed Robinson "to run those bases like lightning. . . . Worry the daylights out of the pitchers."[8] Robinson faked a start for second base on the first pitch. On the next he took off, easily stealing the base. Robinson danced off second in the unnerving style that would become his trademark. Tom Tatum, the Montreal batter, hit a ground ball to third. Robinson stepped backwards, but as the Jersey City fielder released the ball, he broke for third, narrowly beating the return throw.

Robinson had stolen second base and bluffed his way to third. He now determined to steal home to complete the cycle. He took a long lead, prompting Oates to throw to third to hold him on base. On the pitch he started toward home plate, only to stop halfway and dash back. The crowd, viewing the Robinson magic for the first time, roared. On the second pitch Robinson accelerated again, causing Oates to halt his pitching motion in mid-delivery. Oates had balked and the umpire waved Robinson in to score. Earlier Robinson had struck with power; now he had engineered a run with speed. The spectators, delighted with the daring display of baserunning, went wild, screaming, laughing, and stamping their feet. Blacks and whites, Royal fans and Giant fans, baseball buffs and those there to witness history, all joined in the ensuing pandemonium.[9]

One flaw marred Robinson's performance. "By manner of proving that he was only human after all," according to one reporter, Robinson scarred his debut with a fielding error in the bottom of the inning. Acting as middleman in a double play, he unleashed an errant throw that allowed the Giants to score their only run. Otherwise, Robinson affirmed his reputation as an exceptional fielder.[10]

In the seventh inning Robinson triggered yet another Royal rally. He singled sharply to right field, promptly stole another base, and scored on a triple by Johnny Jorgenson. Before the inning had ended two more runs crossed the plate to increase the Royal lead to 10-1. In the eighth frame Robinson again bunted safely, his fourth hit in the contest. Although he did not steal any bases, he scrambled from first to third on an infield hit. Once again he unveiled his act, dashing back and forth along the baseline as the pitcher wound up. Hub Andrews, the third Jersey City pitcher, coped with this tactic no better than his predecessor. Andrews balked and for the second time in the game umpires awarded Robinson home plate. According to a true baseball aficionado, this established "some kind of a record for an opening day game."[11]

The Royals won the game 14-1. Montreal pitcher Barney DeForge threw an effortless eight-hitter and Durrett clubbed two home runs. But, as the Pittsburgh *Courier's* front page headline gleefully announced, JACKIE "STOLE THE SHOW." "He did everything but help the ushers seat the crowd," crowed Bostic. In five trips to the plate Robinson made four hits, including a three-run home run, scored four times, and drove in three runs. He also stole two bases and scored twice by provoking the pitcher to balk. "Eloquent as they were, the cold figures of the box score do not tell the whole story," indicated the New York *Times* reporter in an assessment that proved prophetic of Robinson's baseball career. "He looked as well as acted the part of a real baseball player."[12]

"This would have been a big day for any man," reported the *Times*, "but under the special circumstances, it was a tremendous feat." Joe Bostic, who accompanied his story in the *People's Voice* with a minute-by-minute account of Robinson's feats in the game, waxed lyrical. "Baseball took up the cudgel for Democracy," wrote Bostic, "and an unassuming, but superlative Negro boy ascended the heights of excellence to prove the rightness of the experiment. And prove it in the only correct crucible for such an experiment—the crucible of white hot competition."[13]

II

Two years before Robinson's triumphant Jersey City debut, Swedish sociologist Gunnar Myrdal had published *An American Dilemma*, a landmark study of the race problem in the United States. In it he concluded that "Not since Reconstruction has there been more reason to anticipate fundamental changes in race relations, changes which will involve a development towards the American ideal." Few people shared Myrdal's optimistic viewpoint. His work described a society characterized by northern indifference and ignorance of the plight of blacks and a firmly entrenched system of racial segregation in the South, where Jim Crow laws forbade whites and blacks from attending the same schools, riding in the same sections of trains and buses, receiving treatment in the same hospitals, or competing in the same athletic contests. In Birmingham, Alabama, it was "unlawful for a Negro and white to play together or in the company with each other" at dominoes and checkers. These legal restrictions did not adequately reflect the extent of southern discrimination and segregation. As historian C. Vann Woodward noted, "There is more Jim Crow practiced in the South than there are Jim Crow laws on the books." Common custom required separate toilets and water fountains, entrances and exits, and waiting rooms and ticket windows. "Segregation is becoming so complete," Myrdal discovered, "that the white Southerner practically never sees a Negro except as his servant and in other standardized and formalized caste situations."[14]

Southern whites reinforced this Jim Crow regime with a combination of economic and physical coercion. Blacks who challenged racial conventions jeopardized not only their meager sources of income but their lives as well. Although violence had abated since the early decades of the century when mobs lynched scores of blacks each year, the threat of physical reprisals remained a vivid reality. In 1946 at least nine blacks were lynched; and authorities rescued twenty-one others from angry mobs. Any attempt to dismantle the southern caste system, warned Richmond *Times-Dispatch* editor Virginius Dabney, would result in an "interracial explosion" which would leave "hundreds, if not thousands, killed."[15]

The prevalence of these conditions renders all the more remarkable Myrdal's prescient conclusion. Myrdal argued that during the 1930s, the "popular theory behind race prejudice" in the United States had gradually "decayed." The inclusion of blacks in New Deal relief programs, several Supreme Court decisions limiting discriminatory practices, and a growing exasperation with the South among northern liberals reflected this shift in attitudes. In addition, the growing militancy among blacks, whom, said Myrdal, "America can never more regard . . . as a patient, submissive minority" would contribute to the forthcoming transition. This process would be accelerated by "the world conflict and America's exposed position as the defender of the American faith." Ultimately, Myrdal argued, the opponents of segregation would discover "a powerful tool in the caste struggle" in the "American Creed"—"the glorious American ideals of democracy, liberty, and equality to which America is pledged not only by its political constitution, but also by the severe devotion of its citizens."[16]

In the immediate aftermath of World War II the forces that Myrdal predicted would transform the nation's racial practices merged most dramatically and visibly on the playing fields of America. For a half-century, baseball had provided a mirror image of American society; blacks and whites played in two realms, separate and unequal. Within weeks of the end of the war, Brooklyn Dodger president Branch Rickey announced his intention to end Jim Crow in baseball by signing Jackie Robinson. In the eyes of some contemporary observers, Rickey had initiated a "great" or "noble experiment." Could an American institution, steeped in the traditions of racial prejudice and populated by large numbers of southerners, accept the introduction of blacks peacefully? During the following decade and a half the desegregation experiment unfolded in baseball's major and minor leagues. In a formal sense, it was completed in 1959 when the Boston Red Sox, the last all-white major league team, inserted young Elijah "Pumpsie" Green into a game as a pinch runner. In reality, the experiment continues into the present.

The integration of baseball represented both a symbol of imminent racial challenge and a direct agent of social change. Jackie Robinson's campaign against the color line in 1946–47 captured the imagination of millions of Americans who had previously ignored the nation's racial dilemma. For civil rights advocates the baseball experience offered a model of peaceful transition through militant confrontation, economic pressure, and moral suasion. In 1954 when the Supreme Court declared school segregation illegal in the famous *Brown* v. *Board of Education* decision, a majority of major league teams already fielded black athletes. Minor league integration had penetrated not only the North and West, but most of the South as well. For more than a decade before the explosion of sit-ins and freedom rides of the 1960s challenged Jim Crow accommodations in the Deep South, black athletes had desegregated playing facilities, restaurants, and hotels in many areas of the country.

Baseball was one of the first institutions in modern society to accept blacks on a relatively equal basis. The "noble experiment" thus reflects more than a saga of sport. It offers an opportunity to analyze the integration process in American life. An examination of the forces that led to Robinson's hiring, the reaction among both blacks and whites, the institutional response of the baseball establishment, and the resulting decline of the Jim Crow leagues reveals much about the United States in the 1940s and 1950s. The halting and incomplete nature of baseball's achievement notwithstanding, few other businesses have equalled its performance. The dynamics of interracial relationships among players, coaches, and managers provide rare insights into what occurs when nonwhites are introduced into a previously segregated industry.

"The American Negro problem is a problem in the heart of America," wrote Myrdal. "It is there that interracial tension has its focus. It is there that the decisive struggle goes on."[17] From 1945 to 1959 Jackie Robinson and the blacks who followed him into baseball appealed to the "heart of America." In the process they contributed to the transformation of the national consciousness and helped to usher in a new, if still troubled, age of race relations in the United States.

2

Twilight Ere the Noon

O, minds of fleetful thought!
O, dead who lived too soon!
What pity thou wert brought
To twilight ere the noon!

David Malarcher,
Negro League third baseman,
"Sunset Before Dawn"[1]

I

The "muse" of baseball has a profound sense of irony. In the early twentieth century the mythmakers of our national pastime decreed that the game had its "immaculate conception" on the playing fields of Cooperstown, New York, created fully grown from the head of Civil War hero Abner Doubleday. Evidence that baseball had evolved from earlier contests played by the English and that Doubleday probably never participated in the game did not deter baseball's early historians. They anointed Cooperstown the sport's official birthplace and in later decades the Official Baseball Hall of Fame and Museum was established there.

Baseball, of course, was not born in Cooperstown, but Bud Fowler, one of its unwanted children, was.[2] Fowler was the first black professional baseball player. Born in the small Upstate New York village in 1854, the son of free itinerant workers, Fowler debuted as a paid athlete in 1872. For the next quarter-century he attempted to earn his living in the emerging patchwork of the baseball industry. His experiences provide a microcosm of the black baseball odyssey in the nineteenth century—a composite of grudging acceptance, discrimination, physical abuse, and, ultimately, exclusion.

Fowler made his first professional appearance as the only black player on a team in New Castle, Pennsylvania. For a dozen years he pursued his career in obscurity, leaving no records of his travels. In 1884 he surfaced on a club in Stillwater, Minnesota, in the Northwestern League. *Sporting Life*, a national journal, described him as a pitcher, catcher, and left fielder.

Fowler excelled, however, as a second baseman. By some accounts, he ranked among the best in the game at that position. He began the 1885 season with Keokuk in the Western League, but when that team disbanded, he found difficulty catching on with another. "He is one of the best general players in the country," reported *Sporting Life*, "and if he had a white face would be playing with the best of them." Fowler spent a month in idleness before signing briefly with a club in Pueblo, Colorado. "The poor fellow's skin is against him," *Sporting Life* again sympathized at the year's end. "With his splendid abilities he would long ago have been on some good club had his color been white instead of black. Those who know say there is no better second baseman in the country."

During the next two years, baseball's color line briefly relaxed and as many as twenty blacks were accepted into organized leagues. Fowler batted .309 for Topeka, Kansas, in the Western League in 1886 and the following season signed with the Binghamton, New York, club in the International League.

Fowler's sojourn in the International League typified the hardships of black players of his era. One white who admitted to being "prejudiced against playing on a team with a colored player" painted a dismal portrait of Fowler's ordeal, "Fowler used to play second base with the lower part of his legs encased in wooden guards. He knew that about every player that came down to second base on a steal had it in for him and would, if possible, throw spikes into him. . . . About half the pitchers try their best to hit these colored players." Some baseball historians credit the invention of shin guards to either Fowler or Frank Grant, another black second baseman, for protection against white base runners. By one probably erroneous, but revealing account, white players developed the feet-first slide, "to give the frequent spiking of the darky an appearance of accident."

Despite these difficulties, Fowler performed admirably in the International League. In thirty games in 1887 he batted .350 and stole thirty bases. On July 14, however, league directors, citing complaints that "many of the best players in the League were anxious to leave on account of the colored element," announced that no further contracts with blacks would be accepted. While this ruling was not supposed to affect those blacks already in the League, Binghamton immediately released Fowler and forbade him from signing with any other club in the circuit.

Fowler's release ended his career with white teams. He subsequently joined the Cuban Giants, the leading black team of the era, and for the next decade depended upon the uncertain fortunes of barnstorming for his livelihood. In 1895 Fowler wrote, "It was hard picking for a colored player

this year. I didn't pick up a living; I just existed." He then added, "If I had
not been quite so black, I might have caught on as a Spaniard or something
of that kind. . . . My skin is against me."

To solve his problem, Fowler attempted to combine baseball with
broader forms of entertainment. In 1895 he formed the Page Fence Giants,
described by Robert Peterson as a "judicious blend of showmanship and
good baseball." Before every game the team would ride bicycles through
the streets of whatever town they were appearing in to drum up interest in
the game. In 1899 Fowler assembled a team called the All-American Black
Tourists. The Tourists would arrive in full-dress suits with black pants and
white vests, swallowtail coats, opera hats, and silk umbrellas. After parading
through the community, Fowler would announce "By request of any club,
we will play the game in these suits." No record exists of Fowler's exploits
after the turn of the century.

Fowler's career encapsulized the black baseball experience in America.
Though observers widely acknowledged his talents, he found difficulty gaining acceptance in organized baseball. Torment and uncertainty marred the
years he spent on white teams. Relegated to black barnstorming squads,
Fowler pondered passing as Spanish and injected clowning into his athletic
contests. As the first black professional baseball player, Bud Fowler proved
a living allegory of the history of blacks in baseball in the age of Jim Crow.

II

The formative years of baseball as a professional sport coincided with the
emergence of segregation as an American institution. Ironically, the provision of separate public facilities for blacks and whites had originated not in
the South, where it appeared in its most pronounced form, but in the states
of the antebellum North. Even in the immediate aftermath of the Civil War,
although some southern institutions—most notably schools—immediately became segregated, most areas of southern life remained free from the dictates
of Jim Crow legislation. Although custom and practice in many communities
established the separation of the races, the ironbound barriers characteristic
of the twentieth century had yet to coalesce. Nonetheless, in the years after
Reconstruction the South emerged as an increasingly segregated society and
the North, on the other hand, displayed a growing disinterest in the race
issue.[3]

Concurrent developments in the sphere of baseball reflected the chaotic
throes of the nation's industrial awakening. Like other businesses, the professional game consisted of an unstable array of local enterprise searching
for an organized structure. Teams assembled and disbanded; leagues

formed and fractured. Entrepreneurs, often drawn from the ranks of the players themselves, sought to provide permanence in this fledgling industry. Although the rules of play had taken on a relatively uniform shape, the regulations governing the administration of the game varied from league to league. With regard to the admission of blacks in baseball there was no clear-cut policy, merely a patchwork of local decisions. Like the nation as a whole, baseball entered a period of experimentation regarding the role of black Americans.[4]

The National Association of Base Ball Players, the first organized league, established the initial barrier against blacks in 1867. Founded before the Civil War, the association lasted for nine years without confronting the race question. At its annual convention in 1867, however, "to keep out of the convention the discussion of any subject having a political bearing," the governing committee recommended that all teams "which may be composed of one or more colored persons" be denied admission to the league. When the National Association of Base Ball Players disbanded several years later, the written code of segregation perished with it. Most of its successors relied upon the doctrine of common consent and coercion, the "gentleman's agreement," to exclude nonwhite players.[5]

The National League, baseball's foremost entity in the nineteenth century, utilized this device from its inception in 1876. Though the dominant force in the professional arena, the National League lacked the authority to impose its will upon other circuits. Even those leagues which in 1879 joined the major league in the National Agreement—a pact to respect player contracts and decline from raiding the rosters of other teams—were not required to adopt the racial policies of the major coalition. As a result, Bud Fowler and a handful of others found themselves accepted, if not exactly welcomed, within the boundaries of organized baseball.

Little information exists about blacks who played on white teams in the 1870s, but during the following decade as many as two dozen blacks played on teams in the professional leagues. A pair of brothers, Moses and Weldy Walker, achieved brief major league status in 1884 with Toledo of the American Association. Moses, a catcher, compiled a .263 batting average in forty-two games; Weldy batted .222 in only five appearances. Others registered impressive records and drew accolades for their minor league performances. George Stovey won thirty-three games for Newark in the International League in 1887 and many called Frank Grant one of the finest second basemen of the age.[6]

By the start of the 1887 season prospects for continued integration seemed promising. The League of Colored Base Ball Clubs was recognized as a minor league under the National Agreement, a development that ultimately might have produced a vehicle for black advancement to the majors. In addition, claimed Sol White, the black athlete who in 1906 wrote the first history of black baseball, twenty blacks played in otherwise all-white professional leagues that summer.[7]

But 1887 marked the apex of black acceptance. Events of that year began the precipitous slide that would lead to total exclusion. The League of Colored Base Ball Clubs folded before a single game had been played, and a growing crescendo of complaints by whites about their black teammates and opponents revealed the vulnerability of interracial competition. In June two members of the Syracuse Stars of the International League refused to pose for a team picture with star black pitcher Bob Higgins. A month later, in response to player protests, International League officials issued their edict banning future contracts with blacks.[8]

Within days of the International League announcement, an incident involving George Stovey of Newark further spotlighted the deteriorating position of blacks. Newark scheduled Stovey, the team's top pitcher, to work an exhibition game against the Chicago White Stockings of the National League on July 19. On the day of the game Stovey "complained of sickness" and withdrew. Stovey, however, was not ill. Cap Anson, the manager and star player of the Chicago team, had threatened to withdraw his squad from the contest if Stovey pitched. Four years earlier Anson had presented a similar threat to the Toledo club which included Moses Fleetwood Walker. In that instance the Toledo manager had not only defied Anson's challenge but had deliberately inserted Walker into a game he had not been slated to play. In 1887 Anson prevailed.[9]

Anson was one of the prime architects of baseball's Jim Crow policies, yet the reasons for his intense hostility toward blacks remains unknown. Born in the North, Anson resided in Chicago and played primarily in cities above the Mason-Dixon line. Indeed, few of Anson's contemporaries in baseball were southerners. Most, however, apparently shared his racial attitudes. The athletes' antipathy for interracial competition reflected the "culture of professionalism" emerging in late nineteenth-century America. Practitioners of different occupations formed organizations, established standards of performance, and erected barriers to entry. Racial and ethnic exclusion often constituted a means to define the distinctiveness of a given profession. Membership restrictions appeared in trade unions and professional societies alike.[10] As baseball attempted to establish itself on a secure institutional footing, players and owners defined the attributes of a respectable, professional game. The national pastime would be, at least in the public eye, wholesome, free from the taint of gamblers, and the exclusive preserve of white athletes. By designating some people as unworthy of admission, the baseball community elevated the status of those accepted into the profession. To further distinguish themselves from lesser pretenders, major and minor leagues affiliated under the National Agreement referred to their operations as "organized baseball" and labelled all others "outlaw" leagues.

Blacks in the International League immediately felt the effects of these developments during the 1887 season. Newark dropped Stovey, though the club retained the less talented Walker. Binghamton released Bud Fowler. The following year the Buffalo Bison players refused to pose for a team picture if it included Frank Grant, their leading hitter. Bob Higgins, again the object of teammate abuse, threatened to leave the Syracuse club in mid-season. Neither player returned to the International League in 1889. This left Fleet Walker as the only black in the circuit. Walker batted only .216 and Newark did not invite him to return. Fifty-seven years would pass before another black performed in the International League.[11]

After 1887 the situation rapidly worsened for the few black athletes remaining in organized baseball. An article in the *Sporting News* in 1889 reported, "Race prejudice exists in professional baseball ranks to a marked degree, and the unfortunate son of Africa who makes his living as a member of a team of white professionals has a rocky road to travel." The writer described how whites not only "cut him in a social way" but attempted to " 'job him' out of the business" by giving him wrong instructions and adding errors to his fielding statistics. Pitcher Tony Mullane said of Fleet Walker, "He was the best catcher I ever worked with, but I disliked a Negro and whenever I had to pitch to him I used anything I wanted without looking at his signals."[12]

By the close of the decade only a sprinkling of blacks remained in the minor leagues. In 1889 the Middle States League invited two black clubs, the Gorhams of New York and the Cuban Giants, to enter competition. The following season, the league, renamed the Eastern Interstate League, again included the Giants, as well as a Harrisburg team, which fielded at least two black players. When Harrisburg deserted the circuit to join the Atlantic Association, the league disbanded. Harrisburg retained its two black players and the following year added several others, causing sportswriters to nickname them the "Polka Dots." The Cuban Giants meanwhile enlisted in the Connecticut State League, which also proved short-lived. When the league collapsed in the middle of the 1891 season, the Giants returned to barnstorming, their career in organized baseball at an end.

By 1892 the color line was firmly in place. Despite brief appearances by Sol White and several others in 1895, teams in organized baseball fielded no blacks. Nor did they invite black clubs to join any major or minor leagues. The Acme Colored Giants, who played half a season in Pennsyl-

vania's Iron and Oil League in 1898, represent the sole exception. After winning only eight out of forty-nine games, the team mercifully disbanded. At
the dawn of the twentieth century, the national pastime was a Jim Crow
enterprise.[13]

III

As Bud Fowler, Moses Fleetwood Walker, and others struggled to gain a
toehold in organized baseball, many black athletes formed their own teams.
Competing against both black and white opponents, these squads became
an important component of black culture in the age of Jim Crow. Hidden
or at least obscured from the view of whites, black baseball, like black
newspapers, black universities, and black music, offered a vital, vibrant,
and often innovative alternative for those excluded from the dominant
American institutions.

The first all-black team to achieve widespread recognition was the
Cuban Giants. Formed among the waiters of the Argyle Hotel in Babylon,
New York, in 1885, the Giants toured the East. The players chattered gib-
berish on the field to pass as Cubans and competed against the local semi-pro
teams and even major league clubs. Sometimes, sporting different names,
the club played in the minor leagues. But for the most part the Cuban
Giants held no regular affiliation. They simply played whomever would ante
up money for a game.[14]

The Cuban Giants represented the prototypical black baseball team.
They introduced to the game not only its itinerant style but its most popular name—black baseball abounded with Giants. In 1900 the five major professional teams included the Cuban Giants, the Cuban X Giants, and the
Columbia Giants (formerly the Page Fence Giants). Six years later there
were nine professional teams within a 100-mile radius of Philadelphia, all
dubbed the Giants. For the next two decades these teams led a precarious
existence; unaligned with any league, they traveled the nation in search
of competition.[15]

Even after 1920, when Negro Leagues formed, barnstorming remained
the basis for black baseball. Only a third of a season's 200 games counted
in the league standings. To survive, a team had to travel. Most major franchises were located in the North, but 90 percent of the nation's black
population lived in the South. As author Art Rust has pointed out, black
baseball "was an empire built on poverty. How could poor black fans
finance a wealthy league?"[16]

The level of competition varied considerably from day to day (or, in
some cases, from afternoon to evening). The barnstorming teams might play

other black professional teams, or local semi-pro teams, both black and white, or squads composed of major league all-stars. Before the mid-1920s, when Baseball Commissioner Landis forbade the practice, black teams occasionally pitted themselves against major league clubs. Games were therefore contested under inconsistent conditions. "We would bat from one background in Griffith Stadium on Sunday, then Monday night we were down here in Rocky Mount batting against just any background, sometimes an open field," says Hall of Famer Buck Leonard.[17] Teams rarely kept statistics of these encounters; even if they had been recorded the variable level of competition would have rendered them meaningless.

In an age in which the vast majority of Americans rarely traveled great distances, black ballplayers constituted rare men of the world, or at least of the hemisphere. They journeyed not only throughout the United States but also to Central America and the Caribbean. For most, baseball was a year-round occupation. During the winter months they headed for Cuba, Venezuela, or Mexico where they were welcome additions to the local athletic scene. Caribbean baseball fanatics lavished money, favors, and adulation upon the black North Americans. Beginning in 1939, wealthy Mexican and Venezuelan team owners determined to improve their summer leagues by luring the top stars in the Negro Leagues. The higher salaries and superior treatment attracted many black ballplayers. When shortstop Willie Wells left the Newark Eagles in 1939 to play for Vera Cruz in the Mexican League, he eloquently explained his decision in a letter to Pittsburgh *Courier* sportswriter Wendell Smith:

> Not only do I get more money playing here, but I live like a king.
> . . . I am not faced with the racial problem of Mexico. . . . We live
> in the best hotels, we eat in the best restaurants, and can go anyplace
> we care to. . . . We don't enjoy such privileges in the U.S. . . . I
> didn't quit Newark and join some other team in the United States. I
> quit and left the country. . . . I've found freedom and democracy
> here, something I never found in the United States. . . . Here, in
> Mexico I am a man.[18]

Many recollections of former Negro Leaguers involve their extensive travels. "The schedule was a rugged one," wrote Roy Campanella. "Rarely were we in the same city two days in a row. Mostly we played by day and traveled by night; sometimes we played both day and night and usually in two different cities." The need to maximize their appearance led black teams to introduce night baseball. In April 1930, the Kansas City Monarchs became the first team to play under the lights. By 1935 when the Cincinnati Reds premiered night contests in the major leagues, black clubs were experienced practitioners of baseball after dark. Barnstorming squads carried their own portable lighting systems. "We'd install them on poles all around the outfield," Buck Leonard told John Holway. "A big dynamo out there in the outfield generated the electricity for the lights. After the game was over, we would take down the poles." Thus equipped, black teams could wage an afternoon battle in one community and dash to a nearby town for a night game in another. Nor were three games in a day unusual.[19]

In the days of Rube Foster's Chicago American Giants of the 1910s and 1920s, players traveled comfortably in Pullman cars. But the more common means of transportation was the team bus, or two or more automobiles barely large enough to hold the men and their equipment. During his days with the Baltimore Elite Giants, Campanella recalls, "We traveled in a big bus and many's the time we never bothered to take off our uniforms going from one place to another. . . . The bus was our home, dressing room, dining room, and hotel."[20]

Touring with the Homestead Grays in 1932, Quincy Trouppe lacked even that luxury. In his autobiography Trouppe recalls traveling in two or three seven-passenger cars, "We were so cramped for space that we organized a kind of Notre Dame shift and when the ride became too uncomfortable someone would give the signal and we'd all change positions on the rear and jumper seats. We had little time to waste on the road, so it was a rare treat when the cars would stop at times to let us stretch out and exercise for a few minutes."[21]

Road accommodations usually ranged from the uncomfortable to the uninhabitable. Most major hotels were segregated, requiring blacks to stay at Jim Crow outposts. In areas where no facilities for blacks existed, ballplayers slept on the bus or outside at the ball park. The average black hotel of that era also lacked appeal. "We were continually under attack by bedbugs," says Trouppe. "My roomie and I stayed up many nights in Pittsburgh fighting these monsters until early morning." When critics censured Negro League owners for the poor housing, Effa Manley, the co-owner of the Newark Eagles, responded that they lacked the power to rectify the situation. "Until Congress makes statutory changes on race prejudice in hotels," she argued, "I'm afraid there's little we can do to better such accommodations."[22]

The itinerancy, inconsistent competition, and the need to attract crowds encouraged another controversial element of black baseball—the injection of showboating and clowning into the competition. As early as the 1880s black barnstorming teams became known for their stunts and comedy. During the World War I era, the Lincoln Giants entertained the fans with a pre-game exhibition of juggling, pantomime, hidden-ball tricks, and acrobatic displays of throwing and catching the ball. The Indianapolis Clowns of the 1930s and 1940s, though a serious competitive team in the Negro American League, presented two of their players, Goose Tatum and King Tut, as a comic duo.[23]

Most of the antics took place before the game. In the actual competition the athletes played seriously, particularly against top black clubs or major leaguers. Players only showboated against distinctly inferior semi-pro competition; even then it more often involved the flaunting of superior skills rather than comedic antics. The master showman of black baseball during the 1930s and 1940s was pitcher Leroy "Satchel" Paige. Yet Paige's stunts—guaranteeing that he would strike out the first six or nine men to face him or calling in his outfielders—defied inferior hitters. Paige never attempted these feats against tougher competitors.

At best, teams and players that engaged in clowning simply catered to the whims of the fans and added entertainment; at worst, when their performances took on the stereotyped images of a minstrel show or the Stepin Fetchit characteristics portrayed in the movies, the clowns perpetuated the negative perceptions of blacks common among whites, and cast doubts about the quality of the athletes. Most veterans of the Negro Leagues deeply resent the notion that buffoonery, and not baseball, was their occupation. "If you was black, you was a clown. Because in the movies, the only time you saw a black man he was a comedian or a butler," observes Piper Davis, former player-manager of the Birmingham Black Barons. "But didn't nobody clown in our league but the Indianapolis Clowns. We played baseball."[24]

Black baseball developed stars of indisputable talent as well as a distinctive style of play. In the early decades of the twentieth century black athletes compared favorably with their white counterparts. Observers nicknamed Cuban pitcher Jose Mendez the "Black Matty" after Christy Mathewson. Contemporaries hailed John Henry Lloyd as the "Black Wagner," after Honus Wagner, the Pittsburgh Pirate infielder generally acknowledged as the best at that position. One sportswriter commented that Babe Ruth was the greatest player in organized baseball, but "in all baseball, organized or unorganized, the answer would have to be a colored man named John Henry Lloyd."[25] The list of black players talented enough not only to play in the major leagues but to have excelled is a long one. In the 1920s and 1930s outfielders like Oscar Charleston and James "Cool Papa" Bell, infielders Willie Wells and Ray Dandridge, and the incomparable Pittsburgh Crawford battery of Satchel Paige and Josh Gibson represented only the most obvious examples of players who excelled against all competition.

For their efforts these stars seldom received salaries commensurate with those of white major leaguers. With the exception of Satchel Paige, whose regular paycheck and income from barnstorming and winter baseball totalled an estimated $40,000 a year during the 1940s, most players earned between $125 and $300 a month, less than half the salary of the average white athlete. Like Paige, most supplemented their incomes with post-season barnstorming tours and Caribbean baseball. Playing year round, a black athlete earned far more than the typical black worker in the United States, but far less than white ballplayers of inferior skills.[26]

Despite the presence of indisputable stars, the quality of play in black baseball did not equal that of the white major leagues. Most observers acknowledged that with few exceptions black teams could not have competed in the majors on a day-to-day basis. "On certain days our Negro National or Negro American League clubs could have been major leaguers," Bill Yancey of the Black Yankees told Robert Peterson. "If we played with Bill Holland pitching, we were major league . . . but, if we had some other fella in there, we might be a Double-A club." Ted "Double-Duty" Radcliffe says the black teams of the 1930s and 1940s were "about Triple-A Level. . . . The big leaguers were strong in every position, where most of the colored teams had a few stars but they weren't strong in every position."[27]

Black teams generally employed only seventeen or eighteen players rather than the twenty-five-man roster common in the majors. As a result, many athletes, particularly the pitchers, played more than one position. "Double-Duty" Radcliffe earned his nickname due to his skills as both a pitcher and a catcher. He often hurled the first game of a doubleheader and moved behind the plate for the nightcap. Others, like Martin Dihgo and Leon Day, excelled at virtually every position, though they won their greatest fame as pitchers.

The lack of manpower gave the opportunity for these all-around athletes to display their versatility, but it also represented the primary source of weakness on the black clubs. "The majors had more replacements, more pitchers and more reserves," says star hurler Hilton Smith. Buck Leonard concurs, "We didn't have—as the majors did—two good catchers and six or seven good pitchers and good infielders and outfielders. We had about four good pitchers and about two or three mediocre ones."[28]

Black teams also suffered from inadequate training in fundamentals. "We did not know about backup plays or how valuable they were," explains Buck Leonard. "We weren't told the certain position you were supposed to get in for certain plays." In part this stemmed from the absence of a spring training period. "No sooner did you pull on your uniform and crack a sweat than you were in a game before paying customers," contends Roy Campanella. When Jackie Robinson joined the Kansas City Monarchs, he reported on a Friday, was idled by rain the following day, and played in his first game on Sunday without a single practice session.[29] Since most of the athletes had played winter ball in Latin America, they did not require extensive conditioning. But the absence of training eliminated the possibility of meaningful coaching or instruction.

The lack of training gave black baseball a peculiar caste, at least to white observers nurtured on the orthodox techniques of the major leagues. "So many of [the blacks] were never taught the game by a competent coach," explains author Bill Brashler. "They learned it in a sandlot or by watching the older players, and they picked up bad habits and kept them until someone took the time to show them differently."[30] As a result, black baseball became a more diverse and colorful game than the white variation. Batting styles and fielding habits did not adhere to the proper "form," but they were nonetheless effective and entertaining.

White baseball followed the course of other dominant institutions, becoming more rationalized, more predictable, and less daring. Free from the pressures which dictate conformity, black baseball remained more closely akin to the early days of the game or the contests played on the sandlots—less structured, more ebullient, and more innovative. Since the appearance of Babe Ruth, the home run had dominated organized baseball to the exclusion of the bunt, the stolen base, and the hit-and-run. "They played conservative baseball, waited for the big hit, and they played the percentage," recalls Trouppe. Negro League clubs, on the other hand, combined the best of both worlds. Despite the presence of undisputed power hitters, like Josh Gibson, black teams also emphasized speed, baserunning, and what they called "tricky baseball." "You know in boxing there's two rules, Queensbury and the one they called 'coonsbury,' " explained second baseman Newt Allen. "We played the coonsbury rules. That's just any way you think you can win, any kind of play you think you can get by with."[31]

Black pitchers also developed their own peculiar style. "Anything went in the Negro National League," wrote Campanella. "Spitballs, shine balls, emery balls; pitchers used any and all of them. They nicked and moistened and treated the ball to make it flutter and spin and break." Cool Papa Bell remembers the "Vaseline Ball" which had "so much Vaseline on it, it made you blink your eyes on a sunny day." Not only did the rules allow the doctoring of the baseball, but as Campanella explains, there weren't enough baseballs available to replace the scuffed balls. "I was never sure what the ball would do once it left the pitcher's hand, even when he threw what I called for," recalls the Hall of Fame catcher. Nor was the ball always aimed at the plate. Beanball and brushback pitches were epidemic.[32]

The absence of a substantial league structure facilitated this free-wheeling style. Despite efforts in the 1920s and 1930s to establish leagues parallel to those in organized baseball, black baseball remained, for the most part, a collage of independent enterprises. The first successful attempt to form a Negro League resulted from the labors of Rube Foster. Foster was sculpted from the mold of baseball's early pioneers. Like Spalding, McGraw, and Comiskey he rose from star player to skillful manager to owner and administrator. One of the great pitchers of the early twentieth century, Foster assembled the Chicago American Giants in 1911. Nine years later, after retiring as a player, he created the Negro National League, an association of eight midwestern barnstorming teams. In 1923 a second circuit, the Eastern Colored League was established. After surviving the 1920s, both organizations fell victim to the depression. By 1932 no black major league existed.[33]

The following year Gus Greenlee, the owner of the Pittsburgh Crawfords, launched the second Negro National League. Despite frequent membership changes, the structure established by Greenlee stood for over a dozen years. In 1937 a Negro American League formed; it also survived for over a decade.[34]

The Negro Leagues, however, were leagues in name only. Black teams still derived the bulk of their income from barnstorming games not counted in the standings. The number of games in a season varied from team to team. Unlike their white counterparts, Negro League owners exercised little control over their employees. Athletes repeatedly jumped from team to team or to Latin American clubs and back. Many players worked without contracts. Even those with agreements in writing felt minimal compunction about ignoring them. "They were regular contracts. But we didn't pay too much attention to them," recalls Bill Yancey, who played for the New York Black Yankees, among others, in the 1920s and 1930s. "You signed up for a year . . . but if you felt like jumping the next year, you jumped."[35] Negro League owners regularly imposed fines and suspensions for players who violated their contracts, but they just as regularly voided the punishment if the man wished to return. Nor did the owners themselves always honor the sanctity of the contract.

Black teams rarely owned their own arenas, placing them at the mercy of the major and minor league organizations from whom they rented fields. Negro League rentals represented an important component of organized baseball's income. For some teams, like the New York Yankees, revenues amounted to over $100,000 a year.[36] Nonetheless, the landlords often treated the black clubs cavalierly. They forbade black players from using locker rooms and showers and cancelled scheduled games in favor of prize fights and other more lucrative events.

In addition, major league clubs guaranteed certain booking agents monopoly control over scheduling. The true power in the Negro Leagues rested with these agents. Owners who challenged their authority found themselves banished from their most profitable game locations. While Negro League proprietors included both white and black entrepreneurs, the booking agents who monopolized the leagues, like Abe Saperstein and Eddie Gottlieb, were almost always white. For their compulsory services they demanded 40 percent of the gross receipts.[37] Arrangements such as these led Branch Rickey to brand the Negro Leagues as "rackets."

The action on the field reflected this administrative chaos. Umpires possessed minimal authority over the players. Physical attacks on arbiters occurred frequently. Games, at times, adopted a haphazard countenance. In 1945, for example, a contest between the Kansas City Monarchs and the Baltimore Elite Giants was suspended because the official scorer had departed and no one remained to resolve a dispute over the scoring totals. In 1943 league officials invalidated the results of a World Series game when the Homestead Grays imported three stars from the Newark Eagles to help them win.[38]

Underfinanced and overextended, few, if any, Negro League franchises registered profits before World War II. "We never missed a payday," recalls Effa Manley, who owned the Newark Eagles with her husband Abe. "But we were losing much money and had to go to the bank many times."[39] Under these conditions club owners required finances from other sources. With most legitimate opportunities to wealth blocked for blacks, white sports promoters and black gambling kings frequently emerged as owners.

The mercurial career of Gus Greenlee typified ownership in the Negro Leagues.[40] Greenlee reigned as the black numbers king of Pittsburgh's North Side. His operations emanated from the Crawford Grille, a popular night spot for blacks. In 1931 he acquired a local semi-pro team, named it the Crawfords, and determined to assemble the greatest team in black baseball. He spent $100,000 to build a stadium, a rarity in the Negro Leagues, and proceeded to lure the greatest stars to Pittsburgh. In 1931 he purchased Satchel Paige's contract for $250. The following year he raided the roster of the crosstown Homestead Grays, recruiting, among others, first baseman Oscar Charleston, third baseman Judy Johnson, and catcher Josh Gibson. In 1934 he added James "Cool Papa" Bell, the fleet center fielder from the St. Louis Stars, giving the team five future Hall of Famers. He backed this core with a strong supporting cast and the Crawfords became not simply the best black baseball team in history, but possibly the most outstanding club ever assembled.

Greenlee's Crawfords dominated black baseball during the depression years. Yet despite their great success and popularity, the Crawfords never consistently made profits. When police vice squads closed in on Greenlee's numbers racket, he could no longer pay top salaries to his athletes. The stars he had courted defected to other clubs. The crushing blow came in 1937 when Paige took eight Crawfords with him to play for dictator Rafael Trujillo in the Dominican Republic. The following year Greenlee Stadium was forfeited to a demolition crew and the Crawfords were disbanded.

The rise and fall of the Crawfords illustrate the myriad weaknesses of the Negro Leagues. Created out of the proceeds of Greenlee's gambling operations, the team perished when his shaky empire crumbled. Strengthened by raiding the talents of other clubs, the Crawfords collapsed when its own players disregarded their contracts.

Had Greenlee sustained his dream for several more years he would have shared in the Negro Leagues' only period of prosperity. World War II proved a boon to baseball. "During the war when people couldn't get much gas, that's when our best crowds were," recalls Buck Leonard. "Everybody had money and everybody was looking around for entertainment," adds Satchel Paige. "Even the white folks was coming out big."[41] The growing awareness of the Negro Leagues was evident in the popularity of the East-West All-Star game. Created by Greenlee and his assistant, Roy Sparrow, in 1932, one year before the major leagues instituted their own exhibition, the East-West game became the primary showcase for black players and a popular extravaganza for the fans. Profits from the all-star game frequently represented the difference between solvency and bankruptcy for many clubs. In 1943 the game drew over 51,000 fans and at the war's end, the Negro Leagues reached their peak—a two-million dollar empire, one of the largest black-dominated businesses in the United States. Their moment at the summit, however, was to prove short-lived.[42]

IV

"Baseball has given employment to known epileptics, kleptomaniacs, and a generous scattering of saints and sinners," wrote black sportswriter Sam Lacy in 1945. "A man who is totally lacking in character has turned out to be a star in baseball. A man whose skin is white or red or yellow has been acceptable. But a man whose character may be of the highest and whose ability may be Ruthian has been barred completely from the sport because he is colored."[43]

Lacy's sarcastic jabs underscored the inconsistency and irrationality with which the baseball establishment enforced its color barrier. The major and minor leagues forbade interracial competition, but it occurred regularly on the boundaries of the organized game. In preseason exhibitions, post-season barnstorming tours, and Latin American winter leagues, blacks and whites played together. Within the sacred confines of the major leagues, rumors abounded that light-skinned blacks had infiltrated the game.

"It is no secret that players of suspected Negro parentage have appeared in big league games," wrote sportswriter Joe Williams in 1945. "They were presented as Indians, Cubans, Mexicans, and you name it." Despite the generally accepted notion that some blacks had passed as white to enter organized baseball, no proven instances of this phenomenon exist. The most celebrated case occurred in 1901 when Baltimore Oriole Manager John McGraw attempted to disguise second baseman Charlie Grant as an American Indian. McGraw renamed Grant Chief Tokohama, but the charade fooled neither the black fans who flocked to see Grant play, nor Charles Comiskey, who exposed the scheme. Grant never appeared in a regular season game.[44]

According to historian David Voigt, harassment drove dark-skinned George Treadway of the Brooklyn Dodgers out of baseball at the turn of the century. Fans taunted American Indian catcher "Chief" Meyers with cries of "Nigger!" believing him a black man. Rumors continually circulated that Babe Ruth, considered by many to possess negroid features, was part black. Bing Miller, an outfield contemporary of Ruth, also aroused suspicions. When he played for the St. Louis Browns his manager always referred to him as "Booker T." Miller, due to his dark skin.[45]

Cubans and other Latin athletes always created speculation. By the early twentieth century Latin ballplayers regularly appeared in the national pastime. Yet only those considered to have "pure Caucasian blood in their veins" could play. The color line barred their darker-skinned countrymen. In 1911 when two Cubans entered the Connecticut League, the team manager journeyed to Havana to certify that they were "genuine Caucasians." When the Cincinnati Reds later promoted them, further guarantees were advanced from Cuba.[46]

Clark Griffith, then manager of the Reds and later the owner of the Washington Senators, ranked as the leading importer of Latin talent. Rumors abounded that, as Red Smith so aptly put it, "there was a Senegambian somewhere in the Cuban batpile where Senatorial lumber was seasoned." Washington officials always claimed otherwise. Of catcher Mike Gonzalez it was written, "His people were of pure Spanish blood, not of mongrel Indian or Negro Mixture." Nonetheless, Latin players suffered greatly, not only from the disdain of their teammates and the beanballs of opposing pitchers, but from the insensitive stereotyping and ridicule of the press.[47]

By far the most common contact between athletes of different races occurred in the annual pre- and post-season exhibition games that pitted black and white teams against each other. In the early years of the twentieth century, black clubs played against the regular rosters of major league squads, particularly when teams toured Cuba for spring training. At times these outfits were major league in name only, lacking several top stars or including non-roster players. In other instances the entire team participated. In either event, Cuban and black stars fared well. From 1907 to 1911, according to John Holway, the record of major league teams in Cuba was an even .500, splitting sixty-four games and tying one. Performances such as these led American League President Ban Johnson to denounce these contests. "We want no makeshift club calling themselves the Athletics to go to Cuba to be beaten by colored teams," he proclaimed in 1913.[48]

Nonetheless, games between major league teams and blacks continued until the late 1920s when Baseball Commissioner Kenesaw Mountain Landis forbade clubs from appearing as a unit in the off-season. Hereafter major league all-star squads could barnstorm during the post-season months, though Landis limited the number of players allowed from any individual team. Black players believed that Landis invoked this rule to end the embarrassing defeats they handed championship clubs.

During the first half of the twentieth century barnstorming constituted an integral feature of America's cultural landscape. In an age in which the sixteen major league teams concentrated in eleven northeastern and midwestern cities and when television did not exist to bring the national pastime into the living rooms of America, the vast majority of baseball fans never saw a major league contest. Each fall squads of major leaguers brought baseball to American communities, entertaining the faithful, while supplementing their own incomes. Though billed as all-star teams, they often included only one or two name stars and a variety of lesser lights and minor leaguers. No one complained. When a major league barnstorming team appeared, towns took on a festive air. Businesses closed, schools might be given a half-holiday, and parades welcomed the Olympian visitors.

Contests between the traveling all-stars and teams of Negro Leaguers ranked among the most popular attractions on the barnstorming tour, particularly when Satchel Paige pitched for the black squad. Paige first surfaced on the national scene in the late 1920s. Within a short time, he became a legend. The sources of Paige's remarkable popularity are manifold. A crowd-pleaser, Paige seemed to thrive on the excitement of large throngs and to rise dramatically to challenges. His tall, lanky frame, his unusual nickname, and his seemingly lackadaisical manner readily fitted the popular stereotype of blacks held by whites of the depression era. Former teammate Newt Allen draws the connection directly. "Remembering the comedian Stepin Fetchit," says Allen, "[Satchel] talks and sounds just like him." By the mid-1930s the legends surrounding Paige, whom few had seen, had reached mythic proportions. The names of his pitches (the "bee ball," which, according to Satch, buzzed when he threw it, the "jump ball," and the "trouble ball"), his stunt of calling in his outfielders, and his minstrel show one-liners ("Do you throw that fast consistently?" "No sir. I do it all the time.") all added to the aura surrounding Paige.[49]

Paige's true appeal, however, rested not on myth but on reality. By any standards, he ranks as one of the greatest pitchers in history. Surviving throughout most of his career without a curve ball or effective change of pace (his famous "hesitation pitch" was not developed until the 1940s) Paige relied upon a blazing fastball, impeccable control, and a remarkably resilient arm to defy and usually master any and all opposition. By the mid-1930s Satchel Paige matched against one of the top major league hurlers was the most popular attraction in post-season play. In 1934 and 1935 he toured with Dizzy Dean, generally acknowledged as the best white pitcher of that era. Paige won four of six contests and Dean, never known for his humility or modesty, admitted, "My fastball looks like a change of pace alongside that pistol bullet old Satch shoots up to the plate. . . . That skinny old Satchel Paige with those long arms is my idea of the pitcher with the greatest stuff I ever saw."[50] Ten years later, long after Dean had taken his countrified observations to the announcer's booth, Paige joined Cleveland flame-thrower Bob Feller in one of the most elaborate, well-publicized, and lucrative barnstorming tours in history.

The well-publicized exploits of Paige versus the major league stars, perhaps more than anything else, awakened fans, sportswriters, and baseball officials to the potential of black ballplayers. Few could deny that Paige had major league abilities. The barnstorming tours also gave other Negro League stars the opportunity to showcase their talents, and most took full advantage. "That's when we played the hardest, to let them know, and to let the public know that we had the same talent they did and probably a little better lots of times," asserts Judy Johnson. The determination of the black players and their application of "tricky baseball" often confounded the major league squads. Records compiled by John Holway reveal that in 167 games between blacks and "all-star" barnstorming teams during the 1930s, whites won less than a third of the decisions.[51]

For the Negro League stars, the barnstorming tours confirmed what they already suspected. "We always played the major leaguers and we knew that there wasn't any difference because we used to always beat 'em after the season was over," recalls Gene Benson. Jake Stephens, a black shortstop of an earlier era, goes even further, "You knew you were better than the major leaguers. You just knew it."[52]

Yet the black athletes harbored no illusions about the significance of these contests. They recognized that organized baseball remained closed to them. For most players, the possibility of integration seemed so distant, it was not even discussed. "It was like saying, 'How would you like to be a millionaire?'" explains sportswriter Sam Lacy. "They just didn't expect it. You don't talk about being a millionaire." Although many players dreamed of playing in the major leagues, they accepted the inevitability of segregation. Buck Leonard recalls his reaction when approached by integration advocates from the Communist *Daily Worker*. "We're going to leave that to you all to discuss," Leonard remembers saying. "We're out here to play ball. We're not out here to demonstrate or anything like that." If a tryout could be arranged, asserts Leonard, the athletes would gladly cooperate. But he says, "We didn't think there was anything we could do."[53]

Nonetheless, most Negro League stars were not embittered by their experiences. Almost to a man, the veterans of Jim Crow baseball reject the overtones of tragedy and deprivation inherent in this saga. "I've had a wonderful life," pitching great Bill Foster told Holway. "I don't regret anything at all that I can remember. . . . It just wasn't time then for Negroes in the major leagues." "We didn't have to worry about prejudice and all that stuff because we just loved the game," says Benson. "We had such a lovely game, all we wanted to do was play."[54]

Most of the athletes naturally would have welcomed the chance to play major league ball and collect major league salaries, but they rarely dwell on this issue. Instead they emphasize the joys and advantages that their careers provided. "I'm not bitter," says Ted Page. "I think I'm very lucky to be able to say that I played with all the great ballplayers, with and against them. This is something that is unusual." If the color line limited the fame and fortune of these men, they nonetheless earned far more than they would have in other walks of life; in an age of limited mobility, their travels made them truly unique. "A Negro ball player, playing Negro ball in the United States might not have lived like a king, but he didn't live bad either," writes Roy Campanella. "We had players . . . who came from slum neighborhoods. . . . Playing ball was a way to beat that, to move on to something better." Campanella's fellow catcher, Quincy Trouppe, claims, "Baseball opened doors for me which would have been barred. . . . It revealed new vistas that were more educational than a doctor's degree . . . because of this great national game, I have lived a life comparable to the wealthiest man in the United States."[55]

Within the empire of Jim Crow, black ballplayers carved out their own game, a distinctive entity in which baseball attained some of its greatest moments, only to see them ignored and forgotten. But the ability of people to survive and sustain a flourishing culture in the face of discrimination does not erase the stain. For a half century baseball reflected the racism of American society. The ultimate dissolution of segregation rested not with the athletes, but with the powers of organized baseball and the ability of the advocates of reform to compel them to alter their exclusionist ways.

3

The Conspiracy of Silence

The observer finds that in the North there is actually much unawareness on the part of white people to the extent of social discrimination against Negroes. . . . White northerners are surprised and shocked when they hear about such things. . . . One of the main difficulties for the Negroes in the North is simply lack of publicity. It is convenient for the Northerners' good conscience to forget about the Negro.

Gunnar Myrdal,
An American Dilemma

I

"There is no rule, formal or informal, or any understanding—unwritten, sub-terranean, or sub-anything—against the hiring of Negro players by the teams of organized ball," declared Baseball Commissioner Kenesaw Mountain Landis in 1942.[1] The statement typified the hypocrisy of the baseball establishment. The men who controlled the national pastime in the twentieth century had inherited a system of rigid racial exclusion. Although theirs was a sport played primarily in cities removed from the dictates of Jim Crow, baseball officials religiously policed the color line. Yet as Gunnar Myrdal pointed out, the obvious discrepancy between the ideals of the "American Creed" and the actual status of blacks lay at the heart of the nation's racial dilemma. Baseball executives, even those who privately favored segregation, recognized this conflict in their domain. If baseball was truly the national pastime, it could not exclude a tenth of the population from participation; if baseball embodied the essence of American competition and opportunity, it could not block entry to those who possessed the requisite skills to succeed. Spokesmen dared not portray segregation as correct or proper, nor admit the existence of a color barrier.

Americans accepted the denials of Landis and his colleagues due to what Myrdal called "the convenience of ignorance." To most whites, the "Negro problem" in baseball, as in the broader society, did not exist. But to a growing number of Americans, both black and white, segregation in the national pastime symbolized the inherent injustices of a Jim Crow society. Their efforts to expose the contradictions between baseball rhetoric and reality laid the foundations for the postwar onslaught against the color barrier.

The task of defending the baseball establishment against its critics often fell to Commissioner Landis. In 1921 baseball officials had selected Landis, a federal court judge, to restore the game's tarnished image in the aftermath of the 1919 Black Sox Scandal. The owners granted Landis absolute power to "safeguard the interests of the national game of baseball." In the eyes of the general public, Landis ruled wisely, courageously, and fairly throughout his twenty-three-year reign. Few Americans of the era matched his esteem and popularity. Yet Landis did not warrant this reputation. He brought to baseball a disdain for law and due process characteristic of his judicial career. A "grandstand judge" who won fame in controversial cases like the *Standard Oil Anti-Trust Case* of 1907 and the wartime trials of Industrial Workers of the World leaders, Landis often acted arbitrarily, and higher courts overruled his decisions with "startling frequency" according to one analyst. As baseball commissioner, he imposed life suspension on players accused of gambling, even after the courts had acquitted them. In other instances he ignored similar offenses.[2]

While denying the existence of a color line in baseball, Landis carefully guarded his personal opinions on the race issue. Most contemporaries agreed, however, that he adamantly opposed desegregation. "Judge Landis had convenient hiding places for his ideals," wrote former umpire George Moriarty in a 1947 letter. "If the populace was not looking, he had little compunction about defending the underdog, but if the spotlight were turned on in full focus, he would defend anyone to the last camera." During the mid-1930s, according to then National League President Ford Frick, Landis short-circuited a suggestion by several owners to debate the issue in closed session, ruling that the topic had not properly been placed on the agenda. In 1942 when Brooklyn Dodger Manager Leo Durocher stated that he would sign black players if allowed to, Landis publicly proclaimed, "Negroes are not barred from organized baseball . . . and never have been in the 21 years I have served." The following year, after black leaders addressed a major league meeting, Landis quickly stifled any discussion of their proposals. "The gentlemen asked for an opportunity to address the joint meeting. They were given the opportunity," he told a dissident owner. "What's next on the agenda?"[3]

Landis, however, did not single-handedly perpetuate baseball segregation. No owner raised a significant challenge to his edicts on the issue and
the ban on blacks reflected the prevailing attitudes of the baseball hierarchy.
Unable to acknowledge discrimination, owners developed a series of rationalizations defending the necessity of separate competition. Wherever
possible, they attempted to shift responsibility to other parties or to blame
circumstances beyond their control.

Some baseball "experts" argued that the absence of blacks in the majors
stemmed from their lack of talent, intelligence, and desire. "There is not a
single Negro player with major league possibilities," alleged a *Sporting
News* editorial on the eve of integration. And Cleveland Indians owner
Alva Bradley later asserted, "In 1945 there was only one Negro player
mentioned as being of major league caliber. That was Satchel Paige."[4]
Owners frequently complained about the absence of minor league seasoning
among black athletes, but they never gave them the opportunity to start at
the lower levels and prove their abilities.

More significantly, ample evidence exists that other baseball executives
did not share Bradley's delusion. In 1938 Clark Griffith, owner of the Washington Senators, quite frankly stated, "There are few big league magnates
who are not aware of the fact that the time is not far off when colored
players will take their places beside those of the other races in the major
leagues." In that same year National League League President Ford Frick
spoke of the "inevitability" of integrated baseball, as did Phil Wrigley of
the Chicago Cubs. On numerous occasions owners approached black stars
and informed them of their value to a big league franchise, "If only you
were white." After watching Webster MacDonald outpitch Dizzy Dean in
1935, Connie Mack advised him, "I'm sorry to say this, but I'd give half my
ball club for a man like you." Mrs. Grace Comiskey, who owned the White
Sox, would watch "Sug" Cornelius pitch for the Chicago American Giants
and lament, "Oh, if you were a white boy, what you'd be worth to my club."
The list of these testimonials is endless.[5]

Doubts about the talents of blacks were chimerical, but concern over
the feasibility of interracial competition had a more substantial basis. Approximately one third of all players in organized baseball came from the
South and might object to the presence of blacks. Sportswriter Fred Lieb
claimed that 1920s stars "Gabby" Street, Rogers Hornsby, and Tris Speaker
all told him that they were members of the Ku Klux Klan. Ty Cobb held
blacks in contempt and on one occasion physically attacked a black chamber-
maid. In 1938 New York Yankee outfielder Jake Powell embarrassed the
guardians of the national pastime when he told a radio interviewer that
during the off-season he was a "cop" who derived "pleasure beating up nig-

gers and then throwing them in jail." Several stars like Hornsby and Al Simmons refused to join barnstorming teams that played blacks.[6]

Most major leaguers did not share these sentiments. A poll taken by Wendell Smith in the late 1930s found that four fifths of the National League players and managers had no objections to integration. Southerners, as well as northerners, regularly participated in interracial post-season competition. Even Jake Powell, when not doing police work, could be found on the barnstorming trail. Some, like Dizzy Dean, lavished praise on their opponents. "It's too bad those colored boys don't play in the big league," drawled Dean, "because they sure got some great players."[7]

Athletes who dissented from this consensus could pose no real threat to the owners. In the realm of baseball, management totally dominated labor. The reserve clause bound players to their teams from the moment they signed until the day they were released or traded. For most, baseball provided a higher income and more glamorous life-style than they could have achieved elsewhere. Few players would have sacrificed their careers to block integration. Those who did, regardless of their stature, could have been replaced easily. The introduction of blacks would have raised no significant challenge to this state of affairs.

Another frequently voiced objection involved spring training and minor leagues in the South, where integrated competition would violate local laws and customs. However, baseball had considerable economic muscle in dealing with recalcitrant training locales. The annual spring hiatus in Florida provided an important source of revenue for these communities. Many towns and cities competed to host the preseason camps. Threats of abandonment and agreements to control the conduct of black team members could, and later did, drive a wedge in southern resistance. With regard to the minor leagues, baseball's empire stretched far enough to allow for blacks to be assigned outside of the South during their climb to the major leagues.

Apprehension about the impact of desegregation at the box office constituted perhaps the owners greatest and most understandable fear. Many owners, if not most, favored keeping the game on a segregated footing. But baseball owners were businessmen. If the expectation of profit outweighed the fear of financial loss, some owners might gladly have overcome their prejudices. Until World War II, however, integration held few apparent economic benefits. Three quarters of the nation's black population lived in the South; major league franchises existed only in the North. "Black patronage was negligible," asserts Sam Lacy, "so they didn't feel that it was worthwhile to appease those black customers and run the risk of the white customers who were in the majority of the population."[8]

"Almost everybody is afraid of the unknown," explains Bill Veeck, who

34

EARLY INNINGS

was one of the first owners to employ blacks. "There were a lot of people who the operators thought would not come and they were more than those who would come. So they felt this would weaken their financial returns." Former Baseball Commissioner and National League President Ford Frick agreed. "What baseball operators had done, throughout the years," he wrote in his autobiography, "was bow abjectly to what they thought was overwhelming public opinion. They were afraid to make a move. They were afraid of upsetting the status quo, afraid of alienating the white clientele that largely supported the professional game."[9]

Frick's emphasis on adverse public opinion misinterprets the prevailing attitudes of the era. White indifference, rather than fan hostility, posed the principle obstacle to integration. Northern whites knew that the major leagues were segregated, but the issue seldom intruded upon their thoughts. They were aware of the existence of Negro leagues, but in the absence of press coverage, they possessed only a vague conception of the quality of play. Given these conditions, the forces of inertia overwhelmed those of change. Before World War II no great demand for an end to baseball segregation arose; few critics challenged the rationalizations of the major league owners. Minimal inducements existed for baseball administrators to break with tradition or embark on an economic gamble. Integration awaited an increased public awareness of the inequities of baseball's racial policy.

II

In 1938 New York Yankee outfielder Jake Powell's intemperate radio remarks about "beating niggers over the head" unexpectedly elevated the issue of blacks and baseball into the sports headlines. The Yankees suspended Powell and the chastened player toured Harlem bars apologizing for his comments, but some columnists used the incident to question baseball's racial practices. Westbrook Pegler accused the national pastime of dealing with "Negroes as Adolf Hitler treats the Jews." A *New York Post* writer accused Commissioner Landis of "smug hypocrisy" in his handling of the matter. For the most part, however, the white press downplayed the controversy, dismissing Powell's comments as being in a "jocular vein," (sportswriter Shirley Povich quipped that if Powell was as ineffective with his police clubs as with a bat, Negroes had little to worry about) giving lip service to the story, or ignoring it altogether.[10]

The treatment of the Powell story typified coverage of blacks and baseball in the white press. On occasion some writers might raise the issue, but for the most part it remained alien to the sports pages. In 1931 Pegler and New York *Daily News* reporter Jimmy Powers both urged an end to segregation.

During the next decade both occasionally returned to the subject. "I have seen personally at least ten colored ball players I know who are big leaguers," wrote Powers in 1939. "I am positive that if Josh Gibson were white, he would be a major league star." Two years later Washington *Post* columnist Shirley Povich advised his readers, "There's a couple of million dollars worth of baseball talent on the loose ready for the big leagues, yet unsigned by any major leagues. Only one thing is keeping them out of the big leagues—the color of their skin."[11]

During the mid-1930s the spectacular successes of blacks in other sports provided ammunition for baseball's critics. The emergence of Joe Louis as the world heavyweight boxing champion and a national hero led many Americans to re-evaluate their prejudices. The dramatic triumphs of Jesse Owens at the 1936 Berlin Olympics and his alleged snubbing by Adolph Hitler also injected the race issue into the sports pages. If Americans could cheer the efforts of Joe Louis and Jesse Owens, why should they object to blacks in baseball?

But the arousal of public awareness required more than the achievements of Louis and Owens and the sporadic urgings of Powers, Pegler, and other white sportswriters. A more persistent approach was necessary. Two groups that emerged in the late 1930s provided this impetus: a small coterie of young black sportswriters and the Communist Party, one of the few groups concerned with civil rights issues during the depression years. Although narrow access to the public limited both sets of advocates, they succeeded to a remarkable degree in informing the American people of the existence and injustice of Jim Crow athletics.

Wendell Smith of the Pittsburgh *Courier*, the nation's leading black weekly, represented the most talented and influential of the black sportswriters.[12] An athlete of considerable talent in his youth, Smith found his path to professional sports blocked by the color barrier. In 1933 he pitched his American Legion team to a 1-0 victory in a play-off game. A scout from the Detroit Tigers signed Smith's catcher Mike Tresh, who later played and coached in the majors, as well as the losing pitcher. For Smith, the scout had only wistful words, "I wish I could sign you too kid. But I can't." In later years Smith cited this experience as inspiration for his decision to become a sportswriter and crusade to integrate baseball. He attended West Virginia State College on an athletic scholarship and jointed the Pittsburgh *Courier* in 1937. One year later he became the sports editor. Smith ranked among the nation's best sportswriters. He could be bitterly sarcastic and vitriolic in his rage against Jim Crow, yet lyrical in his descriptive prose. Although his columns tended to run overlong and belabor a point, they nonetheless offered both entertainment and insight.

Two other young black sportswriters who played critical roles in the integration campaign, also appeared at this time. Sam Lacy, a persistent and perceptive critic of the baseball establishment, joined the Washington *Tribune* in 1938 and after brief stints with that paper and the Chicago *Defender,* became the sports editor of the Baltimore *Afro-America* in 1944. In New York, Joe Bostic, the aggressive sports columnist for the *People's Voice,* spearheaded the integration campaign.

The efforts of these and other black writers to integrate sports possessed an element of irony. They too were victims of Jim Crow, who held analogous positions to the athletes they covered. Segregation hid their considerable skills from the larger white audience and severely restricted their income earning potential. Yet they rarely mentioned their own plight. Indeed, the barriers for black journalists lasted long after those for athletes disappeared.

At a time when few whites thought of racial issues, these writers injected the integration controversy not only into the black press, but into the broader public arena. Smith interviewed National League players and managers about their attitudes regarding the entry of blacks into the majors. Lacy attended meetings of baseball executives, demanding—and often obtaining—the opportunity for blacks to plead their case. Bostic, a resident of Brooklyn and a writer for a Harlem-based weekly, represented a persistent thorn in the side of the three New York teams by leading delegations to their offices and challenging them in his columns. At Christmas in 1943 Bostic wrote a seasonal letter entitled "No Room at the Yankee Inn," criticizing the club for its failure to employ blacks. The column garnered Bostic a writing award and banishment from the Yankee press box.[13]

The second group that played a major role in elevating the issue of baseball's racial policies to the level of public consciousness was the American Communist party. The depression years had rejuvenated the radical movement in the United States. While never the threat to the American economic system that they hoped to be, or that their tormentors alleged them to be, the Communists nonetheless played a major role in the formation of the Congress of Industrial Organizations (C.I.O.) and, indirectly, the passage of critical New Deal social legislation. Unlike other political groups of the era, the Communists stressed the necessity of organizing blacks as well as whites. In cases like that of the Scottsboro Boys they provided legal assistance for blacks caught in the web of southern justice. That these activities also publicized the party and accrued to its benefit does not negate the genuine concern that American Communists felt for the black populace.

The Communists naturally seized upon the issue of segregation in baseball. As one of the most readily apparent evidences of racial discrimination, the baseball situation not only offered an opportunity to campaign against injustice, but a highly visible public forum as well. The *Daily Worker,* led by its sports editor, Lester Rodney, unrelentingly attacked the baseball establishment. Negro League games were headlined as CHANCE TO SEE GREAT JIM CROW COLORED STARS. Editorials assaulted "Every rotten Jim Crow excuse and alibi offered by the magnates for this flagrant discrimination," and challenged Commissioner Landis with clippings of black victories over major league stars. "Can you read, Judge Landis?" asked one article. "Why does your silence keep . . . Negro stars from taking their rightful place in our national pastime at a time when we are at war and Negro and whites are fighting and dying together to end Hitlerism?"[14]

The Communists did not confine their campaign to newspaper rhetoric but challenged the baseball executives with political action and direct confrontations as well. Delegations to major league teams demanded tryouts for black players. Petition drives collected signatures to protest discrimination. Elected officials from the Communist and American Labor parties continually pressed the issue. On the opening day of the 1945 season, Communists picketed Yankee Stadium. One of the banners read, "If We Can Stop Bullets, Why Not Balls?"[15]

The participation of the Communist party in the integration campaign often allowed baseball officials to downplay the protests. Larry MacPhail, the Yankee's president, and the *Sporting News* both charged that "agitators" motivated by selfish interest produced the clamor for integration. Wendell Smith later wrote that "the Communists did more to delay the entrance of Negroes in big league baseball than any other single factor."[16] Nonetheless, the success of the Communists in forcing the issue before the American public far outweighed the negative ramifications of their sponsorship. The crusade waged by the Communists, the black press, and a small coterie of white sportswriters helped to alleviate the apathy that nourished baseball segregation.

III

The efforts of integration advocates notwithstanding, World War II, more than any other event, caused Americans to re-evaluate their racial attitudes. Many historians view the war as a watershed in the struggle for civil rights. The conflict against Nazi racism exposed the contradictions of racial practice in the United States. "How can we be trained to protect America, which is called a free nation," asked one black soldier, "when all around us rears the ugly head of segregation?" Blacks subjected to southern mores and nationwide Jim Crow army regulations protested at military bases throughout the United States. Civilian groups also actively campaigned for integration. In 1942 black labor leader A. Phillip Randolph threatened a march on Washington to protest federal job discrimination. The Pittsburgh *Courier* launched a "Double-V" campaign—victory at home, as well as abroad. As former army lieutenant Jackie Robinson wrote of his wartime experiences, "I had learned that I was in two wars, one against a foreign enemy, the other against prejudice at home."[17]

The war also triggered dramatic population shifts. The demand for labor in defense plants lured millions of blacks from the rural South to the nation's industrial belt. Black population in northern states increased by 50 percent during the 1940s. For the first time in the country's history blacks constituted a substantial proportion of northern urban residents. Suddenly, blacks made up a more potent voting bloc and an appealing consumer market. Integration advocates now flourished the carrot of economic benefits and wielded the stick of political retribution.

The impact of both the world conflict and the nation's heightened racial awareness also affected baseball. In January 1942, President Franklin D. Roosevelt quickly eliminated fears that the national pastime might be asked to suspend wartime operations. In his famous "green light" letter, Roosevelt proclaimed, "I honestly think it would be best for the country to keep baseball going."[18] But the draft quickly depleted major league rosters. Teams filled their squads with an unlikely collection of 4–F holdovers, retirement age veterans, and athletes of minor league abilities. Pete Gray, the one-armed outfielder of the 1944 St. Louis Browns, became a dramatic symbol of the wartime manpower shortage.

Organized baseball totally ignored the two-armed, able-bodied Negro League athletes. In light of both the international embarrassment caused by segregation and the need for ballplayers, pressures mounted for baseball to drop its color barrier. C.I.O. unions sent a delegation to Commissioner Landis in 1942 to urge baseball to accept blacks. In New York activists organized a Citizens' Committee to End Jim Crow in Baseball and the state legislature passed the Quinn-Ives Act which banned discrimination in hiring and established a five-man commission to investigate violations.[19] Many people pointed out that baseball was among the most blatant offenders of the new law. In St. Louis the Cardinals and the Browns reacted to these pressures by eliminating segregated sections at Sportsman's Park, the last outpost of Jim Crow seating in the majors.

In response to such developments the *Sporting News* devoted its entire editorial column for August 6, 1942, to a discourse entitled, "NO GOOD FROM RAISING RACE ISSUE." The journal argued that few people, either black or white, favored the mixing of the races on the diamond. Members of each race claimed the *Sporting News,* "prefer to draw their talents from their own ranks and both groups know their crowd psychology and do not care to run the risk of damaging their own game." Citing several erroneous examples of blacks who allegedly favored segregation, the editorial stated that only "agitators, ever ready to seize an issue that will redound to their profit and self-aggrandizement," who were "not looking at the question from the broader point of view or for the ultimate good of either race or the individuals in it" raised the issue. These people ignored the "tragic possibilities" that might emanate in the heat of an interracial contest and the ultimate destruction of the Negro Leagues that would result. "Without a medium for developing [black] talent," predicted the newspaper, "there would be no players who could make the grade, even if given the opportunity." Since their own people were thus "protected," the "agitators" should stop "mak[ing] an issue of a question on which both sides would prefer to be left alone."[20]

The *Sporting News* protests notwithstanding, the color barrier seemed in danger of collapsing. In 1942 Negro League pitcher Nate Moreland and all-American football star Jackie Robinson requested a tryout at the Chicago White Sox Pasadena training camp. White Sox Manager Jimmy Dykes allowed the pair to work out. Although hobbled by a charley horse, Robinson impressed Dykes. "I'd hate to see him on two good legs," exclaimed the White Sox pilot. "He's worth $50,000 of anybody's money. He stole everything but my infielders' gloves." Dykes stated that he was willing to accept black players, but he nonetheless dismissed the two athletes. "I can play in Mexico, but I have to fight for America where I can't play," commented Moreland bitterly.[21]

The following year the Pittsburgh Pirates appeared ready to recruit black ballplayers. For many years the Pirates had seemed the most likely team to field blacks. During the 1930s Pittsburgh was the capital of black baseball. The talented rosters of the Crawfords and the Homestead Grays naturally tempted the Pirates. In addition the local *Courier* repeatedly pressured Pirate owner William Benswanger to hire black players. In later years Benswanger claimed that he attempted to sign Homestead sluggers Josh Gibson and Buck Leonard but the Grays' owner Cum Posey refused to cooperate. "I tried more than once to buy Josh Gibson," asserted Benswanger in 1950, but Posey always replied, "Lay off, will you. If I did it would start a movement that would eventually break up the Negro Leagues."[22]

Speaking when integration was a reality, Benswanger probably exaggerated his ardor for experimentation. Wendell Smith charged him with "unmitigated story-tell[ing]." Nonetheless, in 1940 Benswanger spoke favorably about ending the color line. "If it came to an issue, I'd vote for Negro players," he allowed. "There's no reason why they should be denied the same chance that Negro fighters and musicians are given." Two years later Benswanger stated, "I know there are many problems connected with the question, but after all, somebody has to make the first move."[23]

In July 1943, Benswanger succumbed to pressure from *Daily Worker* sports editor Nat Low and agreed to Forbes Field tryouts for catcher Roy Campanella of the Baltimore Elite Giants and pitcher Dave Barnhill of the New York Cubans. In his autobiography Campanella recalled the invitation proffered by Benswanger. "It contained so many buts that I was discouraged even before I had finished reading the letter," wrote Campanella, who quoted the following passages, "You must understand that you would have to start at the very bottom. . . . It might take many years to reach the major leagues. . . . The pay would be small. . . . There is no guarantee that you would ever make it." The young catcher advised Benswanger that he would gladly work his way up through the minors for a chance to play for the Pirates. A tryout was scheduled for August 4, but it never came to pass. Low received a letter from Benswanger cancelling the audition due to unnamed pressures.[24]

In Washington, D.C. that same season, Senators owner Clark Griffith invited Leonard and Gibson to his office and asked them if they wanted to play in the major leagues. They answered affirmatively and expressed confidence that they could play at that level. Griffith warned Leonard and Gibson that, "If we get you boys, we're going to get the best ones. It's going to break up your league." Leonard replied, "Well, if that's gonna be better for the players, then it's all right by me."[25] Griffith did not pursue the matter and Leonard and Gibson remained with the Grays.

Across the continent, developments in the Pacific Coast League hinted at breakthroughs at the minor league level. Clarence Rowland, the president of the Los Angeles Angels announced that tryouts would be held for three black players. Pressure from other league owners forced him to retreat. Several weeks later, after a local columnist had criticized the Oakland Oaks for their failure to employ blacks, Oakland owner Vince Devincenzi, in what appears to have been a carefully orchestrated charade, ordered his manager to audition two black players. The manager, Johnny Vergez, refused. Despite this act of insubordination, the matter, and not the manager, was dropped.[26]

That same year, Bill Veeck, Jr., who would be a gadfly to the baseball establishment for three and a half decades, presented a more potent challenge to the ban on blacks. Veeck was the twenty-nine-year-old son of the former president of the Chicago Cubs. The father had been dignified, formal, and reserved; the son was exuberant, informal, and iconoclastic. In

1941 he purchased a debt-ridden, last-place minor league franchise in Milwaukee and through wildly imaginative promotions and shrewd player deals transformed it into a profitable pennant-winning enterprise. In 1943 he advanced a more audacious scheme. Veeck sought to purchase the floundering Phillies from Gerry Nugent and stock the team with black players.[27] "The only untapped reservoir of players were some of the blacks who were either older or for one reason or another had not been drafted," explains Veeck. Fielding the cream of the Negro Leagues, Veeck wrote in his autobiography, "I had not the slightest doubt that in 1944, a war year, the Phils would have leaped from seventh place to the pennant."

Veeck experienced no difficulty in attracting financial backers or reaching agreement with Nugent. He made just one fatal error. "Out of my long respect for Judge Landis, I felt he was entitled to prior notification of what I intended to do," wrote Veeck. He traveled to Chicago and unveiled his scheme to the commissioner. Landis listened politely, revealing no reaction.

Veeck returned to Philadelphia, confident that he had purchased the Phillies. When he arrived in the City of Brotherly Love the next morning, he discovered that Nugent had turned the club over to the National League. Shortly thereafter, league President Ford Frick sold the team to William Cox, a wealthy lumber dealer, for half the price that Veeck had offered. Did Landis block the sale of the Phillies to Veeck? "I have no proof of that," says Veeck today. "I can only surmise."[28] Several weeks later Veeck heard that Frick had boasted about stopping the young maverick from "contaminating the league." In the end Frick and Landis proved the victims of the joke. One year later Landis banished the "uncontaminated" Cox from baseball for betting on his own team.

Landis had again protected the racial purity of the game, but even czars are only mortal. Shortly after the 1944 season, the craggy-faced jurist died of a heart attack. The death of Landis removed the symbol of baseball's integrity; it also eliminated one of the most implacable and influential opponents of integration.

To Sam Lacy the departure of Landis presented an opportunity to gain a more open hearing of the case for black players. In 1943 baseball owners had agreed to hear Lacy's plea, but his publisher at the Chicago *Defender* had sent controversial actor Paul Robeson to replace the reporter in hopes of generating more publicity. Robeson, a former all-American football player told the baseball magnates that racial attitudes in America had changed. "They said that America never would stand for my playing Othello with a white cast," he said referring to his current Broadway hit, "but it is the triumph of my life." When Robeson left, Landis curtailed all discussion of the matter.[29]

In March 1945, Lacy sent a letter to each major league owner suggesting the creation of a committee to study "the possibilities and [find] the best way of ironing out the many ramifications" of bringing blacks into the majors. Lacy admitted that "this is a sort of compromise for me as a colored man in that it embraces the element of 'appeasement,'" but he felt "it will be a step in the right direction." Leslie O'Connor, who headed the panel replacing Landis until a new commissioner could be chosen, invited Lacy to address a joint meeting of major league owners on April 24. Lacy presented his proposal and the executives agreed to his plan. A Major League Committee on Baseball Integration was established, including Lacy, team presidents Branch Rickey of the Brooklyn Dodgers and Larry MacPhail of the New York Yankees, and Philadelphia magistrate Joseph H. Rainey. Despite repeated efforts by Rickey and Lacy to convene the group, the committee never met. "MacPhail always had some excuse," recalls Lacy. "Finally Branch Rickey said, 'Well, Sam, maybe we'll forget about Mr. MacPhail. Maybe we'll just give up on him and let nature take its course.'"[30] If Rickey was subtly revealing his future intentions to Lacy, the black reporter did not realize it.

While Lacy struggled to bring the Committee on Integration to life, a new baseball commissioner assumed office. At their April meetings the owners selected A. B. "Happy" Chandler, the United States senator and former governor of the segregated state of Kentucky to succeed Landis. Many reacted with dismay. Joe Bostic wondered about the implications of installing "a government official from Dixie at this critical time." Bat Masterson, Jr., described Chandler as a man "whose racial bias is said to be something out of this world." Although Chandler had claimed to be a benefactor of Negroes while governor of Kentucky, Masterson wrote, "Investigation revealed that the extent of the then governor's benefaction was in having separate schools for Negroes built."[31]

Opponents of integration sensed that they had another sympathizer in their midst. *Sporting News* editor J. Taylor Spink forwarded a copy of Bostic's critical comments to the new commissioner along with a clipping of his own 1942 editorial which he told Chandler "took care of the situation." MacPhail, though publicly favoring integration, wrote to Chandler describing the race issue as "increasingly serious and acute." "The three New York clubs are in a critical position right now," he warned the new commissioner. "We can't stick our heads in the sand and ignore the problem. If we do, we will have colored players in the minor leagues in 1945 and in the major leagues shortly thereafter."[32]

Not all observers felt that Chandler shared this ardor for segregation.

Ric Roberts, a sportswriter for the Pittsburgh *Courier* recalls, "We went right down to see him the morning the story broke. Chandler came out immediately shaking our hands and said, 'If a black boy can make it on Okinawa and Guadalcanal, hell, he can make it in baseball.'" Then, as if to indicate that this was not simply Landis-type rhetoric, Chandler told Roberts and his colleagues, "Once I tell you something, brother, I never change. You can count on me." In a more straightforward statement, the Kentuckian declared "I don't believe in barring Negroes from baseball just because they are Negroes."[33] It remained to be seen if Chandler, unlike Landis, would be true to his words.

IV

When Happy Chandler assumed the commissioner's office, baseball's integration crusade had just entered a new phase. Throughout the war civil rights advocates throughout the nation had become increasingly militant in pressing their demands. A threatened March on Washington in 1941 had forced President Roosevelt to establish a Fair Employment Practices Commission. On military bases, black servicemen refused work in menial Jim Crow jobs and protested segregation at post facilities. In April 1945, the age of confrontation arrived in baseball. In two independent incidents black sportswriters forced major league teams to give tryouts to Negro League stars, focusing added attention on baseball's racial dilemma.

In Boston, the Red Sox and the Braves found themselves in a precarious position as they prepared to start the new season. The city council, under the leadership of Isadore Muchnick, a white politician representing a predominantly black district, was pressuring the two teams to employ blacks. Muchnick threatened to deny the team's annual permit for Sunday baseball. Red Sox General Manager Eddie Collins responded with protests of innocence. "I have been connected with the Red Sox for twelve years and during that time we have never had a single request for a tryout by a colored applicant," wrote Collins. "It is beyond my understanding how anyone can insinuate or believe that all ballplayers, regardless of race, color, or creed, have not been treated in the American way as far as having an equal opportunity to play for the Red Sox."[34]

Wendell Smith contacted Muchnick and promised to provide three major league prospects who would request tryouts with the two Boston clubs. Smith arrived in Boston with Jackie Robinson, who had recently reported for his first season with the Kansas City Monarchs; Sam Jethroe, a fleet outfielder with the Cleveland Buckeyes and the leading hitter in the Negro

Leagues in 1944; and Philadelphia Stars second baseman Marvin Williams, a .338 hitter. All three athletes were in their mid-twenties and near the peak of their abilities.

On April 14 and 15 the trio of aspirants reported to Fenway Park, but tryouts were postponed both days. The following morning, Boston *Daily Record* sportswriter Dave Egan, a longtime advocate of baseball integration, wrote a scathing column criticizing Collins. Egan reminded the Red Sox general manager that he was "living in *anno domini* 1945 and not the dust-covered year 1865," and "residing in the city of Boston, Massachusetts and not in the city of Mobile, Alabama." He outlined the qualifications of the three applicants and reminded Collins of his claim that blacks had never requested a chance with the Red Sox. "If [they] cannot make the grade with that classy aggregation of Red Sox we espied the other day," wrote Egan, "room might be found for [them] in the shabbiest and lowest league in organized baseball, in order that [they] might be given the opportunity to work their way up the ladder."[35]

Confronted with the unrelenting pressure of Muchnick and Egan, the Red Sox held the tryout on April 16. Neither the Red Sox players nor manager Joe Cronin were present. Coaches Hugh Duffy and Larry Woodall handled the audition. "It was kind of a dull day," recalls Jethroe. "There wasn't anything spectacular about it; no fans in the stands, just a few newspaper reporters and a coach or two." Clif Keane, a sportswriter for the Boston *Globe,* later recounted, "I can distinctly remember during the workout somebody yelling 'get those niggers off the field.' I can't recall who yelled it. People used to say it was Collins. But I don't really know."[36]

The players, none of whom ever mentioned the epithet, went through the motions of the tryout. "We shagged some flies in the outfield. Then we hit," remembered Robinson. "Williams batted first and hit the ball hard. Then I batted and hit the ball harder. Jethroe batted and then the old fellow who was running the workout said, 'You boys look like pretty good players. I hope you enjoyed the workout.' That was that." The coach told them that the Red Sox would contact them about their status. Ten days later, having received no word from the Red Sox, Smith wrote to Collins for further information. Collins answered that a broken leg suffered by Manager Joe Cronin shortly after the tryout "threw everything out of gear." He also expressed fears of tampering with players under contract with the Negro Leagues.[37] Neither Smith nor the players heard from the Red Sox again.

Twenty-four years later, Cronin, then the American League president, discussed the tryout with a reporter. "We told them our only farm club available was in Louisville, Kentucky and we didn't think they'd be interested in going there," claimed the former Red Sox manager. "Besides, this was after the season had started and we didn't sign players off tryouts those days to play in the big leagues." As manager, Cronin himself could not have offered them jobs, nor was he inclined to. "We just accepted things the way they were," he recalls. "We all thought that because of the times it was good to have separate leagues."[38]

The results of the Red Sox tryout disappointed Smith and the others. They abandoned efforts to force a confrontation with the Braves and the black players returned to their teams. From a publicity standpoint, the Boston episode also failed dismally. The preceding day, President Roosevelt had died and few people paid attention to the events in Boston.

Ten days earlier, a similar scene had transpired at Bear Mountain where the Dodgers held their wartime training camp. (During the war, travel restrictions prevented the traditional Florida preseason camp.) On April 6, Joe Bostic arrived unannounced at the Dodger base with two Negro League players, pitcher Terris McDuffie and first baseman Dave "Showboat" Thomas, demanding tryouts.[39] "I'd decided I'd gotten all the mileage out of conversation I can," Bostic explains his actions today. "I was knocking on first one door and then the other. The next thing was a concrete move and this would be it." Bostic had previously appeared at the Dodger offices to plead his case. "Always," he recalls, "there was this smooth out that you can't accuse baseball of their having a color line or prejudice, because no one had tried. Finally in '45 I took the bull by the horns."

Bostic experienced difficulty in gathering recruits for the expedition to Bear Mountain, "You'd be surprised at the number of players who were actually afraid to buck the establishment." Bostic canvassed ten or twelve players before settling on McDuffie and Thomas. "McDuffie had all the guts in the world. Nothing scared him," recalls Bostic. A standout pitcher in the Negro Leagues since 1931, McDuffie had pitched twenty-seven complete games in a row for the Newark Eagles in 1938 and posted a 27-5 record for the Homestead Grays in 1941. In 1944, however, he had registered an unimpressive 5-6 mark. At thirty-four years of age, he seemed a doubtful candidate for the major leagues. Thomas, a veteran of over twenty seasons of Negro League ball, was five years older. "I had settled on Thomas," says Bostic, "because Thomas was the best fielding first baseman I knew in America at that time, bar none." Many others shared this verdict. "Thomas I knew would dazzle them and he had a good bat," recalls the black reporter.

Upon arrival with his charges, Bostic received an icy reception. "Rickey went berserk almost, with fury," according to Bostic. "We went into the dining room at the Bear Mountain Inn and he told me that he did not appreciate what I had done." Rickey told Bostic that he had been put on a spot. If he allowed the tryout to proceed, Bostic would get "the sports story of the century." On the other hand, if he turned Bostic down, he would be open to embarrassing criticism. Confronted by this dilemma and enraged for reasons unknown to the others at that time, Rickey allowed the tryout to proceed. McDuffie and Thomas performed for forty-five minutes before Rickey dismissed them.

The athletes' age and the confrontational nature of the encounter led most people to dismiss the tryout as a publicity stunt. The presence of a reporter and a photographer from the *Daily Worker*, according to sportswriter Bill Roeder, added "a sickening Red tinge."[40] Bostic asserts that he honestly felt that McDuffie and Thomas could play for the Dodgers. Nonetheless, he admits that he primarily sought publicity for his cause. "It was the psychological breaking of the conspiracy of silence," he contends. "The real problem was that the press ignored [the issue of integration]."

When the tryout ended, Rickey had one parting comment for Bostic and the others. "I'm more for your cause than anybody else you know, but you are making a mistake using force. You are defeating your own aims." Rickey never forgave the Negro sportswriter for his actions. "He never spoke to me from that day further until the day he died," says Bostic. And as he departed, Bostic considered Branch Rickey the least likely person to leap baseball's color barrier.

4

Oh, They Were a Pair!

*Oh they were a pair, those two! I tell you
the air in that office was electric.*

Dodger scout Clyde Sukeforth
describing Branch Rickey and
Jackie Robinson's first meeting[1]

I

Less than a month after the April 1945 tryouts at Bear Mountain, Branch
Rickey assembled a press conference to address the issue of blacks in baseball. Before an audience of reporters from the black and white media Rickey
quickly dashed any hopes that the Dodgers planned to sign a black player.
The recent agitation, he charged, was communist inspired and harmful to
the cause. Rickey then turned his attention to the Negro Leagues, which he
decried as "rackets." To remedy this situation, Rickey announced the establishment of the "United States League," a new circuit for black players.
The U.S. League would utilize standard contracts, regular schedules, and
superior treatment for the players. The possibility existed, hinted Rickey,
that the best performers in the U.S. League might be recruited by major
league teams.[2]

The response to Rickey's anticlimactic announcement ranged from puzzlement to disappointment. The institution of a new Negro League hardly
seemed the answer to baseball's racial dilemma. Some commentators accused him of aspiring to the "dictatorship" of black baseball. Others saw
this as a subterfuge to evade New York State's Quinn-Ives antidiscrimination act. Black columnist Ludlow W. Werner later wrote, "When I left that
meeting . . . I had formed the opinion that it would be a hot day in December before Rickey would ever have a Negro wear the uniform of organized [white] baseball."[3]

The United States League was indeed a subterfuge, though not of the
kind Rickey's detractors suspected. The Brooklyn Dodger president was
not camouflaging his attempt to perpetuate baseball's color line, but rather

his intention to eliminate it. Behind the facade of looking for talent for this strange new league, Rickey, in reality, was seeking black athletes for the Dodger organization. Though none of those present knew it, they had just witnessed the first act in the drama of baseball integration.

"I couldn't face my God much longer knowing that His black creatures are held separate and distinct from His white creatures in the game that has given me all I own," Rickey later explained his decision. The statement was typical of the man. Religious, righteous, and rhetorical, Rickey was an American original. The product of a pious Methodist upbringing on an Ohio farm, the Dodger president exhibited a strange mixture of moralist and mountebank—a combination, according to *Time*, of "Phineas T. Barnum and Billy Sunday." Throughout his career, both as a symbolic gesture and to honor his mother, Rickey refused to attend Sunday games. But, as his critics frequently pointed out, he had no qualms about listening to the games on the radio or collecting his Sabbath profits. An avowed prohibitionist, he often surrounded himself with intemperate, yet talented employees. He preached honesty but saw no contradiction in stretching or disobeying league rules to strengthen his teams. "I don't think he would lie," said Red Smith, "but he was so good at evasion, at circumlocution, that he didn't have to lie."[4]

Rickey encouraged formality and he received it from most of his subordinates. "We always called him Mr. Rickey. Everyone did," recalls Rachel Robinson. "I think we wanted to hold him in that position of respect and honor. Part of his power was maintaining that mystique about himself."[5]

His manner commanded caricature. He presented a familiar figure to millions of baseball fans—a cigar lodged firmly in the corner of his mouth, a floppy hat pulled down to his bushy eyebrows, wrinkled clothing draped sloppily over his former catcher's frame, and bespectacled eyes gazing intently over the playing field. Rickey perpetuated this mystique with his skillful use of the English language and his theatrical flamboyance. A master of the spoken word, Rickey marked his conversations with rhetorical flourishes and verbose explanations. A New York *Times* reporter captured him in mid-performance:

> Coatless, his unruly hair hanging down over his eyes and his shirt soaked in perspiration, the Mahatma dashed back and forth on the raised platform from the blackboard to the front of the stage, putting on a performance rivalling that of any leading dramatic actor you can name.[6]

The proper way to pick a runner off second base provided the topic of this breathtaking soliloquy.

Rickey's religious allusions and sermonlike speeches led reporters to call him the "Deacon." In 1942 sportswriter Tom Meany dubbed him the "Mahatma," reflecting John Gunther's description of Indian leader Mahatma Gandhi as "a combination of God, your father, and Tammany Hall leader."[7] The nickname was so appropriate that it stuck.

Rickey created this public image. Yet this persona obscured, often deliberately, his private side. "I thought Mr. Rickey got stereotyped, caricatured," says Rachel Robinson. "I saw him in different moods, so it was never just this cigar-chewing, funny-hat guy, who was Bible-thumping and always giving sermons. I saw him more as a total man and I think the legend tends to deny him that totality."[8] Despite his overbearing, sanctimonious manner, Rickey inspired a fierce loyalty and a respect bordering on worship from his associates and players.

For Rickey baseball provided an escape from his midwestern farm background. As a young man he played two seasons in the major leagues as a catcher. He worked his way through law school by coaching college baseball. He graduated near the top of his law school class at the University of Michigan and seemed destined for greater pursuits than baseball. In 1913, however, Robert Hedges, the owner of the St. Louis Browns persuaded him to return to baseball as his personal assistant. Three years later, after Hedges had sold the Browns, Rickey transferred to the crosstown Cardinals. During these early years Rickey served both St. Louis clubs as field manager, but it grew readily apparent that his skills lay not in the dugout but in the front office. After 1925 Rickey permanently shed his uniform and donned his fashionless suit and tie to become the general manager of the Cardinals.

Energy and innovation characterized Rickey's career. A compulsive worker, Rickey routinely labored eighteen-hour days with barely a wasted minute. He dictated letters and memoranda on cars, trains, and planes, and even through the closed door of his toilet stall. Rickey devoted his life to devising ways to perfect the instruction of athletes. He believed the ability to run, hit, and throw constituted God-given talents which could not be taught. The corollary to this axiom was that all other nuances of baseball could be learned. At the start of his managing career in 1914, a sportswriter reported, "He is a Professor of Baseball. His efficiency courses in sliding, baserunning and batting mark a new departure in the game."[9] His schemes ranged from an elaborate preseason "Baseball College" for the instruction of fundamentals to training paraphernalia like sliding pits and batting tees taken for granted today. To Rickey baseball represented a science in which one researched, experimented, and refined techniques for maximum results.

While with the Cardinals Rickey created the farm system, the greatest achievement of his early years.[10] Under this plan a major league club, through either ownership or working agreements, controlled a chain of minor league franchises through which it could cultivate young talent before harvesting the best for the parent team. Through this mechanism Rickey produced not only championship squads for the Cardinals but surplus players who could be sold profitably to other organizations. As a result of his efforts the Cardinals became the most successful franchise in the National League. In 1949 it was estimated that Rickey's farm systems had developed three out of eight major leaguers. Rickey developed not only athletes but administrative talent as well. Many of baseball's leading executives, including Larry MacPhail, Bill DeWitt, and Warren Giles, apprenticed under Rickey. As a reward Rickey earned in excess of $100,000 a year, a remarkable sum during the depression decade of the 1930s.

Rickey's transfer in 1942 to the Brooklyn Dodgers, which led to baseball's integration, was as unlikely as it was unexpected. Most observers deemed it unthinkable that Rickey would relinquish his St. Louis post. Nor did there appear to be an opening in Brooklyn, where MacPhail had rejuvenated a struggling Dodger franchise, transformed it into a pennant contender, and more than doubled attendance in four short years. In the late 1930s, however, personal differences and business disagreements soured relations between Rickey and Cardinal owner Sam Breadon. By 1941 an irreparable breach had emerged. To the surprise of the baseball world Rickey announced the end of his twenty-five-year Cardinal reign. At the same time the abrasive MacPhail had alienated the Dodger owners. When he marched off to Washington to join the war effort, they breathed a sigh of relief, and named Rickey to replace his former protégé as the Dodger general manager.

Rickey and the Brooklyn fans constituted an imperfect match. Rickey was the prototypical midwestern American; Brooklynites were a cynical amalgam of immigrant cultures. To the hardened New Yorkers, Rickey seemed phony and hypocritical. The mischievous New York press corps enhanced this image. Cartoonists delighted in caricaturing the familiar Rickey luring young players to his minor league "chain gang" where they would watch their youth fade and their skills erode. Sports columnists portrayed Rickey as a master of double-talk, dubbing the site where he held his press conferences the "Cave of the Winds" and attacking Rickey as a Scroogelike skinflint, whose low salaries kept his players in poverty.[11]

The most vicious of the attacks emanated from the typewriter of Jimmy Powers of the *Daily News,* the city's leading newspaper. "Jaunty Jimmy never let fact interfere with a good story," charges Harold Parrott, a former Dodger employee. In 1943 Powers began to refer to Rickey as "El Cheapo," a tag which he gleefully used for years. In the latter half of 1946, Powers prodded Rickey almost every other day. According to one account, 74 out of 180 "Powerhouse" columns bore the "El Cheapo" tag. "What shall we do with 'El Cheapo?'" wrote Powers. "Shall we send him over Niagara Falls in a barrel? Shall we maroon him on Bikini Atoll?"[12] As the conflict raged in Europe, Powers, Joe Williams, and other sportswriters waged their own conflict with Rickey, much to the delight of the local fans.

Rickey's strategy for rebuilding the Dodgers provided ample fuel for his critics. He inherited an aging, pennant-winning team and a talent-poor minor league system. The Mahatma determined to re-create his St. Louis success by constructing an extensive farm network. Simultaneously he traded fan favorites like Dolph Camilli and Joe Medwick whom he felt had passed their prime. As the Dodgers sank to seventh place in 1944, the crescendo of criticism from press and public rose. At one point, fans hanged Rickey in effigy in front of Brooklyn's Borough Hall, in full view of the Dodger offices.

Rickey, though irritated, adhered to his strategy for postwar Dodger dominance. Upon his arrival in Brooklyn he had initiated a two-pronged talent search to rebuild the club. The uncertainties produced by the war had led other baseball executives to reduce their scouting operation for fear of losing players to the army. Rickey, expecting an American victory by 1945, took the opposite tack. He quadrupled the size of the Dodger scouting staff and began to sign predraft-age players. In Rickey's wartime "youth brigade," laughed minor league manager Jake Pitler, "We were loaded with comic books and candy bars, but we carried practically no shaving cream."[13] When the war ended the beardless boys had matured into men, and, as a result of Rickey's foresight, the Dodgers possessed the most talent-laden organization in the National League.

The second target of Rickey's massive wartime talent hunt was potentially more controversial. Only a handful of people knew of its existence. Throughout the United States and the Caribbean, Rickey had sent scouts after the last unmined source of baseball talent. They were searching for black players for the Brooklyn Dodgers.

The reasons for Rickey's unilateral action have provoked debate for almost four decades. Rickey frequently related a story that revealed a long-standing commitment to ending segregation. The Deacon's first exposure to racism had occurred in 1904 when he served as the baseball coach at Ohio Wesleyan University.[14] Among his athletes was Charlie Thomas, a black first baseman, whose hitting, according to the school archives, "was feared all over the state." "From the first day at Ohio Wesleyan," Thomas later recalled, "Branch Rickey took a special interest in my welfare." In the spring of 1904 the Wesleyan squad traveled to South Bend, Indiana, to play Notre Dame. The hotel at which the team had reservations refused to allow Thomas to lodge there. Rickey convinced the management to place a cot in his room for Thomas to sleep on, as they would do for a black servant. That night Thomas wept and rubbed his hands as if trying to rub off the color. "Black skin! Black skin!" he said to Rickey. "If I could only make them white."

"That scene haunted me for many years," explained Rickey, "and I vowed that I would always do whatever I could to see that other Americans did not have to face the bitter humiliation that was heaped upon Charles Thomas." While employed in St. Louis, the southernmost city in the major leagues where segregated seating still prevailed, Rickey dared not redeem his pledge. As soon as he joined the Dodgers, Rickey initiated his plan.

The Charlie Thomas story, though based on fact, is vintage Rickey. The allegory is almost biblical and the sermonlike quality of the tale invites skepticism. Many people place little stock in the episode as the primary rationale for his actions. Even if one accepts the Charlie Thomas saga at face value, it does not fully explain why the Dodger president chose to challenge the color barrier four decades later.

Characteristically, Rickey contradicted himself in explaining his motivations. He never tired of repeating the tale of Charlie Thomas, but at the same time, he adamantly denied any noble intentions. In October 1945, he wrote to sportswriter Arthur Mann, "I don't mean to be a crusader. My only purpose is to be fair to all people and my selfish objective is to win baseball games." On numerous occasions, Rickey denied that his rationale lay outside the realm of sports. "The greatest untapped reservoir of raw material in the history of the game is the black race! The Negroes will make us winners for years to come," Rickey told his family, "And for that I will happily bear being called a bleeding heart and a do-gooder and all that humanitarian rot."[15]

Rickey the baseball executive clearly perceived that being the first to sign blacks would propel the Dodgers to pennants. Rickey the businessman might have also seen windfall profits in his future. Sportswriter Bob Addie wrote in 1954 that Rickey's daring breakthrough was "compounded of sincerity and cupidity," the inherent justice of integration made more attractive by the promise of increased black attendance. The economic benefits, however, so obvious in retrospect, were not so assured in the mid-1940s. Although the black population in northern cities had increased dramatically during World War II, no evidence exists that this factor played a role in Rickey's decision. Many contemporary analysts saw grave economic dangers, both at the gate and in the loss of southern white prospects. "Nobody could reasonably suspect materialistic motives," wrote Tim Cohane in Look in March 1946. "In fact, signing [blacks] may cost Rickey money."[16] Baseball executives feared that Rickey's decision endangered the financial stability of the game. If the Dodger president indeed recognized the vast profits that integration would eventually generate, his prescience exceeded that of his fellow owners even more than is generally acknowledged.

Former Negro League star Frank Forbes suggested that another economic consideration motivated Rickey. "I've never been sure Rickey didn't do it to knock us out," contended Forbes. "We were giving him fits at the gate." Forbes noted that in the mid-1940s black teams competed with the Dodgers from two directions. When the Dodgers played at home on Sundays, black teams played doubleheader at Yankee Stadium or the Polo Grounds, attracting 15,000 to 20,000 fans. At the same time the Bushwicks, an independent team located in Brooklyn, drew a similar number of spectators when they played a black squad. These fans might have attended Dodger games instead.[17] Forbes's explanation, while plausible, lacks any substantiation. Even before the advent of integration, Rickey's Dodgers drew consistently well at the box office.

Another intangible factor, in addition to Rickey's youthful vow, his dedication to winning, and the potential of profit, perhaps best explains the Mahatma's revolutionary undertaking. People reminiscing about Rickey emphasize one point with uncanny regularity. Virtually all agree that Rickey, given his energy, innovation, and brilliance, would have been successful in whatever endeavor he had chosen. Yet he had devoted his life to baseball, rather than law, politics, or business. An acknowledged genius in his own domain, Rickey had contributed little outside of the realm of sports. An anecdote that appeared in the *New Yorker* revealed Rickey's frustration. While still with the Cardinals during the 1930s, Rickey unexpectedly began to lecture his son:

> I completed my college course in three years. I was in the top ten percent of my class in law school. I'm a Doctor of Jurisprudence. I am an honorary Doctor of Laws. . . . You have to admit boy that I am an educated man. . . . And I like to believe that I am an intelligent man. . . . Then will you please tell me, why in the name of common sense, I spent four mortal hours today conversing with a person named Dizzy Dean.[18]

By taking the initiative to integrate baseball, Rickey emerged from the limited world of baseball and aspired to influence developments in the broader society.

In discerning Rickey's motivations, however, there is a danger of ignoring the broader social forces that created a conducive atmosphere for the "great experiment." Even if Rickey had not been straitjacketed in St. Louis for a quarter of a century, it seems doubtful that he would have endeavored to end segregation much earlier. Rickey feared that precipitant action was more likely to negate, rather than to advance, the interests of blacks. In 1944 the Deacon contrasted integration with prohibition, which he considered a "most worthy [cause] . . . thrown back a hundred years by the Volstead Act." Rickey feared that, "Very possibly, the introduction of a Negro into baseball, even without force, might similarly throw back their cause of racial equality a quarter century or more."[19] Wartime changes in American attitudes, however, had created a more conducive environment for an integration experiment.

Rickey also believed that the appearance that he had succumbed to external coercion would prove "disastrous" to his efforts. He adamantly insisted that neither the growing protest movement nor the Quinn-Ives antidiscrimination law had influenced him. He had acted, he claimed, "despite the misguided labor of pressure groups." But the impact of the agitation cannot be dismissed so easily. Sociologist Dan Dodson, who assisted Rickey in assembling the blueprint for baseball integration agreed that the image of surrender was undesirable. Nonetheless, Dodson admitted that the Quinn-Ives law and the pressure groups "both contributed to the initiation of the venture and the venture was far less difficult, no doubt, because both were realities."[20] The changes wrought by World War II and the dogged dedication of integration advocates had at last elevated the issue to the forefront of public attention and thereby hastened the end of Jim Crow in baseball. At that point, Branch Rickey seized the initiative.

II

Red Barber was one of the most popular men in Brooklyn. He had broadcast Dodger games on the radio since 1937. As much as any man on the field, Barber could claim responsibility for the club's resurgent appeal. Of southern ancestry, Barber had been born in Mississippi and raised in Florida. "The Negroes who came and went through our lives were always treated with the utmost respect and a great deal of affection," he wrote in his autobiography, "but there was always a line drawn and that line was always there."

In early 1945 in a deserted Brooklyn restaurant Barber sat with his employer, Branch Rickey, and heard a most startling revelation. "There is a Negro player coming to the Dodgers," said Rickey. "I don't know who he is and I don't know where he is, and I don't know when he is coming. But he is coming. And he is coming soon."

"I gave him back no support," says Barber. "I gave him back 100% silence, because he had shaken me. He had shaken me to my heels." The southern-born announcer went home that evening and told his wife that he could no longer work for the Dodgers. He could not be a party to Rickey's outrageous scheme. At his wife's urgings, Barber delayed his decision. "But the thing was gnawing on me," he confesses. "It tortured me. . . . I set out to do a deep self-examination. I attempted to find out who I was." Barber agonized over his predicament. Although he knew that he would be able to find another position, he had no desire to leave Brooklyn. Yet the thought of announcing for an integrated team appalled his southern sensibilities. After months of soul-searching, Barber reached a resolution. His job was to "broadcast the ball," not to worry about who was playing. "I did not care what anybody else said or thought or did about the player who was coming and whose name I did not know," explains Barber. "All I had to do was treat him as a man, a fellow man, treat him as a ballplayer, broadcast the ball."[21]

Barber reacted precisely as Rickey had anticipated he would, bearing out the Mahatma's most deep-seated convictions on the racial issue. Branch Rickey was innovative, but he was not impulsive. He planned things on a grandiose scale, examining the philosophical underpinnings of his actions. He had prepared for the racial breakthrough carefully. Potential problems had to be anticipated, and wherever possible, avoided. Rickey studied the work of historians and sociologists and consulted "experts" in the field of race relations.

The work of Columbia University Professor Frank Tannenbaum particularly impressed him. Tannenbaum contrasted racial attitudes in Latin America and the United States and found that Latin culture had allowed blacks to mix socially, intermarry, and become citizens, whereas Anglo-American culture erected strict racial barriers. The greater "proximity" of blacks and whites encouraged more amicable relations. Tannenbaum's thesis, though disputed by later historians, reinforced Rickey's convictions that individuals, thrust together in pursuit of a common goal, would be able to overcome their racial prejudices. His advance warning to Barber not only alleviated a possible problem from the man who would present the black player to Brooklyn radio audiences, but, in testing the reaction of the southern-born announcer, Rickey confirmed, to his satisfaction, the Tannenbaum theory.[22]

Barber thus became one of only a handful of people aware of Rickey's activities. The need for absolute secrecy obsessed the conspiratorial Mahatma. Premature revelation, he feared, would undermine the entire enterprise. He informed only those for whom he deemed foreknowledge essential. Primary among his select group were the Dodger owners. For over a decade three hostile factions had owned the team. The real authority in the organization, however, rested with the Brooklyn Trust Company which had kept the ball club afloat with generous loans. In 1943 Rickey approached George V. MacLaughlin, the bank's president and a local civic leader, with his plans for rebuilding the Dodgers. Rickey mentioned the possible recruitment of black players. MacLaughlin responded favorably, but added a caveat, "If you find the man who is better than the others, you will beat it; and if you don't you're sunk." With MacLaughlin's support Rickey broached the issue to the Dodger board of directors. All endorsed the plan, although one owner questioned Rickey's "real motive." The owners then swore to guard the secret, withholding the information even from their families.[23]

Rickey also kept his own family, as well as his top aides, in the dark. Harold Parrott, the Dodger traveling secretary, was present at Rickey's home in 1945 when the Mahatma finally elaborated his intentions to his wife and children. Jane Rickey and their daughters feared for the effects on the sixty-four-year-old executive's health and worried that it would provide new ammunition for the press. "Haven't you taken enough abuse about being 'El Cheapo' and about the 'chain gang' and all that?" Parrott remembers Rickey's wife as saying. Branch Jr., the Dodger farm director, nicknamed the "Twig" by sportswriters, also opposed the move. He predicted that Dodger scouting efforts in the South would come to a halt. Parrott added his own misgivings. As the traveling secretary he spoke of the hardships a black player would face on the road.[24] Though none of the group objected to the idea of integration, all felt that Rickey should not accept the burden.

By this time, Rickey's agents had been evaluating black athletes for two years. José Sada, the athletic director of a Puerto Rican school, performed the initial scouting on that island and Robert W. Haig of Columbia University, Rickey's former fraternity brother, checked on prospects in Cuba. Rickey quickly ruled out the possibility of signing a Latin player. "It's tough enough for a colored boy if he can speak the language," one of his aides explained, "so it's going to be doubly tough if he can't."[25] Rickey also concluded that the best black players could be found in the United States.

In this country Rickey assigned his top Dodgers scouts—George Sisler, Wid Matthews, Tom Greenwade, and Clyde Sukeforth—to search for black players. He told them that they were looking for players for a new team alternately called the "Brown Dodgers" or the "Brown Bombers" which would play in Ebbets Field when the Dodgers were on the road. None of them suspected Rickey's true intentions. He instructed them to maintain a low profile so as not to attract attention. "We'd buy our ticket and we'd sit back and we never identified ourselves at all," recalls Sukeforth. "If we saw a good-looking ballplayer we made a report on him, just like a white boy."[26]

Rickey also employed Oscar Charleston, the former Negro League great, to assist in scouting and provide background information on the prospects.

The formation of the United States League in May 1945 enabled Rickey's agents to operate more openly. The Dodger president's true design for this new entity remains unclear. Its primary function was to allow the Dodgers to search for black players, but Rickey also attempted to create a viable league that would compete with the Negro National and American circuits. A successful Brooklyn club in the United States League would have provided a lucrative Ebbets Field tenant when the Dodgers played on the road. Through the United States League, Rickey played both ends against the middle, attempting to gain a slice of the profits from Jim Crow baseball, while simultaneously spearheading the cause of integration. After one lackluster season, the league collapsed.[27]

Rickey also erected additional smokescreens. In the summer of 1945 Rickey recruited an important ally, Dr. Dan Dodson, who established a political diversion.[28] Dodson, a New York University sociologist, was the executive director of the Mayor's Committee on Unity of New York City, a body created to investigate discrimination. In July he requested interviews with officials of the three New York teams. At his meeting with the Yankees, MacPhail denounced him as "a professional do-gooder" who knew nothing about baseball. A different reception awaited him at the Dodger offices. He discovered that he, and not Rickey, was under scrutiny. Rickey had investigated Dodson carefully and quizzed him for thirty minutes. He then regaled Dodson with the story of Charlie Thomas. Moments later, Rickey unveiled his intention to end baseball segregation. The Dodger president asked Dodson to contribute his advice and expertise to this venture. More importantly, Rickey requested Dodson's assistance in camouflaging his activities. The Mahatma asked Dodson to organize a committee to investigate the feasibility of baseball integration and offer the illusion of action, while Rickey labored behind the scenes to conclude his preparations.

"This was one of the toughest decisions I ever had to make while in office," Dodson later admitted. "The major purpose I could see for the committee was that it was a stall for time. . . . Yet had Mr. Rickey not delivered—had he been bluffing, as so many contended—I would have been totally discredited and the Mayor's Committee on Unity would have been impaired immeasurably through the loss of public confidence."

Dodson gambled on Rickey's integrity and arranged the formation of the Mayor's Committee on Baseball to study the issue of blacks and baseball. The new organization, assembled in late August, included Rickey, MacPhail, Dodson, and eight others. The presence of only two blacks, Dr. John

Johnson, a Harlem minister, and Bill Robinson, the entertainer, typified the white-dominated human rights agencies of the era. With the exception of Rickey and Dodson, committee members remained unaware that theirs was a token venture.

As Rickey and Dodson erected their political facade, Dodger scouts filed reports on black players. Rickey wanted not one, but several prospects whom he could recruit simultaneously, garnering the most promising black athletes before other teams entered the market. Among this first group of pioneers, however, the Dodger president had determined that there must be one player who would occupy center stage and upon whose performance the success or failure of the "noble experiment" would rest.

The Mahatma had given careful thought about the type of man he required for this role. The candidate did not have to be the best black ballplayer, though he naturally needed superior skills. Rather, he had to be the most likely to maintain his talents at a competitive peak while withstanding pressure and abuse. He needed the self-control to avoid reacting to his tormentors without sacrificing his dignity. "How can a man of worth and human dignity and unsullied personality bend enough?" Rickey later explained his thinking. "How could a man with distinctive personality successfully keep it unscraped with constant absorption of attacks calculated to absorb his self-respect?" In addition to his composure on the field, the candidate had to be an exemplary individual off the field as well. "We could know about his playing ability in uniform," reasoned Rickey, "but what about out of uniform? . . . his associates, his character, his education, his intelligence." When Rickey had completed the portrait of the ideal path breaker, he concluded, "There were just not very many such humans."[29]

Rickey reviewed the reports accumulated by his scouts and weighed the merits of the candidates. The initial black player would probably spend several years in the minor leagues, making anyone over thirty a risky proposition. Many of the top stars in the Negro Leagues, like Satchel Paige and Josh Gibson, were thereby eliminated due to age. On the other hand, many of the younger Negro League stars lacked the maturity necessary for the role. Others, like Monte Irvin, whom many observers deemed the best prospect for major league stardom, were in the army. Second baseman Lorenzo "Piper" Davis of the Birmingham Black Barons ranked high on the lists of several scouts, although some questioned his hitting ability. Catcher Roy Campanella of the Baltimore Elite Giants and pitcher Don Newcombe of the Newark Eagles were both judged potential major leaguers, but Rickey felt that neither matched his stringent requirements for the pivotal role.[30]

Increasingly, Rickey's attention became riveted on Jackie Robinson, the shortstop of the Kansas City Monarchs. In May, following the United States

League press conference, he had quizzed Wendell Smith about potential players for his new team. Smith unhesitatingly mentioned Robinson. Reports from three of his scouts all spoke highly of the athlete. Tom Greenwade called him the best bunter in baseball. Wid Matthews, a southerner, who would likely have resigned had he known Rickey's intentions, said the black prospect, though "strictly the showboat type" was "one of the best two-strike hitters he had seen in a long time." George Sisler doubted that Robinson had a strong enough arm to play shortstop in the majors, but expressed confidence that he could be a standout at second base.[31] On the basis of these reports, Rickey traveled to California and inquired into Robinson's background. He determined that the infielder fulfilled all of his requirements. Only one final test, a face-to-face meeting at which the Mahatma could meet and assess the candidate, remained. In late August, just as the Mayor's Committee on Baseball held its first meetings, Rickey dispatched Clyde Sukeforth to locate Robinson and bring him to Brooklyn.

III

One year earlier baseball had lain distant from Jackie Robinson's thoughts. A lieutenant in the United States Army, Robinson sat in a military courtroom at Fort Hood, Texas, facing a court-martial for insubordination.[32] Robinson's troubles had begun on July 6, 1944, when he defied a southern bus drvier's command to "get to the back of the bus where the colored people belong." The black lieutenant, aware that the army had recently ordered the desegregation of military buses, refused. When military police and the base provost marshal took the side of the driver, Robinson objected vehemently. Four weeks later, he found himself on trial, the prospect of a dishonorable discharge dangling over his head.

Robinson escaped conviction at his court-martial. An able defense lawyer, a modicum of pretrial publicity, and the weakness of the case against him led the army judges to rule that he had acted within his rights in his refusal to bow to southern tradition. The incident, however, illustrates the character of the man whom Branch Rickey had chosen as his standard bearer. Proud, courageous, and defiant, Robinson was never reluctant to assert his rights as an American and as a black man, even in the face of personal risk. To many, Robinson's wartime protest might have seemed unpatriotic and unpalatable. Indeed, for several years after the war accounts of Robinson's life never mentioned this episode. But to Rickey, Robinson's bold stand against segregation symbolized the spirit required for the undertaking ahead.

Even in 1944 Jackie Robinson was not simply another unknown soldier.

His prewar collegiate athletic career at U.C.L.A. had established him as the nation's outstanding all-around athlete, "the Jim Thorpe of his race,"[33] according to sportswriter Vincent X. Flaherty. In 1940 and 1941, after transferring to U.C.L.A. from a junior college, he emerged as the school's first four-letter man, starring in football, basketball, track, and baseball. Twice he led the Pacific Coast Conference in basketball scoring, leading one coach to call him "the best basketball player in the United States." In his junior year, he averaged eleven yards a carry in football, teaming in an all-American backfield with Kenny Washington, who later became one of the first blacks to play in the National Football League. "He is probably the greatest ball carrier on the gridiron today," wrote Maxwell Stiles in *Sports Weekly*. Robinson, who held the national junior college broad jump record, was also the NCAA champion in that event in 1940. During his college years, baseball was one of Jackie's lesser sports, though Ned Cronin reported in 1940, "Had it not been for the policy prohibiting Negroes in organized baseball, he would have been sought by half a dozen major league scouts."

Robinson had not confined his competitive fires to the major college sports. All athletic events came within his realm. He tried his hand at golf and won the Pacific Coast intercollegiate golf championship; he won swimming championships at U.C.L.A.; in tennis he reached the semifinals of the national Negro tournament. It is probable that no other athlete, including Jim Thorpe, has ever competed as effectively in as broad a range of sports.

Sportswriters in 1945 frequently commented that Robinson, raised in the Far West, had escaped the ravages of American racism. California, it is true, was not Georgia, Robinson's birthplace, but life in the Golden State still exacted a toll upon its black citizens. He had arrived in California in 1920 at the age of fourteen months, the youngest of five children of Mallie and Jerry Robinson. Eight months earlier, his father, discouraged by the life of a sharecropper, had deserted the family. Mallie Robinson, a devoutly religious, indomitable woman, determined to provide a decent home for her children. California, she hoped, would offer more opportunities than the Deep South.

The family settled in Pasadena, an affluent suburb of Los Angeles, and Mallie struggled to support Jackie and his brothers and sisters with the meager wages she earned as a domestic. Her heroic efforts notwithstanding, the children grew up in poverty. "Sometimes there were only two meals a day," Jackie later wrote, "and some days we wouldn't have eaten at all if it hadn't been for the leftovers my mother was able to bring home from her job."[34] With the help of the welfare agency, Mallie Robinson purchased a house on Pepper Street in a white Pasadena community. The neighbors petitioned to have the Robinsons removed and when this failed, they offered to buy out the black family. But Mallie was determined to keep her home. Residents subjected the Robinson family to abuse and harassment for several years, but the house on Pepper Street remained the physical and spiritual shelter for the close-knit Robinson clan.

"Pasadena regarded us as intruders," Jackie wrote of his childhood. "My brothers and I were in many a fight that started with a racial slur on the very street we lived on. We saw movies from segregated balconies, swam in the municipal pool only on Tuesdays, and were permitted in the YMCA only one night a week." In 1936 when a judge ordered Pasadena pools to allow blacks, the city government responded by purging all blacks from its payrolls. Among those fired was Jackie's older brother Mack, who had recently returned from the Berlin Olympic Games where he won a silver medal, finishing second to Jesse Owens in the 200-meter dash.[35]

For Jackie, as for his brother, athletics had become a passion. Even in the world of sports, he faced discrimination and racism. "Jack had some pretty rough treatment from narrow-minded sportsmen wherever he's gone," reported one writer. In his senior year at U.C.L.A., despite leading the basketball conference in scoring for the second straight season, Robinson failed to be named to either the first, second, or third all-division teams, prompting one person to comment, "It's purely the case of a coach refusing to recognize a player's ability purely out of prejudice."[36]

Robinson endured not only overt abuses but the more subtle understanding that despite his great fame and ability, no career in professional sports awaited him outside the Jim Crow leagues. Other opportunities also seemed limited. His brother Mack had found only janitorial work available after college. Jackie's obvious gate appeal reinforced the irony of his situation. Wherever he performed attendance skyrocketed. At a Chicago track meet, a sell-out crowd materialized for his appearance and an additional 10,000 people—mostly blacks—were turned away. At the All-Star football game in Chicago, 20,000 blacks paid to watch him play. Promoters of an exhibition football contest in Hawaii distributed handbills advertising Robinson, "the sensational All-American halfback," as the primary attraction.[37]

Robinson dropped out of U.C.L.A. during his senior year due to financial difficulties and a desire to support his mother. He worked as an athletic coach for the National Youth Administration and supplemented his income playing for the Los Angeles Bulldogs, a barnstorming football squad. In the spring of 1942 the army drafted him.

Even before his altercation with a Texas bus driver, Robinson experienced repeated confrontations with military Jim Crow.[38] At Fort Riley, Kansas, officials denied him entry to Officers' Candidate School (OCS) despite his college background. Robinson protested to another black athlete stationed at the base—Joe Louis, the heavyweight champion of the world. Louis informed Truman Gibson, a black advisor to the Department of War, who forced a reversal of the Fort Riley policy. Upon graduation from OCS, Robinson faced another dilemma. Fort Riley had an athletic double standard. The football team, which challenged not only other military bases, but colleges as well, accepted blacks; the baseball squad did not. Robinson's attempt to join the baseball team met with rebuff. Pete Reiser, a team member and later Robinson's colleague on the Dodgers, vividly remembered the scene:

> One day a Negro lieutenant came out for the ball team. An officer told him he couldn't play. "You have to play with the colored team," the officer said. That was a joke. There was no colored team. The lieutenant didn't say anything. He stood there for a while watching us work out. Then he turned and walked away. I didn't know who he was then, but that was the first time I saw Jackie Robinson. I can still remember him walking away by himself.[39]

Though barred from playing baseball, the football coach actively solicited the former all-American running back. Offended by the blatant discrimination, Robinson refused to suit up, even after a colonel threatened to order him to play.

Robinson's military stint continued to be a stormy affair. As morale officer for the black troops at Fort Riley, he attempted to increase the number of seats provided for black soldiers at the segregated PX. He succeeded, but not before he had engaged in a shouting match over the phone with an officer who had asked him, "How would you like to have your wife sitting next to a nigger?"[40] Shortly thereafter, the army transferred Robinson to Fort Hood, Texas, where the events leading to his court-martial occurred. In November 1944, he received an honorable discharge, bringing his turbulent military career to an end.

The Robinson personality had been created by these experiences. His fierce competitive passions combined with the scars imbedded by America's racism to produce a proud, yet tempestuous individual. A victim of prejudice, he reacted vehemently when he perceived a racially-motivated slight. His driving desire for excellence and his keen sense of injustice created an explosive urge. "He was the kind of man who had to make his presence felt," says his friend and teammate Don Newcombe. "He sometimes overdid it. Like a boiler he could not keep it all inside him." When Branch Rickey traveled to California to investigate Robinson's background, some people warned him that "Robinson's number one trouble was that he would argue with and talk back to white officials and players" and that as a youth Robinson had difficulties with the police because he was always "shooting off his mouth about his constitutional rights." "He wasn't the most popular man on the campus and off," wrote columnist Will Connolly. "Jackie had a genius for getting into extra-curricular scrapes." Both Rickey and Connolly dismissed this behavior as only unacceptable because of Robinson's race. "If he had done the things people are criticizing him for as a white player he would have been praised to the skies as a fighter, a holler guy, a real competitor, a ballplayer's ballplayer," explained Rickey. "But because he's black his aggressiveness is offensive to some white people."[41]

If Rickey actually believed this, he had sorely misjudged Robinson. For Robinson, as Rickey and so many others learned, was the most aggressive of men, white or black. This characteristic nurtured his greatness and encouraged him to rise to challenges and advance where others might retreat. But this same coiled tension, increased by Robinson's constant and justifiable suspicions of racism, led to eruptions of rage and defiance, which at times exceeded accepted—and even necessary—bounds.

In 1945 Robinson joined the Kansas City Monarchs with whom he spent an unhappy season barnstorming through the nation. The educated Robinson, a nondrinker and nonsmoker, never quite fit into the boisterous life of the Negro Leagues. Accustomed to the discipline and structure of intercollegiate athletics, Robinson found the loose scheduling and erratic play appalling. Nor did he hide his distaste for being relegated to a Jim Crow league. Though most black ballplayers resigned themselves to their segregated status, Robinson often spoke of impending integration. Teammate Othello Renfroe recalls, "We'd ride miles and miles on the bus and his whole talk was 'Well you guys better get ready because pretty soon baseball's going to sign one of us.' " When faced by the indignities of southern segregation, Jackie would grow livid. "We . . . pulled up in service stations in Mississippi where drinking fountains said black and white and a couple of times we had to leave without our change, he'd get so mad," Renfroe recalls.[42]

Robinson's hair-trigger disposition led many Negro League players to doubt that he would be able to withstand the pressures of racial pioneering. "It was hard to anticipate seeing any black player crack the major leagues," writes Quincy Trouppe, "and with Jackie's temper being the way it was, it didn't seem likely that a major league team would be willing to take a chance with him."[43]

Others, however, quickly saw Robinson as the perfect candidate to cross the color line. In private conversations before Robinson had even played a game for the Monarchs, sportswriters Wendell Smith and Sam Lacy agreed that Robinson could succeed in the majors. In a preseason article in 1945 in *Negro Baseball*, Lacy named several prospective major league players, calling Robinson the "ideal man to pace the experiment." Lacy noted that Robinson's college experience made him no stranger to interracial competition. "He would have neither the inferiority complex we should steer away from," wrote Lacy, "nor would he have the cocky bulldozing attitude we likewise must avoid."[44] When Smith offered to recruit players for the Red Sox tryout, he made Robinson his first choice.

By August 1945, Branch Rickey also felt that Robinson satisfied his specifications. Although neither Rickey's scouts nor other black players considered Robinson the best player in the Negro Leagues, few questioned his superb competitive skills. More importantly, he met the Mahatma's other qualifications. He was college-educated, unusual for a baseball player of that era, and had played with white teammates in the past. Destined for the spotlight of publicity, Robinson was articulate, intelligent, and witty. He had served as an officer during the war, which made his claim to equality on the baseball diamond all the more persuasive. And, as his actions in the military had proven, he had the courage and convictions necessary for the undertaking. Robinson's temperament remained the sole question mark. Rickey could only hope that the athlete would understand the need for self-control and possess the ability to exercise it.

Jackie Robinson's personal life also matched Rickey's demands. Off-the-field scandals involving liquor or women might undermine the great experiment, but Rickey's investigations revealed that he had little to fear along these lines. Like Rickey, Robinson was a Methodist who neither smoked nor drank. Although single, his social life revolved around one woman, Rachel Isum. Jackie had met Rachel while both attended U.C.L.A. Intelligent, poised, and beautiful, Rachel had been born and raised in Los Angeles, the product of a black middle-class upbringing. War and Jackie's athletic travels had delayed their marriage, which had been rescheduled to follow the 1945 baseball season. As Rickey studied the scouting reports on his desk, his good fortune must have surprised him. His lengthy search and careful planning notwithstanding, even the considerable imagination of Branch Rickey could not have envisioned a more suitable candidate than Jackie Robinson.

IV

Clyde Sukeforth had spent most of his adult life in baseball. A native New Englander, he had played in the major leagues for ten years. After his retirement in 1934 he worked in the Dodger organization as coach, minor league manager, and scout. Since Rickey's arrival in Brooklyn he had become one of the Mahatma's most trusted assistants. Throughout the 1945 season Sukeforth had scouted the Negro Leagues in the name of the Brown Dodgers, with no suspicions of Rickey's purpose. In late August, however, when Rickey dispatched him to Chicago to meet with Jackie Robinson, Sukeforth realized the magnitude of his journey. Rickey instructed him to watch Robinson at shortstop to see if he could make the long throw required for that position. If Sukeforth was satisfied with his arm, he was to bring him to Brooklyn. Then Rickey added, "If his schedule won't permit it, if he can't come in, then make an appointment for me and I'll go out there."[45]

"Mr. Rickey go out there? To see if some guy named Robinson was good enough to play shortstop for the Brooklyn Brown Bombers?" Sukeforth later told interviewer Donald Honig. "Well, I'm not the smartest guy in the world, but I said to myself, *this could be the real thing.*"[46]

Sukeforth approached Robinson at Comiskey Park before a scheduled Monarchs' contest and found the player wary and guarded. The scout explained that he worked for the Brooklyn Dodgers and had instructions to observe Robinson's throwing abilities. Unfortunately, Robinson had injured his shoulder earlier in the week and could not play. Nonetheless, Sukeforth decided to invite Robinson to Brooklyn. Other scouts had issued laudatory reports and Rickey seemed anxious to meet the black shortstop. Since Robinson would be sidelined for several days by his injury, the moment appeared ideal.

Robinson always claimed that Rickey's revelation that he had chosen him to integrate baseball totally surprised him. But Sukeforth is not convinced. In Sukeforth's hotel room that night, Robinson pressed the scout for more details. "Why is Mr. Rickey interested in my arm? Why does he want to see me?" demanded Robinson. Sukeforth repeated his instructions including Rickey's offer to come to Robinson. "The significance of that last part wasn't lost on him. I could see that," asserts Sukeforth.[47]

"The more we talked, the better I liked him," says the former Dodger scout. "There was something about that man that just gripped you. He was tough, he was intelligent, and he was proud."[48]

Sukeforth had Robinson meet him in Toledo, where he had to scout another player. "I look up between games of a doubleheader," recalls Sukeforth, "and there's Robinson, sitting back in the stands watching me. I don't know how long he's been there, his eyes on me."[49] The two men traveled together to New York where on August 28, 1945, Sukeforth ushered Robinson into Rickey's office.

The meeting between Branch Rickey and Jackie Robinson has passed into the folklore of American sports. Sukeforth introduced the two men, warning Rickey that he had not watched Robinson throw. "But the old man was so engrossed in Robinson by that time, he didn't hear a damn word I said," remembers Sukeforth. "When Rickey met somebody he was interested in, he studied them in the most profound way. He just sat and stared. And that's what he did with Robinson—stared at him as if he were trying to get inside the man. And Jack stared right back at him." Robinson also recalls that moment, "His piercing eyes roamed over me with such meticulous care, I almost felt naked."[50]

Rickey saw a good-looking, broad-shouldered man, one half inch shy of six feet tall. Robinson possessed, by one description, "a sensitive, intelligent, face, with strong features, a high forehead, wide and somewhat brooding eyes, a full mouth, and determined chin." His skin was uncompromisingly dark. Columnist John Crosby called him, "the blackest black man, as well as one of the handsomest, I ever saw."[51]

Rickey told Robinson of his extensive research into the athlete's career and personal life. He then revealed the purpose of the meeting. Robinson, despite any earlier suspicions, was nonetheless jolted. He also remained skeptical. "It took me a long time to convince myself that Rickey was not just making a gesture," he told Wendell Smith. For three hours, Rickey harangued Robinson on the responsibilities incumbent upon the first black player, graphically illustrating the difficulties that Robinson might face. He portrayed the hostile teammate, the abusive opponent, the insulting fan, the obstinate hotel clerk. Rickey challenged the black man with racial epithets and verbally transplanted him into ugly confrontations. "His acting was so convincing that I found myself chain-gripping my fingers behind my back," wrote Robinson.[52]

In the face of this onslaught Robinson finally responded, "Mr. Rickey, do you want a ballplayer who's afraid to fight back?" The Mahatma had awaited this moment. "I want a player with guts enough not to fight back," he roared.[53]

The purpose of Rickey's theatrics grew apparent to Robinson. When the Dodger president posed as a player who had just punched Robinson in the cheek, the man who had fought Jim Crow in the army replied, "I get it. What you want me to say is that I've got another cheek." Rickey produced a copy of Papini's *Life of Christ* and asked Robinson to read the sections on "Nonresistance." He impressed upon the black athlete the necessity to retreat from all confrontations until he had established himself in the major leagues.[54]

Robinson did not accept the challenge hastily. Sukeforth, the sole witness to this historic meeting, later told Rickey, "I was impressed with the fellow and the way he handled himself. He would not go off half-cocked. He gave your questions serious thought before he answered them." It seemed to Sukeforth like a full five minutes before Robinson responded to Rickey's appeal. The black athlete finally replied, "Mr. Rickey, I think I can play ball in Montreal. I think I can play ball in Brooklyn. But, you're a better judge of that than I am. If you want to take this gamble, I will promise you there will be no incident."[55]

Thus began one of the most remarkable relationships in sports history, one which Rachel Robinson feels people have misunderstood. "The things that have been reported about it make it sound very paternalistic on Mr. Rickey's part as though he directed everything," asserts Rachel. "There was much more of an attitude of their being collaborators and conspirators. . . . There was an alliance between them and a kind of mutual respect."[56] Both Robinsons agreed with Rickey as to the need for care and caution lest the great experiment fail. The central figures in the venture had no major disagreements.

Before leaving Rickey's office Robinson signed an agreement to accept a bonus of $3,500 and a salary of $600 a month which would be offered by the Montreal Royals, the top Dodger farm club, by November 1. He also averred that he had no written or oral obligation to any other club. Rickey swore Robinson to secrecy, with exceptions made for Rachel and his mother. The momentous news would remain hoarded until Rickey deemed a public announcement appropriate.

With Robinson in the fold, Rickey had to complete numerous other preparations. He considered the proper timing of the announcement. Dodson urged Rickey to make his intentions public after the baseball season, but before players signed their contracts for 1946. In this way people in the Dodger organization would know that they might be playing with a black man before committing themselves for another season. Rickey, on the other hand sought to delay publicity longer, possibly until the New Year. For one thing, he hoped to sign several other black players for Dodger minor league teams "and make one complete break of the story." In addition, he felt that the story would receive more attention once the football season had ended.[57]

Rickey informed sportswriter Arthur Mann of his plans and asked him to write an authorized story describing the reasons for signing black players and the search for the right pioneer. On October 7, however, Rickey wrote to Mann, "We just can't go with the article. . . . We can't go with any publicity at this time." Rickey stated that he would be unable to clear the contracts of the additional players until December at the earliest and that he hoped to extend the deadline on signing Robinson from November 1 until January 1. "It might not be so good to sign Robinson with other and better players unsigned," he explained.[58]

The black athletes who most interested Rickey were catcher Roy Campanella and pitcher Don Newcombe. Campanella was the more established of the two. The son of an Italian father and an Afro-American mother, Campanella had grown up in a relatively integrated environment in Philadelphia. Like Robinson, he had experience competing among whites. "I always played on white teams in my whole younger years," says Campanella. "Until I went into the all-black leagues, I never played on any all-black teams." Unlike the college-trained Robinson, Campanella received his education in the buses and ball parks of the Negro Leagues. Although only twenty-four, he had already played nine seasons with the Baltimore Elite Giants. Dodger scouts unanimously praised Campanella for his fielding and throwing abilities. A squat 5'9" and 215 pounds, he was an unlikely looking baseball player. But he ran with surprising speed and hit with tremendous power. "We were all in on scouting Campanella," recalls Sukeforth. "You couldn't go wrong there."[59]

Newcombe, a Sukeforth discovery, represented a far greater risk. Like both Robinson and Campanella, Newcombe came from a nonsouthern, urban environment. Only nineteen-years old, the tall, husky New Jerseyite had much to learn about pitching. He possessed a major league fastball, but he lacked control and discipline. Nonetheless, Newcombe had recorded a 14-4 mark for the Newark Eagles in 1945. "He wasn't by any means the best pitcher in Negro baseball," wrote Wendell Smith, "but Rickey signed him because he's young, big, and has all the natural ability necessary to get him into the big leagues."[60]

Both Campanella and Newcombe appeared at Ebbets Field in a black versus white all-star game in mid-October. Newcombe had pitched two innings on a cold, rainy Sunday when a sore arm forced his removal from the contest. "I'll never forget. This man walked in, this white man, and I was in there crying because I thought my baseball career was over," relates Newcombe. The man was Clyde Sukeforth and he asked Newcombe to report the following day to the Dodger offices, where the pitcher signed an agreement which he believed obligated him to play for the Brooklyn Brown Dodgers.[61]

Later that week, Campanella journeyed to Montague Street in downtown Brooklyn. He arrived at 10 in the morning and left at two in the afternoon. "We talked," he later told Robinson, "or rather Mr. Rickey did. Man, he's the talkingest man I ever did see." Rickey questioned Campanella about his weight and age. He reviewed the details of Campanella's life and baseball career. "He had everything down there that I had ever done," recalls Campanella, "at home, at school, about my parents, my family, everything." After several hours, Rickey finally asked Campanella if he would like to play in the Dodger organization. The catcher, who for years had sought an opportunity in organized baseball, assumed that Rickey meant the Brown Dodgers. Campanella explained that he already received one of the highest salaries in the Negro Leagues and expressed reluctance to risk that status on a precarious new venture. He declined Rickey's offer. Before he left, however, Rickey had Campanella promise not to sign with another team before speaking again with the Dodgers.[62]

Meanwhile, pressures on the New York baseball teams to end Jim Crow mounted. Several political candidates had injected this issue into their 1945 campaigns. Communist City Councilman Ben Davis, a former college football star running for re-election, distributed a flyer featuring two blacks, one a dead soldier, the other a baseball player. The caption read, "Good enough to die for his country, but not good enough for organized baseball." A state delegation investigating violations of the Quinn-Ives Act called upon the three major league owners in October and demanded that they sign a pledge not to discriminate in hiring. The baseball executives refused and an indignant Horace Stoneham of the Giants denounced the delegation for their coercive attempt to force the issue at election time.[63]

In early October Yankee General Manager Larry MacPhail offered his solution to the race problem. Privately, MacPhail opposed integration and the plan exposed his Machiavellian personality. ("The Redhead is so careful of the truth," observed one writer of MacPhail, "he used it very sparingly.") MacPhail condemned "political and social-minded drum beaters" for stirring up the issue. He emphasized the need to strengthen and preserve the Negro Leagues. Once this had been accomplished, a few blacks who had established their "ability and character" in their own league might advance to the majors.[64] If implemented, MacPhail's proposal would have created an illusion of progress while indefinitely delaying the advent of blacks.

Mayor La Guardia also joined in the clamor. He boasted about the work of the Mayor's Committee on Baseball on his Sunday radio program. Suddenly, the panel, created as a benign subterfuge by Rickey and Dodson, became a liability. Both Rickey and MacPhail had resigned, the former in order not to compromise himself, the latter to issue his own report. The remaining members, unaware of their role as a stalling device, prepared to issue a report criticizing the three New York teams and calling for immediate action. Mayor La Guardia requested that the committee allow him to report that "baseball would shortly begin signing Negro players" as a result of their work. "Our committee's become an election football," confessed one member, neatly mixing athletic metaphors.[65]

Confronted with these developments, Rickey feared that people would view the Robinson signing as a forced action rather than a carefully planned project. He asked the mayor to postpone his announcement for one week and contacted Robinson. Rickey instructed the former all-American to fly directly to Montreal for a press conference the following afternoon.

For almost two months Jackie Robinson had kept the news bottled inside him. Only his family and fiancée knew that Rickey had tapped him to break the color line. Now, with the signing one day off, he had to share his thoughts. Robinson was staying at the Woodside Hotel in Harlem awaiting departure on a barnstorming tour in Venezuela. He knew that Campanella, one of his teammates, had met with Rickey the preceding week. The two athletes scarcely knew each other, but Robinson invited the catcher to his room to play cards. After the first hand Robinson questioned Campanella about his visit with Rickey. Then he informed the Negro League star that he had signed. Campanella said he had no interest in playing for the Brown Dodgers.

"Did Mr. Rickey tell you that he wanted you for the Brown Dodgers?" asked Jackie.

Campanella realized that Rickey had never mentioned which team he desired him to join. Robinson suddenly exploded with excitement. "I didn't sign with the Brown Dodgers," he told the startled Campanella. "I'm going to play for Montreal. . . . I'm going to be the first Negro in organized baseball. I'm flying up to Montreal tomorrow for the official signing ceremony. It's going to be a big thing—cameras and everything."[66]

Campanella sat dumbfounded, hoping that he had not destroyed his opportunity to play in the major leagues. Robinson did not seem to notice. He was talking about the future.

5

It Won't Work Out!

Everybody in baseball from the batboy up is expressing an opinion on Robinson's chances of making good.

Wendell Smith, 1945[1]

I

On Tuesday, October 23, 1945, President Hector Racine of the Montreal Royals called a press conference at Delormier Downs, the club's home ball-park. Racine stated that the Royals would make "a very important announcement," one which would affect baseball from "coast to coast." He suggested that photographers as well as reporters should be on hand. The content of the forthcoming story bewildered the Canadian press. Harold Atkins of the Montreal *Daily Star* speculated that Montreal would get a big league team. "Only a big league franchise would cause such a furor," wrote Atkins. Another reporter suggested that the Royals would name a legendary star like Babe Ruth as manager.[2]

At the appointed time over two dozen newspaper and radio men crowded into the Royal offices. Racine entered the room accompanied by Lt. Colonel Romeo Gavreau, the Royals' vice-president, Branch Rickey, Jr., the director of the Dodger farm system, and an unidentified, broad-shouldered black man. Racine introduced the mystery figure as Jackie Robinson and announced that the Royals had signed him to a contract.

The news, according to one writer, "exploded" on the assemblage. A moment of "stunned silence" ensued before the reporters dashed for telephones to relay the startling story to their newspapers and radio stations.[3] Several minutes transpired before Racine could restore order and resume the press conference.

"We made this step for two reasons," Racine informed the reporters. "First, we are signing this boy because we think of him primarily as a ball player. Secondly, we think it a point of fairness." Racine stressed that although the Royals would back Robinson fully, "he will have to fight for his place at training camp like every other rookie." Rickey, Jr., reviewed the process through which the Dodgers had selected the black player. He described Robinson as a former army officer and "a fine type of young man, intelligent and college bred." The "Twig" predicted that his father, who had remained in Brooklyn, would be "severely criticized in some sections of the United States where racial prejudice was rampant." He acknowledged that southern ballplayers might "steer away" from signing Dodger contracts. Some athletes might go so far as to quit the game. "But," remonstrated Rickey, Jr., "they'll be back in baseball after they work a year or two in a cotton mill."[4]

Throughout these pronouncements, the eyes of the reporters naturally shifted to Robinson, the focus of the afternoon's drama. "This Robinson is definitely dark," wrote Al Parsley of the Montreal *Herald* the following day. "His color is the hue of ebony. By no means can he be called a brown bomber or a chocolate soldier." Outwardly, Robinson appeared calm and confident, though behind this facade, he later wrote, "I was nervous as the devil."[5] When Racine and Rickey, Jr., had finished speaking, Robinson addressed the reporters.

Jokingly referring to himself as a "guinea pig," Robinson expressed delight with being chosen to break the color line. He noted that with the exception of his season with the Kansas City Monarchs, most of his considerable athletic experience had been with mixed, not segregated, teams. The new Royal admitted that he expected problems with accommodations and from fans and other players. "But, I'm ready to take the chance," he asserted. "Maybe I'm doing something for my race."[6]

Jackie's performance received rave reviews from the reporters. "He talked with that easy fluency of an educated man," wrote Parsley. "Jack answered a dozen questions fired at him . . . with easy confidence, but no cocksureness, nor braggadocio." At one point, Robinson displayed a "toothy grin that was really fetching."[7] Robinson had passed his first test. Now he and the officials of the Brooklyn and Montreal teams sat back and waited for the waves of reaction.

II

In his initial *Sporting News* column following the Robinson signing, Dan Daniel eavesdropped on a discussion in the imaginary "Bijou Tonsorial Parlor, Jem Miggs, Prop., in Anyoldtown, U.S.A."

HIGGLEBOTTOM: I see how the Dodgers have signed a Negro ballplayer. First thing you know, we'll have Old Black Joe McCarthy managing the Yankees.

SNORT: And the club turned into a minstrel show. That MacPhail is always looking for something different, here's his chance.

MIGGS: At 2:30 in the afternoon, or at 8:30 before night games, the umpire won't call "play ball." He will holler "Gentlemen be seated!"

JASPER: The time will come when white players will have to cork up to stay in the major leagues.

CHEERBYL: You men make me sick. You cheer for Negro players on college football teams. You think its okay to have Negro players on National Football League teams. You are willing to let Negro athletes win olympic championships and you think its great for Joe Louis to be heavyweight champion of the World. Why not Negro ball players?

MOANS: Well, it ain't never been done before.

CHEERBYL: We never threw an atomic bomb before either. Wake up Willie, this is 1945. Negroes helped win the war.

JASPER: Well, if the Negro ball players—granted there are any good enough to make the grade, which they say they ain't—want to put up with the hardships they will run into in the big time, let them take their medicine.[8]

In a few short lines Daniel encapsulated the debate over baseball integration as well as the racial and political tenor of the times. His characters move from insensitive racial stereotyping to a discussion of the pros and cons of the Robinson signing. They invoke many of the major themes underpinning the "noble experiment": the athletic double standard posed by baseball segregation, the wartime sacrifices of black soldiers, and the dawning of a new era. This barbershop sextet seems skeptical that blacks possessed the talent or wherewithal to survive the forthcoming ordeal, but they willingly offer them the opportunity. One senses, on the part of Parker, a reluctant acceptance of the inevitability of the events that have shaken his familiar world.

Daniel's barbershop libretto reflected the intense reaction generated by the Montreal announcement. Newspapers relegated the story to the sports pages, where writers accustomed to predicting athletic outcomes speculated about the most dramatic racial development of the era. Nonetheless the Robinson saga immediately captured nationwide attention. The *Sporting News* decried the uproar as "out of proportion to the actual vitality of the story."[9] Yet the "Bible of Baseball" devoted almost four full pages to the development, presenting reactions from major sportswriters, different sections of the country, the black press, other players, and baseball executives. The range of these responses reveals the racial perspectives of postwar America and the magnitude of the venture initiated by Rickey and Robinson.

Many commentators openly questioned Rickey's wisdom and motives. Cleveland sportswriter Ed McAuley saw the race issue as "an aspect of a grave social question" and doubted that baseball dugouts, "seldom operated on the highest level of mental maturity," were "the places to seek the answer." In a lengthy editorial, the *Sporting News* argued that Rickey's surprise announcement left "the racial problem in baseball as far from a satisfactory solution as ever." The Dodgers had signed Robinson, alleged the journal, primarily as a "legalistic move" to evade New York State's Quinn-Ives bill. True integration remained impractical if not impossible.[10]

"Some of his contemporaries doubt Rickey's sincerity in the whole matter and put it down as a publicity dodge," said Dan Parker. In Montreal Sam Maltin discovered "a heavy fog of suspicion . . . that Robinson will never wear a Montreal uniform." Rickey's old nemesis Jimmy Powers charged, "We question Branch Rickey's statements that he is another Abraham Lincoln and that he has a heart as big as a watermelon and that he loves all mankind." Black sportswriter Joe Bostic also possessed doubts. "I thought it was a trick," he recalls. "I thought Rickey was strictly a tricky man. I just wouldn't accept that it would be real."[11]

Several southern sportswriters objected vehemently to the integration breakthrough. "I don't see why a top flight Negro ballplayer would be so anxious to play in the white leagues when he is doing so well in his own organization," wrote Atlanta *Journal* sports editor Ed Danforth. Danforth warned that "the only menace to peace between the races is the carpetbagger white press and agitators in the Negro press who capitalize on racial issues." George White of the Dallas *News* described the Dodger action as "unfair" to both Robinson and the South, where an established way of life was threatened. "Segregation in the South will continue," added Bud Seifert of Spartanburg, South Carolina. "We live happier with segregation in athletics as well as all other activities."[12]

Rickey's supporters, however, easily outnumbered his detractors. To many Americans the lessons of World War II dictated more liberal racial policies. "Those who were good enough to fight and die by the side of whites," stated Elmer Ferguson of the Montreal *Herald*, "are plenty good to play by the side of whites." Black Congressman Adam Clayton Powell called the Robinson signing, "a definite step toward winning the peace." Lee Dunbar of the Oakland *Tribune* saw it "fitting that the end of baseball's Jim Crow law should follow the conclusion of a great war to preserve liberty, equality and decency."[13]

The end of baseball's color line appeared in some accounts as comparable to the freeing of the slaves. Reporters and cartoonists caricatured Rickey as another Abraham Lincoln. A cartoon from the Montreal *Gazette* showed

Rickey with the Emancipation Proclamation in hand, gazing up at Lincoln, and musing, "Wonder how I'd look in a stovepipe hat?" Dan Parker wrote, only partly in jest, "Any resemblance between Branch Rickey and Abraham Lincoln is purely coincidental. . . . True [Rickey] is given to making addresses, but he modestly disclaims credit for having topped Honest Abe's Gettysburg effort, at least to date."[14]

Voices of acceptance emerged even amidst the chorus of southern dissent. "The Negro and the white man are opponents in the ring, why not the baseball diamond?" reasoned Durham (N.C.) *Sun* sports editor Hugo Germinio. W. N. Cox of Norfolk, Virginia, reduced the issue to one of performance. "I guarantee that if Jackie Robinson hits homers and plays a whale of a game for Montreal that the fans will lose sight of his color," he predicted. Sports director Fred Maley of the San Antonio *News* agreed. "A star is a star no matter what his race," asserted Maley, "and I am not apprehensive over the consequences of the signing of Robinson."[15]

Robinson himself became the object of national interest. "I am happy for the event," wrote black columnist Ludlow Werner, "but I'm sorry for Jackie. He will be haunted by the expectations of his race." Sam Lacy cast Robinson in the role of a greater "national benefactor" than President Truman. "Alone, Robinson represents a weapon far more potent than the combined forces of all our liberal legislation," contended Lacy. Robinson, observed Wendell Smith, "has the hopes, aspirations and ambitions of thirteen million black Americans heaped upon his broad, sturdy shoulders."[16]

In light of these responsibilities, many writers—both black and white— urged Robinson to emulate the most well known and popular black man in America, Heavyweight Champion Joe Louis. "None of our scholars, scientists, artists or writers has received the popular accolades or acclaim that has been the swarthy heavyweight champion's," wrote Pittsburgh *Courier* columnist Joseph D. Bibb. During the past decade Louis had transcended the sports world to become a genuine folk hero. To blacks he represented racial pride and prowess. To whites he appeared the ideal Negro—polite, well mannered, one who knew his place—in short, a "credit to his race." Louis's 1938 ring triumph over the German Max Schmelling and his wartime fund raising had elevated him to the height of his popularity. Louis, asserted Bibb, "has given a wonderful example of the value of superior conduct and spotless behavior," one which Robinson might profit from. Robinson sounded the same theme, "I'll try to do as good a job as Joe Louis has done. . . . He has done a great job for us and I will try to carry on."[17]

Many observers doubted that Robinson could assume the Louis mantle. San Francisco sportswriter Will Connally reported that in California, many people felt that Rickey had chosen the wrong man. They considered Robinson's former U.C.L.A. teammate Kenny Washington a superior pioneer. "Kenny is a 'white man,' a nice guy," Connally quoted Californians as saying, "Robinson, he's a troublemaker."[18]

An even more fundamental question about Robinson underlay this speculation: Was he talented enough to survive in organized baseball? Although few people had actually seen him play, there existed no absence of expertise on this issue. Jimmy Powers, the influential New York *Daily News* sports columnist fired the opening salvo. "We would like to see him make good," wrote Powers, suddenly less enthusiastic about baseball integration, "but it is unfair to build up hopes and then dash them down. . . . Robinson is a 1000-1 shot to make the grade." Powers argued illogically that if Robinson "couldn't muscle into the major league line-ups when 43-year old outfielders patrolled the grass for pennant winners and one-armed men and callow 4–F's were stumbling around," he had little chance now that baseball teams had a "backlog of talent, proven stars returning from the war."[19]

The *Sporting News,* in its editorial column, pursued a similar line of reasoning. Robinson, contended the Baseball Bible, "is reported to possess baseball abilities which, were he white, would make him eligible for a trial with, let us say, the Brooklyn Dodger Class C farm at Newport News, if he were six years younger." Like Powers, the *Sporting News* noted that with the war's end, Robinson would be "thrown into competition with a vast number of younger, more skilled, and more experienced players." A year earlier, perhaps, Robinson would have had a chance, but now, "the waters of competition in the International League will flood far over his head."[20]

Cleveland Indian star Bob Feller, considered an expert on the Negro Leagues due to his post-season barnstorming tours, agreed with these assessments. He asserted that of those Negro League players he had watched only Paige and Josh Gibson might qualify for the majors. As for Robinson, Feller "could not foresee any future . . . in big league baseball." The former U.C.L.A. all-American, said the Cleveland hurler, had "football shoulders and couldn't hit an inside pitch to save his neck. If he were a white man, I doubt if they would consider him big league material." Feller fended off criticism by telling Wendell Smith, "I hope he makes good. But I don't think he will."[21]

Reporters and fans, usually unaware that Negro League all-stars competed evenly with Feller's major league squads, generally accepted his comments. Robinson, on the other hand, vehemently objected to this appraisal. "I played two games against Feller on the coast last month," he told Jimmy Cannon, "but if you lined up ten of us [Negroes], I'll bet he couldn't pick me out of the bunch."[22]

The reactions of most white players, other than Feller, remained private and guarded. For the reserve army of old-timers, 4Fs, and minor league talents who had sustained baseball during the war years, returning servicemen posed a greater threat to their jobs than a solitary black shortstop. Those discharged from the military were anxious to resume their interrupted careers without further distractions. Reporters evidenced no interest in the feelings of northern players, even those likely to be Robinson's teammates, and few athletes unwisely volunteered their opinions.

On the other hand, the press besieged several southerners for reactions. The most ominous and most widely quoted comments emanated from Alabama native Dixie Walker, the popular Brooklyn Dodger outfielder. "As long as he isn't with the Dodgers," stated Dixie, "I'm not worried." Rogers Hornsby, the Texas-bred, Hall of Fame slugger and former manager bluntly predicted, "It won't work out." Hornsby contended that a "mixed baseball team differs from other sports because ball players on the road live much closer together. It's going to be more difficult for the Negro player to adjust himself to the life of a major league club, than for the white players to accept him."[23]

Detroit Tiger first baseman Rudy York, alone among the southern players, publicly deviated from the consensus. York, from Cartersville, Georgia, said of Robinson, "I wish him all the luck in the world and hope he makes good." For his encouragement, York received a letter from the NAACP, praising him for his stand, which probably did little to further endear him to his neighbors.[24]

Pee Wee Reese, the Kentucky-born Dodger shortstop, heard the news while returning from Guam on a naval vessel. "Hey, Pee Wee," shouted one of his fellow sailors, "the Dodgers have signed a nigger to play baseball." Reese took considerable ribbing from crew members when they heard that Robinson played shortstop. Surrounded by the vast Pacific Ocean, Reese had the opportunity to think about the unexpected development before facing reporters. By the time he reached the United States, he had resolved that the matter did not concern him. He remained the Dodgers' regular shortstop and if anybody, either black or white, could replace him, the more power to him. When asked for a comment upon reaching San Francisco, Reese was his usual puckish, confident self. "Just my luck" he joked, "the first Negro to be signed to a contract in modern Organized Baseball not only had to be signed by the Brooklyn organization, but he also had to be a shortstop."[25]

Surprisingly, the prospect of integration did not generate as heated a reaction among southerners as Branch Rickey, Jr.'s, comment which implied that the region's ballplayers had emerged from cotton mills. The southern caste system deemed mill workers inferior to those who worked the soil. Bill Werber, a former major league infielder, wrote a letter to Rickey, Sr., criticizing "the attitude that your son has assumed," as a "definite insult to every southern boy." Werber charged that Rickey's effort to force southerners to grant social acceptance to Negroes was "highly distasteful" and that the Dodgers were in fact "for some unaccountable reason, discriminating against the majority." The remark also rankled a group of cotton mill owners who threatened to sue the Dodgers for slander.[26]

To gauge the response among Negro League players, reporters naturally turned to Satchel Paige. When informed of the comments of Feller, his barnstorming rival, Paige countered, "They didn't make a mistake in signing Robinson. He's a No. 1 professional player. They couldn't have picked a better man." Paige's flattery, however, masked a cauldron of conflicting emotions. Thrilled that the color line had at last fallen, the failure to be selected as the standard-bearer disappointed the aging hurler. "Signing Jackie like they did still hurt me deep down," Paige wrote in his autobiography. "I'd been the guy who started all that big talk about letting us in the big time. . . . I'd been the one the white boys wanted to barnstorm against. I'd been the one everybody said should be in the majors. . . . It was still me that ought to have been first."[27] Despite his disappointment, Paige presented a public face of uncompromising support for his former Monarch teammate.

In his ardor to help the "great experiment," Paige called Robinson "the greatest colored player I've ever seen." Either Paige had engaged in hyperbole or he saw something that most of his Negro League colleagues did not. "Robinson was never really spoken of as a superstar," recalled Newark Eagle owner Effa Manley. Buck Leonard asserts, "When the Dodgers signed Robinson, we didn't think he was that good."[28] Indeed, some black athletes feared that Rickey had chosen Robinson precisely because of his lack of ability. By hiring a ballplayer of inferior talent, the Dodgers could guarantee failure and would be able to retreat to their segregated ways.

Several factors account for the relatively low esteem in which Negro League players held Robinson. While jealousy may have played a minor role, the brevity of Robinson's career with the Monarchs constituted a more important consideration. A team member for less than a full season, at least part of which he spent as the second-string shortstop, Robinson had neither established himself as a "star," nor as "one of the boys." Nonetheless, the haphazard statistics of the Negro Leagues credited Robinson with a .340 batting average and he started at shortstop in the East-West All-Star Game. Even if the players did not fully appreciate Robinson's talent, the prospect of integration brought unmistakable joy to their ranks.

The sense of celebration pervaded black America. Unlike the white press, black newspapers placed the Robinson story on the front page, hailed the breakthrough in their editorials, and devoted a substantial proportion of their papers to the event. Robinson immediately joined Joe Louis atop the pantheon of black heroes, while Rickey became one of the most popular white men in black communities. To young blacks the news provided inspiration. "I was 16 and already dreaming of a baseball career, but not in organized ball." recalled St. Louis native Elston Howard. "A friend of mine came into the store and said 'Ellie, have you heard the news? Branch Rickey has signed one of our boys. His name is Jackie Robinson.' I felt like dancing all over that floor. The path was opening up. Maybe I could become a major league player."[29]

Few white Americans shared Howard's jubilation. Yet despite scattered criticism, the decision to integrate baseball seemed a popular one. Dodger Manager Leo Durocher, touring military bases in the Pacific for the USO, reported that American troops expressed considerable interest in the story and thought the news was "really great." As election day approached in New York City, according to one observer, there ensued "a mad race among the various pressure groups, sportswriters, and other lesser fry to convince the public that they alone were responsible for the signing of Jackie Robinson."[30] Even those who voiced doubts and skepticism seemed resigned to the inevitability of desegregation in the national pastime, if not through Rickey's "noble experiment," then sometime in the near future.

Baseball executives, however, numbered among the minority who did not share this sentiment. Minor league officials openly criticized Rickey's *fait accompli.* "Very surprising. It's hard to believe. I can't understand it," remarked Joseph A. Brown whose Buffalo Bisons competed against Montreal in the International League. Herb Armstrong, business manager of the rival Baltimore Orioles, suggested legislation to prohibit the signing of black players. Eastern League President Thomas Richardson wired Commissioner Chandler suggesting that Robinson be sent "right back to the Kansas City club where he belongs." Referring to Rickey, Richardson added, "Some of these fellows lay the eggs and after they're broke they expect someone else to take them and put them back together."[31]

W. G. Bramham, the influential president of the National Association of Professional Baseball Leagues, the governing body of the minors, offered the most colorful commentary. "Whenever I hear a white man . . . broadcasting what a Moses he is to the Negro race," exhorted the North Carolina-based Bramham, "right then I know the latter needs a bodyguard." Bramham criticized those of the "carpetbagger stripe," who "under the guise of helping" really used blacks "for their own selfish interests that retard the race." Bramham aimed his most sarcastic barb directly at Rickey. "Father Divine will have to look to his laurels," he joked, "for we can expect Rickey Temple to be in the course of construction in Harlem soon."[32]

Major league executives, concentrated in media centers and vulnerable to criticism, displayed more caution in their reactions. Commissioner Chandler, National League President Frick, and American League President Will Harridge were all "unavailable for comment." Athletics' owner Connie Mack tersely stated, "I'm not familiar with the move and don't know Robinson. I wouldn't care to comment." Alva Bradley, owner of the Cleveland Indians, and Eddie Collins, general manager of the Red Sox, denied the existence of a color line. Collins noted Robinson's tryout with the Red Sox, adding, despite all evidence to the contrary, "Of course, they always have a chance to prove themselves in the minors." Bradley pursued a similar tack. "Colored players have never been discriminated against in the major leagues," he argued. "They have simply never been able to get into the minor leagues to get the proper training for major league competition." Most other executives remained noncommittal. Only Horace Stoneham of the Giants, under pressure from New York politicians, gave even a qualified endorsement of the Dodger action. "It is a fine way to start the program," he stated. "But we have hundreds of returning servicemen and only if they fail to make the grade will we have room for new players."[33]

The public response of major league officials revealed little about their perceptions of Rickey's bold action. Behind the scenes, however, the Robinson controversy elicited greater concern, as the baseball hierarchy attempted to adjust to the new reality thrust upon them.

III

On February 16, 1948, two and a half years after he had signed Jackie Robinson, Branch Rickey recounted the integration saga in a speech at Wilberforce State University, a black college in Ohio. After reviewing the, by then, familiar details of the story, Rickey unexpectedly charged that his fellow owners, in a secret 1946 report, had condemned his efforts. At a meeting of major league officials, alleged Rickey, "after I had signed Robinson and before he had played a game," copies of a document criticizing him were handed out and then carefully collected. "Each copy bore the name of the man to whom it was handed," Rickey told his predominantly black audience. "After we read them they were collected. [National League President] Frick checked off the names to see that he had all the copies." The report stated that, "However well intentioned, the use of Negro players would hazard all the physical properties of baseball."[34] The other owners, according to Rickey, unanimously approved this document.

"You can't find a copy of that report anywhere," contended the Mahatma, implying a cover-up. "I've tried to get a copy of the report but league officials tell me they were all destroyed. But let them deny that they adopted such a report if they dare. I'd like to see the color of the man's eyes who would deny it."

The baseball hierarchy adamantly refuted Rickey's allegation. Bob Carpenter, owner of the Phillies, called them "ridiculous." Clark Griffith of the Senators claimed that he had never heard of the report, commenting, "The door has always been open to those boys if they were good enough to make it into the big leagues." The most vicious attack came from Larry MacPhail, Rickey's arch rival. MacPhail, who had retired from baseball after the 1947 season, described Rickey's statements as "false and inflammatory." The Dodger president, MacPhail charged, had "double-crossed his associates for his own personal advantage, raided the Negro leagues, and took players without adequately compensating them." Rickey's speech, said MacPhail, was "an attempt to glorify himself. Churchill must have had Rickey in mind when he said, 'There but for the grace of God goes God.' "[35]

Rickey rejected MacPhail's response as "typically MacPhailian distortions, untruths, and inventions." Nonetheless, Rickey retreated from his earlier statements. Although he maintained that his account was substantially correct, he allowed that some of the owners might have overlooked the anti-black comments because they had been appended to a larger report that dealt with other issues. He admitted that there might have been "other reasons than the so-called Negro reference for removing the report from publicity."[36]

The short-lived Wilberforce controversy proved inconclusive. Rickey's charges, which became part of the Robinson legend, remained unsubstantiated. The owners' denials, despite their unanimity, failed to convince many Rickey partisans.

Many years later, Commissioner Chandler, deposed by the owners in 1951, endorsed Rickey's version of the 1946 events. Chandler asserted that the owners had condemned Rickey for breaking the color barrier by a 15-1 vote. "You wouldn't believe some of the things said at that meeting," recalled the former commissioner in 1972. "One of them flat out said that if we let Robinson play they'd burn down the Polo Grounds the first time the Dodgers came in there for a series." Chandler could not recall the exact nature of the vote, whether it was directed at Robinson, or blacks in general, or perhaps Rickey. Chandler described his own role as passive. "I made no comment," the former commissioner recounted. "For one thing, the press didn't know about it and I didn't consider that vote an order, only an expression of their sentiment."[37]

Chandler claims that several weeks after the vote, Rickey came to see him at his home in Kentucky, beseeching him for support. "Happy, I want

Robinson to play," Chandler quotes Rickey as saying, "but I can't bring him in unless you go along with me." At this point, according to Chandler, "I looked the old gent right in the eye and said, 'Bring him in. He'll play if he's got the capacity to play.' "

Chandler's version of this story fails to resolve the controversy. While supporting Rickey's allegations, Chandler portrays himself as a major actor in the integration drama, an image that he has repeatedly sought to perpetuate. "I've always thought that it was something kind of wonderful," he told a reporter, "that a fellow like me, a Confederate, a Democrat, a southerner, and man whose grandaddy was in Morgan's cavalry was the one who made it possible for the first black to play big league baseball."[38] Yet Chandler's attempts at self-glorification cannot be substantiated. Although he had earlier endorsed the idea of baseball integration, contemporary reports reveal no record of Chandler's reaction to the Robinson signing. The episode posed a sensitive issue for the Kentucky politician. Nationally, a ruling against Robinson would have raised loud cries of discrimination. In Kentucky, however, where Chandler might again seek office, a public stance might have threatened his popularity. "Chandler is political minded," wrote Milton Gross, "and his Southern constituents back home will remember. Happy needs the wisdom of a Solomon."[39] Instead, Chandler chose the discretion of a mute. He remained uncommitted in the public eye, neither giving Rickey's actions his approval, nor using his powers to oppose them. No confirmation exists of his private encouragement to Rickey. At best, one can describe Chandler's role as endorsement by abstinence. Chandler's own claims to posterity notwithstanding, he appears as no more than a bit player in these historic events.

If Chandler's recollections remain unreliable, additional evidence exists supporting Rickey's contentions. In 1951 a House of Representatives Subcommittee chaired by Emmanuel Celler of Brooklyn investigated baseball's monopoly status. Committee attorneys uncovered a 1946 report thought to have been destroyed by baseball officials, which dealt, in part, with the race issue. Celler's committee, primarily interested in the business operations of the national pastime, ignored the sections pertaining to integration. Other contemporary observers also failed to mention these passages. Yet the report is a remarkable and revealing document and lends credence to Rickey's Wilberforce charges.

On July 8, 1946, more than eight months after Rickey had signed Robinson and two months after the black athlete had played his first game for Montreal, the National and American Leagues established a joint steering committee "to consider and test all matters of Major League interest and report its conclusions and recommendations." MacPhail was elected chair-

man of the committee, which also included both league presidents, Tom
Yawkey of the Boston Red Sox, Sam Breadon of the St. Louis Cardinals, and
Phil Wrigley of the Chicago Cubs. The committee, mainly concerned with
player relations, met seven times during the next month. MacPhail then
drafted a report of the panel's conclusions for presentation to the major
league owners at their August meetings in Chicago. The document examined a broad range of issues including rule changes, player raids by the
Mexican leagues, means to counteract charges of an illegal monopoly, methods to prevent "outsiders from being successful in attempts to organize
players into unions," a player pension plan, and problems relating to schedules, ticket prices, and bonuses for first-year players.[40] In addition, MacPhail
analyzed the "Race Question."

The manner in which MacPhail defined the "Race Question" illustrates
his perspective. His stated objective was not how to bring blacks into baseball, but rather to suggest "Methods to protect baseball from charges that
it is fostering unfair discrimination against the Negro by reason of his race
and color." This evaluation had become necessary for several reasons.
Negroes were among the game's "most loyal supporters," and blacks had
already "enriched" college football, boxing, and the Olympic Games. Furthermore, many black baseball players had served in the armed forces
during the war.

MacPhail dismissed the demands of integration advocates as representative of "certain groups in this country including political and social-minded
drum beaters." Neither professional baseball nor the lot of black ballplayers
interested these protestors. "They know little about baseball and nothing
about the business end of its operation," argued the report. "They single
out baseball for attack because it offers a good publicity medium. These
people who charge that baseball is flying a Jim Crow flag at its masthead—
or that racial discrimination is the basic reason for the failure of the major
leagues to give employment to Negroes—are talking through their individual
or collective hats."

In one of its most revealing passages, the report predicted the potential
economic repercussions of integration. Noting that baseball, like any other
business enterprise, depended upon profits for its existence, MacPhail questioned whether the sport desired added Negro attendance. The Robinson
experience had already resulted in a "tremendous increase" in black patrons
in the International League. "The percentage of Negro attendance at some
games at Newark and Baltimore was in excess of 50%," according to the
report. Rather than view this as a spur to added profits, MacPhail expressed
fears, much as Rickey later charged, that "a situation might be presented,
if Negroes participate in Major League games, in which the preponderance

of Negro attendance in parks such as the Yankee Stadium, the Polo Grounds, and Comiskey Park could conceivably threaten the value of Major League franchises owned by these clubs."

Despite this problem, "Every American boy, without regard to his race or color or creed, should have a fair chance at baseball." But signing a few players would simply be a "gesture" contributing "little or nothing to the solution of the real problem." This "real problem" lay not so much with organized baseball, as with the black athletes and the Negro Leagues, as could be understood by looking at the "facts."

"A major league baseball player must have something besides great natural ability. He must possess the technique, the coordination, the competitive attitude and the discipline, which is usually acquired only after years of training in the minor leagues," explained MacPhail. The average big leaguer, he contended, spent seven years in the lower ranks. But, MacPhail argued somewhat circuitously, since Negroes had never had a chance in the minor leagues, "comparatively few good young Negro players are being developed." Thus, few black players met major league standards.

To support this position, MacPhail quoted none other than Sam Lacy, one of integration's most ardent proponents. Lacy and other black writers frequently criticized the absence of fundamentals in the Negro Leagues. Some black athletes excelled in hitting or fielding or baserunning, Lacy contended, but few demonstrated the all-around talent necessary for success in the majors. He concluded, "I am reluctant to say that we haven't a single man in the ranks of colored baseball who could step into the major league uniform and disport himself after the fashion of a big leaguer." It was an unfortunate piece of writing, one which the black sportswriter later regretted. Aimed at improving the quality of play in the Negro Leagues, the frequently reprinted passage had overshot its mark and became valuable ammunition for those who sought to keep blacks out of baseball. MacPhail quoted Lacy at length and concluded, "Mr. Lacy's opinions are shared by almost everyone, Negro or White, competent to appraise the qualifications of Negro players."

Even if the major leagues could find talented players, the report continued, the Negro Leagues still presented a problem. Black baseball was a $2,000,000 business; the twenty-four major and minor league teams employed 400 athletes. "If the major leagues and big minors of Professional Baseball raid these leagues and take their best players—the Negro leagues will eventually fold up—the investments of their club owners will be wiped out—and a lot of professional Negro players will lose their jobs," worried MacPhail. But organized baseball would also suffer, since some clubs derived a substantial part of their revenues from rentals by black teams. The

Yankees, for example, received $100,000 a year from the Negro Leagues for the use of Yankee Stadium and their minor league parks in Newark, Kansas City, and Norfolk. "Club owners are reluctant to give up revenues amounting to hundreds of thousands of dollars every year. They naturally want the Negro Leagues to continue," MacPhail frankly admitted.

Shifting arguments in mid-paragraph, the report raised the issue of player contracts in the Negro Leagues. Major league teams "do not sign, and cannot properly sign players under contract to Negro clubs," but not because of "racial discrimination." Organized baseball was "simply respecting the contractual relationship between the Negro leagues and their players." The report did not consider the possibility of signing blacks before they entered the rival organization or once their contracts had expired.

After thus defining the problem and laying out the "facts," the committee in its summation failed to make any concrete recommendations other than calling for efforts to "arrive at a fair and just solution—compatible with good business judgment and the principles of good sportsmanship." Instead, MacPhail vented a thinly veiled attack on Branch Rickey. "Your Committee does not desire to question the motives of any organization or individual who is sincerely opposed to segregation or who believes that such a policy is detrimental in the best interest of Professional Baseball," wrote MacPhail in a left-handed denial of intent. Nonetheless, "The individual action of any one club may exert tremendous pressures on the whole structure of Professional Baseball, and could conceivably result in lessening the value of several Major League franchises."

The "Report of the Major League Steering Committee" is a damning document. Couched in palatable phrases defending the rights of all men to enter the national pastime, MacPhail sought, through often dubious logic, to explain away the absence of blacks in their leagues. Blame rested not with the baseball establishment, which was free of prejudice, but with ignorant protestors, inadequate black athletes, and selfish Negro League owners. The threat of financial loss, largely unsubstantiated, also prevented an end to segregation. The report suggests no methods to bring blacks into the major leagues, nor any desire to do so. For Rickey, who had dared to confront the problem unilaterally, the document expressed nothing but mildly concealed contempt and condemnation.

The final disposition of the 1946 report remains unclear. At the Celler hearings baseball spokesmen testified that the steering committee had rejected MacPhail's draft. Lacking time to rewrite it, "they submitted their report as a cut-up document, deleting certain paragraphs and other materials." The owners then "recaptured" the "mutilated documents" and destroyed them.[41] Some sections of the report, released to the press in 1946, became the basis for revisions in the standard player contract and a major league pension fund. But baseball officials could produce no copies of the final version for the Celler Committee.

Had the owners accepted MacPhail's controversial analysis of the "Race Question?" In 1951 congressmen did not raise this issue. Rickey, in his Wilberforce speech, indicated that the baseball executives approved these passages. Chandler supported this account. Other owners either denied these charges or remained silent. Perhaps their subsequent actions speak for them. Two years would pass before any of the owners present at that meeting, other than Rickey, would sign blacks. At the time of the Celler hearings, most had not yet integrated their teams.

IV

Most of MacPhail's rationalizations for the perpetuation of segregation possessed little validity. Another body of athletic entrepreneurs, however, shared his concerns about the fate of the Negro Leagues and the contractual status of black players. The owners of black baseball franchises, most of whom ideologically supported integration, confronted a major crisis. "If the Negro ballplayer had a chance in organized baseball," Dan Daniel had predicted several months before the Robinson signing, "the Negro League would be forced out of business."[42] For organized baseball the admission of Robinson heralded a new age; for black baseball it marked the dawn of destruction.

The Kansas City Monarchs, Robinson's former employers, immediately protested his signing. "We won't take it lying down," exclaimed Tom Baird, one of the white owners of the Monarchs. "Robinson signed a contract with us last year and I feel he is our property."[43] Baird carefully stressed that he did not object to Robinson crossing the color line, but to the manner of his signing. Rickey had dealt directly with the athlete without prior purchase of his contract from the Monarchs. The Negro League owner threatened to appeal to baseball's commissioner and, if not granted satisfaction, to appeal his case to the courts.

Rickey might have avoided the thorny issue of Robinson's contractual status had he sought agreement with the Monarchs before recruiting Robinson. The ever penurious Dodger president, however, had already spent a considerable sum in scouting black players and in bypassing the Monarchs saved a substantial amount of money. Kansas City might have demanded a prohibitive payment for Robinson's services. Furthermore, prior negotiations with the black team might have threatened the impenetrable secrecy that Rickey deemed necessary for his strategy. Both Rickey and Robinson firmly believed that the black shortstop had no legal obligation to the Monarchs. Robinson contended that a handshake constituted his only agreement with the Kansas City club. Rickey claimed that in his extensive study of the Negro Leagues, "I failed to find a single player under uniform contract and I learned that players of all teams become free agents at the end of each season, with no written guarantee or consideration."[44]

From a strictly legal and literal standpoint, Rickey may have been right. The operative word in his statement was "uniform." The Mahatma had not denied that the Negro League players signed contracts, but rather, that unlike organized baseball, no standard agreement existed between employer and employee. Of greater importance, the Negro Leagues did not employ the "reserve clause" in its contracts. This highly unorthodox provision bound major league players to their original employers in perpetuity. Owners could automatically renew the contract each year, trade players at will, or terminate the agreement with only ten days' notice. In the absence of the reserve clause, argued Rickey, Negro League players became available to the highest bidder at the end of each season. Personnel practices in black baseball sustained Rickey's position. If executives within the Negro Leagues could lure players to their teams without compensation to their former clubs, why couldn't Rickey do the same?

Nonetheless, the Monarch protest had considerable merit. Negro league clubs had invested time and money in the development of their players. Baird and the other owners felt that they should be allowed to sell the contracts of their players in the same manner as the white minor leagues. Most people in organized baseball shared this opinion. They found the concept of "raiding" other leagues without offering proper compensation highly distasteful and threatening, particularly at a time when the Mexican Leagues were offering large sums of money to entice players to abandon major league teams and play south of the border.

For those opposed to signing black players, the issue provided a convenient target to attack. "While it is true that we have no agreement with the Negro Leagues," argued Clark Griffith, "we still can't act like outlaws in taking their stars." The notion that Negro League contracts could be ignored, objected MacPhail, might be "fine and dandy for folks without any financial interest in baseball . . . but I'm not looking for any costly lawsuits."[45]

The lords of baseball also feared that a lawsuit by Baird might threaten the reserve clause, the contractual cornerstone of their fiefdom. "If Baird brings legal action against the Dodgers," warned Milton Gross of the New York *Post*, "baseball faces the prospect of players winning the right to shop around from team to team after each season, or the necessity of signing each man to a long-term contract." Since, he added, the legality of the reserve clause was questionable, "The one thing baseball men have not wanted in the past, do not want now, or in the future, is the airing of player contract matters."[46]

Rickey, however, doubted that Negro league owners would pursue their claims. "We were in no position to protest and he knew it," Effa Manley of the Newark Eagles complained heatedly thirty years later. "He had us over a barrel in a way. The fans would never have forvigen us plus it would have been wrong to have prevented [the players] from going to the major leagues."[47] For Manley, Baird, and their colleagues in black baseball, the Robinson signing posed a classic dilemma. For years they had decried the color line which provided the basis for their own existence. The spectre of integration threatened their interests, yet opposition to it would expose them to the wrath of their fans. By failing to reimburse the Monarchs for Robinson's services, Rickey had salted their wounds. With baseball integrated, the sale of their athletes to organized baseball represented the only hope of the Negro Leagues to offset their inevitable decline. Yet Rickey had declared all black players free agents and the owners dared not oppose him.

Recognizing the futility and potentially negative effects of their appeal, the Kansas City Monarchs withdrew their protest almost as rapidly as they had issued it. On October 25, J. L. Wilkinson, Baird's partner, denied that his team would attempt to reclaim Robinson. "I want to see Jackie make good," declared Wilkinson. "I would never do anything to mar his chances."[48]

Even this hasty Monarch retreat proved too late. The challenge to Rickey's cavalier conduct evoked a torrent of criticism from the black fans and press. The Pittsburgh *Courier* in a November 3 editorial on the sports page wrote, "We do not approve of raiding or any other unfair practices" and said that the paper "does not intend to jeopardize the best interests of Negro baseball in any way." But cutting to the heart of the matter, the *Courier* argued, "We did feel, however, that the signing of Jackie Robinson by the Brooklyn farm club transcended anything else at this particular time." In subsequent weeks and months, the black press pilloried the barons of Negro baseball. A letter to the Chicago *Defender* called Negro League owners "as selfish as any plantation owner of the slavery bound men in the days prior to the Civil War." A Pittsburgh *Courier* editorial entitled "A Foolish Protest," advised the Monarchs that "Instead of trying to hamper those who have made a step forward, let us help them as much as we can."[49]

Assaulted on one flank by the black press, the embattled Negro League owners also faced an onslaught from the formidable Rickey. The Mahatma had anticipated a protest from the Monarchs and prepared a rebuttal. "They're simply a booking agents' paradise," stormed the Dodger president.

"They are not leagues and have no right to expect organized baseball to respect them."[50]

Confronted by these attacks, the Negro League owners reappraised their future. Could they fit into the newly integrated structure of the national pastime? Or, as a correspondent to the Chicago *Defender* optimistically predicted, would "the use or need of the Negro Leagues [soon be] eradicated?" Black baseball officials considered several alternatives. A. B. Martin, president of the Negro National League, speculated that integration might actually increase interest in black baseball.[51] Perhaps the Negro circuits might be incorporated into organized baseball as minor leagues which developed talent and then sold players to the majors. The possibility of working agreements with specific big league clubs was also suggested.

At the urging of Clark Griffith, the self-appointed defender of black baseball, club owners of the Negro National and Negro American leagues convened in Harlem on November 9, 1945, to discuss their future. Griffith, in a letter to Homestead Gray owner Cum Posey, encouraged the officials to file a formal protest with the baseball commissioner, asking for a ruling that would protect the rights of Negro League clubs. Adhering to Griffith's advice, the joint committee drafted a protest to Commissioner Chandler calling for an end to the raiding of the Negro Leagues. "We are glad to see our players get the opportunity to play in white baseball," they contended. "We are simply protesting the way it was done."[52] Citing the expenses involved in operating the leagues and developing players, the owners requested that player deals be negotiated with the respective clubs rather than the individual players.

The Negro Leagues continued their courtship of organized baseball at their December 13 gathering. The owners adopted verbatim the bylaws of the major leagues, changing only the names of the leagues in the original documents, and agreed to adopt standard major league contracts. "The new contracts carry a reserve clause," announced Martin, essentially conceding Rickey's charges against the old player pacts. "It now appears that our contracts are as iron-clad as those of organized baseball."[53]

With this minor face-lift accomplished, Martin and Tom Wilson, the president of the Negro American League, met with Chandler to discuss the entry of their leagues into organized baseball. Chandler, the veteran Kentucky politician, responded with a masterful piece of political equivocation, opening the door with one hand while kicking it shut with his foot. "I will be glad to arrange an alliance between organized baseball and the Negro Leagues, when you can come to me with a clean bill of health. You must clean out the gamblers. You must establish your game on a fair and honest footing and develop your umpires to the levels of high respect which the decision callers hold in Organized Baseball." Chandler suggested that the Negro Leagues build their own stadiums as soon as possible, an almost impossible task for the financially precarious operations.[54] In short, Chandler told black baseball, "Get your house in order," before serious consideration would be given to their request.

The Negro League pilgrimage to the baseball commissioner failed to mute attacks on them. In an editorial, the *Sporting News* endorsed Chandler's position, claiming that although "Baseball is thoroughly American [and] it wants to do the fair and square thing. . . . Organized Baseball cannot afford to tie up with any ally with less than rigid standards." The black press unleashed a cascade of criticism aimed at Martin and Wilson. Sam Lacy called the whole affair "pitifully sad" because the Negro League owners did not realize that Chandler was "simply pulling their legs." Wendell Smith portrayed Martin and Wilson as "whimpering" to Chandler. "All they cared about was the perpetuation of the slave trade they had developed. . . . [They'll] shout to the high heavens that racial progress comes first and baseball next. But actually the preservation of their shaky, littered, infested, segregated baseball domicile comes first last and always."[55]

Smith also speculated that if accepted by organized baseball, Negro League owners might unite with "reactionary forces already there" to "hamper the advancement of the Negro player to the majors." The Chicago *Defender* expressed similar fears, wondering if "a deal was made . . . whereby Negro baseball will be put on a 'respectable basis' and the doors to the Big Leagues will be closed to Negro players." Ideally, argued the Chicago weekly, the Negro Leagues would ultimately be eliminated. "No selfishness on the part of Negro ownership, nor appeasement . . . to the Southern reactionaries in baseball must stand in the way of the advancement of qualified Negro players."[56]

In the end, the posturings of organized baseball and the Negro Leagues proved little more than a shadow dance. Black baseball made few further efforts at "housecleaning," the commissioner's office took no steps toward consolidation, and the critical issue, that of compensation for black players signed by the major leagues, remained unresolved. For Negro League owners, the lesson was clear. With the prospect of integration hanging in the air, neither their friends nor their foes cared about their fate.

V

In January 1946, Oakland *Tribune* sportswriter Lee Dunbar reported that "veteran baseball men" had told a "friend recently returned from the East" that Robinson would be barred from performing in at least two cities. Dunbar also reported that "a deal is already cooking among International League club owners to raise a jackpot and hand it to Robinson if he will consent to transfer to another league." In Montgomery, Alabama, sportswriter Sam Adams predicted, "It's going to lead to trouble. Players are corresponding on it and there may be a sit-down strike in the spring."[57]

These and other rumors attested to the continuing interest in the integration saga throughout the winter of 1945–46. The prospect of integration triggered controversy not only among officials of both black and white baseball, but it had repercussions beyond the boundaries of the national pastime as well. Prodded by the Dodger action, numerous athletic agencies re-examined their racial policies. In December 1945, the National Baseball Congress, the governing body for semi-professional baseball announced that it would allow Negro and mixed teams winning state titles to participate in its national championship. In March blacks picketed an event sponsored by the American Bowling Congress in Buffalo, New York, calling for an end to its whites-only policy.[58]

The most significant breakthrough occurred in professional football. A clear-cut color line had never existed on the gridiron. In the collegiate ranks, black stars were common, but no professional team had fielded a black since Joe Lillard had played for the Philadelphia Eagles in 1933. Encouraged by local fans, the Los Angeles Rams, recently transplanted from Cleveland, announced the signing of Robinson's former U.C.L.A. teammates, Kenny Washington and Woody Strode, in March 1946. In the All-America Conference, a new league competing for attention with the National Football League, coach Paul Brown of Cleveland signed Bill Willis, a black lineman, and Marion Motley, a fullback.[59]

The collegiate game also experienced changes. In May the Big Six Conference put its "gentleman's agreement" regarding black athletes into writing, leaving participation of nonwhites up to individual institutions in accordance with state laws. The student councils at Big Six schools—Kansas, Nebraska, Iowa State, and Kansas State—passed resolutions requesting the inclusion of blacks in athletic programs. In the Ivy League, Yale University announced that Levi Jackson would become that institution's first black football player.[60]

In baseball other major league owners showed no inclination to follow Rickey's lead, but some stirrings occurred on the periphery of the national pastime. As spring training began stories of token integration trickled in. Jess Brooks, a former Kansas City Monarchs infielder worked out with Tacoma in the Western International League. Some speculated that the new Havana team in the Florida State League might be permitted to field Cuban blacks. From the Negro Leagues came the improbable saga of Eddie

Klepp. A white pitcher, Klepp reported to spring training with the Cleveland Buckeyes of the Negro American League and became a Jackie Robinson in reverse. As the Buckeyes traveled through the South, Klepp was barred from eating or staying with his teammates. Before an exhibition game in Birmingham, city officials chased Klepp from the field and when he tried to sit behind the Buckeye dugout, they ordered him to sit in the white section. Klepp remained with the Cleveland team for the 1946 season.[61]

In New York integration posed a dilemma for baseball writers. At their annual dinner and show in February, always an iconoclastic and free-wheeling affair, some writers were leery of approaching an issue as delicate as the Robinson debate. Arthur Mann, on the other hand, the guiding spirit behind the show and a close friend and confidant of Branch Rickey, saw little reason to refrain from poking fun at the latest Dodger controversy.[62] The resulting performance dramatically demonstrated the racial perspectives of liberals in the postwar age.

The curtain rose on a southern mansion, the Kentucky home of Commissioner Chandler. On the stage, a "darky" in satin knee breeches stood dusting a table, his back facing the audience. He turned slowly to reveal that the upper part of his costume was a Montreal Royals uniform. "Looks lak de massa will be late dis evening," commented the black-faced house servant. Later in the show Chandler and his butler engaged in the following exchange:

CHANDLER: (Claps hands and calls) "Robbie-eee! Robiee!

BUTLER: Yassah Massa. Here ah is.

CHANDLER: Ah! There you are Jackie, Jackie you ole wooly-headed rascal, how long you been in the family.

BUTLER: Long time, Kun'l. Marty long time. Ebber since Marse Rickey bought me from da Kansas City Monarchs.

CHANDLER: To be sure, Jackie, to be sure. How could I forget that Massa Rickey brought you to our house. (Aside) Rickey—that no good carpetbagger. What could he be thinking of?[63]

At another point in the show, Mann, renowned for his Branch Rickey impersonation, dressed up as the Dodger president, and surrounded by a quartet of four black-faced field hands sang a parody written to the tune of "The Battle Hymn of the Republic" entitled "Glory, Glory, Massa Rickey."

The Sporting News hailed the 1946 writers' show as the "best yet." "It was all such lampoonery," wrote Arthur Daley of the New York Times, "that no one's feelings were really hurt." Wendell Smith voiced the only dissent, labelling the show a "Nazi Opera" and accusing the writers of giving vent to their true opposition to Rickey's venture which they dared not express in their papers.[64]

In reality the 1946 writers' show stands as a tribute to the insensitivity of mid-twentieth-century America. The participation of Mann, an unreserved supporter of baseball integration who soon joined the official Dodger family and later authored biographies of both Rickey and Robinson, indicates that the show's racial stereotypes stemmed more from misguided mischief than malevolence. Sportswriters, reflecting the era in which they lived, frequently filled their columns by making fun of long ethnic names, the accents of Latin ballplayers, and the presumed personality attributes of various nationalities. Cleveland *Press* columnist Jimmy Doyle regularly quoted a character named "Ku Klux Clancy, the Invisible Umpire." This brand of racism, rarely given a second thought, spoke for an age in which as "invisible men," blacks could feel no pain and well-intentioned whites had little sense of the harm which they inflicted.

The objects of the baseball writers' satire spent the winter preparing for their forthcoming ordeal. For Rickey 1945 had been a momentous year. Throughout the summer, while the Dodgers fruitlessly chased the Chicago Cubs for the National League pennant, Rickey negotiated the purchase of a large block of shares in the Brooklyn club. By the end of the season he owned 25 percent of the team. The purchase left him deeply in debt and no sooner had he closed the deal than the furor over Robinson erupted.

The tensions took their toll on the sixty-five-year-old Rickey. In December at the major league meetings in Chicago, he suffered dizzy spells. On the train heading back to New York he experienced a second, more serious attack requiring hospitalization. Rickey's condition baffled doctors. For two weeks he underwent tests until a prominent brain specialist diagnosed Meniere's disease, a permanent disorder characterized by vertigo, nausea, and vomiting. The condition usually remained dormant, but it could appear at any time without prior warning. Doctors knew no cure, but advised that the disease could be contained if the patient reduced his activities and led a more restful life. For the dynamic Rickey, facing what he perceived as the most important challenge of his life, this offered no solution. He remained hospitalized for five weeks, emerging in time to open the Dodger's special Florida pre-training camp on February 1. Though few people knew of his disability, attacks of Meniere's disease plagued him for the rest of his life.[65]

Jackie Robinson passed through an equally eventful winter. No stranger to public attention and adulation, Robinson's new celebrity status dwarfed his earlier fame. Newspapers and radio shows ardently pursued him for interviews. Honors flowed in for both him and Rickey. High schools devoted publications to the "Fair Deal for the Negro in Baseball," while *Picture News*, a new comic book, contained the story of his life, entitled "The California Flash."[66]

In December Robinson traveled to Venezuela where he had previously agreed to play winter baseball. Robinson played shortstop for the "American All-Stars," a team of Negro League standouts including the great Buck Leonard and future major leaguers Roy Campanella, Sam Jethroe, and Quincy Trouppe. Even in Venezuela Robinson no longer traveled as just another baseball player. *Mundo Reportiva*, a Caracas journal, devoted its entire back page to a feature on Robinson, *"El primer hombre de color en 'Las Grandes Ligas' Americans."* A large, illustrated caricature of Robinson was surrounded by comments reviewing his career as a collegiate athlete and as *"un soldado de 'Tio Sam' "* He had, read the text, opened the doors of white baseball and if successful would eloquently demonstrate to the world the *"estupido prejuico racial"* that disgraced the great American nation.[67]

While Robinson barnstormed through Venezuela, Rachel Isum, his fiancée, made her acquaintance with New York City. Born and raised in Los Angeles where she had expected to settle, Rachel had previously decided to spend her final winter as a single woman exploring New York. At the time, she had no idea that her adult life would be centered in the eastern metropolis. Rachel found employment as a nurse at the Joint Disease Hospital and, for variety, as a hostess in a luxurious Park Avenue restaurant; she saved her money to pay for a bridal gown and veil.

Jackie and Rachel had been engaged for almost five years. Military service and Jackie's travels as a baseball player had delayed the wedding for a seemingly interminable period. Even before the paternalistic Rickey had advised Robinson to marry, they had set a wedding date. "We didn't get married as the result of Mr. Rickey's directive," laughs Rachel. "Let's not perpetuate the myth that Mr. Rickey directed our lives to that extent."[68]

For Jackie and Rachel personal and practical considerations eclipsed the implications of the approaching baseball season. "I don't think I, at that time, fully appreciated what it meant," recalls Rachel. "We were excited that we had a job opportunity. It wasn't just having an opportunity to engage in any major social change. [Jackie] had this fantastic job and clearly he had to make it, so there was nothing guaranteed in it. There was that kind of tension around 'could he do it?' and 'were these people sincere?' "[69]

In many respects the excitement over their oft-postponed marriage took their minds off the challenges that awaited them during the upcoming baseball season. "We'd waited a long time to get married and nothing could overshadow that," recalls Rachel. "We were just not out of our minds about this opportunity because we had a bigger thing happening."[70] Amidst the details of planning for the wedding, they temporarily forgot their fears for the future. With wartime shortages still a reality, finding a pair of nylon stockings to wear to the wedding concerned Rachel more than their impending trip to spring training. On February 10, 1946, Jackie Robinson married Rachel Isum at a large church wedding in Los Angeles. Two weeks later they left for Florida to launch the great experiment.

II

RUNS, HITS, AND ERRORS

6

If They Come Here,
They Can't Play

> Probably the first headache will come
> next spring . . . in Daytona Beach, Fla.
> and anyone who has traveled that far
> South can't help but wonder just how
> things can be arranged. Fundamental
> things such as where he will sleep and
> where he will eat. Not to mention what
> traveling accommodations they'll let him
> have in deepest Dixie.
>
> Tommy Holmes,
> *Brooklyn Eagle,* October 24, 1945

I

In the waning days of February 1946, Jackie and Rachel Robinson boarded
an American Airlines plane in Los Angeles; their destination, the Brooklyn
Dodger training camp at Daytona Beach, Florida. Eight years would pass
before the Supreme Court's school desegregation decision would begin to
unravel the threads of racial discrimination, nineteen before Congress would
pass a comprehensive Civil Rights Act. For Rachel, married but a few weeks
and raised in California, it would be her first exposure to southern society
and she approached the journey with trepidation. "I had heard so many
stories about the treatment of Negroes in the Deep South that I was bewildered," she later recalled. Rachel also knew of "how quickly Jack's
temper could flare up in the face of a racial insult. . . . I could not be sure
but what some incident might occur in which we would both be harmed
or killed."[1]

In the unsettled environment of the postwar South, Rachel's fears of
physical harm were well founded. Although southerners did not repeat the
orgy of violence that had left scores of blacks murdered after World War I,
reports of atrocities still emanated from the region. At least thirty lynching
attempts occurred in 1946. As if to reinforce the Robinsons's apprehensions,

one of the worst outbreaks of anti-black rioting had erupted in Columbia, Tennessee, that week. Before it ended, one hundred blacks would be summarily arrested and two killed "while trying to escape."[2]

To reach Daytona Beach, the Robinsons took an all-night flight to New Orleans where they were to change planes. In New Orleans, however, they encountered a seemingly innocuous obstacle. Bumped off their connecting flight, they had to wait for another plane. Stranded at the airport, Jackie and Rachel made the acquaintance of Jim Crow. They discovered that none of the restaurants would serve blacks unless they took their food elsewhere to eat. The Robinsons, related Jackie, "decided to skip food until we reached a place where we could be treated like human beings." Since the airport provided no places for blacks to rest, they went to a nearby hotel. "We entered this place," Rachel vividly remembered, "and I was almost nauseated. It was a dirty, dreadful place and they had plastic mattress covers. Lying on the bed was like trying to sleep on newspapers." Twelve hours passed before they resumed their journey.[3]

The Robinsons's ordeal had just begun. At Pensacola airline officials instructed them to deplane "so more fuel could be added on." Two white passengers replaced them. Despite Jackie's vociferous protestations, the Robinsons were helpless. Needing a place to stay overnight, the Robinsons sought to rent a room in a home recommended by a cab driver. When they arrived they found the house "overrun with children." Rather than impose upon the occupants and anxious about their already delayed arrival at the training camp, the couple decided to ride a bus to Jacksonville, where they could make connections to Daytona Beach.

On the bus Jackie and Rachel sat down in reclining seats and tried to sleep. Within a few miles the driver stopped the bus and motioned them to the rear. "The seats at the back," wrote Robinson many years later, "were reserved seats—reserved for Negroes—and they were straight backed. No little buttons to push. No reclining seats." For Rachel, on her first visit to the South, the trip seemed a nightmare. "For sixteen hours we bounced and jogged at the back of the bus and often I was almost nauseated by the engine fumes that wafted in through the open window. . . . The Jim Crow section got so jammed that we took turns standing and sitting, although there were several empty seats in the white section."[4]

At Jacksonville they waited in a bus station that Rachel described as a "wretched hell hole," crowded into a black waiting room with few seats and numerous flies. Unwilling to ask for food at the back doors and windows of restaurants, the Robinsons went hungry throughout the long ordeal. Finally, Wendell Smith and Pittsburgh *Courier* photographer Billy Rowe drove from Daytona Beach to pick them up and deliver them to the Dodger camp.

As they arrived three days late, Robinson exclaimed, "Well I finally made it, but I never want another trip like this one."[5]

II

Four months had elapsed since the Brooklyn Dodgers had shocked the nation with the announcement of Robinson's signing. Team President Branch Rickey, the architect of the integration strategy, had carefully planned each aspect of the historic breakthrough, seeking to minimize wherever possible the difficulties that Robinson would face. He assigned Robinson to the Montreal Royals, a team which ventured no farther south than Baltimore during the regular season. But Robinson's baptism under fire would nonetheless take place not in the friendly environment of Canada or the northern United States, but in Florida, where the white baseball leagues held their annual preseason training.

Florida, like other southern states, enforced a strict code of segregation that applied to travel accommodations, eating places, and recreational facilities. Most communities forbade interracial competition. "Never before in this state, or any other Southern state," commented the New York *Times*, "has a Negro played with whites in organized baseball, nor [in Daytona Beach] have Negro teams been pitted against white teams."[6] In the best of circumstances blacks watched exhibition games from small Jim Crow seating areas; in some cities, officials barred blacks from the ball park.

These conditions led to substantial speculation about Robinson's fate in Florida. "If Branch Rickey could set up his training camp for his Montreal Royals in a more democratic environment," wrote Sam Lacy, "I'd be clamoring for him to abandon Daytona Beach and so would the rest of us." In the *Sporting News,* Harold C. Burr called the situation "a powder magazine that may explode any minute" and urged that it be "handled with diplomacy and delicacy."[7]

A muted, but ominous tone characterized the initial Florida reaction to the Robinson signing. Most Florida newspapers simply printed the story as it came over the wire services without comment. The Deland *Sun News* headlined its story: NEGRO PLAYER WILL TRAIN AT DAYTONA, but when asked by the Chicago *Defender* for a comment, the *Sun News* sports editor replied, "Opinion here is divided on whether it will work or not. Some are bitterly opposed to the idea, while many want to see the boy get a chance. Sports fans in general like to see a fair deal and a good player, whatever his race or peculiarities."[8]

Other reports from Florida took on a less moderate tone. In Miami where the New York Giants trained, civic leaders were reported to be in a "mild fever over the possibility that the Dodgers might bring colored players along." One of them told Giant manager Mel Ott, "I don't want to embarrass any ball club, but if they come here, they can't play and that's flat." Daytona Beach City Manager Jim Titus, representing the resort area in its negotiations with the Dodgers, reminded them that "Robinson will run into some strict segregation laws if he arrives with the Montreal team. He will not be allowed to stay in the same hotel with the white players and will be forced to use . . . other services set aside for Negroes only." At the hotel where the Royals would reside, officials reiterated their policy of segregation. According to Red Smith, news of the signing prompted the beach club where Dodger officials had booked rooms to abruptly cancel their reservations.[9]

Rickey and Robinson both tried to downplay the significance of Jim Crow regulations in Daytona Beach. "We are not going down to . . . try and change the law," stated Rickey. "I can't go to the Florida legislature and say, 'Look here, now, you've got to change your laws because Montreal has a colored player on the team.'" Robinson's comment was, "I'm going there to play ball, not to live. . . . I'll be down there strictly as a ballplayer and will act accordingly."[10]

For Rickey and other Dodger officials the interval between Robinson's signing and his arrival in Florida entailed unusually intense preparation. Baseball's 1946 spring training camps represented a microcosm of the chaos created by postwar reconversion throughout the nation. Teams returned to Florida for the first time since wartime travel restrictions had confined them to northern locales. Hundreds of returning veterans flooded into the camps hoping to reclaim their prewar positions. Facilities opened a month early to help teams sort out the new and returning players.[11]

The presence of the Robinsons posed additional problems. Dodger officials had to find accommodations for the black couple and facilitate their acceptance at Daytona Beach. Rickey deemed it essential that the Robinsons not be isolated from other blacks during their southern sojourn. He arranged for them to stay at the home of Joe Harris, a highly respected black Daytona Beach politician. Rickey also recruited journalists Smith and Rowe to accompany Robinson throughout spring training.[12] In addition, Rickey conducted a search for a second black athlete to share Robinson's trials.

From the moment of Robinson's signing, rumors had spread that at least one other black player would join Robinson on the Montreal roster. "It would be a wise move on the part of the Brooklyn organization," wrote Harold C. Burr in the Sporting News. "Robinson would be a lonely boy without a member of his race around." The task fell to a little-known pitcher named John Wright.[13] Scouts described Wright, a "willowy right-handed pitcher," as having good control, a live fastball, and a wide variety of curves, knucklers, and sinkers in his repertoire. At twenty-seven, he had pitched for the New Orleans Zulus, a novelty team in his hometown, as well as for the Newark Eagles, Toledo Crawfords, and Homestead Grays of the Negro Leagues. In 1943 he had won twenty-five games for the Grays, while losing only four. In 1944 Wright had joined the navy and like so many other ballplayers, fought his military battles on baseball diamonds. Pitching for the all-black Great Lakes Naval Station team, Wright compiled a 15-4 record, including a no-hit game, and posted the lowest earned run average of any pitcher in the armed forces.

"Wright doesn't boast the college background that is Jackie's," wrote Sam Lacy, "but he possesses something equally valuable—a level head and the knack of seeing things objectively. He is a realist in a role which demands divorce from sentimentality." Wright put it another way: "I am a Southerner. I have always lived in the South, so I know what is coming. I have been black for 27 years and I will remain like that for a long time."[14]

It is unclear where Wright fit into Rickey's grand scheme. "I don't think that the reports indicated that Johnny Wright was an outstanding pitcher," recalls Clyde Sukeforth, "but apparently Mr. Rickey thought he would be an excellent companion." Yet Wright possessed considerable talent. Several major leaguers who had played against both rated Wright a better prospect than Robinson. Alex Pompez, owner of the Cuban Stars, doubted that Robinson was ready for the "fast company" of the International League, but he predicted that Wright would win fifteen games for the Royals.[15] Numerous reports emanating from Florida touted Wright as the "sleeper" in the great experiment.

Rickey also had to select a manager for the Montreal Royals. His choice surprised the baseball world. In December 1945, he announced that Clay Hopper, a forty-four-year-old cotton broker from Greenwood, Mississippi, would manage the Royals. "Hopper is a gent with a drawl from the deep South and he is going to have to handle Jackie Robinson," noted Canadian sportswriter Baz O'Meara. "Oh! Oh!" commented the Baltimore *Afro-American*.[16]

Two frequently cited quotations illustrate Hopper's alleged distaste for his new assignment. The Mississippian, it is said, pleaded with Rickey to send Robinson elsewhere. "Please don't do this to me," he reputedly told Rickey. "I'm white and I've lived in Mississippi all my life. If you're going to do this, you're going to force me to move my family and home out of

Mississippi." On a later occasion, when Rickey described a Robinson catch as a "superhuman play," Hopper reportedly responded, "Mr. Rickey, do you really think a nigger's a human being?"[17]

These stories may be true, but Rickey, who had so carefully orchestrated the integration scenario, had not rashly cast Hopper in this critical role. The new Royal manager epitomized the career baseball man. Since graduating from Mississippi A. & M. he had played for or piloted nineteen different teams before coming to Montreal. Although a spectacular slugger, an almost total inadequacy in the field had short-circuited Hopper's playing career. Rickey, while still directing the St. Louis Cardinal organization, had spotted young Hopper's leadership qualities. He handed the Mississippian the reigns of his first minor league club in 1929, when Hopper was only twenty-seven years old. For the next seventeen years Hopper could be found at the helm of a Rickey farm club. In 1942 when Rickey moved to Brooklyn, Hopper followed him into the Dodger organization.[18] Soft-spoken with a good sense of humor, Hopper earned a reputation for handling and developing young players. Eight times he rewarded Rickey with championship teams.

Rickey knew Hopper well and trusted the integrity of his longtime confederate. He also hoped that Hopper's Mississippi origins might mute dissension and serve as an example of a white southerner willing to accept blacks on his team. Nor does it appear that Rickey forced the role of civil rights pioneer on Hopper. Hopper earned a substantial income from his cotton enterprises and did not depend upon baseball for his livelihood. The timing of his appointment is equally significant. He agreed to manage the Royals after the Dodgers had publicized their integration venture. "We signed Robinson before we signed Hopper," said Rickey, Jr., "so he must have been forewarned."[19]

Personnel matters notwithstanding, the most important preparations concerned Robinson's reception in Florida. Rickey and the Dodgers had little influence over what would happen in most Florida cities, but they made every effort to minimize problems at Daytona Beach. A typical Florida resort town located on the banks of the Halifax River, "this picturesque, tropical city," according to Wendell Smith, was "steeped in the traditions and customs of the Old South."[20] Although segregation prevailed in Daytona Beach, the efforts of two local blacks had mitigated tensions. Famed educator and NAACP leader Mary McCleod Bethune had founded Bethune-Cookman College in the city and politician Joe Harris, Robinson's host, had given blacks a modicum of influence.

The Brooklyn club had started negotiations to establish a training camp before revealing Robinson's recruitment, but the announcement had no effect on city officials. "We knew Robinson would be with Montreal long before the city signed a contract," City Manager Titus told Smith. "In fact, we were working on the contract when Robinson was signed. If we were going to raise an objection, we would have raised it then. We would have torn up the contract and forgotten the whole thing."[21]

Titus and Mayor William Perry gave Rickey wholehearted cooperation in his efforts to reduce friction at Daytona Beach. "No one objects to Jackie Robinson and John Wright training here with the Montreal baseball club," proclaimed Mayor Perry in a public statement. "The city officials and the population in general simply regard them as two more ballplayers conditioning themselves here. We welcome them and wish them the best of luck." Perry, in an exclusive interview with Wendell Smith, described Robinson and Wright as "entertainers." Show business represented an accepted arena for black participation. "No one gets excited when Cab Calloway comes here," explained the mayor.[22]

With city officials on their side, Rickey and his aides launched a "tolerance" program in Daytona Beach and the surrounding areas. According to Robinson, Rickey spent the winter months "persuading, bullying, lecturing, and pulling strings behind the scenes" to guarantee a fair reception for the black athletes. Bob Finch, Rickey's secretary, addressed local groups like the Rotary Club of nearby Deland, speaking on "the touchy subject of equality for all men." Finch told the Deland businessmen that "Robinson and Wright were symbolic of what all Americans want, an opportunity for everyone," and warned his audience that activities to prevent this "would be a reflection on the democracy under which we live." Finch claimed that the crowd of well-to-do southerners enthusiastically accepted his speech.[23]

While Finch wooed the local business community, Rickey prepared the athletes gathered at the Dodger camp. Rickey normally began daily activities with a lecture on the finer points of baseball. But on February 28, the day before the scheduled arrival of Robinson and Wright, the Mahatma's early morning oration dealt not with athletics but race relations. Rickey denied signing Robinson and Wright due to political pressures and said that his only consideration was to bring Brooklyn a winning team. "I would have signed an elephant to play shortstop," exclaimed the flamboyant Rickey, "if the elephant could have done it better than anyone else." He pointed out Clay Hopper's acceptance of Robinson despite his Mississippi origins and asked the Dodger prospects to be "gentlemen."[24]

By March 1 Robinson's scheduled arrival date, Dodger officials hoped that they had minimized potential spring training problems. Only Robinson, desperately trying to reach Daytona Beach, was missing.

III

On March 4 Robinson and Wright made their long-awaited spring training debut. The Dodgers had directed preparations for their stay in Florida primarily at Daytona Beach, where most workouts would take place. But their initial brush with southern hospitality occurred at the Dodger pre-training camp at Sanford, a small celery-growing town, twenty miles from the central Brooklyn outpost.

Barred from the Mayfair hotel where other Dodger hopefuls boarded, Robinson and Wright donned their Montreal uniforms at the home of David Brock, a local black doctor, before proceeding to the Sanford training grounds. "I didn't need an introduction when [Robinson] came through that door," Hopper later told Red Barber. "I said to myself, 'Well, when Mr. Rickey picked one he sure picked a black one.'" The Mississippian shook Robinson's hand and greeted him pleasantly. "I was relieved to see him stick out his hand," recalled Robinson, "for even in those days a great number of southerners would under no circumstances shake hands with a Negro."[25]

On his first day Robinson's rendezvous was neither with destiny nor baseball players, but with the media. Newsmen surrounded Robinson and fired a myriad of questions, while photographers demanded dozens of poses. Few expressed interest in Wright; Robinson was the center of attention. The shortstop fielded their inquiries with grace and wit, commenting on his chances for success, his experiences playing winter ball in Venezuela, his golf matches with Joe Louis, and even his excess weight. ("It's all in my feet," he laughed, when told it didn't show.[26]) Robinson did manage to get in a few swings at the batting cage and Wright played "pepper" and threw to a few hitters. Overall, the day passed without incident.

The following day included fewer questions and more baseball as events seemed to be progressing smoothly. But at the Brock home, Robinson and Wright found black newspapermen Smith and Rowe anxiously awaiting their return. Several times Smith made phone calls to Rickey. Suddenly he turned to the Robinsons and Wright and told them, "Pack your bags, we're going to Daytona Beach." Robinson feared that Rickey had decided to end the experiment and inwardly fumed as he gathered his belongings. As the carload of blacks left Sanford, Smith explained the reason for the hurried flight. A delegation from the town had told Rickey that they would not allow blacks and whites on the same field. They demanded that the Robinsons and Wright, as well as Smith and Rowe, leave Sanford.[27]

The Dodgers did not release details of the expulsions nor those of the

Robinsons's travel ordeal to the press. The New York papers attributed Robinson's late arrival at Daytona Beach to bad weather. The black papers mentioned that Robinson had been "bumped from his plane" but did not cite racial reasons; perhaps their patrons could read between the lines. The media reported Robinson's early departure from Sanford as necessary to allow him and Wright to get settled in Daytona Beach. According to Smith, an integral member of Rickey's strategy circle, the Dodgers did not reveal the Sanford situation "because it was feared the power of suggestion might create a similar development elsewhere with the result that Robinson and Wright would eventually be on the outside looking in altogether."[28]

These early difficulties failed to discourage the Robinsons. "What it did for us," recalls Rachel, "was not only enlighten us and open our eyes to what things were going to be like, but it also mobilized a lot of fight in us. We were not willing to think about going back. It gave us the kind of anger and the rage to move ahead with real determination." In addition the experiences strengthened their relationship. "Because we were a newly married couple," she relates, "I think it had a lot to do with quickly solidifying our marriage."[29]

Following the hurried departure from Sanford the Robinsons and Wright settled into Daytona Beach. The Dodgers had divided their training base in the resort community into two camps. Ironically, the parent club worked out on the white side of town, while the Royals practiced in the black district. Local officials raised no objections to Robinson and Wright training in Daytona Beach, but widespread speculation persisted that they would be barred from actual competition. The test occurred on March 17 when the Royals and Dodgers met in an exhibition clash.

"Southern tradition and precedent will go by the boards," reported the New York *Times* that morning. But rumors flew that the game would be cancelled. Robinson himself doubted that city officials would allow him to perform. New York sportswriter Bill Corum, a part-time Daytona Beach resident who had encouraged Rickey to encamp in the city, also "began to worry . . . that some untoward incident" might occur. Four thousand fans, including an overflow crowd in the section reserved for blacks, poured into the ball park to witness events.[30]

Robinson took the field "thinking so many other things, I didn't know what I was doing." When he strode to the plate in the second inning, he expected to be jeered. Corum, fearing the same thing, had recruited a contingent of friends "to cheer him no matter what." Corum's precautions proved unnecessary. Widespread applause drowned out scattered boos leaving Robinson "with a warm glow of hope and confidence." He played

108   RUNS, HITS, AND ERRORS

five relatively uneventful innings. "Aside from the fact that one man on the ballfield had a complexion shades darker than every other player present," commented Buster Miller in the New York *Age*, "there was absolutely nothing to remind the observer that 'something different' was occurring."[31]

"Something different," however, happened in Jacksonville, where the Royals were scheduled to play against the Jersey City Giants on March 23. The *Florida Times-Union*, the local newspaper, noted the probability that Robinson would be in the lineup, marking "the first time a member of his race had played with white ball players at the Jacksonville park." In a city in which blacks constituted almost half the population and substantial numbers of blacks attended baseball games, the *Times-Union* predicted "one of the largest crowds ever to see an exhibition game will turn out . . ." and that the "colored stands" would probably prove inadequate to handle the local black fans.[32]

The problem of seating Jacksonville's black spectators never had to be faced, as another Robinson entered the picture. Two days before the scheduled game, George C. Robinson, the executive secretary of the Jacksonville Playground and Recreation Commission, announced that Robinson and Wright would not be permitted to play. "It is part of the rules and regulations of the Recreational Department that Negroes and whites cannot compete against each other on a city-owned playground,"[33] he told the *Times*.

Initially the Dodgers offered a conciliatory response. Rickey announced that the Dodgers "have no intention of attempting to go counter to any government's laws and regulations. If we are notified that Robinson cannot play at Jacksonville, of course he cannot play." The Giants requested that the Royals leave Robinson and Wright at Daytona Beach. Rickey countered with a demand that he be notified of the ruling on the "official stationery of the city of Jacksonville" so that "neither the Montreal club nor the Brooklyn club would bear the onus."[34] Instead, the Jacksonville Parks Commission voted unanimously to cancel the game.

The barring of Robinson and Wright drew widespread criticism throughout the North. "Jacksonville got more bad press banning [them] than any city in Florida has experienced since the Jesse Payne lynching at Madison, Florida last October," wrote Wendell Smith. New York and Boston writers were described as "quite upset," while the Brooklyn *Eagle* decried the act as "deplorable." Baz O'Meara of the Montreal *Daily Star* called it a "terrible thing" but noted that Canadians "can hardly appraise these things from an American standpoint." Fifty-eight members of a northern Presbyterian church wrote a letter protesting the Jacksonville decision as a "great injury to democracy and brotherhood" in violation of the "Gospel of Jesus Christ."

Robinson commented philosophically, "Well, I think all of us will sleep just as well tonight, eat just as well tomorrow and feel just as good the next day. I think the world will keep moving in the same general direction—forward."[35]

Two days later, however, on March 25 the Royals arrived at Deland, Florida, to find the game cancelled due to a malfunction in the lighting system; the game had been scheduled for the afternoon. The *Eagle* reported that "Officials of Southern cities are uniting today in a lockout campaign against the Montreal Royals." Red Smith recalls that before a scheduled Dodger-Athletics contest at West Palm Beach, a sportswriter asked Connie Mack, "Suppose they bring Jackie Robinson along?" Mack angrily flared, "I wouldn't play him. I used to have respect for Rickey. I don't anymore." Another reporter convinced Mack to take these comments "off the record" and the outburst received no publicity.[36]

Later that week Hopper and his team journeyed to Jacksonville hoping to play their scheduled game despite the earlier cancellation. Outside the stadium they found a large crowd awaiting them, but the park itself, wrote Wendell Smith "was as closed and quiet as a funeral parlor at three o'clock in the morning." City officials had padlocked the gate and a contingent of city police barred further entry. When Montreal General Manager Mel Jones telephoned for an explanation, the receiver went dead.[37] The Royals reluctantly retreated to Daytona Beach.

Undeterred, the Montreal club again tried to play outside of Daytona Beach. On April 7 the Royals were scheduled to play the St. Paul Saints at Sanford, where townspeople had expelled Robinson and Wright earlier. City officials asked Rickey to leave the black second baseman at the Dodger camp. Rickey ignored the request and the Royals again boarded their little-used bus for the twenty-mile ride to Sanford. Robinson nervously took batting practice and, to everyone's surprise, appeared in the starting lineup. As the second batter in the first inning Robinson beat out an infield single. He proceeded to dance off first base to the chagrin of the distracted pitcher. As the hurler threw to the plate, Robinson broke for second, stealing the base easily. When the next batter singled, the former track star flashed around third base and headed for a close play at the plate. With the crowd roaring, Robinson slid safely under the tag with the first run of the game.[38]

Basking in the moment and the cheers of the Florida fans, Robinson fielded his position in both of the first two innings. As he returned to the dugout at the end of the second frame, his reverie came to an abrupt end. "Vicious old man Jim Crow stepped right on the baseball diamond," wrote Wendell Smith.[39] The chief of police walked on to the field and informed Manager Hopper that Robinson and Wright had to be removed from the ball park. Caught in the middle of a game, Hopper saw little point in resistance and the two blacks withdrew from the dugout.

Robinson's appearance at Sanford and the Royals' abortive trek to Deland and Jacksonville marked a distinct shift in Rickey's strategy. Initially, he had pledged not to take the black athletes where they were unwanted. After the first Jacksonville ban, however, Dodger spokesmen became more strident and militant. "We don't care if we fail to play another single exhibition game," declared Mel Jones. "If they don't want to play us with our full team, they can pull out of the games." Club President Hector Racine proclaimed, "It will be all or nothing with the Montreal club. Jackie Robinson and John Wright go with the team, or there's no game."[40] In assessing his position, Rickey had undoubtedly realized that he held a strong hand. With national public opinion on his side, he could force the issue and shift responsibility for any incidents to Florida city officials. Nor did the Montreal club suffer. The Royals simply transferred their road games to Daytona Beach and missed few training contests.

Amidst the storm of cancellations and lockouts, Daytona Beach stood as an island of enlightenment in a sea of bigotry. City officials chose to defy southern convention and open their arms, if not their hotels, to Robinson and Wright. A decidedly economic rationalization accounted for this tradition-breaking policy. "The Dodgers are big business and there's no mistaking that," wrote local sports reporter Bernard Kahn. "They live the life of O'Reilly at the best hotels and buy the finest of everything." The influx of hundreds of players, trainers and executives, provided a "tidy income" for local businessmen.[41]

Immediate revenues provided only the tip of the iceberg for the civic well-being of Daytona Beach. The postwar era marked a second chance for the economic boosters of Florida's resort cities. The abortive land boom of the 1920s had awakened the nation to Florida's potentialities as a recreation and retirement community. Overspeculation, however, had brought the dizzying inflation of real estate values to a halt and tarnished the Florida dream. The collapse of the land bubble heralded future hard times. Neither depression nor war had offered inducements for the establishment of a resort mecca. With the war's end, Florida businessmen sought to rejuvenate the dream.

"Daytona Beach has just one thing to sell," boasted an editorial in the local *Evening News,* "tourist entertainment in the broadest sense of the word."[42] What better way could this message be publicized than through the medium of a major league baseball team which sent back daily reports to the nation's largest city? Sportswriter Kahn elaborated on the value of the Dodger presence:

Daytona Beach is getting its name printed daily in the newspapers printed all over the United States. . . . Daytona Beach has also appeared in the motion picture newsreels and let's not forget such topline radio announcers as Red Barber and Harry Wismer, who hobnob around the Dodger camp. . . . The ten big name baseball reporters here . . . have an accredited audience of 9,413,505 subscribers. Thanks to the Brooklyn Dodgers, Daytona Beach is getting more than its share of the baseball publicity.[43]

The added attention created by the presence of Robinson and Wright and the favorable reports on the city's tolerance, especially in contrast to competing Florida locales, only enhanced baseball's value to the community.

Local newspapers demonstrated the importance of baseball to Daytona Beach. In the fall of 1945 news of negotiations between city officials and Dodger management had appeared on the front page. Stories hailed Rickey as the "foster father of baseball in Daytona Beach." The *Evening News* ranked the announcement that the Brooklyn club would train in the city as one of the "Top Ten Daytona Beach Stories of 1945."[44] These optimistic dispatches included no negative references to the presence of blacks in the Dodger entourage.

Throughout the spring of 1946 Daytona Beach officials and citizens courted Rickey and the Dodgers in an effort to obtain a five-year contract with the team. The business community overwhelmingly favored the return of the Dodgers. As spring training drew to a close, two full pages of advertisements in the *Evening News* invited the Brooklyn team to visit again in 1947. "We'll all worry about worse than rainy weather, if we don't get 'dem good old bums' back next spring," read the ad from the all-weather tire store. The local Packard dealer warned, "Don't get any ideas that we aren't for the boys from Brooklyn." Other establishments echoed these sentiments, while Mayor Perry hailed the Dodgers as "a fine group of sportsmen" who have provided "high-class entertainment which filled a need here." The Daytona Beach Ministerial Association joined the chorus, urging the city "to leave no stone unturned in getting the Dodgers to return here for spring training next year."[45]

Other Florida communities also sought to entice the Dodgers for the following season. Black athletes notwithstanding, West Palm Beach, Fort Lauderdale, and even Deland, which had barred Robinson from playing, wooed the Brooklyn club. The mere rumor of a contract with Deland produced a banner front-page headline, RICKEY MAY BRING DODGERS HERE.[46] In many Florida cities, farsighted boosters did not allow race taboos to stand in the way of urban growth and profits.

IV

The flood of criticism generated by Robinson's treatment in Florida offered an indication of the intense national interest in his progress. The manner in which both mainstream and black newspapers chronicled his exploits provides a further demonstration. As Sam Lacy noted, the Washington *Post* captioned most training camp stories by reporting teams and scores: "Bosox 7-1 Victors;" "Bucs Top Chisox." On the Montreal-Brooklyn game, however, the headline read ROBINSON HITLESS. As if to reiterate Lacy's point, next to his column in the Baltimore *Afro-American*, the banner blared, "Jackie's Fielding Flawless as Royals Best Dodgers." The Pittsburgh *Courier* ran first-page accounts of Robinson's activities while a front-page box promised an "Exclusive Picture Story of Jackie Robinson and Johnny Wright as they Worked Out with the Montreal Royals in Florida." Wendell Smith's eyewitness accounts boosted *Courier* circulation by 100,000.[47]

Florida newspapers, on the other hand, attempted to downplay the story and in some instances suppressed word of the controversy. While the Daytona Beach *Evening News* treated the story fairly, newspapers from Jacksonville, Deland, and Miami either carried releases from the wire services or ignored the story entirely. The *Florida Times-Union* of Jacksonville imposed a veritable cover-up of the lock-out controversy. On March 23 a small item announced the game cancellation but made no mention of the race issue. Two days before a second scheduled contest at Jacksonville the paper reported that Robinson and Wright "would not be available." When officials blocked this game as well, the *Times-Union* reinstituted the cloak of secrecy, noting the cancellation but offering no explanation. According to the city's foremost daily, the Jacksonville lockout, which had received widespread treatment in the national press, had not occurred.[48]

A similar situation existed in Deland. Papers reported news of cancellations in Jacksonville, but when Deland itself barred Robinson and Wright the *Sun-News* simply recorded the official explanation that the stadium lights needed repairs.[49] Two weeks later, the *Sun-News* did print a letter from local blacks protesting the city's action. The journal did not respond, but it offered the following cryptic comment in an editorial:

We see where the Brooklyn Dodgers' "varsity" is traveling North by Pullman, while the second squad is making the trip by bus.

We hope for the sake of the Ebbets Field faithful that the second stringers don't follow the custom of bringing charges of a "caste system" and perhaps even inciting open mutiny among the Beloved Bums of Flatbush.[50]

If the guarded coverage of the integration issue in the Florida press reflected the selective "invisibility" of blacks in Southern society, the treatment of the Robinson story by two New York sports columnists demonstrated northern racial attitudes. Writing from a supposedly sympathetic standpoint, Jimmy Powers of the *Daily News* and Dan Parker of the *Daily Mirror,* both of whom had clamored for an end to sports segregation a year earlier, wrote columns that implicitly questioned the wisdom of Branch Rickey's "noble experiment."[51]

Parker likened the Dodger president to Abraham Lincoln, then noted that many baseball people considered the whole affair a "publicity dodge." He described Robinson and Wright as "going through the motions" with the Royals in the Negro district of Daytona Beach, while the Dodgers worked out "across the tracks with the white folks." Both players, wrote Parker, received the same treatment as "their pink cuticled brethren under the skin." He bemoaned the lot of Robinson who "isn't living up to his extravagant advance billing" and concluded stereotypically, "One gets the idea that, although there has been no unpleasantness, on the surface at least, Robinson and Wright are vaguely unhappy about the whole business. They certainly aren't having as much fun as they would with their rollicking teammates in Negro baseball."

Parker confined his comments to the realm of sports; Powers took the opportunity to analyze the dilemma of race relations in the South. The *Daily News* columnist attacked "liberals" who "frame pretty press releases primarily to make money out of colored people and colored athletes," and expressed fears that their calls for "mixed gatherings" at athletic events would lead to race riots. Powers invited northerners to cross the Mason-Dixon line and witness the racial progress being made in both the athletic and social arenas. "We remember when colored garbage collectors were paid five dollars a week here," he wrote with sincerity. "Now colored garbage collectors receive $5.50 for a seven-hour day. . . . There are more colored colleges with larger enrollments, more colored athletes hitting the headlines."

For Powers, writing in 1946, progress could be measured by the wages of black garbagemen and the existence of segregated colleges. As Wendell Smith pointed out in a scathing rebuttal to the posturing of Powers and Parker, Powers "fail[ed] to mention that a lot of the fabulously 'rich' colored garbage collectors hold degrees from the 'big' colored colleges, but can't get anything better because the South is progressing so rapidly."[52] Power's message, like Parker's, went out to millions of New York readers; only the *Courier's* primarily black patrons saw Smith's retort.

The success or failure of the integration experiment, however, would be determined not in newsprint but in Florida's baseball stadiums. Much rested upon the acceptance of Robinson and Wright by the fans and their fellow athletes. Serious doubts existed about the nature of Robinson's reception by white fans. Some northern writers feared for Robinson's safety. As sportswriter Tommy Holmes noted, baseball officials could not "guarantee protection from the hoodlum in the bleachers,"[53]

But Florida fans seemed to welcome the presence of the black ballplayers. White fans turned out in large numbers for scheduled Royal games. Last-minute cancellations turned many people away. Referring to the Jacksonville lock-out Robinson commented, "We did have one consolation: a big crowd had been waiting to see the game. . . . Had the decision been left to all those people in line the game would have been played." Cheers, rather than jeers, commonly greeted Robinson. For decades baseball owners had placed partial blame for the ban on blacks on the fans, but as Buster Miller of the New York *Age* wrote, the Florida experience answered those "who've screamed for years that putting Negroes and Whites on the same battlefield would be like setting a match to kerosene."[54] Outward opposition came not from the fans, but from public officials who doubtless feared the potential political consequences of cooperation.

If the reaction of white fans proved heartening, the response from blacks overwhelmed Robinson. The Jim Crow stands filled to overflowing for Jackie's appearances. In his first game against the Dodgers one thousand blacks jammed the segregated section in right field, with hundreds standing behind the foul pole where they could barely see the action. A contingent of blacks from West Palm Beach made the 200-mile trek to Daytona Beach to witness a Robinson performance.[55] Countless others traveled equally long distances to share in the historic breakthrough.

"The coop-like wooden stands for colored people, out beyond the right-field wing of the local grandstand, literally shook with a spasm of hysteria as Jackie Roosevelt Robinson came up with his first base hit of the spring training exhibition scheduled here," reported Tommy Holmes from Daytona Beach. The crowd lived and died with Robinson's every action. His second time up he hit a long, hard foul down the left field line just out of the reach of the opposing outfielder. "When that foul fell to the ground," wrote Holmes, "the gasp of relief from the Negro section indicated that everyone in the coop held his breath throughout the lone flight of the ball. It meant another chance for their standard bearer."[56]

Sam Lacy, the black sportswriter, portraying his own intense involvement with Robinson's performance in Florida, perhaps best illustrated the emotions of the black fans. "I felt a lump in my throat each time a ball was hit in his direction. I experienced a sort of emptiness in the bottom of my stomach whenever he took a swing in batting practice. I was constantly in fear of his muffing an easy roller. . . . And I uttered a silent prayer of thanks, as with closed eyes, I heard the whack of Robinson's bat against the ball."[57]

Robinson welcomed the support of the black fans, but, he confessed to Wendell Smith, they kept him under tremendous pressure. "I could hear them shouting in the stands, and I wanted to produce so much that I was tense and over-anxious. . . . I started swinging at bad balls and doing a lot of things I would not have done under ordinary circumstances. I wanted to get a hit for them because they were pulling so hard for me."[58]

In at least one instance, black Floridians raised their voices not to cheer, but to protest the treatment accorded Robinson and Wright. In Deland, ninety-four blacks signed a letter appealing the city's action in barring Robinson and called for a second scheduled game to be allowed to occur. "These things are very distressing to us," read the plaintive letter. "There is a feeling of uncertainty and having been let down." The blacks expressed shock that this could have happened in Deland where they had been "loyal and enthusiastic" citizens who had "boasted to others of the tolerance, liberalism, and unprejudiced behavior here." They called upon "the White Citizens of Deland to rectify a condition which robs us of a feeling of security and happiness."[59] The black protest fell upon deaf ears. The second game was transferred to Daytona Beach.

Dodger strategists had feared fan reaction in Florida, but they also worried about the response of white athletes. Under the best of circumstances, spring training represents a difficult period for baseball players. For all but a handful of established major leaguers, the Florida camps are pressure-filled testing grounds in which career hopes may be realized or dashed. The crowded postwar Dodger camp intensified competition and the presence of Robinson and Wright added disruptive elements. Yet little outward evidence of resentment surfaced among white players.

With Robinson and Wright in camp, Royal aspirants found an element of uncertainty injected into their already difficult trials. Montreal players were shuttled like pawns to and from padlocked stadiums, unaware if their scheduled contests would take place. Yet resentment against the two blacks seems to have diminished, rather than increased, as the spring wore on. During the early days of March, Lacy noticed an "unmistakable aloofness" on the part of many white players, particularly the southerners. For their part, Robinson and Wright stayed to themselves and did not speak unless spoken to. By the end of the month, however, Robinson reported, "All the fellows seem to be pulling for us," and Lacy noted that the whites had stopped avoiding the two newcomers and in many instances could be found in amiable conversations with them.[60] Robinson, for whom playing with whites was not a novelty, proved particularly adept at making those who approached him feel at ease.

Several players went out of their way to assist the two blacks. "Everyone has been helpful," said Robinson. "I've been told how to play different hitters and John here picked up a lot of pointers on pitching." Lacy cited the example of one unnamed player who initially refused to have his picture taken with the blacks but later could be seen passing along helpful hints. Robinson seemed to be most readily accepted by those with whom he directly competed. Signed as a shortstop, Jackie was quickly introduced to Stan Breard, the popular French-Canadian who had starred at that position for the Royals in 1945. Robinson posed for pictures with Breard and his wife. Later, when a ground ball took a bad hop and slammed Robinson in the face, Breard ran over to make sure his rival was uninjured, offering words of reassurance. After the Royals switched Robinson to second base, Lou Rochelli, a returning war veteran and one of the top candidates at that position, instructed Robinson in his new assignment.[61]

According to a story told by Hopper, one southern opponent assisted Robinson in an unusual way. Paul Derringer, a thirty-nine-year-old former major league hurler who had won 223 games over his fifteen-year career, faced Robinson in an April exhibition game. The Kentucky-born player told Hopper that he would test the black athlete. The first time Robinson came to the plate, Derringer hurled a fastball at his head. "He knocked him down all right," said Hopper, "forced him to put his chin right in the dirt." Robinson stepped back in and Derringer threw a second pitch that headed at him and then broke sharply over the inside corner. Robinson lashed the ball on a line over the third baseman's head for a single. Two innings later, Derringer again decked Robinson. This time the angry batter drove the next pitch into left-center field for a triple. After the game Derringer confided to Hopper, one southerner to another, "Clay, your colored boy is going to do all right."[62]

The case of Clay Hopper, whom Rickey hired as Montreal manager despite his southern background, typified the response of baseball people. Whatever Hopper's personal feelings, he did not display them. He treated both Robinson and Wright fairly. He never spoke out publicly against the experiment and when called upon to take his integrated squad to various Florida cities, he did not balk. By the time the Royals arrived in Montreal, Hopper spoke glowingly of Robinson, calling the black second baseman a "regular fella and a regular member of my baseball club." While skeptical about Robinson's hitting abilities, Hopper regaled Montreal reporters with stories of Robinson's fielding and base running prowess. When the Montreal *Daily Star* ran an opening day layout picturing Abraham Lincoln surrounded by Rickey, Racine, Robinson, and Hopper, the southerner asked for the original for his home in Mississippi.[63]

The ultimate measure of the spring efforts, however, lay not with the manager, nor the white players, nor the fans, but in the performances of the two black athletes. "Mr. Rickey never over-assured us," says Rachel Robinson. "He never said, 'Look, I'll fix it.' He implied quite the contrary. Jackie would have to make a place for himself on the team." In his desire to impress, Robinson quickly developed a sore arm that plagued him through much of spring training. Unable to make the long throw required of a shortstop, Robinson shifted to second base, a move that Rickey had planned all along. But, with his arm "throbbing like a sore thumb," he proved equally ineffective at that position.[64] It appeared that the injury might curtail Robinson's career.

But Rickey would not allow a minor ailment to undermine his efforts. He handed Robinson a first baseman's mitt and ordered Hopper to play him at that position where he would not have to throw. As a result, Robinson made his Florida debut at first base, the position, ironically, at which he would begin his major league career a year later. A full week passed before Robinson could return to second base.

As Robinson's arm healed, his poor hitting posed a more serious problem. Robinson failed to bat safely in his first seven times up in intrasquad games and also went hitless in another four-game stretch. His early performances seemed to confirm the standing opinion that Robinson was a "sunbeam afield, but not too husky a hitter." A Montreal writer reported that Jackie "chases the curve à la Jim Thorpe," the great Indian athlete who had failed to achieve stardom in baseball. After viewing Robinson's early efforts, a sportswriter wrote, "It is do-gooders like Rickey that hurt the Negro because they force inferior Negroes on whites and everybody loses. Take this guy Robinson. If he was white they'd have booted him out of camp a long time ago."[65]

"Jackie couldn't perform well that spring," recalled Rachel, "because the pressure was unbearable. . . . He was trying too hard; he was overswinging; he couldn't sleep at night; he had great difficulty concentrating." But Robinson resourcefully compensated for his slump. In his first game against the Dodgers he reached base on a fielder's choice, stole second, and scored a run. A similar sequence occurred in his aborted Sanford appearance. The black speedster fattened his average with bunt singles and infield hits, always an important facet of the Robinson diet and treated Florida observers to a preview of the baserunning excitement that would characterize his career. In one game opponents caught Robinson between first and second and according to Hopper, "The whole ball club . . . tried to run him down. . . . None of us was surprised when he reached second base safely; we'd have been surprised if they'd got him out."[66]

By the beginning of April, Robinson had "shed his early spring nervousness" and showed daily improvement. In the Royals last game against the parent Dodger club, Robinson slashed two singles against major league pitchers and threw "like a man with a brand new arm."[67] Facing the Jersey City Giants, he tripled and scored. In another contest he stroked two hits against St. Paul. While his performance had not erased all doubts about his hitting ability, when the Royals headed north, Robinson had clearly earned a slot in the starting lineup.

John Wright also experienced spring difficulties. The lanky pitcher drew raves for his "zeal and determination," but this performance on the mound left much to be desired. Wright relied on sharp control but according to Robinson, "every time he stepped out there he seemed to lose that fineness and he tried a little bit harder than he was capable of playing." Wright pitched well in his first intrasquad game, but against the Dodgers he surrendered eight runs and ten hits in five innings. In another intrasquad game, he walked four men in four innings and gave up two runs on three hits, including a single by Robinson. In his last Florida appearance, Wright was "wilder than an Egyptian Zebra," according to Smith, walking four batters and hitting another in the only inning he pitched.[68] Nonetheless, Wright accompanied the Montreal squad northward.

Before the teams broke camp, Branch Rickey assessed Robinson's first spring training. "I'm not discouraged," said Rickey. "I was told that Robinson and Wright would be reviled and shunned by other ball players. They haven't been. I was told that they would be thrown at and spiked. That hasn't happened. I was told that they couldn't live down here . . . that I couldn't get transportation for them in the South . . . that fans would boo them off the field, but the crowds treated them with no discourtesy." Rickey's actions, however, speak louder than his optimistic words. He cancelled plans to bring Don Newcombe and Roy Campanella to spring training. Fearing further incidents, the Royals called off scheduled exhibition games in Georgia and Virginia.[69] The following year when Rickey prepared to promote Robinson to the Dodgers, he set up training camp in Havana, Cuba, rather than in Florida.

Robinson himself, while embittered by his Florida experiences, always contended that he had drawn strength from the positive responses of the players and fans. Rachel Robinson had no such consolation. "I soon learned," she later said, "that all the books in the world cannot really make one understand what it means to be a Negro with dignity and self-respect in an area where segregation is entrenched by custom and supported by a maze of laws. . . . These were painful things for me, but particularly painful for Jackie, because he was such an assertive person and was very sure of his manhood. . . . To have to see him kowtow and submit to these indignities was abominable."[70]

Beyond the human drama of the Robinsons and John Wright, what stands out in retrospect is the extent to which baseball's first integrated spring training unveiled a strategy for later civil rights advocates. Aided and abetted by sympathetic whites, a handful of individual blacks shouldered the physical risks inherent in a policy of direct confrontation with the institutions of Jim Crow. In the face of opposition from local public officials, baseball's integration coalition refused to retreat.

"If . . . Montreal had capitulated and left the Negro players behind," argued the Chicago *Defender* after the Jacksonville lock-out, "the setback would have encouraged obstructionists to close the gates tight against any additional dark aspirants."[71] Instead, Rickey and Robinson relied heavily on the powers of the northern press to evoke sympathy for the victims of southern racism. This adverse publicity hit directly at the weakest link in the southern armor. The hopes of Florida businessmen for economic expansion rested heavily on the influx of northern capital and population. Far-sighted members of the business community recognized that for these dreams to reach fruition, Jim Crow had to end.

As the Royals departed Florida in mid-April, many doubts remained. Spring training rarely provides an accurate indicator of regular-season performance. The true challenge, "the crucible of white-hot competition" of International League play, still awaited Robinson, starting on April 18 in Jersey City.

7

Il a gagné ses épaulettes

*It is ironical that America, supposedly
the cradle of democracy, is forced to send
the first two Negroes in baseball to Canada in order for them to be accepted.*

Chicago *Defender* editorial,
April 13, 1946

I

JIM CROW DIES AT SECOND[1] hailed a newspaper headline in the aftermath of
Jackie Robinson's heroic 1946 opening day performance. Yet Robinson's dramatic debut resolved neither the issue of blacks in baseball nor his future
with the Montreal Royals. In athletics one day's triumph may be washed
away in the daily flood of competition that follows. By June the Royals had
released pitcher Barney DeForge, the first-game victor; Red Durrett who
contributed two home runs to the initial Montreal triumph, appeared in
the starting lineup for only a few weeks. Robinson's inaugural achievement
notwithstanding, the recurrent pressures of the lengthy International League
campaign confronted him with an ongoing test of his abilities, stamina, and
perseverance.

League schedulers had stiffened Robinson's task by placing the Royals
on the road for the first two weeks of the season. After a pair of games at
Jersey City, the Royals would travel to Newark, Syracuse, and Baltimore,
the league's southernmost locale, before arriving in Montreal.

Robinson faced his first crisis in Newark, the second stop on the Royals
itinerary. Following a Sunday doubleheader against Montreal, Newark
Bears outfielder Leon Treadway jumped the club. Many assumed that
Treadway, a North Carolinian who had spent the preceding two seasons
with the Yankees, refused to play against Robinson. International League
officials, registering "considerable consternation," offered two alternative
explanations for Treadway's defection. They reported that Treadway had
quit the team in "disgust" because he could not find an apartment in Newark
and that he had opted to play in the Mexican League. These versions of the

Treadway disappearance failed to convince many reporters. Several days later the outfielder requested a demotion to the segregated South Atlantic League, thus lending credence to earlier speculation.[2] Despite several successful minor league seasons, Treadway never again reached the Triple-A classification. The furor that inevitably followed Robinson notwithstanding, he continued to perform well. In five games against the two New Jersey teams he batted .417, scoring ten runs and driving in five.

The Royals migrated northward to Syracuse where cold weather and an even chillier reception for Robinson and Wright greeted them. With the exception of Baltimore, Syracuse proved the most inhospitable of cities. Fans booed Robinson when he appeared at the plate and the Chiefs players jeered him mercilessly from the dugout. As Robinson knelt in the batter's circle waiting to hit, a Syracuse player pushed a black cat in his direction, shouting, "Hey Jackie, there's your cousin clowning on the field."[3] The umpire stopped the game and ordered the Syracuse manager to silence Robinson's tormentors. The first contest against the Chiefs marked the first game in which Robinson failed to hit safely; the second night he rebounded with two hits in five at-bats.

The Syracuse series also marked the International League debut of John Wright. Wendell Smith described the "modest and inconspicuous" Wright as "more or less in the shadows of the dugout and bullpen." In his first game, the Chiefs accorded him a "rough reception."[4] In three and a third innings of relief work he yielded four runs on five hits. Control problems, which had plagued him throughout spring training, continued to limit his effectiveness.

Wright and Robinson had one further port of call before finding safe harbor in Montreal. Their opening odyssey concluded in Baltimore. Even before the season had begun, International League President Frank Shaughnessy had telephoned Rickey and begged him not to bring the black players to the southern city. Predicting "rioting and bloodshed" that would "wreck organized baseball in that city," Shaughnessy beseeched Rickey, "For God's sake, Branch, don't let that colored boy go to Baltimore. There's a lot of trouble brewing down there." The two baseball officials met on opening day at Jersey City and Shaughnessy reiterated his plea. When the Mahatma dismissed his fears with one of his customary sermons, Shaughnessy exploded, warning the Dodger executive that "this is not the time for philosophical mouthings and silly platitudes. The people are up in arms in Baltimore."[5]

Rickey later admitted that had he believed that a serious possibility of violence and bloodshed existed he doubtless would have retreated. He felt, however, that Shaughnessy had greatly exaggerated the dangers. "We solve nothing by backing away," he told the league president. "In fact, we'll encourage every agitator in Maryland if we show fear."[6] In Baltimore, Oriole officials seemed more concerned with the financial consequences of Robinson's presence than with the prospect of violence. Rumors abounded in the city of a threatened fan boycott.

On a frigid April Saturday night Robinson debuted in Baltimore. "You know they told me this was the Southernmost city in the league," he remarked, "but last night I thought I was playing in Alaska." Only 3,415 "frozen fans" attended the game, reinforcing reports of a boycott. Those who appeared made their presence known. For Rachel Robinson, sitting behind the Royal dugout, this experience seemed worse than the humiliating journey to Florida. When Jackie appeared on the field, the man sitting behind her shouted, "Here comes that nigger son of a bitch. Let's give it to him now." The Baltimore fans unleashed an unending torrent of abuse. All around her people engaged "in the worst kind of name-calling and attacks on Jackie that I had to sit through." For one of the few times Rachel feared for Jackie's physical safety. That night as she cried in their hotel room, Rachel thought that perhaps Jackie should withdraw from the integration venture.[7]

John Wright also faced the jeers of the Baltimore fans. In the sixth inning, with the bases loaded and a five-run deficit, the Royals inserted Wright in relief. The black hurler retired the side without allowing a run. He completed the game, allowing no hits in a losing cause.

The following day, with warmer weather and a Sunday doubleheader in the offing, Baltimore fans dispelled all fears of a boycott. Over 25,000 people filled the stadium, including an estimated 10,000 blacks. The volume of insults increased as white fans roundly booed Robinson. Unlike opening day, Robinson did not respond to the Baltimore challenge with his best performance. During the first three games of the series he registered only two hits in ten at-bats and committed two errors. The Royals lost the second game of the Sunday doubleheader due to Robinson's poor fielding.

The following night, in the series finale, Robinson atoned for his earlier showing. He had three hits in three official times at bat, scoring four runs to pace the Royals to a 10-0 victory. He also received his unofficial baptism into organized baseball when a fastball by pitcher Paul Calvert smashed him on the wrist. Whether negative feelings or simply Robinson's effectiveness at the plate motivated Calvert (ironically a Montreal native) is impossible to determine.

The Monday night triumph over Baltimore concluded the grueling two-week road trip. For the beleaguered Robinson the tour represented a spectacular success. Despite the pressure of the Jersey City opener, the Treadway desertion in Newark, and the hostility of fans and players in Baltimore and Syracuse, he performed remarkably well. While the Royal team compiled only a 6-6 record, Robinson had hit safely in ten of the twelve contests and boasted a 372 batting average. He had scored seventeen runs and stolen eight bases. As April drew to a close, and with spring training and the initial road trip behind him, Jackie Robinson finally arrived in Montreal.

I I

Robinson's presence in Canada posed an unmistakable irony: the integration of baseball, the national pastime of the United States, would be enacted largely outside that country's borders. Canadians, observes historian Robin Winks, "[tend] to view their neighbors in the midst of their racial dilemma with a certain air of moral superiority." They therefore reacted with a mixture of puzzlement and pride. "Local sports fans didn't seem to appreciate how monumental and revolutionary a move the Brooklyn and Montreal clubs had made," reported Montreal sportswriter Dink Carroll, adding, "The absence here of an anti-Negro sentiment among sports fans . . . was what Mr. Rickey doubtless had in mind when he chose Montreal as the locale of his history-making experiment."[8]

Their nationalistic breast-beating notwithstanding, Canadians did not lack racial prejudice. Blacks in Canada, like those in the United States, lived in distinct communities and tended to concentrate on the lower end of the economic scale. A history of discrimination and prejudice pervaded many Canadian provinces. Even in Montreal, only one hotel regularly accepted blacks as late as 1941. Never representing more than 2 percent of the population, blacks were, according to Winks, "forgotten, hidden, or overridden." Prejudice against them was "the product of indifference . . . [and] of far more generalized and thus far less identifiable assumptions about race held widely in the Western world."[9] Nonetheless, after the horrors of Florida, Syracuse, and Baltimore, the less race-conscious environment of Montreal provided a welcome respite for the Robinsons and Wright.

French Canadians predominated in Montreal, accounting for 75 percent of the population, and their influence permeated the city. In Delormier Downs, the ball park where the Montreal populace lavished fanatic affection on the hometown Royals, the public address announcer spoke both French and English and signs were translated into both languages.[10] French-Canadians Stan Breard and Jean Pierre Roy had ranked as the most popular players the previous year.

Only 10,000 blacks lived in Montreal in 1946 and the relative absence of prejudice in the city grew apparent to the Robinsons as they searched for lodgings. As in the United States, Canadian cities suffered housing shortages during postwar reconversion. For Wright, whose family had remained in New Orleans, a rooming house proved adequate. But, the newlywed Robinsons, expecting their first child, anxiously desired to establish their first home. After spending several weeks in an ill-heated hotel, they decided to find an apartment.

"The club gave out these three-by-five cards which said, 'These are the apartments for rent that we have scouted,'" recalls Rachel Robinson. "Jack didn't have the time to look for a house, so I took the cards and went out." Rachel's only frame of reference for apartment hunting derived from the United States, where blacks faced exclusion in most desirable neighborhoods. "I really expected the doors to be shut in my face." The Robinsons located an apartment that met their financial and living requirements in a French-Canadian district somewhat distant from the ball park. To Rachel's surprise, the landlady greeted her warmly, inviting her for tea, and gladly offered her the rooms. "The first apartment that I said I wanted, I got," remembers Rachel. "That alone was very exciting."[11]

"All of the people up there were French and couldn't speak a word of English and we didn't know anything about French," Jackie told an interviewer in 1972, "but we communicated." Canadians, writes Robin Winks, due to their unfamiliarity with blacks, view them as "exotics" alien to the natural landscape. The Robinsons represented a curiosity to their French-Canadian neighbors. "They called us everything from Black Dutchman to anything else," said Jackie. "They didn't know what we were; they'd never seen anything like us before."[12]

The Robinsons found unmistakable affection in their new neighborhood. Shortly after they moved in, a delegation of women visited Rachel. With food rationing still the rule in Canada, the women, noticing that she was pregnant, offered her additional ration coupons should she run short. "When I'd go off on the road," recalled Jackie, "if they didn't see her for a day or so, they'd come knocking on the door to find out where she was."[13] The children of the neighborhood also visited frequently, offering to shop or carry heavy packages for Rachel. As Jackie left for the ball park they lined the streets to watch him. Undoubtedly, Robinson's celebrity status accounted for some of the warmth, but the young couple sensed a genuine acceptance among their French-Canadian neighbors unlike anything they had experienced among whites in the United States.

The hospitality that the Robinsons received in their neighborhood was, in part, an extension of the adulation at Delormier Downs. From the first, the French-Canadian fans had taken to Robinson. Despite his impressive play on the first road trip, many in Montreal still questioned his abilities and staying power when the Royals arrived in Canada. Local sportswriters doubted that Robinson would hit well enough to maintain a position with the International League club. Lloyd McGowan wrote that Robinson had been "fattening up" on left-handed pitching and predicted that his average would drop when he faced righties. As late as May 16 Baz O'Meara of the *Star* wrote, "There's a widespread belief that in a month or so, Jackie will not be hitting with any degree of consistency."[14]

Throughout the month of May, Robinson silenced his detractors. "The critics have cowered, scampered for cover," wrote McGowan on May 28. "Robinson has proved that there is nothing he can't do on the diamond with a fair amount of éclat, not to mention elan." The "dark destroyer" continued to hit at an impressive pace, his average consistently above the .340 mark. He impressed observers even more with his baserunning and fielding skills. Robinson ranked second in the league in stolen bases and, after committing seven errors in the first three weeks of the season, he began a string of seventy-nine errorless games. Robinson's growing skill as a pivot man on double plays also evoked praise. Before joining the Royals, Robinson had always played shortstop. Yet once he adjusted to fielding at second base, few matched him at turning the double play. In the team's twenty home games during May, Robinson, working with two different shortstops, engineered thirty-two double plays prompting McGowan to boast, "Nobody can chase Robbie off his keystone job—nobody you've seen playing baseball lately."[15]

The quality of Robinson's Royal teammates facilitated his own efforts. The 1946 Montreal Royals rank as one of the greatest teams in minor league annals. As the premier farm club in Rickey's bountiful Brooklyn chain, the Royals included both Dodger veterans like pitcher Curt Davis and catcher Herman Franks and prospects awaiting imminent promotion like outfielders Marvin Rackley and Tom Tatum. Montreal boasted a potent offense, batting close to .300 as a team and running the bases with abandon. Averaging better than seven runs a game, the Royals' final tallies often resembled football, rather than baseball, totals. The thorough dominance of the Canadian club in the International League had a salutory effect on the black second baseman. Relieved of the pressures of a pennant race, Robinson concentrated completely on his own performance, which, amidst the galaxy of stellar displays, lost little of its lustre.

Supplementing their winning ways with an exciting style (within one two-day period, for example, four different players, including Robinson, stole home safely), the Royals attracted Montreal fans in record numbers. Robinson provided the primary lure. "The Canadian people loved him," remembers shortstop Al Campanis. "He would prepare a show for them. He'd be on first base and he'd hear the chant 'Allez! Steal that base.'" Commenting on the fanaticism surrounding Robinson, a visiting sportswriter remarked, "Montreal fans are as fair and generous as any I've ever seen, but they don't seem to be helping Robinson by making that furor over him every time he comes to bat."[16]

His admirers followed the easily recognizable Robinson wherever he went. Pittsburgh *Courier* correspondent Sam Maltin reported, "On the street-car, on the way home from the stadium, Jackie is surrounded by admirers. . . . In restaurants, Jackie's food gets cold. He's too busy signing autographs, never refusing requests for his signature. He's in great demand as a speaker at youth gatherings." In mid-June he joined a contingent of the Montreal Canadiens, the reigning world hockey champions, in a visit to ailing servicemen. Even among the heroes of Canada's own national pastime, Robinson remained the prime attraction.[17]

While Robinson savored the fruits of stardom, John Wright quietly faded from the scene. His early season performance in Baltimore had evoked optimism from Wendell Smith, who predicted that "the lean righthander from New Orleans will get the call from Manager Hopper regularly now." Smith's forecast could not have been more inaccurate. Wright saw no action during the next two weeks. The pitcher himself made no public protest, never showing "an inkling of resentment or jealousy," according to Smith. For the *Courier* correspondent, on the other hand, Wright's absence from the mound represented "the one big mystery on the Montreal team." Hopper's sole comment was "Johnny's not ready yet," to which Smith replied, "Certainly he can't get ready riding the bench."[18] The Baltimore game proved Wright's valedictory appearance as a Royal. On May 14 the Royals demoted him to Three Rivers in the Canadian-American League.

Wright's failure provoked considerable speculation. The United Press reported that he lacked an adequate fastball. Sam Lacy rejected this notion, attributing the demotion to the overabundance of right-handed pitching on the Royal club. Lacy claimed that he was "reasonably satisfied that race had nothing to do with the fact that Montreal Manager Clay Hopper did not use [Wright] as regularly or as often as he might have used him," and concluded "Wright did not have the chance many of us had hoped he would have, nor did he prove any ball of fire when the opportunity presented itself."[19]

Assessing John Wright's talents, Don Newcombe recalls, "I don't know if he had that kind of ability that would warrant his being a major league pitcher. . . . He didn't have a major league fastball. . . . He worked hard and he tried, but he was tense." Jackie Robinson attributed Wright's ineffectiveness to the difficulties of pioneering. "John couldn't stand the pressure of going into the new league and being one of the first," Robinson later asserted. "The things that went on up there were too much for him."[20]

"[Wright's] fall was cushioned somewhat, insofar as race-conscious followers of the Royals are concerned," according to Lacy, by the simultaneous signing of black pitcher Roy Partlow to replace him. A Negro League standout since 1934, Partlow had spent most of his career with the Homestead Grays. Like most black ballplayers, he had also pitched throughout Latin America and the Caribbean. In 1945 he had posted a 9-4 record for the Grays and had reigned as the "strikeout king of the Negro National League." "There's no man I can think of who had better stuff than Roy Partlow when he wanted to pitch," asserts Newcombe. A superb hitter, Partlow batted a league-leading .455 in Puerto Rican winter ball in 1947.[21]

Rickey signed Partlow in mid-season off the roster of the Philadelphia Stars. As a result, the Dodger president paid $1,000 to the Stars for Partlow's contract.[22] Rickey denied that this marked a departure from his earlier policies on the signing of black players. Unlike Robinson and the others, whom he recruited in the off-season, Partlow was clearly obligated to another team and not a free agent.

The press reported Partlow to be thirty years old. In reality he was at least thirty-six, a fact apparently known to the Dodgers. It appears that like Wright, his assignment was more to accompany Robinson than to pitch for the Royals. The Dodgers never expected to elevate Partlow to the majors.

Like Wright, Partlow found himself relegated to bench duty. "Right now, I've got seven starting pitchers and not enough work for them," explained Manager Hopper. "I'm winning ballgames and therefore I don't feel like complicating matters by experimenting with Partlow."[23] For two weeks the black left-hander remained untried. Finally, on June 5 Hopper named him as starting pitcher against the second-place Syracuse Chiefs. Future major league star Hank Sauer greeted Partlow in the first inning with a two-run home run. A two-out Syracuse rally in the fifth inning ended Partlow's inauspicious debut. The Royals lost, although Partlow was not the pitcher of record.

The following night Partlow pitched effectively in relief and for the next few weeks the bespectacled southpaw became an important member in the Royal bullpen. In this role, Partlow hurled nine scoreless innings, prompting the *Sporting News* to report, "Roy Partlow has developed into one of the club's best relief chuckers." Hopper rewarded Partlow with a starting assignment on June 24 against the Jersey City Giants. The black pitcher registered his first win in organized baseball, hurling a five-hitter as the Royals coasted to a 16-2 victory. "My colored boy looked pretty good last night," said Hopper. "He has been a little nervous. Now he seems to have overcome it. I figure he can be a regular starter now."[24]

Partlow's next two starts, however, proved disastrous. On June 29 the

Baltimore Orioles chased him in the second inning; four days later the Buffalo Bisons knocked him out in the third. In both instances, Montreal rallies prevented Partlow from being a losing pitcher, but Hopper again dropped the left-hander from the starting rotation. Partlow made two more relief appearances with the Royals, registering a victory over Toronto and pitching two hitless innings in an exhibition game against the Dodgers. Several days after the Dodger visit, the Royals dispatched him to Three Rivers to join John Wright.

Partlow lasted longer than John Wright had at Montreal and experienced more success. He survived at the Triple-A level for almost two months, hurling in ten games and demonstrating some flashes of talent. Like Wright, he had been prone to wildness. Although he won two contests while losing none, he compiled a disappointing 5.59 earned run average. His departure marked another turning point for Jackie Robinson. The Royals did not replace Partlow with another black athlete "to keep Jackie company." By mid-July Robinson had assured his position. Rickey no longer deemed it necessary to provide him with black companionship. For the remainder of the season, Robinson remained the lone black athlete in the International League.

III

As long as Jackie Robinson remained anchored at Montreal, the travails of racial pioneering seemed less ominous. For both him and Rachel the interludes in Canada provided a necessary, if limited, respite from the seasonal tempests. In other cities, however, Robinson's reception remained unpredictable and threatening.

Buffalo ranked perhaps as the most hospitable of other International League cities. On Jackie's initial appearance, according to a Buffalo sportswriter, "He received an ovation he can never forget." Between games of a June doubleheader, the president of the Buffalo City Council hosted a ceremony honoring Robinson and Partlow. The two men received gifts including cash, wallets, wrist watches, and traveling bags.[25] Throughout the season Robinson could depend upon a warm reception in Buffalo.

On the other hand, Syracuse, the league's other New York city, persisted as one of Robinson's worst stops. The problem arose not from the fans, but from the opposing athletes. Bench jockeying was common practice in baseball, but directed at Robinson, its ugly racial overtones exceeded the accepted bounds of propriety. At the season's end Montreal General Manager Jones berated his Syracuse counterpart for the Chiefs' treatment of Robinson. "You've got the worst bunch of jockeys in the league from your club," fumed Jones. "He had to take a worse ride from your club than any other."[26]

The taunts of the Syracuse players paled beside the threats of violence that always accompanied a trip to Baltimore. "There was a lot of tension there," recalls teammate Johnny "Spider" Jorgenson. "People no doubt liked to see him play, but there was still that tension there that anything could happen." The ominous crowd reaction that had so terrified Rachel Robinson during the first series in Baltimore resumed in each of the Royals subsequent appearances. On the second journey to the southern city, Robinson, injured earlier, appeared in only one game. On the final play of that contest a brawl erupted at home plate and fans came pouring out of the stands in support of the hometown Orioles. Robinson had already reached the clubhouse when the melee began, but fans surrounded the dressing room. "Those fans were there, I would say, until one o'clock in the morning," remembers Jorgenson, "and they'd say 'Come out here Robinson, you son of a bitch. We know you're up there. We're gonna get you.'" Jorgenson and two other players, southerners Tatum and Rackley, remained with Robinson until the crowd had dispersed and then, unable to get a cab, they escorted Robinson to his hotel on a city bus.[27]

Epithets and threats of fan violence also marred Robinson's final visit to Baltimore in early August. "Throughout the series Jackie was chided by a number of ignorant, unreconstructed whites and made the target of the 'unfunny humor' of others," reported Lacy. A patron seated near the sportswriter cracked that Robinson "oughta be behind a pair of mules." Oriole Manager Tommy Thomas persistently tormented Robinson. "You let him in and they'll all be coming in now," Thomas shouted to the Royal players. "You'll all be out of a job." A close play at home plate in the first game of the series inspired another riot. Fans invaded the playing field in protest and four police radio cars, two traffic cruisers, ten foot-police officers, and motorcycle policemen arrived to control the crowd. Umpire Gus Winters, not Robinson, who had hit a home run, two singles, and stolen home during the contest, was the target of their wrath.[28] Nonetheless, the memories of the earlier confrontation and fears for Robinson's safety haunted the black athlete and his Royal teammates.

The games at Baltimore displayed the terrors of baseball integration; they also demonstrated the undeniable economic benefits. "Although many of them came for the sole purpose of booing him," wrote Lacy, "it remains a matter of record that Jackie Robinson was the outstanding factor which drew more than 67,000 fans to the city stadium last week." Long before the final series at Baltimore, Robinson had become the leading drawing card in minor league baseball. "Not since Dizzy Dean has Rickey had a man in the fold with as much crowd appeal," reported J. Taylor Spink in the *Sporting News*. The Royals shattered International League attendance records in the wake of Robinson's march through the circuit. Montreal established a new standard for home attendance, but on the road Robinson had an even more dramatic impact. Almost three times as many fans in other cities saw Montreal play in 1946 as had appeared the preceding year. Baltimore, largely on the strength of its contests with Montreal, attracted more fans than any club in International League history. Counting the regular schedule and post-season play-offs, over a million people saw the Royals perform in 1946, a remarkable figure in a minor league in which most arenas seated between ten and twenty thousand spectators.[29]

Robinson had not accounted for the entire attendance surge. "Remember, we've had very few postponements, marvelous weather, and a great team," Montreal General Manager Mel Jones explained. "I don't want to take anything away from Robby . . . but he is not the reason for the big crowds." Jones also pointed out that the end of the war had triggered a tremendous sports boom which had sent attendance skyrocketing throughout the major and minor leagues.[30] During World War II personal income in both Canada and the United States had risen dramatically at the same time that consumer production had been curtailed. A spectacular increase in savings resulted. While businesses rushed to convert their plants back to peacetime production, the entertainment industries reaped the benefits of consumer demand. Movies, theaters, and sporting events prospered during the postwar years as never before.

Recognizing these trends, however, does not negate the Robinson phenomenon. Postwar prosperity did not create the interest and curiosity in the first black players; it merely gave it a fertile soil in which to flourish. People in the International League ball parks, both black and white, came to see Jackie Robinson. Dink Carroll, commenting on the record attendance pace established by Baltimore pointed out, "The Orioles are not the attraction away from home that the Royals are—nor is any other club in the league. There are a couple of reasons for this—first, the Royals are the league leaders . . . and second, they have Jackie Robinson. . . . Everyone wants to see him after reading so much about him."[31]

No one wanted to see Robinson more than his fellow black Americans. Large numbers of blacks flooded International League ball parks wherever Robinson appeared. On his first road trip thousands of blacks descended upon tiny Ruppert Stadium in Newark for the initial contest between the Royals and the Bears. In Buffalo and Baltimore blacks consistently accounted for between 40 and 50 percent of the throngs who massed at the playing fields.

Many blacks went to great lengths to witness a Robinson performance. Frank Ellis, the rotund director of an Elks Lodge in Syracuse, led a delegation of his black fraternal brethren to see Robinson's first game in that city. Several days later in Baltimore, Ellis again appeared as Jackie made his tumultuous debut in the southern city. And, when Wright and Robinson arrived in Montreal, Ellis greeted them, beaming his "broad winning smile." John R. Williams, a black sports promoter in Detroit, arranged buses to Toronto for the Royals' first game against the Maple Leafs. Five hundred blacks signed up for the trip. Later in the season the Frederick Douglass Non-Partisan Civic League of Detroit sponsored a sightseeing and lecture tour of Montreal. The major advertised attraction of the junket was an afternoon at Delormier Downs to see Jackie Robinson. When the main train scheduled to transport them was cancelled, half of the disappointed 300 blacks made other arrangements and came on their own. Robinson rewarded their dedication by stroking the game-winning hit.[32]

Millions of black Americans would have gladly exchanged places with Ellis, Williams, and the hundreds of Detroiters who journeyed to Canada. The broad-shouldered black athlete had struck an unmistakable chord in the Afro-American communities of the United States. The unbridled emotions generated by the integration experiment evoked repeated warnings from a fearful black press. "Too many demonstrations, too much autograph signing, etc., wherever he makes his appearance, although well meant, will do him more harm than good," wrote W. L. Gibson in the Baltimore *Afro-American*. "For his sake we should temper our enthusiasm and keep our exuberance within bounds." "Let's not make him a race problem; he's just a ballplayer," admonished the Chicago *Defender*.[33]

Black fans found it difficult to restrain the pride and sense of achievement engendered by Robinson's performance. "Fans here and everywhere he goes are simply idolizing him," wrote Sam Lacy in Baltimore. "They yell to him from the stands, want to talk to him, want to shake his hand, etc."[34] At the ball parks, people shoved gifts at Robinson, who finally asked Lacy to inform his admirers that he could be fined $25 for conversing or fraternizing with people in the stands.

Lacy also embarked upon a campaign to have Robinson treated "as another player," not just by the fans but by his teammates, manager, and opposing players as well. After Robinson's errors led to an early season loss in Baltimore, Lacy composed a "Letter to Clay Hopper" urging him to "bawl out" Jackie for his mistakes. "I am hopeful that you didn't 'bend over backwards' in this case simply because it was Jackie," wrote Lacy. "If you didn't give him hell, you should have. Jackie's people don't want him treated any different than the rest." Two weeks later Lacy defended the right of the fans to boo Robinson in the name of "freedom of expression." "No fan exercises like the baseball fan what he considers an inalienable right to cheer or jeer as he sees fit," explained Lacy.[35]

In print the black press failed to heed its own warnings. The excitement of the season and the magnetism of Robinson's play and personality enchanted black sportswriters as well as fans. In addition, Robinson sold newspapers. His exploits frequently appeared on the front page and he quickly rivalled Joe Louis as the most photographed black personality. Black sports pages included accounts, statistics, and box scores of Montreal contests, analyzing every nuance of Robinson's performance.

In the eyes of black America, Robinson became a larger-than-life figure. On May 18 Sam Lacy described his hopes for his son's future. "I'd want him to combine the wisdom of Joe Louis with the courage of Jackie Robinson," eulogized Lacy. "I'd hope for him to have Jackie's ability to hold his head high in adversity, the willingness to withstand the butts and digs and meanness of those who envy him." A prominent society of blacks selected Robinson as one of the ten great Negroes of his era. Rachel Robinson was also elevated to the pinnacle of black worship. An article by Lula Jones Garrett about the wife of the pioneer athlete concluded, "The only person I know who can equal her is that first citizen of the world, Mrs. Eleanor Roosevelt."[36]

In International League grandstands, Robinson could rely on his black supporters to partially offset white hostility; on the playing field, he stood alone. When confronted by opposing players who objected to his presence, Robinson relied on his own skills and self-control to withstand their onslaughts. Verbal taunts and bench jockeying could be ignored or silently absorbed. But the physical weapons in a ballplayer's arsenal could be less readily dismissed.

The brushback pitch, a fastball thrown right at the batter at speeds approaching or exceeding 90 miles an hour, represents baseball's ultimate intimidator. The inability to recover from the fear implanted by the brushback has ruined many promising careers. Pitchers commonly test young players by throwing at their heads, but in Robinson's case, the consequences of this test were magnified. In the eyes of many, not only was Robinson's personal courage in question, but that of all ballplayers of his race.

"He's been thrown at more than any batter in the league," said teammate Curt Davis, a veteran of thirteen years in the majors. "If he hasn't been then there are a flock of pitchers in this league who have inexplicable lapses in control." Larry MacPhail later admitted to Wendell Smith that he ordered pitchers on the Yankees' Newark farm team to throw at Robinson. One anonymous manager stated, "I offered to buy a suit of clothes for any pitcher on our club who knocks him down."[37]

Statistics do not entirely bear out these reports. Pitchers hit Robinson only six times during the season, with hurlers on Baltimore and MacPhail's Newark franchise striking him three times each. Statistics, however, can be misleading. One cannot determine how often Robinson relied on his agile reflexes to duck out of the way of the oncoming pitch. "I've seen him dusted off at least 30 times," reported Joe Page, a veteran Royal rooter who attended most of their home games. His experiences in one late season game illustrate the point. In a game at Montreal, Oriole pitcher Stan West, who had hit Robinson once earlier in the season, forced Robinson to fall to the dirt in his first at bat and hit him on the wrist in his second time up. On his next appearance at the plate, West threw two more fastballs aimed at Robinson, drawing the vocal wrath of the Montreal fans.[38]

The brushback pitch is intended to intimidate the batter and make him less effective at the plate. With Robinson it usually achieved the opposite effect. "Jackie can take it," related teammate Davis. "He brushes himself off and comes back as if nothing happened." "He always picked himself up smiling," said Page. The manager who offered a suit of clothes for knocking down Robinson found no takers. "We had a tough enough time with the colored boy to get him without wasting pitches," complained one hurler. Robinson explained his counter strategy as follows: "After you have ducked away from a close one, you can expect a curve ball. Nine out of ten pitchers come back to the plate after they drive you away from the plate."[39]

Some of Robinson's teammates did not agree that pitchers targeted Jackie more than others. "He got knocked down a lot," recalls Tom Tatum, "but so did I, so did several of the good ballplayers who were hurting the clubs with their hitting." Jackie, at least in his public statements, agreed. "I don't think they have thrown at me any more than they would anyone else who was hot at the plate," he told J. Taylor Spink.[40] Indeed, five out of the six hit-by-pitch incidents occurred in games in which he had two or more hits. The sixth occasion followed a period in which Robinson had pounded twenty hits over a nine-game span. Racial considerations undoubtedly inspired many of his "dustings," but Robinson also paid a price for his success at the plate.

"They might have throwed at him a little more," concedes Tatum, "but they took potshots more at second base." A second baseman is in a highly vulnerable position. In making the pivot on the double play, he generally has his back to the runner, who attempts to prevent the fielder from completing the throw to first base. In this situation baserunners unleashed their aggressions against Robinson. "I've seen the time when if it'd been me, well, the fight would've started," recalls Tatum. Robinson, however, usually went out of his way to stress that the rough-and-tumble play at second base was a part of the game. After one incident in which Robinson had to be helped from the field, he defended the baserunner. "He didn't rough me up," said Robinson, "he only came in hard and fast. That's the way to play baseball."[41]

But several times plays around second base sorely tested Robinson's self-discipline and promise to Branch Rickey. "You could see sometimes that he'd like to, oh boy . . . ," muses Tatum. Al Campanis recalls one instance in which an opposing player "really wanted to get him at second base, but [Robinson] was too quick." Robinson grew furious and Campanis quickly intervened. "I threw my glove down," relates the current vice-president of the Los Angeles Dodgers. "I said, 'You want to challenge somebody?'" The baserunner backed off. "I think that time [Robinson] might have wanted to beat the hell out of him," says Campanis, "but he just walked around in front of him and got about five yards away and got a grip on himself and backed off." On another occasion, Jackie exchanged words with Baltimore first baseman Eddie Robinson, whom he accused of kicking him in the back on a double play. The Oriole Robinson claimed that the blow had been accidental and the incident passed without further conflict.[42]

The tight pitches and jarring collisions at second exacted a toll on Robinson. Struck on the wrist by a pitch in late April, Robinson missed one game after playing two others with a bandaged left hand. In early June, while in the midst of a twelve-game hitting streak, a more serious injury felled him. Initially reported as a charley horse but later described as a "mysterious ailment" afflicting his thigh, the injury sidelined Robinson for all but two games during the next three weeks. X rays revealed no fractures or bone disturbance, but according to the Royal trainer, Robinson's leg was in "bad shape." "It is blue as well as black," reported the Montreal *Daily Star*.[43]

Robinson in action had produced reams of news copy; Robinson's inaction also made headlines. Reports of his injury-induced idleness provoked widespread speculation as to whether his legs could withstand the daily punishment required in organized baseball. Manager Clay Hopper stoked the controversy when he stated, "He's sure enough a big league second baseman, but his legs are not holding up. . . . He's played in only about half of our games on account of his legs." Abe Saperstein, who booked games for the Negro Leagues, commented that Robinson's football playing days had weakened his ankles. This speculation irritated Robinson. When sportswriter Red Smith traveled to Jersey City to interview Robinson, the black athlete charmed him until Smith mentioned reports that the second baseman was injury prone. "This made him indignant. He defended himself, I think angrily," recalled Smith.[44] Both Sam Lacy and Lloyd McGowan saw the reports of leg problems as efforts of anti-integrationists to belittle Robinson.

"The true greatness of an athlete, his real worth to a team, is often never really appreciated until he's missing," noted Montreal sportswriter Al Parsley. The Royals clearly felt Robinson's absence. In addition, the injury dramatized Robinson's improved relationship with his teammates. Players who earlier in the season had avoided him or been uncomfortable with him, now stopped to ask about his leg. "Even catcher Herman Franks," reported the *Courier,* "who seldom smiles and gives the impression of a sourpuss, was giving Jackie's leg a look-see."[45]

Indeed, by June, Robinson had won most of his teammates over with his quiet courage and determined play. Tom Tatum admitted that at the start of the season many of the players were concerned about having a black man on the team. "There's some of the boys that were uptight maybe a little because they were from the South." Robinson felt that the Southerners "didn't know how to take me at first." Those who objected, however, kept their misgivings private. "If they don't like the notion of his being on the club," wrote Dink Carroll, "they are hiding their true feelings successfully."[46]

Robinson always exercised diplomacy in discussing his teammates with the press. After the opening game he credited their support for his outstanding performance. Later in the season, he told J. Taylor Spink, "It wasn't a question of the players getting along with me. I was on the spot to see if I could get along with them." Speaking of the southern players, he added, "It wasn't my privilege to make friends with them at first."[47]

Robinson never forced himself on his teammates. "He was very quiet, never said much," recalls Spider Jorgenson. Campanis remembers the team stopping for a meal at a cafeteria in Buffalo during the early part of the season. After Robinson came through the food line, he hesitated before choosing a table until Campanis invited Jackie to join him. As shortstop and second baseman, the two men talked frequently on the field. "But he still had that respect that maybe this guy doesn't want to eat with me," says Campanis. "I think he wanted to be asked rather than come right over. . . . He didn't want to sit there unless somebody wanted him there." As the season progressed, the Royals accepted Robinson more readily. "As soon as he won his first ballgame for us, they started pulling for him," says Tatum, "especially when he'd get knocked down at second base or thrown at at the plate."[48]

The relationship between Tatum and Robinson illustrated the racial dynamics on the Royals. The Texas-born Tatum, a top prospect before the war, had injured his arm in the military, severely hampering his throwing ability. Although somewhat reluctant about playing on a team with blacks, the resumption of his own playing career concerned Tatum far more. As the season progressed, Tatum came to like and respect Robinson. "I didn't pursue Robinson to be close to him or anything like that. Just during the season, if we'd come together, we'd talk together." On the road, both Robinson and Tatum tended to linger in the clubhouse longer than most players and would fall into discussions. "I enjoyed talking to him," recalls the Texan. "He was smarter than a lot of the ballplayers. Hell, I had a high school education. He was a lot smarter than me as far as common sense and learning and books."[49]

Speculating on how teammates would receive Robinson, Dink Carroll accurately predicted, "Baseball is their bread and butter and they aren't likely to risk the displeasure of Mr. Rickey by being openly hostile." But the sentiments of the ballplayers went beyond this. In the highly competitive baseball universe, most athletes quickly lost interest in the color of their teammates. Spider Jorgenson has only scattered memories of Robinson as a Royal. "I don't remember the other stuff that went on," he says today. "I was fighting for my life myself." Tom Tatum exclaims, "Why, I was doing it for a living. If they could help me and help the ball club win games, that's more money in my pocket, if you want to put it down to the money part of it."[50]

It would be a mistake to romanticize Robinson's relationships with his teammates. Robinson's friendships on the Royals remained within the confines of the playing field and the clubhouse. Choice and circumstance accounted for this as much as the unfamiliarity of interracial socializing. Friendships rarely form in the transient environment of the minor leagues. "It was a kind of funny club," asserts Campanis. "We all worked together once we got to the ball field, but then we went apart. We lived in different areas and other than once in awhile, we didn't socialize." Rachel Robinson confirms this. "In Montreal, because we lived way out in the French-Canadian neighborhood, we had a long trip. We had to take a trolley and two buses so there was no socializing between us." Nor, at that time, did the Robinsons desire more contact with the other Royals. "There was as much holding out from the players and their families, in a social sense, on our side, as there was from their side," recalls Rachel.[51]

Even at the ball park the Royals probably never unanimously accepted Robinson. But none of them voiced complaints, either publicly, or, according to those interviewed, privately. By mid-season, Robinson felt comfortable enough to join groups of players at meals without being asked and by the end of the campaign, the competition-loving Robinson could be found playing cards with his teammates. Robinson had become a bona fide member of the Royals.

Robinson and Manager Hopper had cemented their relationship during spring training. By the time the team had reached Montreal, the Mississippi-born pilot had apparently achieved peace with his conscience. "He's doing even better than I thought he would," Hopper confessed in early May. "When a man is hitting like he is, all the manager can do is nod his head and smile." As the season progressed, Hopper continued to laud his star. Robinson "has all the qualifications of a great ballplayer," Hopper told Dink Carroll. "If he was white, he'd be a cinch to go anywhere." When quizzed about the prospects of other blacks, however, Hopper expressed less certainty. "There's only one Jackie Robinson."[52]

IV

One Jackie Robinson was not enough for Jersey City manager Bruno Betzel. "I'd like to have nine Robinsons," Betzel told J. Taylor Spink. "If I had one Jackie, I'd room with him myself and put him to bed nights to make sure nothing happened to him." Betzel's enthusiastic appraisal echoed the sentiments of most observers who had watched Jackie slash his way through the International League. "The greatest performance being put on anywhere in sport," wrote newsman Ted Reeves, "is being supplied by colored boy Jackie Robinson of Montreal." "Robinson has been the 'fair haired' lad of the league champions," Sam Lacy wrote, tongue lodged comfortably in cheek.[53]

Robinson's statistics at Montreal still speak eloquently of his triumphant season. He led the league in hitting with a .349 average and in runs scored with 113. He finished second in stolen bases and drove in sixty-six runs, a remarkable figure for a player batting second in the lineup. He also recorded the highest fielding percentage of any International League second baseman. Yet these statistics fail to provide an adequate measure of Robinson's performance. Robinson missed almost thirty games due to injury and played many others in less than complete health. As late as mid-August he was batting in the .370s before a late slump dropped his average. "There doesn't seem to be anything he can't do," marvelled Dink Carroll.[54]

In all departments, Robinson drew accolades. "His most obvious stock in trade is his noodle," lauded Joe Page. "I don't think there is a smarter player in the International League." "Much of his popularity is due to the fact that Robbie is always coming up with something new," wrote Lacy after Robinson evaded a rundown play by confounding Jersey City third baseman Bobby Thomson with a "football roll" that sent Thomson hurtling over him without making the tag. Robinson's running skills awed his admirers. "The real trouble starts when he gets on base," said Page. "Then the boys start throwing the ball around trying to get him. He seems to have the knack of sensing what the pitcher is going to do, like Cobb used to."[55]

Robinson reminded many observers of Ty Cobb, the Georgia-born baseball great who had had little use for blacks. The analogy seemed particularly appropriate with regard to Robinson's bunting abilities. Betzel called him a better bunter than the legendary "Georgia Peach." Hopper described him as a "real artist" in his ability to lay the ball down. By one account, bunts accounted for almost 20 percent of Robinson's hits. While some saw this as a sign of weakness at the plate, most dismissed this criticism. "He can hit the curve and while a natural right-handed pull-hitter, he can power the ball to all fields and has proved he can hit behind the runner," wrote McGowan.[56]

"Like plastics and penicillin, it seems like Jackie is here to stay," commented one writer in mid-season. By that time the question was no longer whether he could make the grade with the Royals, but how he would fare with the Dodgers. One group of "serious thinkers" calculated that Robinson could play second base for twelve of the sixteen major league clubs. "He bunts better than 90 percent of the big league players and runs better than 75 percent," exclaimed Mel Jones. "What can't he do but eat in the dining room of the Waldorf?"[57]

Throughout the season, rumors abounded that the Dodgers would promote Robinson. Despite a performance that might normally have merited such a step, the Dodgers never contemplated Robinson's elevation during the 1946 season. Rickey's master plan called for a full season at Montreal. In late August Mel Jones ended all speculation. "He's passed the test in the International and he shouldn't have to go through all that again in the big league," stated Jones. The Montreal *Gazette* supplemented Jones's comments with a cartoon depicting a player hefting a boulder labelled "International League Pressure." Alongside, on the ground, was a larger boulder marked, "National League Pressure." The accompanying caption read, "Too much in the same season."[58]

The cartoon possessed more truth than most people realized. Outwardly, Robinson had borne his ordeal with "effortless dignity," as Jimmy Cannon remarked. Robinson's composure, however, masked the tremendous strain that he had endured. "All season I have been under terrific pressure," he admitted in October. "It required all my stamina and determination to justify the faith Mr. Rickey and others had in my ability. I knew that every move was being watched and everything I did required deepest concentration." Rachel Robinson recalls that although she and Jackie faced minimal frustrations after spring training, "There were the stresses of just knowing that you were pulling a big weight of a whole lot of people on your back. . . . I think Jackie really felt, and I agreed, that there would be serious consequences if he didn't succeed and that one of them would be that nobody would try again for a long time." Jones also knew of the pressures affecting Robinson. "He came into my office more than once," said the Montreal general manager, "and he'd say, 'Nobody knows what I'm going through.' But he never mentioned quitting."[59]

At home, Rachel knew that her husband was not well. Unable to eat or sleep, Jackie often felt nauseated. In late August both she and Hopper urged the second baseman to see a doctor. The physician concluded that Jackie verged on a nervous breakdown. Since the club had already clinched the pennant, the doctor ordered Robinson to remain home for ten days. Two playing days after his rest period began, however, Robinson returned to action. Two factors motivated his hasty return. As the league's leading hitter, he feared speculation that he was protecting his average in order to win the batting title. More importantly, the doctor's diagnosis had provided its own relief. "As soon as the doctor told me that I wasn't dying of anything horrible, like cancer, that it was just my nerves," Robinson told Hopper, "I was all right. I wasn't nervous anymore."[60]

The ordeal also adversely affected Rachel Robinson. Twenty-three years old, newly married, and expecting her first child, events had thrust Rachel into the alien, if hospitable, environment of Montreal, far from her friends and relatives and removed from other blacks. Since the Robinsons lived far from the ball park and rarely socialized with the other Royals, Rachel lived in relative isolation, especially when Jackie was on the road. Pittsburgh *Courier* correspondent Sam Maltin and his wife Belle provided her major source of companionship.

"The way I handled my anxiety," remembers Rachel, "was to work very hard in my apartment to make it right. . . . I did a lot of knitting for the first baby." For the young Mrs. Robinson, whose later life was to include careers as a professor at Yale and as a successful New York businesswoman, this state of affairs seemed perfectly natural. She says today, "I had been trained to be an excellent homemaker, more than [for] a career, so that wasn't hard to do."[61]

Rachel attended every Royal home game. When the team traveled, however, the strain she felt manifested itself. "I exhibited symptoms I still don't understand," she explains. "I was pregnant and from the third month on I had this fever of undetermined origins. Even the doctors didn't know what to attribute it to." The fever would reach 104 degrees. "It always coincided with the two weeks [Jackie] was on the road, so it looked a little psychosomatic," says Rachel, "but it was a fever." Rachel kept Jackie unaware of these problems. "I felt I was supposed to manage my own anxiety without burdening him and that I was also supposed to protect him from any concern about me." By her own admission, she carried this behavior to "ridiculous proportions." At one point, she required a minor operation and tried to hide the fact from Jackie. The doctor, however, refused to operate without her husband's consent and Jackie had to be called to the hospital.

Despite their anxiety and health problems, Rachel enjoyed the season in Montreal. The French-Canadian hospitality and Jackie's success overshadowed the difficulties. Through it all, she and Jackie still shared the excitement of newlyweds. "I can't convey how much of a pair we were," she reminisces. "The pairing was very intense, as if we were a part of each other." Rachel relates one incident when she was seven months pregnant and Jackie was about to leave on a road trip. "I remember him calling me from the railroad station . . . and saying 'I don't want to make this trip without you, come on down.' And I just packed a bag and went. I was delighted to be asked. . . . The porters were horrified because we had to take an upper berth and they did not want me to climb to an upper berth. But we were as happy as June bugs."

V

The Montreal Royals won the International League pennant by nineteen and one-half games. In the play-offs they experienced no difficulty defeating the Newark Bears and Syracuse Chiefs to emerge as league champions. The Little World Series, which pitted the victors in the International League against the American Association for the championship of the minors, remained their only test. In 1946 the Louisville Colonels won the American Association title. Jackie Robinson headed South once again.

Jim Crow adopted a hybrid form in Louisville, Kentucky. Schools were segregated, but streetcars were not. Blacks and whites went to separate theaters but shopped in the same stores. At Parkway Field, segregation existed both on and off the baseball diamond. Blacks could pay admission and watch the proceedings from a small Jim Crow section down the right-field line, but only whites played the game. "You're smitten with the brazen inconsistency here," observed Lacy.[62]

As the likelihood of a Louisville-Montreal series grew apparent, many expressed concern that Robinson might be barred from playing in the southern city. Bruce Dudley, the president of the Colonels, had opposed the Robinson signing the previous year. Nonetheless, he quickly squelched rumors that the black second baseman would not be allowed to participate.

As long as organized baseball accepted Robinson, reasoned Dudley, he could appear in the Louisville Stadium.[63]

Local officials could not as easily resolve the problem of handling the massive demand for play-off tickets among the black community. The Jim Crow section of Parkway Field held only 466 people and the Colonels' management, citing fears of racial violence, refused to make accommodations for those who wished to see Robinson. "I saw thousands turned away," protested a letter writer in the Louisville *Courier-Journal*, "yet there were plenty of seats in the bleachers. But they were held for white patrons." Even the black press faced similar difficulties. Sam Lacy had telephoned ahead several days earlier for a press reservation. At the ball park, however, he found that a "'press' ticket entitles you to a spot, smack dab against the rightfield wall . . . located at the extreme end of the covered stands . . . which are 'reserved for colored.' "[64]

Louisville blacks resourcefully overcame these obstacles. Some paid high prices to whites for their tickets. Others sought vantage points outside the ball park. One person climbed a telephone pole beyond the center-field fence. About 300 others were "clinging precariously to the sloping roof of a dilapidated shack in view of the rightfield wall." A similar number stood atop a tool house of the L & N Railroad, while another group climbed some freight cars on a siding behind them.[65]

Lacy, sitting in his "spot" in the right-field stands, knew precisely when Robinson entered the playing area from the "crescendo of boos emanating from the huge amphitheater," which struck him "with the force and positive meaning of a punch in the nose." The black sportswriter likened the southern response to a baby forced to take cod-liver oil or a drinker faced with an inferior brew. "It amuses you to see them turn up their noses and move to push the stuff away when they're forced to try a blend after so many years of having it 100 proof," he jibed.[66]

"They called him everything under the sun," recalls John Welaj, who played for the Colonels. "They probably called him watermelon eater, chicken thief, crap shooter, nigger, everything." The abuse came predominantly from the fans rather than the players, who had been warned not to harass Robinson by a representative from the commissioner's office. Nonetheless, an incident before the second game demonstrated the uncertainty surrounding the series. The game began twenty-five minutes late when the Colonels refused to take the field. The cause of the protest was unannounced and rumors spread through the stadium. It finally developed that league officials had suspended the Louisville manager for berating an umpire in the first game. The players had struck until he was reinstated. For Robinson it constituted an anxious moment. "I was afraid I was in the middle of it," he later confessed to Dink Carroll.[67]

Each time Robinson came to the plate during the three games at Louisville a chorus of boos rained down on him from the almost all-white stands. "He took it most gracefully and conducted himself in his every move as a gentleman," said Tommy Fitzgerald, a sympathetic Louisville sportswriter.[68] The tension of the series, however, affected Robinson's play. In three games he stroked only one hit, though he did turn in several stunning fielding plays. Deprived of Robinson's demoralizing speed on the bases, the Royals lost two of the three contests played in the southern city.

Robinson's treatment by Louisville fans and the Colonels' limitation on black spectators drew criticism from a number of local sources. Several letters in the Louisville *Courier-Journal* chastised the white fans for their behavior. "We like to consider Louisville a more enlightened part of the South," wrote Junius E. Hankins in decrying "the petty-prejudice of witch-hunting bigots." Another letter, from "A Group of Fort Knox GI'S" said the reception accorded Robinson caused them to change their opinion of Louisville, which they now viewed, "as a city of obnoxious futility, and in this respect as deteriorated to a comparison of the state of Mississippi." The *Courier-Journal*, in a news editorial denounced "the blight" that had tarnished an otherwise successful season. "The blight was inflicted partly by the demonstrations of prejudice against Montreal's fine second baseman," argued the paper, "But . . . a more deeply bitter taste, which may last a long time, came of the management's policies toward Negro patrons." The *Courier-Journal* cited the "extra-special interest" that the series held for blacks and criticized the "brusque refusal to accommodate many of them." The editorial denied the right of the Colonel management to "decree who shall not be permitted to see the show."[69]

"Robinson hasn't played too well down here," Al Campanis warned the Colonels as the teams departed Louisville. "Wait until you see him in Montreal where the fans are his friends."[70] In Montreal a seven-inch blanket of snow awaited the teams. Delormier Downs, appropriately laid out for the football season, had snow piled along the foul lines. Despite the cold weather, a large crowd appeared to wreak vengeance on Louisville players for Robinson's treatment in Kentucky. As each Colonel approached the plate, they roundly jeered him.

Nonetheless, it appeared that the Colonels would easily register their third victory of the series. At the end of four and one-half innings they led 4-0 and going into the bottom of the ninth, they still held a 5-3 lead. A streak of wildness by Louisville pitchers, however, allowed Montreal to even the score, with Robinson scoring the tying run. In the bottom of the tenth

inning, an error, fielder's choice and a sacrifice, placed Royal runners on
second and third. The Colonels elected to walk Marv Rackley intentionally
to load the bases and pitch to Robinson. Then, as Tommy Fitzgerald described it, "On this frigid, football striped baseball diamond tonight, Jackie
Robinson, former All-American halfback at Southern California [sic] intercepted one of Mel Deutsch's pitches from the 15-yard line to give Montreal
a 6-5 victory over Louisville."[71]

The Montreal *Gazette* called Robinson's game winning single "revenge,"
but his retribution had just begun. The next night the "dark destroyer"
slashed a double in the first inning and scored the first Royal run. With the
score tied 3-3 in the seventh, he led off the inning with a booming triple
and then scored on a double by Lew Riggs. In the eighth inning, with the
bases loaded and two out, Robinson surprised everyone with a squeeze
bunt, which scored Campanis from third with the final run in the Royals
5-3 victory. "Quicker than you can say Jack Robinson, the Colonels have
changed from favorites to underdogs in the Little World Series," lamented
Fitzgerald.[72]

For the sixth game, over 19,000 people jammed Delormier Downs in the
hopes that the Royals would bring the momentous season to a close. Forty-
two-year-old pitcher Curt Davis obliged with a 2-0 shutout. Robinson collected two of Montreal's six hits and started two rally-ending double plays,
including one in the ninth with two runners on base. The Royals reigned
as Little World Series Champions.

As the spectators poured onto the field Robinson fought his way to the
clubhouse to join the Royal celebration. The French-Canadian fans refused
to leave, chanting for Robinson to rejoin them and singing "*Il a gagné ses
epaulettes.*" When he appeared in his street clothes they gathered around
him, kissing and hugging him, and tearing at his street clothes. As they
lifted Robinson to their shoulders, tears appeared in his eyes. The crowd
remained after he retrieved his belongings from the locker room and they
chased him deliriously for three blocks as he attempted to leave. A passing
motorist finally rescued Robinson and spirited him home. To Sam Maltin,
who had shared so much of the magical season with Jackie and Rachel, it
provided a fitting climax. "It was probably the only day in history," he
wrote, "that a black man ran from a white mob with love, instead of lynching on its mind."[73]

8

They Don't Want Me?

I was proud to be one of the first black players . . . This to me means more than just about anything I've ever done. I doubt if many of the black players to-day can remember Jackie Robinson, New-combe, and Campanella. But this is how it started and thanks to the Dodgers for giving us that opportunity.

Roy Campanella, 1980[1]

I

Roy Campanella spent an anxious winter. Since the night in October 1945, at Harlem's Woodside Hotel when Jackie Robinson had disrupted their card game with the revelation that he would soon cross baseball's color line, Campanella experienced the gnawing fear that when he had declined Branch Rickey's contract offer, he had lost his opportunity to play in the major leagues. What if the talkative Rickey had not been offering him a job with the Brooklyn Brown Dodgers? What if he had wanted him to play with Robinson at Montreal? On the night of his arrival in Venezuela, where he, Robinson, and a team of black all-stars were to play winter ball, Campanella wrote a letter to Rickey, informing the Dodger president of his address and expressing a desire to play in organized baseball. He then awaited a response.[2]

"Campanella was just living to get a chance with the Dodgers," recalls Quincy Trouppe, who shared the catching chores on the barnstorming team. "It was all he thought about and talked about."[3]

The United States All-Stars eased through their schedule, winning eighteen of twenty games. Campanella, however, batted only .211, his anxiety apparent in his performance. The Dodgers had still not contacted him. In January Robinson and several team members returned to the United States, while Campanella and others remained in Venezuela for the regular winter league season. Catching regularly for the Vargas team, Campy maintained his vigil. Finally on March 1, the date of Robinson's scheduled arrival in Florida, Campanella received a cable from the Dodgers:

PLEASE REPORT BROOKLYN OFFICE BY MARCH 10. VERY IMPORTANT.

BRANCH RICKEY.

"When that letter from the Dodger organization arrived," recalls Trouppe, "that guy was the happiest person in the hotel."[4] Within a day of receiving the telegram, Roy was en route for Brooklyn.

Campanella was one of four black ballplayers who, in addition to Jackie Robinson, appeared in organized baseball in 1946. Robinson's dramatic breakthrough at Montreal and the force of his personality so dominate the integration saga that the experiences of Campanella, Don Newcombe, John Wright, and Roy Partlow are often forgotten. These four athletes also pioneered in the white baseball wilderness. Their stories, along with Robinson's, reveal the dynamics of desegregation in the national pastime.

Jackie Robinson was the primary figure in Rickey's assault on the color line; Campanella and Newcombe represented a second line of attack. According to Rickey's master plan, the catcher and pitcher would work together at a lower level of the Dodger chain and progress through the farm system in Robinson's wake. Ultimately they would join him on the Brooklyn club, the dark heart of Rickey's envisioned dynasty. The careful planning that had gone into Robinson's future, however, seems to have been lacking in the preparations for Campanella and Newcombe. When the stocky catcher arrived at the Dodger offices, he learned that due to Robinson's problems in Florida, he and Newcombe would not report to spring training. In addition, the Dodgers had not yet determined their destination.

With Campanella present, Bob Finch, one of Rickey's assistants, began to call teams in the Dodger system to see who would accept the two blacks. Actually, few options existed. Given the pair's talent and experience, the Dodgers did not wish to assign them below the Class-B level. Indeed, Campanella probably could have played for the Brooklyn club without minor league seasoning. Above Class B, the Dodgers had few teams located outside of the South. The Dodgers sponsored Double-A operations in Mobile and Fort Worth, and three of the five B-league teams also played in segregated states. Only Danville, Illinois, and Nashua, New Hampshire, offered real possibilities.

Campanella sat nervously as Finch spoke to the general manager of the Danville team. Danville competed in the Three-I League which played its games in Illinois, Iowa, and Indiana. Most considered this region "redneck" territory, a difficult one in which to have blacks break in. From the look on Finch's face and the tone of the conversation, Campanella knew he would not be playing at Danville. "They don't want me?" he half asked and half stated as the Dodger official hung up. Finch confirmed this conclusion. "In retrospect, I wonder just what we were thought of," says Newcombe today. "What kind of animals were we that nobody wanted us?"[5]

Finch phoned Rickey in Florida who told him to try Nashua. Campanella was shocked. He thought Finch had said Nashville in Tennessee. Finch allayed his fears and called Buzzie Bavasi, the young general manager at Nashua in the New England League. Bavasi, one of the bright young men in the Dodger organization, was starting his career as a baseball executive. When confronted with the prospect of fielding two black players, Bavasi's response was crucial; if he refused the Dodgers might have had to delay or abandon the signing of Campanella and Newcombe. "If they can play ball better than what we have," Bavasi told Finch, "then we don't care what color they are."[6]

The announcement that Campanella and Newcombe had signed contracts with the Dodger organization naturally created less of a stir than had the earthshaking news regarding Robinson five months earlier. In both the white and black communities, it reaffirmed Rickey's sincerity in his efforts to integrate baseball. Fred H. Dobens, the president of the Nashua Dodgers, explained that the parent club was "carrying out its plan to give deserving Negro players a chance to make good in organized baseball down through its farm clubs." The press adopted this theme. The Brooklyn *Eagle* commented that when the Dodgers had signed John Wright, "the boys in the back room" had scoffed, "He's there to keep Jackie Robinson company. There'll be no more Negroes in organized baseball." The signing of Newcombe and Campanella proved they were "whistling off key." They could no longer dismiss Rickey's activities as a publicity gimmick.[7]

The black press, while welcoming the latest development, debated the wisdom of the choices. The Pittsburgh *Courier* hyperbolically described Campanella as "the best hitting catcher in Negro baseball" and Newcombe as "the most promising hurler." Sam Lacy displayed less enthusiasm. Largely unfamiliar with Newcombe, he withheld comment, but he expressed skepticism about Campanella's talents. If the Dodgers had indeed obtained the services of "the best catcher in colored baseball," Lacy saw this as a "distinction that is definitely on the dubious side," given the poor quality of catching in the Negro Leagues.[8]

The signing of two more black players once again reopened the issue of compensation to their former clubs. The Baltimore Elite Giants raised no protest over the loss of Campanella. The Newark Eagles, on the other hand, reacted with fury to losing Newcombe. Club owner Effa Manley wrote several letters to Rickey asking him to discuss Newcombe's status, but she received no answer. Fearing the adverse consequences of a public protest, Manley remained silent. Several months later, when she saw the Dodger president at a Negro League game, she chastised the obviously discomforted Rickey. "I hope you're not going to grab any more of our players," she told him. "You know Mr. Rickey, we could make trouble for you on the Newcombe transaction if we wanted to." Even thirty years after the fact, Mrs. Manley remained bitter. "Every time I see the Dodgers get beat," she told an interviewer, "I say they don't deserve to win for what they did to Negro baseball."[9]

With the formalities of their signing and its attendant publicity at an end, Campanella and Newcombe embarked for Nashua. They constituted an odd couple. Campanella hardly looked like a baseball player. He stood 5'9" and weighed over 200 pounds, a "sumo wrestler pared to catcher's size," according to Roger Kahn. Newcombe, at 6'4" towered over his companion. A gangling giant, the young pitcher had the long arms and broad shoulders characteristic of his trade. Campanella, although only twenty-five years old, was a confident, relatively mature veteran of nine Negro League seasons. Nineteen-year-old Newcombe possessed doubts about his talents. "I never really thought I had that kind of ability," he admits today. "[They] liked me because I was so big and could throw the ball hard. But I was always wild. I didn't know where the ball was going."[10]

Campanella and Newcombe, thrust together as the only blacks in New England baseball, became close friends. Campanella radiated an infectious enthusiasm and love for baseball. "He had a dash that was always a pleasure to share," wrote Lacy.[11] He also possessed a willingness to ignore any insults and endure any hardships in order to achieve his lifelong dream of playing in the major leagues.

Rickey did not indoctrinate Campanella and Newcombe as thoroughly as he had Robinson, but he gave them careful instructions on how to behave. Campanella received a letter from Rickey advising him to avoid disputes, ignore taunts and sarcasm, and simply play ball. Before their departure for Nashua, the pitcher and catcher met with Robinson in New York to discuss the coming season. "The three of us got together because we were embarking on this new idea and we had to have sort of a game plan to find out how we were going to operate as players," relates Newcombe. The trio of athletes discussed the difficulties that they might face and agreed to abide by the rules set down by Rickey. Their primary concern lay with the challenge confronting Robinson in Montreal rather than the second front in New England. Throughout the season, according to Newcombe, he and Campanella kept in contact with Robinson exchanging ideas and comparing experiences.[12]

Nashua, New Hampshire, according to Wendell Smith, was "a typical New England town, quiet, liberal, and staid in its ways." Located forty miles north of Boston, Nashua residents seemed to have no qualms about welcoming the two black athletes. "These people are wonderful," reported the ebullient Campanella. "Newcombe and I go any place we want to, do anything we please, and are treated like long lost sons." Newcombe and Campanella and their wives constituted the entire black population of Nashua. They rarely saw the other blacks in the area, who lived at a lumber mill several miles outside of town. "We even had to go to the white barber shop," recalls Newcombe. "He didn't know how to cut black hair. We got scalped many times by the barber who tried. . . . He could have said, 'No, I don't cut black people's hair,' but he tried." Bad haircuts, however, seemed a small price to pay. The two black families had no trouble finding lodgings and experienced no problems in restaurants or at the stadium. "We were very lucky to play in that area," says Newcombe.[13]

Newcombe and Campanella found themselves under the command of manager Walter Alston. Destined to become one of baseball's most famous managers, Alston was, like Bavasi, in the early stages of his ascent through the Dodger organization. In 1946 the soft-spoken, thirty-five-year-old Ohio native faced a crossroads in his life. As player-manager of the Nashua Dodgers he was concluding an unsuccessful career on the field and commencing his life in the dugout. Alston had played more than a decade in the minor leagues. In 1936 in his only at-bat in the majors, he had struck out. In 1944 Rickey, who had originally signed him to a St. Louis contract, offered him a job as player-manager of the Brooklyn farm club at Trenton, New Jersey. After two years piloting Trenton, in 1946 the Dodgers reassigned Alston to Nashua.

Rickey did not consult Alston about whether he would accept the two black players, nor did he give him any special instructions. "Nobody asked me a thing and I never said a word about it," recalls Alston. "They sent me Newcombe and Campanella and I didn't think too much about it except wondering how good ballplayers they were. I was wondering if they could help our club."[14]

The two players quickly erased any doubts that Alston might have harbored. "They weren't around very long before I knew they were both good ballplayers and good guys," states Alston. "They were anxious to do well, do anything they could to help win a ball game. . . . When I saw them play a few games I was glad I had them on my club."[15]

Alston had good reason to be pleased. Both Campanella and Newcombe started strongly at Nashua. Before the first game, the powerfully-built catcher, recalling Robinson's debut in Jersey City, commented, "I only hope that I can make as good a start. I don't ask for the sensational kind of day Jackie had, that's expecting too much."[16] Campanella's performance did not match Robinson's; but he did not miss by a wide margin. After grounding out in his first plate appearance, Campy stroked two singles and walked in his next at bats. In the eighth inning, with a man on base, Campanella unloaded a 440-foot home run, the game winning hit in Nashua's 4-3 victory over the Lynn Red Sox.

Newcombe proved equally impressive in his preview performance. He retired the first eight men in a row en route to a seven-hit, 3-0 shutout over the Pawtucket Slaters. The big right-hander won his first four games before losing a 1-0 decision on June 29. Nashua fans enjoyed Newcombe's pitching, but they seemed more delighted with his hitting. "They want to know," wrote Lacy, " 'Is this guy a pitcher or a hitter?' "[17] Newcombe collected two hits in his first game and thereafter became Alston's most reliable pinch-hitter. During one week in June he had two game-winning doubles and a game-tying, two-run home run. In one July game Newcombe provided a sparkling demonstration of his combined talents. Despite complaining of a sore arm, he tossed a four-hit 7-1 victory striking out fourteen men. In addition, he drove in two runs with a single and two more with a home run. In early August his pitching record stood at 8-3 and his batting average at .349.

Unlike Newcombe, Campanella did not enjoy uninterrupted success at Nashua. After a strong start, his hitting declined. An ankle injury, which kept him out of several early season games, contributed to his slump. In mid-June his average stood at only .235. A twenty-one-game hitting streak in July, however, raised his average close to .300 and propelled the powerful catcher into the team lead in home runs and runs batted in.

Home runs did not come easily in the New England League. Most parks, including Nashua, had more distant fences than the cozy major league stadiums of the era. "It was practically impossible to hit one over the fence, because the outfield stretched nearly to the horizon," wrote Campanella in his autobiography. A local poultry farmer named Jack Fallgren, expecting few balls to be hit over the fence, offered 100 baby chicks for every home run hit by a Nashua player. He did not expect Roy Campanella to be playing for Nashua. The fences usually proved too forbidding for even Campy's extraordinary strength, but the catcher's squat powerful build belied a surprising capacity for speed. Campanella stole sixteen bases in his season at Nashua, including home on one occasion. His running ability added to his home run total, as he registered most of his homers on inside-the-park drives. In early August the Baltimore *Afro-American* jested that Campanella "might start a poultry farm any day now."[18] At the season's end, Roy did just that. Having earned fourteen home runs worth of chickens, he shipped them to his father in Philadelphia who started a farm on the outskirts of town.

Campanella and Newcombe found racial pioneering in the New England League relatively easy, "nothing compared to what Jackie was going through," according to Newcombe. If any of their teammates objected to their presence, neither the players nor manager Alston heard complaints. "There was no problem at all that I can recall," says Alston. "I think they all appreciated them." Newcombe remembers that Larry Sheppard, a fellow pitcher who later became a major league coach, "was one of our biggest boosters." "We had a lot of fun," says the black hurler. "I used to drive the team bus. One night . . . the guys were all singing and I'm driving and all of a sudden I go into this dark area and lights started going off and on. I'd driven up to this graveyard where everyone was making love. They saw this big bus running right up in the graveyard. I'll never forget Roy saying, 'Get out from under that wheel, you're going to kill us all.' "[19]

In the New England League, where most of the players were beginning their careers, the experienced Campanella provided a steadying influence. "I was glad to have Campanella on my club," states Alston "especially catching where he could quarterback the team." A few weeks into the season, Alston approached Campanella with an unexpected proposition. "Roy, you're a bit older than the other fellows on this club and a great deal more experienced. They respect you," Campanella records the manager as saying. "If I'm ever thrown out of the game, I want you to run things." Campanella, though hesitant to accept, was extremely pleased. Thereafter, according to the *Afro-American,* he became Alston's chief adviser, having much to do with "the handling and removal of pitchers, injection of pinch hitters, and the selection of relief moundsmen."[20]

In mid-June, during a game with the Lawrence Millionaires, umpires ejected Alston in the sixth inning for arguing a called strike. He handed over the lineup card to Campanella and departed. The following inning, with a man on base and Nashua trailing by two runs, Manager Campanella made his first strategic move. He sent his roommate to the plate to pinch-hit. Newcombe responded with a home run to tie the game and Nashua proceeded to win, 7-5.[21] Campanella's career as the first black manager produced a perfect 1-0 record.

Alston's faith in Campanella had another significant result. Before the season, the catcher had received a lucrative offer from Jorge Pasquel to play in the Mexican League. Unsure of how he would be accepted in organized baseball, Campanella had kept Pasquel's telegram as a contingency against failure. The day after Alston had made him assistant manager, he handed the telegram to Bavasi and told him that he did not need it anymore. His future, Campanella knew, now lay with the Dodgers.[22]

The only area of conflict occurred with opposing players and managers. Unlike Robinson, Campanella and Newcombe experienced few beanballs and brushback pitches. This resulted, at least in part, from the presence of Newcombe in the regular pitching rotation. "I had the ball in my hand," explains Newcombe. "Nobody was going to bother me." On occasion, opposition bench jockeys would unleash a torrent of racial abuse and invective at Campanella, Newcombe, and Manager Alston, who advised his players to ignore the taunts; if the insults proved too difficult for them to handle, Alston, as manager, would attempt to curtail them. Both players ignored the name-calling. "There wasn't much that happened," asserts Alston, a verdict supported by both Campanella and Newcombe.[23]

Nonetheless, a lingering fear of violence always remained. In an early season game Sal Yvars, a hard-nosed catcher for the Manchester Giants, deliberately picked up a handful of dirt and threw it into Campanella's face as the latter squatted behind the plate. "Man, I was burning," wrote Campanella of this episode. He forgot Rickey's remonstrations against retaliation and turned on Yvars. "Try that again and I'll beat you to a pulp," threatened the angry catcher. Yvars retreated and the incident ended.[24] It marked the only overt challenge faced by either of the two blacks.

Later in the season, General Manager Bavasi found himself in an angry confrontation at Lynn, Massachusetts. The second place Nashua Dodgers, paced by Campanella's hitting and Newcombe's pitching, had just beaten the league-leading Lynn Red Sox in a critical game between the pennant contenders. "If it wasn't for them niggers, you wouldn't have beat us," barked Lynn's general manager when Bavasi went to pick up the gate receipts. Incensed, Bavasi charged his counterpart, and the players had to separate the battling executives.[25]

The essential story of the Nashua Dodgers involved neither Bavasi's battle nor the taunts of the opposition, but the continued excellence of Newcombe and Campanella in the competitive setting. The youthful, weak-hitting Nashua team had opened the season poorly, falling thirteen games behind Lynn by mid-June. Campanella's slugging and Newcombe's hurling, however, spearheaded a revival for Alston's club in July and August. Although unable to catch the Red Sox, the Dodgers finished in second place, one game behind the leaders and qualified for the play-offs.

In the semifinal series the Dodgers faced the Pawtucket Slaters. In the first game Campanella broke up a scoreless tie in the bottom of the ninth inning with a run-scoring double. In the second contest he had three hits

in four at bats to lead Nashua to a 3-1 triumph. The following day, Newcombe tossed a shut-out victory to give the Dodgers a sweep of the series.
The duo continued their outstanding performances in the championship
play-offs against Lynn. Campanella powered a game-winning home run in
the third game and Newcombe was an easy victor in the fifth. In the sixth
and final contest, Campanella's bases-loaded double in the first inning provided the key blow in an 8-2 Nashua win. Though only second in league
play, Nashua garnered the New England League Championship.

For both Newcombe and Campanella the 1946 season proved triumphant. Newcombe won fourteen out of eighteen decisions and two more
games in the play-offs. He registered an impressive 2.21 earned run average.
He also demonstrated the batting talents that would make him one of the
best hitting pitchers in baseball history. Campanella impressed all observers,
not only with his hitting, but with his defensive skills and handling of
pitchers. A unanimous choice as all-league catcher, he finished the season
with a .290 batting average and led the team with fourteen home runs and
ninety-six runs batted in. The *Sporting News* called him the "outstanding
star in the play-offs" Stories in the black press touted Campy as the Brooklyn catcher in 1947, perhaps reaching the parent club before Robinson. The
Sporting News, while more conservative, still labelled Campanella and
Newcombe "two of the top prospects in the Brooklyn chain."[26]

The national press largely ignored the events at Nashua. The spotlight
in 1946 justifiably belonged to Jackie Robinson. But Rickey's "second front"
in the integration battle was as successful as the primary staging ground in
Montreal. Both the performances of the black athletes and the absence of
major difficulties had confirmed Rickey's strategy. "Campanella and Newcombe were ideal men to start the thing because they were outstanding
ballplayers and they handled themselves as well as you can expect," says
Alston in retrospect.[27] For Alston and Bavasi, the season at Nashua also had
important ramifications. It is probably not coincidental that the two men
who had ably handled their duties in the face of the new challenge, became
the principal figures in the Dodger organization during the following decades. Certainly their performances did little to impede their progress. Alston
and Bavasi, as well as Campanella and Newcombe, had passed the test.

II

The successes of Robinson, Campanella, and Newcombe during the 1946
season constituted the most significant developments in the campaign to
desegregate baseball. However, a "third front," generally ignored at the
time, and largely forgotten today, also existed. In the small French-Cana-

dian city of Three Rivers (Trois-Rivières), pitchers John Wright and Roy Partlow, both of whom had had brief trials with Montreal, completed their seasons in the Class-C Canadian-American League, forgotten pioneers of baseball integration.

Three Rivers is a French-Canadian industrial city seventy miles north of Montreal on the St. Lawrence River. The local baseball team had just joined the extensive Dodger farm system in 1946 and the 50,000 residents seemed to share in the postwar baseball fervor sweeping the United States and Canada. Fans flocked to the ball park and townspeople supported the team in a variety of ways. Merchants provided prizes for the slightest feat by a ball player. A base hit would win a free meal; a double produced a steak dinner. "The kids, every time they came to bat, could win a prize," recalls Manager Frenchy Bordagaray. "They gave so many prizes, the merchants did, that the kids ate free most of the time."[28]

In Bordagaray, Rickey had provided the new Dodger affiliate with one of baseball's master showmen. A major league player for over a decade, Bordagaray had served with five different teams. While never one of the game's leading stars, he had twice batted over .300 and ranked as one of baseball's greatest pinch hitters. His playing skills notwithstanding, Bordagaray won more renown for his sense of humor and colorful character as a member of both the "Daffiness Boys" of the Brooklyn Dodgers and the "Gas House Gang" of the St. Louis Cardinals during the 1930s. In 1936 he had scandalized the baseball establishment by showing up at the Dodger spring training camp with a goatee and a mustache. After several seasons in exile with other teams, he returned to Brooklyn in 1942 where he remained throughout the war years.

In 1946 the thirty-four-year-old Bordagaray had reached the end of his major league career. With so many veterans returning from the war, Rickey asked Bordagaray to retire and manage in the Dodger system. But Bordagaray believed that he could still play in the majors. Furthermore, he needed to collect only one more paycheck to qualify for the newly established major league pension. Rickey discounted his fears for the future. The pension, argued the Dodger executive, was a passing thing; it would never pay off any benefits. The persuasive Rickey won out, though his bad advice later cost Bordagaray thousands of dollars in retirement benefits.[29]

Both Buzzie Bavasi at Nashua and Marcel Dufresne, the general manager at Three Rivers, had requested Bordagaray as manager. Rickey assigned him to the latter to please the French-Canadian population. The starting left fielder, as well as the manager, Bordagaray became an instant fan favorite. Playing at the Class C level, only one year removed from the majors, he hit .375 and won the league's Most Valuable Player Award.

In mid-May the Royals assigned John Wright to the Three Rivers squad. Like Walter Alston at Nashua, Bordagaray received neither consultation nor special instructions. "They didn't ask me nothing," says Frenchy. "They just sent him. They said they were sending me a ballplayer." On the Three Rivers team, recalls Bordagaray, "We had all nationalities: blacks, whites, dagoes, Frenchmen, Jewish boys. We had the whole works. The funny thing about it was I never thought of him as black. I just thought of him as a ballplayer." Raised in the small town of Coalinga, California, the Three Rivers manager had little previous exposure to nonwhites. "I didn't know anything about blacks," he admits. "I was born in a town where I never saw a black."[30]

Wright's own reaction to his new surroundings remained private. Cut from the Montreal team and demoted to the C Leagues, the only black in the Canadian-American circuit and the town of Three Rivers, Wright may well have regretted leaving the Negro Leagues. If so, he never mentioned it. His indifferent performance, however, may indicate his disappointment. Pitching against younger and less experienced players, the man who had won twenty-five games for the Homestead Grays three years earlier struggled through the Canadian-American League. At times he sparkled, as in a four-hit shutout against Schenectady in early June. Yet a week earlier he had failed to last the second inning in an 11-0 shellacking. When Partlow arrived, Wright had pitched for Three Rivers for almost two months and his record hovered near the .500 mark.

Roy Partlow had not wanted to go to Three Rivers. When the orders announcing his demotion reached him in Montreal, he deserted the Royals and disappeared. Two days later he requested an audience with Rickey in Brooklyn. After a brief meeting, Partlow agreed to join Wright in the Canadian-American League.

The refusal of a player to accept assignment normally constitutes a minor incident, but Wendell Smith magnified Partlow's rebellion into a serious threat to the "great experiment." Smith devoted his weekly column of July 20 to an attack on the former Negro League star and a sermon on the responsibility of racial pioneering. "It looks as though Partlow has turned out to be an eccentric 'prima donna' and a problem child of no small means," wrote Smith. "Apparently he fails to realize that whatever he does, good or bad, is a reflection on Negro ballplayers." The *Courier* columnist predicted that thousands of people would welcome Partlow's defection with "glee" and say, "See, I told you Negro players can't take it in organized baseball." Smith contrasted Partlow's behavior with that of Johnny Wright, who, when ordered to Three Rivers, had accepted his demotion "like a trooper . . . carrying on like a real ballplayer should."

"Partlow, it appears, needs to sit down and think about the significance of his position," concluded Smith. "He needs to think [more] about those 14 million Negroes from coast to coast who are pulling for him to make good in white organized baseball . . . and less about himself."[31]

In all likelihood, Smith overreacted to the Partlow incident. Even Montreal newspapers paid minimal attention to it. Yet despite Robinson's spectacular success with the Royals, the architects of baseball integration still perceived the experiment as fragile. They saw little room for error or unexpected controversy on the part of one of the minor actors.

In explaining Partlow's failure at Montreal, Rickey revealed his own attitudes about the difficulties inherent in integration. Partlow had shown signs of being a good pitcher, asserted Rickey, but control problems had led to his downfall. Assuring the *Afro-American* that he had not given up on either Wright or Partlow, Rickey commented, "They both have too much ability for that. Both Wright and Partlow are promising and make no mistake about it, they DON'T need experience. What they need more than anything else is orientation." Rickey's final assessment, whether or not accurate, reflected the thinking of the period. "Against colored competition they are both cracker jack pitchers," said the veteran baseball executive, "but from all appearances they suffer a terrific inferiority complex when they are facing white boys."[32]

Another factor might have motivated Rickey's decision to dispatch Partlow to Three Rivers. The Dodger president believed that successful farm franchises produced a winning spirit throughout the organization, resulting in major league pennants. He often sent players, particularly older ones, a notch or two below their talent level to guarantee championships for the Dodger affiliates. Manager Bordagaray, his team languishing in fourth place far behind league leading Pittsfield, had appealed for assistance. "Rickey said he was going to send me someone who was going to win the pennant for me," recalls Bordagaray. "He sent me Partlow."[33]

The presence of two black pitchers on the team posed no problem for Bordagaray. "The blacks, the ones that Rickey sent out at the beginning, they were all gentlemen," asserts Frenchy. At Montreal, Partlow's reticent manner had earned him the nickname "Silent Roy." Both he and Wright continued this policy at Three Rivers. "These black guys who came up didn't say much," remembers Bordagaray. "They were quiet. I think Rickey had 'em schooled." Although their teammates seemed to accept them, Wright and Partlow generally kept to themselves.[34]

Bordagaray recalls only one incident which marred the team's outward tranquility. In a late season game he removed one of his starting pitchers and replaced him with Wright. The displaced hurler, a former Triple-A pitcher from the South, protested, "Why did you have to bring in that jigger?" Wright, who had overheard the comment, asked "What did he say?" Bordagaray quickly doused the sparks. "He didn't say anything," he told Wright. "He's just mad because he couldn't get this last guy out. All you gotta do is get this last guy out and we'll win the ball game." Wright retired the batter and nothing further came of the incident. Bordagaray never heard of any other intrasquad confrontations.[35]

In almost all instances Wright and Partlow received the same treatment as their teammates. "We dressed together. We were all in the same place together. We took showers together," says Bordagaray. In every city except Schenectady the black pitchers stayed in the same hotel as their teammates. In Schenectady, where the hotel barred blacks, Bordagaray instructed them to make their own arrangements. "I didn't even bother them. They were on their own," remembers the manager. "They were old enough anyhow, so you didn't have to worry about them." In Three Rivers itself, Partlow and Wright were highly popular. Although no black women lived in the city, the two black athletes, according to Bordagaray, could be frequently seen with French-Canadian women. Neither the townspeople nor the ballclub raised any objections.[36]

Wherever they played Wright and Partlow faced minimal abuse from fans and opposing players. Bordagaray heard little in the way of name-calling or bench jockeying directed at the black athletes, nor could he recall any instances in which pitchers threw at them. "They were all afraid of [Partlow]," claims Frenchy. "He didn't throw very hard, but nobody wanted to hit against him. He knew how to pitch, especially to those young kids. They didn't have a chance."[37]

Partlow came to Three Rivers with a reputation of being difficult to manage. "Roy was the kind of man who had his own attitude," says Don Newcombe in retrospect, "and his attitude was he'd pitch like he wanted to pitch, not like he had to pitch." Bordagaray, however, had little difficulty with the lefty. "He was a little stubborn with me, but I didn't pay any attention to him," says the man who also had been accused of being a difficult player to handle. "I used to play him in the outfield. He didn't want to play the outfield. I'd say you get out there and play. He'd go and play." Partlow also tended to "sulk a little bit," which his manager readily understood. "I mean here was a guy who had big league aspirations," empathizes Frenchy. "My God, he was a big league ballplayer playing in C League. I was a big league ballplayer in a C League too."[38]

Whatever emotions churned inside of Partlow, when he stepped on the mound in the Canadian-American League, he proved virtually unbeatable. The black southpaw started his first game for Three Rivers on July 16 and walked the first three batters to face him. Perhaps at that moment the veteran lefty decided to demonstrate his true abilities. Partlow struck out the next three batters and proceeded to fan a total of ten men before yielding to relief from Wright in the seventh. The two black hurlers combined for a 7-4 win.

Partlow won nine straight games before losing, finishing the season with a 10-1 record. In the week ending August 24 he was named the Player of the Week in the Canadian-American League ("first time for a Negro," the *Sporting News* dutifully reported[39]) after he fired two five-hitters and a three-hitter. In the eleven games that he started, he completed nine. Partlow also demonstrated his batting talents, compiling a .404 average. Partlow's arrival seemed to inspire Wright. He registered five straight victories, improving his record from 6-7 to 12-8 at the end of the campaign. Partlow's appearance also marked a turning point for the Three Rivers team, just as Rickey had promised. Behind the pitching of the two blacks, Three Rivers closed the gap on Pittsfield. On the final day of the season the Dodger farm club prevailed in a tight four-team race.

The pennant-winning performance propelled Three Rivers into the playoffs where Partlow continued his rampage. In the seven-game series against Rome, Partlow threw three of his club's four victories. The left-hander won the opener 12-1 on a four-hitter, was a 13-3 winner in the fourth game and hurled another four-hitter in the seventh and deciding contest, a 10-1 triumph. In the fifth game Wright registered his only decision, a 4-2 loss in relief.

Three Rivers faced Pittsfield in the championship series. The teams split the first two games. In the third contest, Partlow took over. Making his first pitching appearance of the series, the black pitcher tossed a six-hit, 11-1 victory. The next day he appeared as a pinch hitter in the eleventh inning with the score tied 6-6 and two men on base. He slashed a two-run triple to win the game. Wright, the beneficiary of his companion's clutch performance, received credit for the win. In the fifth game, Partlow stroked another pinch hit and scored the winning tally in a four-run inning which enabled Three Rivers to gain a 9-6 come-from-behind triumph. For the second game in a row, Wright prevailed as winning pitcher. Three Rivers captured the series four games to one with Partlow and Wright sharing the spotlight. Partlow was named the outstanding athlete in the Canadian-American League championships.

Their performances at Three Rivers gave the two pitchers reason for optimism. Thirty-five years later, Bordagaray still speaks enthusiastically of Partlow. "My goodness," says the ever effervescent Frenchy, "He had all the talent in the world. He was good enough to play on the Montreal ball club. In fact he was superior to most of those ball players." At the close of the season, Wright summed up his experiences for Wendell Smith as follows: "Pitched most of the year at Three Rivers, Quebec and had a swell time. . . . I would just like to get another chance at Montreal. I don't know just what I'll be doing next season, however."[40]

Despite his high hopes, the Canadian-American League play-offs marked the end of Wright's career in organized baseball. He barnstormed the nation in the fall of 1946 with the Jackie Robinson All-Stars and played winter ball in Puerto Rico. In January 1947, the Dodgers released him. He rejoined the Homestead Grays and pitched two more years in the Negro Leagues. Partlow, on the other hand, had earned an invitation to return to spring training with Montreal in 1947.

The championship season at Three Rivers rounded out the first year of integrated baseball. The experiment had proved an unqualified success. After the Florida cancellations, no major adverse incidents occurred involving any of the black players. Each of baseball's first three interracial teams won their league championships. Yet, despite this uniform record of achievement, baseball executives failed to follow the Dodger example. Further integration awaited the final phase of Rickey's "noble experiment": the elevation of Jackie Robinson to the major leagues.

9

The Most Costly Trial
Ever Given a Player

> *Vice is a monster of so frightful mien,*
> *As to be hated, needs but to be seen;*
> *Yet seen too oft, familiar with her face,*
> *We first endure, then pity, then embrace.*

> Alexander Pope,
> "Essay on Man"
> often recited by Branch Rickey[1]

I

On September 6, 1946, as Jackie Robinson concluded his triumphant season at Montreal, President Harry S Truman hosted a delegation from the National Emergency Committee Against Mob Violence. The Missouri-born Truman had previously demonstrated minimal interest in the plight of the nation's black population. Like many Americans of the era, Truman believed that blacks and whites alike favored a segregated society. The half-dozen civil rights leaders who now confronted him entertained no delusions that they could spur the president to change his mind. At best, they hoped to evoke a public statement condemning lynching and the Ku Klux Klan. NAACP executive secretary, Walter White, presented Truman with a graphic portrayal of life for southern blacks—lynching, torture, and intimidation. When White concluded his gory tale, the president responded, "My God! I had no idea it was as terrible as that. We've got to do something." Two months later, Truman announced the appointment of a Committee on Civil Rights, empowered to investigate violations against black Americans and make recommendations for remedial legislation.[2] Truman's edict represented a small, though significant step. Although directed at the most grievous depredations against black Americans, it completely ignored the issue of segregation. The federal government thus began its halting, tenuous, and painfully deliberate attack against racial discrimination.

At the same time, major league baseball braced for a direct confrontation with Jim Crow. During the winter of 1946, the uncertain future of Jackie Robinson loomed as the most heated topic in baseball's off-season hot stove league. Brooklyn sportswriter Harold Burr chided that Robinson appeared in the papers almost as often as President Truman.[3]

The first edition of the 1947 *Sporting News* devoted a full page to the controversy. In separate columns Lloyd McGowan of the Montreal *Daily Star* and Cy Kritzer of the *Buffalo Evening News,* two veteran International League sportswriters, assessed Robinson's prospects for the coming season. Kritzer, citing Robinson's age, injury-prone legs, and lack of experience, doubted that the second baseman was ready for the Brooklyn Dodgers. Robinson's league-leading batting in 1946, argued Kritzer, had been more the product of his "crusading zeal" than his talents. "In time," observed the Buffalo scribe, "like an old-fashioned alarm clock, such things as inspiration, zeal, ardor, all run down." McGowan, like so many others who had been captivated by Robinson's Canadian exploits, disagreed. "Unless Jackie gets the brush-off, the runaround, the once-over lightly, and the old business, he should be queueing up with the Dodgers each payday," asserted McGowan. "Install him at second base and you've got a Flatbush favorite, Mr. Rickey."[4]

The McGowan-Kritzer exchange reflected the debate raging in the sporting domain. As the Montreal reporter implied, not only Robinson's abilities on the baseball diamond, but a range of other considerations—Rickey's sincerity in fulfilling his mission, the reaction of the Dodgers and other major league athletes, and the ability of Robinson to withstand the pressures of spring training—remained at issue.

In the 1946 post-season, the spectre of Robinson trailed major leaguers around the barnstorming circuit. Reporters repeatedly asked about Robinson's chances. Several players responded negatively. Bob Feller, engaged in another record-breaking tour with the Satchel Paige All-Stars, reiterated his dire prognosis for black ballplayers. When asked if any could make the big league grade, Feller replied, "Haven't seen one. Maybe Paige when he was young. When you name him, you're done." Pressed on the prospects of the Montreal second baseman, Feller added, "Not even Jackie Robinson."[5]

The integration drama also attracted scholarly analysis. The City College of New York Social Research Laboratory issued a study of anticipated reactions to Robinson's promotion, concluding that while southern players would be hostile, they would not actively oppose the presence of a black teammate. Indifference would characterize the northerners' response to the issue. The authors further predicted that "because of the conspicuous position of professional baseball . . . the results of establishing equal opportunities for Negroes in Organized Baseball would be significant for better race relations in general."[6]

The great experiment, however, had produced few results inside organized baseball itself. None of Rickey's fellow executives showed any inclination to follow his lead in recruiting blacks. At the annual meetings in Los Angeles, officials expressed interest in Robinson's progress, and some, like Connie Mack, ending a public silence on the matter, hailed a "new day" in the national pastime. But, neither Mack, nor any others, went beyond rhetoric. The black press, quick to report rumors of the signing of Negro League stars by the Dodger organization, uncovered no rustlings on the part of other teams. Only Bill Veeck, who had recently purchased the Cleveland Indians, was mentioned as a possible candidate to hire blacks. The ominous silence led Wendell Smith to fear a counter-revolution by baseball's palace guard. Smith made unsubstantiated charges that the owners of the Negro Leagues and the majors were "working hard behind closed doors" to block further defections from one organization to another.[7]

Critics also questioned Rickey's sincerity about promoting Robinson. The conspicuous absence of Robinson's name on the 1947 Dodger roster puzzled many observers. Dodger officials hastened to explain that Robinson, unlike other prospects, had played in the Brooklyn organization for only one year and was ineligible for the minor league draft. By leaving him on the Montreal roster, the Dodgers could protect a more vulnerable player. "Robbie can't help us now," explained club spokesman Fresco Thompson. "He can't score a run or make a hit. He can't steal a base or start a double play. In short, he can't help the Dodgers at all until April 15."[8] Nonetheless, some judged the omission of the black player as evidence that Robinson would be deprived of a fair trial.

The roster controversy did not perturb Rickey. Robinson's reception in Brooklyn and other National League cities concerned him more. Rickey had long believed that the primary threat to Robinson's success lay not with the white fans, but blacks. He felt that an overzealous reaction to the first major league player of their race could prove not only embarrassing, but it might create volatile racial confrontations. Before his departure for spring training, Rickey launched a campaign to prepare the nation's black populace for the advent of integration.

On February 5 Rickey addressed a meeting of Afro-American civic leaders at the predominantly black Carlton Branch of the Brooklyn YMCA.[9] Rickey's guest list reveals both the composition of the urban black bourgeoisie and contemporary perceptions of leadership and influence in the black community. The invitees included doctors, dentists, lawyers, public

service employees, realtors, teachers, morticians, and a minister. An architect, a haberdasher, and a judge rounded out the gathering. No representatives of the black working class were requested to attend. The invitation
from the YMCA had promised that the Dodger president would discuss
"the things which are on his mind as well as ours, in connection with the
projection of what seems to be inevitable." This veiled inference that Robinson's promotion would be announced guaranteed the attendance of most
invitees. Rickey, his assistant Arthur Mann, and Dan Dodson and Judge
Edward Lanzansky of the now-defunct Mayor's Committee on Discrimination in Baseball were the only whites present.

After a dinner provided by the Dodger organization Rickey rose to speak.
Confronted by a sea of black faces, the normally eloquent Rickey seemed
uncharacteristically nervous and hesitant. He quickly departed from his
prepared text and spoke extemporaneously, asking his audience to keep his
remarks secret. Rickey refused to promise that Jackie Robinson would be
elevated to the Dodgers. But, in words that might have offended a less
middle-class gathering, he told his audience that if Robinson did become
the first black major leaguer, "The biggest threat to his success—is the Negro people themselves." Rickey predicted the response of the black community:

> Every one of you will go out and form parades and welcoming com-
> mittees. You'll strut. You'll wear badges. You'll hold Jackie Robinson
> Days . . . and Jackie Robinson nights. You'll get drunk. You'll fight.
> You'll be arrested. You'll wine and dine the player until he is fat and
> futile. You'll symbolize his importance into a national comedy . . .
> and an ultimate tragedy.

Rickey proceeded with an incongruous threat that "If any individual,
group, or segment of Negro society," portrayed the Robinson breakthrough
"as a symbol of social 'ism' or schism, a triumph of race over race, I will
curse the day I signed him to a contract." Rickey warned that he personally
would guarantee that "baseball is never so abused and misrepresented
again." The Dodgers executive called upon the black community to police
itself so as to avoid "spoiling Jackie's chances."

The black middle-class congregation readily accepted Rickey's assertions, which closely matched their own preconceptions of the growing black
urban proletariat in postwar America. The "community leaders" greeted
Rickey's remarkable oration with what Mann described as "deafening applause." Before the gathering had ended they appointed a "Master Committee" to coordinate a campaign to control the enthusiasm of the black masses.

Not all blacks agreed with this approach. Sportswriter Joe Bostic, who had enraged Rickey at Bear Mountain a year earlier and had been omitted from the guest list, reacted angrily when he learned what had transpired. "I've never forgiven any of those guys for either attending or those who did attend for not showing their resentment and indignation at the effrontery," says Bostic. "These were adults. These were educated and intelligent people. And you're going to tell them how to act in a public place?"[10]

Apparently, Bostic espoused a minority opinion within the black bourgeoisie. The Master Committee fanned out through New York's black community promoting the slogan: Don't Spoil Jackie's Chances! Preachers carried the message to their congregations, black newspapers to their readers, and social leaders to their fraternal lodges and clubs. Bartenders reportedly advised customers not to attend ball games while intoxicated. Blacks in all National League cities established similar committees and curtailed plans to honor Robinson at local ball parks.[11]

Although both Rickey and Robinson always maintained that the campaign to harness black enthusiasm was essential to the success of the experiment, the efforts of black leaders now seem excessive and embarrassing. At their best, the appeals not to cheer too loudly or at inappropriate moments and advice like that of William G. Nunn to "learn something about the game in order that we . . . won't humiliate Jackie by our lack of knowledge," patronized blacks. At their worst, these warnings reproduced the crudest of racial stereotypes. "We can get full of Sneaky Pete before we go to Ebbets Field," admonished black sportswriter Dan Burley, "or we can take our Sneaky Pete and watermelons with us as we do at some of the more sociable events." Burley warned against "transferring our Yankee Stadium routines" to Ebbets Field:

> You know of the Yankee Stadium routines, don't you? They are unique, they are staged with beer and pop bottles. Knives, sometimes. Once in a while they use blackjacks for props. . . . The variations are when two big, fat, ugly women get to wrestling with each other in the grandstands sweating and cussing like sailor-trained parrots.[12]

Burley's comments were extreme, but they aptly demonstrate the condescending attitudes of the black middle class toward the black populace newly arrived in northern cities.

In Los Angeles, meanwhile, the object of these precautionary measures waited anxiously at his home. After the Little World Series Robinson had assembled an all-star barnstorming squad. Composed primarily of blacks, the club also included Robinson's white Montreal teammates, Al Campanis and Marvin Rackley. Robinson also appeared in several basketball games with the Los Angeles Red Devils, a professional team which included two

other future major league baseball players, Irv Noren, a white, and George
Crowe, a black.[13] The highlight of the off-season, however, occurred in November with the birth of Jackie, Jr., the Robinsons' first child.

Robinson, like others speculating about his future, had little indication
of Rickey's plans. Robinson trusted the Dodger president and was confident
of a fair chance to make the Brooklyn team. But there existed a strong possibility that Rickey would return Robinson to Montreal. To Rachel Robinson, this was not an unwelcome prospect. "I wouldn't have minded going
back to Montreal," she recalls. "Montreal was safe and secure. I loved that
year at Montreal and really looked forward to that if it was necessary."[14]
Unlike 1946 Rachel would not be able to accompany Jackie to spring training. Financial realities and the presence of four-month-old Jackie, Jr., forced
her to remain in California, awaiting word on whether her summer home
would be in Montreal or Brooklyn.

As the Robinsons prepared for the final act in the assault on baseball's
color line, another event passed almost unnoticed. On January 20, 1947,
Josh Gibson collapsed and died near his home in Pittsburgh. In the pantheon of Negro League heroes, Gibson ranked second to only Satchel Paige.
Throughout the United States and the Caribbean, his batting prowess and
tape-measure home runs inspired awe and adulation. For several years, Gibson had battled a series of baffling ailments, both physical and psychological. The powerful catcher, a heavy drinker, complained of persistent head-
aches. In 1943 he lapsed into a coma for several hours. Nonetheless, he
continued to perform admirably on the playing field. In 1945 he led the
Negro National League with a .393 batting average. But the ravages of
chronic hypertension and alcoholism eroded his once bountiful constitution.
His weight dropped from 220 to 180 pounds and he suffered from head-
aches, depression, and blackouts. Gibson died at the age of thirty-seven;
his body was interred in a gravesite marked not by a tombstone, but by an
impersonal number.[15] Robinson's fate notwithstanding, Josh Gibson, the
"Black Babe Ruth," would never play in the major leagues.

II

Branch Rickey planned the 1947 Dodger spring training camp with pains-
taking care. The primary consideration in his preparations was the smooth
elevation of Jackie Robinson to the Brooklyn club. To avoid southern segregation, Rickey transferred the Dodger base from Florida to Cuba and scheduled additional games in Panama. He devised schemes to make the players
more receptive to the presence of a black teammate. He maintained Robinson on the Montreal roster and scheduled numerous games between the

Dodgers and Royals in which the black star could display his talents. This, Rickey hoped, would spark a groundswell of support among the major leaguers, who would storm his office and demand Robinson's promotion. But all of the Mahatma's machinations dissolved in the hot Caribbean sun. There would be no easy path to the major leagues for Jackie Robinson.

The Caribbean junket presented severe logistical and financial difficulties for the Dodger organization. Higher transportation and lodging expenses, as well as the cost of importing major league competition from the mainland increased monetary outlays. Observers estimated that the Dodgers would lose $50,000 by training in Cuba. But Cuba was not without its attractions. "I had heard that Cubans are a deeply religious people," wrote Sam Lacy. "In two days here I have learned that baseball is their religion."[16] El Gran Stadium in Havana accommodated 35,000 people and Rickey hoped that the prospect of major league play would attract large crowds. Furthermore, Cuban fans idolized Robinson. His success, they anticipated, would pave the way for black Cuban stars to join their light-skinned countrymen in the major leagues.

Cuba's relative interracial harmony also appealed to Rickey. The Dodger president hoped the example of greater tolerance on the island would enlighten the Dodger players. The presence of integrated teams from the Cuban winter leagues would offer the Dodgers the opportunity to compete against integrated squads, acquainting them with the talents of black athletes and the existence of interracial play.

From the moment Robinson arrived in Havana, however, Rickey's master plan began to unravel. Robinson was one of four black players assigned to Montreal, along with Roy Campanella, Don Newcombe, and Roy Partlow. Although the Dodgers accommodated their athletes at the luxurious Hotel Nacional and housed the white Royals at the recently constructed Havana Military Academy, "a plush school for the sons of rich Cubans," Robinson and the other blacks were relegated to a "musty, third-rate hotel." While the white players dined on steaks flown in from the mainland, the blacks received a meal allowance to spend at Havana's restaurants and cafés.. Robinson was furious. "I thought we left Florida to train in Cuba so we could get away from Jim Crow," he protested. He learned to his chagrin that the Dodger organization, not Cuban officials, had requested segregated arrangements.[17] The ever-cautious Rickey, fearing disruptive racial incidents in the Royal camp, had opted for separate facilities.

In banishing the black athletes from the Royal camp, Rickey had gravely miscalculated. Campanella alone possessed even a limited command of Spanish, but when he was unavailable the others felt helpless. "At times we almost went berserk because none of the hotel employees spoke English," wrote Wendell Smith, who accompanied the athletes. A more severe problem resulted from the steady diet of restaurant food consumed by the foursome. Cuban cookery consisted of an unending array of fried foods rarely supplemented by green vegetables. Nor were sanitary conditions the rule in Havana's downtown eateries. "One night I sat in the restaurant next to the hotel eating a bowl of soup," recalls Newcombe, "and I stirred the soup and a cockroach came up out of it. I threw up everything I had in me all over the counter." Robinson experienced the most severe reaction to the Cuban diet, which left him, according to Lacy, "hanging on the ropes and holding his tummy."[18]

Not only did Rickey's strategic segregation fail, but his vision of large Cuban turnouts also proved myopic. The Cuban Winter League completed its play-offs just as the Dodgers and Royals began conditioning sessions. Overflow crowds packed El Gran Stadium each day to watch the championship competition. Dodger exhibition games, on the other hand, held scant appeal for the Cubans. After seeing their local heroes in peak form, watching major leaguers play themselves into shape did not impress the demanding fans. The player who most interested them was Robinson, but he was not yet on the Dodger roster. Low attendance marked Dodger games against the Braves and Yankees and a third series with the St. Louis Browns was cancelled due to lack of interest. Even those games including Robinson failed to excite Cuban baseball aficionados. Press reports had heralded Robinson as an infield phenomenon. Instead, fans observed a ballplayer weakened by dysentery and far from mid-season condition. The tumultuous cheering that greeted his initial appearance changed to whistles, the Cuban equivalent of boos.[19]

Robinson's place in the Dodger future remained unclear during the early weeks in Cuba. To some extent, his fate lay in the hands of Brooklyn manager Leo Durocher. Few people doubted that Durocher would give Robinson a fair trial. One of baseball's most colorful figures, Durocher had played with the Yankees of the 1920s and won fame as the shortstop on Branch Rickey's "Gas House Gang" in St. Louis during the 1930s. Never a good hitter, Durocher had offered solid defense and a hard-nosed, aggressive style. In 1938 he joined the Dodgers, where the following year, at Rickey's suggestion, Larry MacPhail named him player-manager.

When Rickey arrived, he inherited the stormy petrel as manager. Many expected their liaison to be short-lived. Durocher represented the perfect antithesis to the Deacon. Off the field, he dressed sharply and mixed with the stars of Hollywood and Broadway, as well as some of the more unsavory characters who often followed in their wake. He took great pride in his reputation as a ladies' man. In 1947 his marriage to actress Laraine Day, whose divorce from her former husband was not legally accepted in California, produced headlines in all the tabloids. But Rickey never imposed his own moralism on his employees and no one questioned Durocher's first-rate baseball mind or his ability to motivate players and attract fans to the ball park. Furthermore, Durocher possessed, according to Harold Parrott, "the kind of outrageous gall that Rickey seemed to look for in ballplayers, possibly because he was short of it himself." In 1947 the Rickey-Durocher alliance entered its sixth and most promising year. Nor did the Robinson issue threaten to disrupt their relationship. Baz O'Meara echoed the common consensus, when he wrote that Durocher "was the kind of person who wouldn't bar any color, nationality, or creed so long as he can produce base hits."[20]

Where Robinson would break into the Dodger lineup posed a more critical question. It seemed unlikely, as Lacy pointed out, that Rickey and Durocher would "risk destruction of Dodger morale" by bringing up Robinson to warm the Brooklyn bench. But the talent-laden starting nine offered few openings. Robinson had played shortstop in the Negro Leagues, but his arm was considered inadequate for that position in the majors. Furthermore, the Dodgers had no intention of replacing Pee Wee Reese. Second base, where Jackie had excelled at Montreal was the logical position, but few believed he would be able to displace incumbent Eddie Stanky. Stanky, not unlike his manager, was a brash man of subtle talents. "He can't hit, he can't field, he can't throw," Rickey was fond of saying. "All he can do is beat you."[21]

Most observers expected Robinson to be tested at third base where Brooklyn was weak. He had played that position in Montreal at the close of the 1946 season and it seemed likely that Rickey planned to introduce him into the starting lineup there. Anticipating Rickey's strategy, however, was always a hazardous proposition. First base represented another Dodger weakness and conversations between Rickey and Durocher determined that that position offered Robinson his best opportunity.

Robinson first learned of this decision when he arrived in Havana. The prospect of learning another new position did not please him. The preceding season he had mastered second base. Now, in addition to the considerable pressures inherent in his situation, Rickey required Robinson to make yet another transition. "Not only did I not know anything about the position, but I was not anxious to learn," Robinson later confessed.[22]

Characteristically, Rickey ordered news of the shift concealed from the public. During exhibition games in Cuba, Robinson would not play first base; his workouts there would be dismissed as "an experiment of no significance." Only when the Royals arrived in Panama for their games with the parent Dodgers would Montreal Manager Clay Hopper display Robinson at

first base for the benefit of his future teammates. Hopper, who knew that
Robinson would not be his regular season first baseman, protested. He urged
Rickey to place Robinson on the Dodgers immediately, so that the Royals
could prepare properly for their own campaign. Rickey adamantly refused,
fearing premature promotion would further interfere with his already disrupted plans.[23]

The Dodger equipment man unearthed a secondhand first base mitt for
Robinson and Hall of Famer George Sisler presented a crash-course in the
fundamentals of fielding the position. Asked if the glove fit, Robinson in-
accurately retorted, "I honestly wouldn't know, I never had one on before."
Robinson had reported to training with a sore back and a painful callous
on the first toe of his left foot. The quick stops and starts and constant bend-
ing required at first base aggravated these ailments. His stomach troubles
and segregated living quarters added to his irritation. "When I arrived in
Panama to meet the Dodgers," he later commented, "I was a disgruntled
ballplayer."[24]

III

Jackie Robinson was not the only disgruntled ballplayer in Panama. A few
nights after the Dodgers arrived in the Caribbean nation, Traveling Secretary Harold Parrott found pitcher Kirby Higbe drinking heavily in a local
bar. The South Carolina-born pitcher had joined the Dodgers in 1941 after
an undistinguished pitching career with the Cubs and Phillies. The shift to
Brooklyn transformed him into one of baseball's best hurlers, and Higbe
responded with devotion to Rickey and the Dodgers. But Robinson's imminent promotion put his loyalties to a severe test. His tongue loosened by
alcohol, Higbe confessed to Parrott, "Ol' Hig just won't do it. The ol' man
[Rickey] has been fair to Ol' Hig. So Ol' Hig ain't going to join any petition
to keep anybody off the club."[25]

Branch Rickey had anticipated opposition from members of the Brooklyn club, but the revelation that Dodger players were circulating an anti-
Robinson petition challenged both his fundamental integration strategy and
his most deep-seated beliefs about race relations. "The players could decide
Robinson's fate," Rickey had predicted in January. "It's what I'd prefer—
that the Dodger players make their own decision after seeing him in action."[26] Prejudice, Rickey believed, reflecting the attitudes of many northern
liberals, was born of ignorance. Exposure to the folly of bigotry would dissolve opposition and encourage cooperation. Once the Dodgers saw Robinson play and realized that his presence could assist them in their quest for
the pennant, they would not only accept the black athlete, but ultimately

demand that Rickey promote him. At that moment, Ricky would "reluc-tantly" submit to their requests.

Rickey recognized that for several of the southern-born Dodgers playing alongside Robinson entailed a major cultural adjustment. "In the park that I grew up in, there were no blacks allowed," recalls Pee Wee Reese, a na-tive Kentuckian. "Blacks got in the back of the buses, they had a special fountain to drink from. I don't guess that I ever shook the hand of a black person." Reese doubted that Robinson would succeed because, as all white southerners knew, blacks could not handle pressure situations. "You hear this all your life, you believe it," explains Reese today.[27]

Others had more strongly negative feelings than Reese. Higbe expressed his racist attitudes frankly. "We were southerners who had never lived or played with Negroes and didn't see any reason to start then," he wrote in his autobiography. Once, in a radio interview, Higbe, when asked how he had developed such a strong arm, had responded that it came from throw-ing rocks at Negroes. Higbe was immediately cut off the air, but he felt that the announcer simply did not understand. "We didn't hate Negroes," con-tended the pitcher. "The rock fights were more of a game on both sides. . . . They threw as many rocks as we did, sometimes more."[28]

In addition to Reese and Higbe, several other Dodger regulars lived in the South. Eddie Stanky, outfielder Dixie Walker, and reserve catcher Bobby Bragan came from Alabama. Pitchers Hugh Casey and Ed Head had grown up in Georgia and Louisiana respectively. And Ed Stevens, one of Robin-son's rivals at first base, was a Texan.

Rickey did not lack sympathy for the dilemma these athletes faced. All, he felt, were inherently decent men, victims of a southern upbringing. Rickey conceived several strategies to overcome their ignorance and accus-tom them to interracial conditions while the team trained in Havana. Dodger officials hired a bus to transport players to integrated Cuban League play-off games. In early March they arranged a tryout for Roberto Avila, a Cuban League second baseman. Reporters described Avila as "one of the swarthier Mexicans." Both Lacy and Smith speculated that the Dodgers designed Avila's presence in the camp as a "barometer" to measure the reaction to a dark-skinned second baseman. Lacy described Avila as "an ordinary player" whereas Smith dismissed him as "definitely not big league material."[29] (They were wrong. Although the Dodgers did not sign Avila, two years later he surfaced as the Cleveland Indian second baseman, his first name anglicized to "Bobby," and his batting skills sufficient to lead the American League in 1954.)

Durocher also attempted to divert dissension. According to Higbe, the Dodger manager invited Reese and him to dinner in Havana to discuss the situation. Durocher and Laraine Day urged the two men to give Robinson a chance. Leo argued that Robinson could win the pennant for the Dodgers, while Laraine stressed that Robinson was "a nice quiet guy that we wouldn't have to associate with off the field."[30]

These efforts, however, failed to ward off the impending revolt. At Montreal the preceding season, Robinson had played among minor leaguers whose precarious futures dictated against rebellion. The Dodger stars, on the other hand, possessed more security. Their major league status, and in some cases, extreme popularity with the Brooklyn fans established a firmer platform from which to voice their objections.

Veteran outfielder Dixie Walker, the most popular of the Dodger players, determined to rally the dissidents. Known in Flatbush as "The People's Cherce," Walker had joined the Dodgers in 1940 and helped win a pennant the following year. Already in his thirties and exempt from military service, Dixie became the standout performer on the draft-ravaged Dodger teams of the war years. A consistent .300 hitter, Walker paced the National League with a .357 average in 1944. Walker loved the Dodgers and their fans, and many people speculated that upon retirement he might become the manager of the club. At thirty-six years of age, Walker sincerely desired to conclude his career in Brooklyn. But the proud Alabaman could not accept the distasteful prospect of playing alongside a black man. When Robinson had signed in 1945, Walker had told reporters that as long as a black player was not on his team, he would continue to play. With Robinson's ascension to the Dodgers imminent, Walker initiated a protest petition to block the infielder's path.[31]

Upon learning of Higbe's confession from Parrott, both Rickey and Durocher attempted to quell the uprising. Durocher gathered the Dodger players for a midnight meeting in a kitchen behind the mess hall where the team ate its meals. With sleepy athletes sitting on chopping blocks and counters or leaning against stoves and refrigerators, Durocher, bedecked in pajamas and a bright yellow bathrobe, harangued his troops about the Robinson situation. "I don't care if a guy is yellow or black, or if he has stripes like a fuckin' zebra," Parrott quotes Durocher as saying. "I'm the manager of this team and I say he plays." Durocher barked to the rebels to take the petition and "wipe your ass with it," because Robinson was "going to put money in your pockets and money in mine."[32] The manager threatened to trade any players who persisted in their protest.

The following evening Rickey ordered the players suspected of supporting Walker's petition to report to his hotel room. "I have always believed," he later explained, "that a little show of force at the right time is necessary when there's a deliberate violation of law." Arthur Mann also attended these stormy sessions. Rickey, according to Mann, "outdid Stentor at his best, as he hurled some of his best verbiage into the tropical night." The Mahatma lectured the athletes on "Americanism" and offered each the option of being traded if they did not wish to play with Robinson. The Dodger executive had little difficulty with outfielder Carl Furillo, the sole northerner in the group, or Hugh Casey, the pitcher from Georgia. Higbe and Bobby Bragan were not so easily placated.[33]

Higbe, despite his late night confession, still opposed Robinson's elevation. "I loved Brooklyn and Brooklyn loved me," Higbe later wrote. "I knew what a great ball club we had and that it was going to cost me plenty to be traded away." Nonetheless, explains Higbe, "If I could have looked ahead and seen all the change that was coming, I think I still would have done what I did. I was brought up to stand by what you said and believed in even if you were the last one standing there."[34] Higbe does not say that he asked to be traded, but he sensed that his Dodger days were numbered.

The most heated exchange involved Bragan, the pugnacious third-string catcher from Birmingham. Unlike some of the others, Bragan refused to be intimidated by Rickey. The fiery southerner, who had not been approached with a formal petition, denied being a part of a conspiracy. But when Rickey ended his lengthy tirade and asked him if he wished to play on the same team as Robinson, Bragan declared defiantly, "No, I do not! I wouldn't want to be the scapegoat, Mr. Rickey, but I'd just as soon be traded." Rickey shouted back, "Then I may accommodate you, sir!" and dismissed the catcher. The emotions of the argument, according to Mann, left Rickey visibly shaken when Bragan stormed out of the room.[35]

Even without the actions of Rickey and Durocher, the mutiny likely would have failed. Northern players had no interest in the protest and some key southerners had refused to support it. Missouri-born Pete Reiser told one of the petitioners that while in the army he had entrusted his daughter's health to a physician whose name he had discovered in the telephone directory. The doctor turned out to be black. Reiser asked the mutineer what he would have done and the player replied, "I would have turned around and walked away from that neighborhood." "I told him I thought he was a goddam fool," says Reiser, "and then I told him what he could do with his petition."[36]

The protestors also approached Reese, but the soft-spoken shortstop and team leader declined, despite his southern upbringing. "I wasn't trying to think of myself as the Great White Father," he recalls. "I just wanted to play the game, especially after being in the Navy for three years and needing the money." Reese's refusal, perhaps more than any other, doomed the petition.[37]

Ironically, Dixie Walker, who had initiated the uprising, left Panama before the storm broke. A family illness had called him back to the United States. From his home in Birmingham, he wrote to Rickey advising him, "Recently the thought has occurred to me that a change of ball clubs would benefit both the Brooklyn Baseball Club and myself." Walker asked to be traded as soon as possible. "My association with you, the people of Brooklyn, the press and radio has been very pleasant and one I can truthfully say I am sorry has to end," wrote Walker poignantly. "For reasons I don't care to go into I feel my decision is best for all concerned."[38]

Rickey moved quickly to accommodate those who had asked to be traded. Bragan had changed his mind and withdrawn his request, but within three days of receiving Walker's letter, Rickey arranged an exchange with Pittsburgh that would have sent "The People's Cherce" to the Pirates for two part-time players and $40,000. Before the transaction could be consummated, Rickey's baseball instincts surfaced and he reneged. Walker was worth a great deal more. When the outfielder rejoined the club, he asked Rickey to return his letter, explaining that he was willing to remain a Dodger if it was in the best interests of the team. Nonetheless, Rickey, realizing that the situation placed the players under a great strain, persisted in his efforts to trade the dissidents. Shortly after the start of the season, Rickey shipped Higbe to Pittsburgh; Walker, at least for the time being, remained with the Dodgers.[39]

Rickey's attempts to trade the two players were neither retaliatory nor punitive. The Dodger president recognized the burden that he had placed upon these men and he respected the courage and determination of those who had spoken out most forcefully. "He didn't take offense at what I'd said," recalls Bragan, "because he knew that I'd grown up surrounded by a way of thinking that had been there long before I came on the scene and couldn't help but have it imparted to me." Rickey later wrote of Walker, "In my book he is a high-class gentleman. . . . He was bold enough, strong enough to write me that long-hand letter asking me to trade him and then to come to me to ask me to give the letter back."[40] Rickey did not hesitate to hire Walker as a minor league manager in the Dodger system when Dixie's playing career had ended.

For Bobby Bragan, the explosive confrontation in Rickey's hotel room proved a turning point. The following day Mann told Bragan how much Rickey appreciated his honesty. "That was the start of a great friendship between Mr. Rickey and me," says Bragan.[41] In 1948 when a position opened up managing the Dodgers' Fort Worth farm club, Rickey offered Bragan the job, the first of many major and minor league positions that Bragan enjoyed. In 1954 as general manager at Pittsburgh, Rickey gave Bragan his first opportunity as a major league manager.

The anti-Robinson campaign had failed due to the prompt and firm response by Dodger officials and the unwillingness of most players to support Walker's petition. Lack of sympathy for the segregationist argument, fears for their futures, and the general sense of loyalty that Rickey had engendered in the Dodger organization, all contributed to the refusal of the players to join the conspiracy. Nonetheless, the brief and abortive rebellion demonstrated Rickey's naïveté about the depth of player feeling. Even before the black infielder's first appearance against the Dodgers, it had grown obvious that Robinson would receive no groundswell of support from his fellow athletes. If his performance merited promotion to the Dodgers, it would be Rickey and Durocher, and not the white players, who would usher him into the big leagues.

IV

The arrival of the dissension-ridden Dodgers in Panama marked the beginning of a critical period for Jackie Robinson. During the next two weeks, the Montreal Royals were scheduled to play a series of eleven games against the Dodgers in Panama, Cuba, and finally Brooklyn. Robinson's performance in these contests would determine his fate for the 1947 season. Before the first game, Rickey called Robinson aside for instructions. "I want you to be a whirling demon against the Dodgers," exhorted the Deacon. "I want you to concentrate, to hit that ball, to get on base by any means. I want you to run wild, to steal the pants off them, to be the most conspicuous player on the field."[42]

As in Cuba, Jackie and his black Montreal teammates merited top billing in Panama. Local officials had guaranteed the Dodgers $35,000 if Robinson accompanied the team. Repeated photographs in newspapers had made the black Royals so familiar that they attracted crowds wherever they went. When the Dodgers appeared against General Electric, the champions of the Panama Professional League, only 2,000 spectators attended. More than three times that number witnessed the Royals against the same club, overflowing the tiny wooden stadium. Smith noted the irony that black athletes were "accorded better treatment here than they have ever experienced from their own countrymen."[43]

On March 17 Robinson confronted the Dodgers for the first time that spring. Once again Rickey's plans drifted off course. The Mahatma had stressed that the final decision on Robinson would be made by Durocher, but the Dodger manager had disappeared. "Why wasn't Durocher around to look at his latest and most spectacular candidate?" wondered sportswriter Bill Roeder.[44] The "Lip" had hastened to Los Angeles, where a judicial hearing on the legality of his marriage to Laraine Day was in progress.

Despite Durocher's absence, Robinson displayed his prowess to the Dodger players. In the first contest, he pounded a pair of hits against pitcher Hal Gregg. The following day he added three more singles without hitting the ball out of the infield. Two of the hits came on bunts. After dropping one ball expertly down the third baseline, Robinson bluffed in that direction on his next at-bat and then pushed the ball to the left of the pitcher and toward Stanky, the second baseman, who had no play on the speedy Robinson. This so frustrated Stanky that he called time, picked up the ball, and heaved it over the grandstand and out on to the street. "It was the worst thing I ever seen on a ballfield," Campanella later stated. With Georgian Hugh Casey on the mound, many of the Royal players expected a retaliatory brushback pitch the next time Robinson appeared at the plate. "Everybody said he'd knock his own mother down," remembers Johnny Jorgenson of Casey. "Well the next time, we thought he was going to drill Robinson with a pitch. There was a little moment of silence: 'Here it is. Let's see what happens here.' Instead, Casey went right along and pitched to him."[45]

Under the intense scrutiny of the Dodgers, Royals, reporters, and fans, Robinson staged remarkable performances in Panama. When the Royals returned to Cuba, Robinson had appeared in a dozen games against either the Dodgers or local clubs and had batted .519, easily the best figure of any Brooklyn or Montreal player. Nonetheless, he remained a Royal. In Cuba, Durocher, who had missed all of the Panama games, would hopefully get a chance to see Robinson play first base. But the fates continued to conspire against the athlete. His recurrent stomach problems threatened to sideline him from the important series with the Dodgers. He competed in the first contest on March 27 in a severely weakened condition and committed two errors that enabled the Dodgers to triumph. The following night his ailment forced him to sit out the game.

Robinson returned to the lineup on April 1. To the surprise of everyone, he was stationed not at first, but at his old second base position, leading to speculation that Rickey had abandoned the spring experiment. In reality, Montreal Manager Hopper had dictated the switch. Hopper wanted to test several other prospective first basemen (including Chuck Connors, destined more for television than major league fame). Rickey, furious at Hopper's insubordination, announced, "Robinson will return to first base tonight and play there every remaining game with Montreal." Nonetheless, in the next game, Hopper again defied Rickey and placed Robinson at second. On April 4 Robinson reappeared at first base, but misfortune continued to plague him. A collision with catcher Bruce Edwards during a mid-game rundown injured Robinson's back, and Robinson failed to appear in any of the remaining games in Cuba.[46]

Rickey intended the Dodger-Royal competition as a showcase for Robinson's talents and value to the team. Instead, confusion characterized the games. Durocher's absence in Panama, Robinson's stomach ailments, Hopper's insistence on preparing other first basemen, and the collision with Edwards left the situation uncertain. Although Robinson had batted well, his struggle to learn a new position produced erratic fielding. The resulting spectacle puzzled sportswriters. The New York *Post* headlined its April 5 story, "No Fair Trial for Jackie Robinson," reporting that "The lack of a consistent policy . . . has led everyone to believe that Robbie is getting the proverbial runaround." Sam Lacy shifted from optimism to pessimism and back as Robinson shuttled from position to position. He finally concluded that the whole scenario was "another clever maneuver on the part of Rickey" who planned to introduce Robinson not as a Dodger regular but as "an all-around utility infielder," who would be able to fill in at four different positions. *World-Telegram* sportswriter Mike Gaven agreed, adding, "It probably would be safe to say that he will do a lot of pinch-running."[47]

To produce this "utility infielder" noted Gaven, the Dodgers had staged "the most costly trial ever given a player." The $50,000 deficit, he wrote "will be itemized as spring training expenses. But . . . the red ink will always spell Jackie Robinson. It will be an indelible mark that baseball will never forget." Gaven pointed out that in the end, Robinson had never "don[ned] the uniform of the club he was trying to make" and that he had only "casually [met] less than half of his potential teammates." Gaven saw no indication of diminished resentment against Robinson among the Dodgers.[48] Despite Rickey's carefully laid plans, Robinson left the Caribbean much as he had arrived there—a member of the Montreal Royals with an uncertain future.

Throughout the spring, the primary focus of attention had centered on Robinson. Campanella, Newcombe, and Partlow, his three black teammates, toiled in relative obscurity as they struggled to make the Montreal club. Upon arrival in Havana, Campanella developed a sore arm, and for a time it seemed doubtful that he would be promoted. But the ailment subsided and he clearly earned the first string catcher's role with the Royals. Newcombe, ordered to lose weight during training and further weakened by his bouts with Cuban food, contributed an unimpressive spring. "I got so weak I could hardly swell up your lip if I hit you with a fast ball," he recalls.[49]

As a result, the Dodgers returned Newcombe to Nashua for another year of seasoning.

Partlow continued to pose a problem for the Dodger management. He reported late to Havana and rumors circulated that he was holding out for a better contract. When he appeared, he offered no explanation for his tardiness. Partlow's behavior drew a sharp rebuke from Robinson who complained that although Partlow was "one of the greatest lefthanded pitchers in the game . . . unless he gets the feeling that he wants to play he may as well forget about the game from the standpoint of organized ball." Partlow pitched poorly in Cuba and shortly after the teams arrived in Panama, he received his unconditional release. The *Courier* noted that like John Wright, Partlow "seemed to have a tendency to choke up while laboring among the caucasians."[50] The left-handed pitcher immediately rejoined the Philadelphia Stars, his brief chance in white baseball at an end.

The Dodgers and Royals played their final game in Havana on April 6 with the injured Robinson watching from the sidelines. While the two clubs leisurely traveled northward, stopping for workouts in southern cities, Robinson and Campanella proceeded directly to New York. The Dodgers and their farm team would clash again in Brooklyn for a pair of exhibition games, at which time a decision on Robinson would be made. Rickey still grasped at the hope that it would not appear that he had forced Robinson on an unwilling Dodger team. He no longer deluded himself that the players would demand Robinson's elevation. Before leaving Havana, he announced, "The players will have no voice in the selection of Dodger regulars. That is up to Durocher alone."[51] Rickey's final scheme called for Durocher to apply "pressure" on him to "force" him to promote Robinson. On April 9 the manager would tell reporters that Robinson was the first baseman required by the Dodgers to bring the pennant to Brooklyn. The following day, Rickey would "succumb" and "allow" Durocher to have Robinson.

Rickey's strategies had consistently misfired throughout the spring and the Durocher ploy proved no exception. On the morning of April 9, before the manager could issue his request, Baseball Commissioner Happy Chandler shocked the baseball world by suspending Durocher for one year for "conduct detrimental to baseball." Durocher was the unfortunate victim of a long-simmering feud between Rickey and Yankee President Larry Mac-Phail, a conflict which had been deepened, though not created, by their differences over the race issue. Several years earlier, Commissioner Landis had warned Durocher against consorting with known gamblers. In response, he had presented the commissioner with a list of people with whom he would no longer socialize. When two of the people on Durocher's untouchable list appeared in MacPhail's box at a Yankee game, both Durocher and Rickey attacked the hypocrisy of the situation. MacPhail, who had orchestrated Chandler's selection as commissioner, cried slander and demanded an investigation of the charges. Few people expected any major developments to occur. Nonetheless, with the opening of the baseball season less than a week away, Chandler levied fines on both clubs and suspended the Dodger manager.[52]

Although the controversial decision did not mention the Robinson situation, several observers saw Rickey's assault on the color line as the underlying cause of the Durocher suspension. "Many of us will always believe that it was Chandler's way of getting at Rickey, whom he could not touch personally but whose manager was vulnerable," wrote Dan Dodson. Harold Parrott has charged that the lords of baseball, by eliminating Durocher, had conspired to make Robinson's ordeal more difficult. "What the black man needed behind him was Durocher's bark and brass and bellow" to ease the pressure from opposing players, managers, and even umpires, asserts Parrott.[53] It is unlikely, however, that the racial issue constituted a primary, or even a major element in the Durocher case. No evidence exists that Chandler strongly opposed the decision to hire Robinson. The entire affair reflects the unwise decision of an insecure new commissioner. The absence of Durocher certainly disrupted the already confused Dodger picture and made Robinson's path more arduous, but it seems dubious that the commissioner intended this. Chandler, at the urging of his patron MacPhail, simply sought to assert his recently acquired authority.

For the moment, the Durocher controversy overshadowed the Robinson story. Though dismayed by the commissioner's action, Rickey realized that he could no longer delay Robinson's promotion. On the morning of April 10 he informed Robinson that the afternoon game would be his last as a Royal. With Robinson at bat in the sixth inning, the Dodgers announced his promotion. Robinson, unaware that the news was public, ingloriously bunted into a double play to the cheers of his Royal teammates.

After eighteen months of speculation, Robinson's ascension to the Dodgers seemed anticlimactic. Editorials in the New York press welcomed the event. "If Robinson was a white man, his name would have been there long before this," commented the New York *Times*. The New York *Post* expressed a "particular satisfaction" and predicted that most local fans "will be rooting for him to make a good showing." In most other cities newspapers confined their analyses to the sports sections. "This of course is just a token victory," commented Boston sportswriter Dave Egan. "The war against bigotry in baseball will not be won until every team in the major leagues judges every man on his ability to play ball."[54]

At Ebbets Field, fans greeted Robinson's initial appearances as the Brooklyn Dodger first baseman nonchalantly. "No buildings collapsed either from the reverberations caused by the epochal event or from the power of Robinson's hitting," remarked Dan Daniel after Robinson's Dodger debut in an exhibition game against the Yankees. The crowd, wrote Daniel, "took the event in stride."[55]

For blacks, the moment held more significance. TRIUMPH OF WHOLE RACE SEEN IN JACKIE'S DEBUT IN MAJOR LEAGUE BALL, boasted a Boston *Chronicle* headline. From the first Brooklyn-Montreal contest, black fans had turned out at Ebbets Field in large numbers, at times constituting a majority of the spectators. They wildly cheered Robinson, while Dixie Walker, the rumors of his protest having reached New York, was "greeted with a deluge of boos and catcalls." The public chastisement of the former "People's Cherce" drew reprimands from both the black and white press. "Thoughtless booing of Dixie for his own private opinion isn't going to make Jackie's chances of being welcomed into the Brooklyn Dodger fold any better," warned black writer Dan Burley. The harassment of Walker quickly ceased.[56]

The Baltimore *Afro-American* highlighted Robinson's three preseason performances against the Yankees in two boxes. The first presented a meticulous account of each plate appearance. The second offered an inning by inning description of "Robbie's First Day on the Dodger Bench," informing the reader that in the sixth inning Robinson was "first to bench, was joined by Boris Woyt, rookie outfielder; Vic Lombardi, pitcher, started to take the next seat, changed his mind and wedged in between two other players. Later Ed Stanky dropped on the bench beside Jackie."[57]

On the field, Robinson produced no heroics in these final exhibition contests. In the three-game series against the Yankees he collected only two hits, although he drove in four runs. He handled thirty-six fielding chances without an error. Nonetheless, the Yankees concluded that his awkwardness would soon banish him to the Brooklyn bench.[58]

On April 15 the Dodgers opened their regular season against the Braves at Ebbets Field with Clyde Sukeforth serving as interim manager. Robinson started at first base. Little of the tension that had characterized Robinson's Montreal debut a year earlier resurfaced. The surprising lack of excitement that had characterized the Yankee series continued. Although an estimated 14,000 black fans flooded through the turnstiles, the arena filled to only two thirds of capacity. Arthur Daley recorded the event as "quite uneventful."[59]

Rachel Robinson, possessing a more personal interest in the activities, disagreed. She and Jackie, Jr., had joined Jackie when he arrived in New York. Still uncertain as to whether they would be living in Brooklyn or Montreal, the young family had taken a room at the McAlpin Hotel in Manhattan. With no friends in New York to care for Jackie, Jr., they took turns eating meals in the coffee shop, unable to leave the room at the same time. "The reporters were around all the time and I'm trying to make diapers and formula," recalls Rachel. To make matters worse, the change of water from California to New York had given the baby diarrhea.[60]

Nonetheless, Rachel was determined to attend Opening Day. "I packed up the baby, went downstairs, and couldn't get a taxi that would go to Brooklyn," she recalls. "I thought I was going to be late." A cold, gray pallor enveloped Ebbets Field and on arrival, Rachel divided her time "worrying about the baby catching cold and worrying about Jack's performance." She sat with the Campanella family and Roy's mother sheltered young Jackie in her fur coat while Rachel heated his milk bottles at the hot dog stand. "I was very, very excited and very, very nervous," says Rachel. But the thoughts running through her mind were the same as those of thousands of other onlookers: "I was trying to figure out which players were going to be friendly and how he was going to make out."[61]

10

A Lone Negro in the Game

> A lone Negro in the game will face caustic comments. He will be made the target of cruel, filthy epithets. Of course, I know the time will come when the ice will have to be broken. Both by the organized game and by the colored player who is willing to volunteer and thus become a sort of martyr to the cause.
>
> Washington Senators owner
> Clark Griffith, 1938[1]

I

The Brooklyn baseball club acquired its unusual nickname in the early twentieth century. Electrified streetcars in New York's largest borough were so dangerous, joked the residents, that one had to become a skilled "trolley dodger" to survive. Brooklynites appended the name to the local baseball team and later shortened it to "Dodgers." Throughout the next several decades the team preserved the borough's identity. Brooklyn, a gathering of three million people of diverse ethnicity, populous enough to be the nation's fourth largest city, had been incorporated in 1898, against the will of most of its residents, into Greater New York. Brooklyn retained its independence from the parent metropolis only in the public mind—a community characterized by aggressive, colorful residents, distinctive Brooklyn accents, and most of all, the baseball team. In the major leagues, the Dodgers were the only franchise that hoisted the banner of a borough, rather than a city.

When Jackie Robinson arrived in Brooklyn in 1947, gasoline-powered buses were replacing the electric trolleys which had given the team its name. These two developments—the appearance of a black baseball player and the invasion of the internal combustion engine—symbolized the forces transforming Brooklyn. Wartime migrations had sprinkled the borough's predominantly white, middle-class population with blacks from the South and Latins from Puerto Rico. At the same time, the greater availability of the automobile and the rapid construction of highways facilitated the exodus of the expanding white middle class to the suburbs, and points farther west. The Robinsons journeyed from California to New York; many more people traveled in the other direction. At the dawning of the age of Jackie Robinson, Brooklyn had entered its twilight era, a victim of the postwar transition affecting America's venerable industrial regions. Within a decade these changes would realign the borough's ethnic and racial composition, undermine its local economy, and, to emphasize the decline, banish its baseball club to a land of freeways. What meaning hath the term "Dodgers" in a city with no trolleys?

There is a myth which has flourished about the Brooklyn fans. It is said that they supported their team faithfully and fanatically. Through lean years and fat years, they flooded into tiny Ebbets Field, the legendary arena at the intersection of Empire Boulevard and Bedford Avenue. ("There was never another ball park like Ebbets Field," writes Red Barber. "A little small, outmoded, oldfashioned. . . . You were practically playing second base, the stands were so close to the field."[2]) The myth nonetheless is hollow. As the Dodgers floundered in or near the second division in the 1920s and 1930s, fans stayed away in droves. By 1937 when Larry MacPhail took over the Dodgers, the team verged on bankruptcy. MacPhail rejuvenated the franchise on the field and at the box office, before turning over the reins to Rickey. The MacPhail-Rickey years marked the golden age of Brooklyn Dodger baseball. Dodger devotees flocked to Ebbets Field in record numbers and dying Hollywood soldiers asked for Brooklyn scores before passing on to their next feature film. At the war's end the Dodgers had reached the peak of their popularity.

Robinson joined a Dodger squad that had set a new Brooklyn attendance record as it tied for first place in 1946. A play-off loss to the Cardinals kept Brooklyn out of the World Series. Few people, however, predicted that the team would re-emerge as a contender. "Brooklyn is the one club which appears to lack peace of mind," wrote J. Taylor Spink in the *Sporting News*, picking the club for fifth place. "Durocher's suspension has not helped. Neither has the in-again, out-again business with Jackie Robinson." After the second game of the season, Rickey replaced Durocher with Burt Shotton, who had served as the Deacon's "Sunday Manager" in St. Louis. Shotton confronted the Dodger players, accustomed to Durocher's brassy direction, as a grandfatherly figure who wore a business suit in the dugout rather than a uniform. Unlike Durocher, writes Harold Parrott, Shotton "hardly ever raised his voice enough to be heard at the other end of the dugout, much less by an umpire; and what he did say wouldn't upset a Sunday school."[3]

For Jackie Robinson, relative tranquility characterized the initial week of the 1947 season. In the first two contests, facing the Boston Braves, the rookie first baseman eked out one bunt single. "He seemed frantic with eagerness, restless as a can of worms," observed a Boston correspondent.[4] On April 18 the Dodgers crossed the East River to play the New York Giants. Over 37,000 people flocked to the Polo Grounds to witness Robinson's first appearance outside of Brooklyn. Robinson responded with his first major league home run. The following day the largest Saturday afternoon crowd in National League history, more than 52,000 spectators, jammed into the Giants' ball park. Robinson stroked three hits in four at-bats in a losing cause. Rain postponed a two-game set in Boston, and on April 22 Robinson and the Dodgers returned to Brooklyn, where a swirl of events abruptly shattered the brief honeymoon. The next three weeks thrust Robinson, his family, his teammates, and baseball into a period of unrelenting crises and tension.

The Dodgers' first opponents on the homestand were the Philadelphia Phillies, managed by Alabaman Ben Chapman. While playing for the Yankees in the 1930s Chapman had gained a measure of notoriety for his anti-Semitic shouting jousts with spectators. Now he ordered his players to challenge Robinson with a stream of verbal racial taunts "to see if he can take it." From the moment the two clubs took the field for their first contest, the Phillies, led by Chapman, unleashed a torrent of insults at the black athlete. "At no time in my life have I heard racial venom and dugout abuse to match the abuse that Ben sprayed on Robinson that night," writes Harold Parrott. "Chapman mentioned everything from thick lips to the supposedly extra-thick Negro skull . . . [and] the repulsive sores and diseases he said Robinson's teammates would become infected with if they touched the towels or the combs he used."[5] The onslaught continued throughout the series.

Bench jockeying always comprised an integral part of the national pastime. "Probably the greatest cruelty in the American sports picture is the abuse that is showered on players from the rival dugout," explained sportswriter J. Roy Stockton. These exchanges held no topic sacred. Frequent targets included personal problems, appearance, ethnicity, and race. Athletes often subjected Latin-American opponents to racial barbs. In the 1935 World Series, according to umpire George Moriarty, the Chicago Cubs "crucif[ied] Hank Greenberg for being a Jew" and taunted Jewish umpire Dolly Stark as a "Christ-killer."[6]

The Phillies verbal assault on Robinson in 1947 exceeded even baseball's broadly defined sense of propriety. Fans seated near the Phillies dugout wrote letters of protest to Commissioner Chandler, and newsman Walter Winchell attacked Chapman on his national Sunday night radio broadcast. Chandler notified Philadelphia owner Robert Carpenter that the harassment of Robinson must cease or he would be forced to invoke punitive measures.

Chapman, while accepting Chandler's edict, defended his actions. "We will treat Robinson the same as we do Hank Greenberg of the Pirates, Clint Hartung of the Giants, Joe Garagiola of the Cardinals, Connie Ryan of the Braves, or any other man who is likely to step to the plate and beat us," said Chapman, listing some regular targets of ethnic insults. "There is not a man who has come to the big leagues since baseball has been played who has not been ridden." During his own playing career, alleged Chapman, "I received a verbal barrage from the benches that would curl your hair. . . . They wanted to see if I would lose my temper and forget to play ball." Robinson, argued Chapman, "did not want to be patronized" and had received the same test administered to all rookies.[7]

Chapman's defense drew support from many fans and sportswriters. According to the *Sporting News*, the Phillies received "an avalanche of letters and telephone calls . . . commending Chapman for his fair stand toward Robinson." Several sportswriters also accepted Chapman's explanation. J. Roy Stockton concluded, "If the dugouts treat Jackie just as they treat any other enemy player, especially the good ones, they'll give him a riding eventually. That's baseball." Even Sam Lacy indirectly approved Chapman's stance. Lacy turned his column over to a "friend," who argued that Chapman "seems to have a pretty good explanation to me." The friend condemned Lacy and other writers who "keep on crying that you want Jackie treated like every other ballplayer. . . . The Phillies and Chapman took you at your word."[8]

The general consensus, however, judged the Phillie behavior unacceptable. Robinson's Dodger teammates led the protest. By the second day of the series they lashed back at Chapman demanding that he cease baiting Robinson. Chapman's fellow Alabamans marched in the forefront of Robinson's defenders. Eddie Stanky called him a "coward" and challenged him to "pick on somebody who can fight back." Even Dixie Walker reprimanded Chapman, a close personal friend. Rickey later claimed that this incident, more than any other, cemented Dodger support for Robinson. "When [Chapman] poured out that string of unconscionable abuse he solidified and unified thirty men, not one of whom was willing to sit by and see someone kick around a man who had his hands tied behind his back," asserted Rickey.[9]

Robinson publicly downplayed the incident. In his "Jackie Robinson Says" column which appeared in the Pittsburgh *Courier*, the Dodger first baseman wrote, "Some of the Phillies' bench jockeys tried to get me upset last week, but it didn't really bother me." The following week he added, "I don't think [Chapman] was really shouting at me the first time we played Philadelphia." Several writers praised Robinson for his restraint. In later years he revealed his true emotions as he withstood the barrage of insults. "I have to admit that this day of all the unpleasant days of my life brought me nearer to cracking up than I have ever been," he wrote in 1972. "For one wild and rage-crazed minute I thought, 'To hell with Mr. Rickey's "noble experiment." ' " The ordeal tempted Robinson to "stride over to that Phillies dugout, grab one of those white sons of bitches and smash his teeth with my despised black fist."[10]

Robinson enjoyed a taste of revenge in the initial game against Philadelphia. In the eighth inning, with the teams deadlocked in a scoreless tie, he singled, stole second, and moved to third when the catcher heaved the ball into centerfield. Gene Hermanski followed with a single and Robinson answered his tormentors with the game's only run. But the final two games of the Philadelphia series marked the beginning of a prolonged batting drought. Over the next week, Robinson, plagued by a sore shoulder, failed to get a hit in twenty times at bat and rumors had him destined for the Dodger bench.

Hitting slumps are an integral part of baseball, but Robinson's early season problems came at an inopportune moment. His batting skein stemmed not only from the adjustment to major league pitching and the harassment by opponents but from the outside pressures that gathered about him. "He's not a ballplayer," complained Rickey, "He's a sideshow attraction." Even before the season had started, Rickey reported, Robinson had received 5,000 invitations to appear "at all sorts of events." "There are too many well-wishers and too many seeking to exploit him," said the Dodger president. In addition, Robinson and his wife felt obligated to answer all of the encouraging mail, making further demands on his time. "The boy is on the road to complete prostration," worried Rickey.[11]

The daily flood of mail included not only congratulatory messages, but threats of violence. In early May, the Dodgers turned several of these notes over to the police. The letters, according to Robinson, advised "that 'somebody' was going to get hurt if I didn't get out of baseball," and "promised to kill any n——s who interfered with me." In the aftermath of the threats and in light of the burden that answering the mail placed on the Robinsons, Rickey requested that they allow the Dodgers to open and answer all correspondence.[12] In addition, Robinson agreed to refuse all invitations to speak or be honored as well as opportunities for commercial endorsements.

The Dodgers released details of the threatening letters to the press on May 9. On that same day Robinson faced other unpublicized challenges in Philadelphia, the initial stop on the club's first extended road trip. Rickey had been forewarned that Robinson would not get a warm reception in Philadelphia. Herb Pennock, the former major league pitcher who served as the Phillies general manager, had called Rickey demanding that Robinson remain in Brooklyn. "[You] just can't bring that nigger here with the rest of your team, Branch. We're just not ready for that sort of thing yet," exhorted Pennock, according to Parrott who listened on the line. Pennock threatened that the Phillies would boycott the game. Rickey called Pennock's bluff and calmly responded that the Dodgers would accept a forfeit victory. The Phillie executive retreated.[13]

When the Dodgers arrived in Philadelphia on May 9, the Benjamin Franklin Hotel, where the club had lodged for several years, refused to accept Robinson. Team officials had anticipated problems in St. Louis and Cincinnati, but not in the City of Brotherly Love. The preceding year, a local judge had cited the Benjamin Franklin for discrimination and the owners had signed a pledge disavowing this behavior. Before their arrival, the Dodgers had included Robinson's name on the reservation list and hotel officials raised no objections. Nonetheless, when the Brooklyn club appeared, the hotel denied Robinson entry. Rather than force a confrontation, Robinson arranged for alternative quarters. On subsequent trips, the Dodgers transferred their Philadelphia headquarters to the more expensive Warwick hotel.[14]

At Shibe Park, Robinson endured another distasteful chore. The negative publicity inspired by the Phillies' treatment of him in Brooklyn had led both team owners to request a conciliatory photograph of Robinson and Chapman shaking hands. Chapman, pressured by the Phillies' ownership, went so far as to say that he would "be glad to have a colored player" on his team, though he continued to maintain that he had treated Robinson fairly. For Robinson the journey to the Philadelphia dugout to pose with Chapman entailed a painful necessity. "I can think of no occasion where I had more difficulty in swallowing my pride and doing what seemed best for baseball and the cause of the Negro in baseball than in agreeing to pose for a photograph with a man for whom I had only the very lowest regard," he later confessed.[15]

Chapman's public moderation notwithstanding, the Phillies resumed their earlier harassment. Although Commissioner Chandler had limited their racial repertoire, Phillie bench jockeys replaced it with an act inspired by the recent death threats. "Some of these grown men sat in the dugout and pointed bats at me and made machine gun-like noises," Robinson later recounted.[16]

A third, more ominous development, which also surfaced on May 9, overshadowed these incidents. New York *Herald Tribune* sports editor Stanley Woodward unveiled an alleged plot by National League players, led by the St. Louis Cardinals, to strike against Robinson. Woodward charged that the Cardinals, at the urgings of a Dodger player, had planned a strike during the first Dodger-Cardinal confrontation three days earlier. Only the stalwart actions of National League President Ford Frick and Cardinal owner Sam Breadon had averted the walkout, wrote Woodward. The two executives had confronted the players and Frick had delivered, "in effect," the following ultimatum:

> If you do this you will be suspended from the league. You will find that the friends you think you have in the press box will not support you, that you will be outcasts. I do not care if half the league strikes. Those who do it will encounter quick retribution. They will be suspended, and I don't care if it wrecks the National League for five years. This is the United States of America, and one citizen has as much right to play as another.

> The National League will go down the line with Robinson whatever the consequence. You will find that if you go through with your intention that you have been guilty of madness.[17]

Cardinal officials immediately denied the report. Breadon called the story "ridiculous" and Manager Eddie Dyer dismissed it as "absurd." St. Louis players also refuted Woodward's charges and to this day, most team members steadfastly reject stories of a conspiracy against Robinson. "I know that there was a lot of things being written that we objected to playing against the Dodgers being Jackie Robinson was there," recalls Red Schoendienst. "But it wasn't true at all. I can't remember anybody talking about Jackie Robinson or the Dodgers for bringing up Robinson." Marty Marion, Stan Musial, and Enos Slaughter also deny contemplating a strike. "I've read stories that a strike was imminent, but I don't remember that at all," Marion told interviewer Bill Marshall.[18]

The St. Louis Cardinal strike, although generally accepted as an integral part of the Jackie Robinson legend, remains an extremely elusive topic. Woodward's initial dispatch consisted of vague generalities. He named no names and revealed few specifics. Woodward described his story as "factually and thoroughly substantiated," but the following day he retracted major segments of his allegations. Frick, it turned out, never had met with the Cardinals and never voiced the words that Woodward attributed to him, still cited by many baseball histories as the finest utterance of Frick's long career. Nonetheless, Woodward maintained his story was "essentially right and factual" and boasted, "It can now be honestly doubted that the boys from the Hookworm Belt will have the nerve to hoist their quaint sectional folklore on the rest of the country."[19]

Reconstructed thirty-five years later, the strike saga amounts to somewhat more than the denials of the players would indicate, but quite a bit less than Woodward's allegations implied. Robinson's promotion undeniably aroused considerable discontent among the Cardinals and other teams. The idea of organizing a strike probably surfaced. Cardinal captain Terry Moore admitted as much the day the story broke. He told St. Louis sportswriter Bob Broeg that he did not doubt that there had been "high-sounding strike talk that meant nothing." How far this talk actually proceeded is difficult to discern. Dick Sisler, a rookie on the Cardinals in 1947, recalls, "Very definitely there was something going on at the time whereby they said they weren't going to play." The planning, says Sisler, was done "by a lot of the older players. I don't think the younger fellows had anything at all to say."[20]

The Cardinal club seemed a logical fulcrum for the strike movement. Most of the Cardinal regulars came from the South, including Moore, Marion, and Slaughter, usually identified as the ringleaders of the conspiracy. The animosity between the Dodgers and Cardinals, who had tied for first place in 1946 and expected to contend for the pennant again, was well known. Branch Rickey had assembled both teams and both bore his aggressive, hard-nosed trademark. "The Brooklyn Dodgers and Cardinals were kind of enemies," recalls Marion. "I don't think we had any personal love for anybody on the club and I don't think they had any for us."[21] In addition, the Cardinals had started poorly, losing eleven of their first thirteen games, prompting many observers, including owner Breadon, to surmise that something other than baseball had disrupted the team.

Rumors of the impending mutiny reached Breadon in St. Louis and on May 1 he flew to New York where the Cardinals were playing the Giants. Breadon informed National League President Frick of the strike rumors. Frick, in less eloquent terms than attributed to him by Woodward, advised Breadon to warn the Cardinals that the National League would defend Robinson's right to play and that a refusal to take the field would lead to their suspensions. Breadon conferred with player representatives Moore and Marion, both of whom denied the rumors. According to Frick, Breadon reported back, "It was just a tempest in a teapot. A few of the players were upset and popping off a bit. They didn't really mean it."[22] If an uprising indeed had been brewing, it ended with these discussions. On May 6 the Cardinals appeared as scheduled at Ebbets Field and lost to Robinson and the Dodgers.

Both Frick and Breadon assumed that this closed the matter. Meanwhile, Woodward had learned of the strike rumors and received confirmation from Frick of the warnings issued to the Cardinals. On May 9, the day after the completion of the St. Louis series, Woodward broke the story.

Woodward often receives credit for averting a player rebellion. This was not the case. As Wendell Smith wrote, the incident was "greatly exaggerated and it made a better newspaper story than anything else."[23] If the discontent in the Cardinal locker room had reached the point of conspiratorial action, and no firm evidence exists to support this, the actions of Frick and Breadon, and not the belated revelations of the sportswriter, effectively crushed the revolt.

Nonetheless, Woodward's allegations, exaggerated or not, marked a significant turning point. The account of Frick's steadfast renunciation of all efforts to displace the black athlete, following so closely after Chandler's warning to Chapman, placed the baseball hierarchy openly in support of Robinson. In addition, the uproar created by the Woodward story dashed any lingering hopes among dissident players that public opinion, at least as reflected in the press, endorsed their opinions.

The prospect of a player strike, unlike the Chapman episode, inspired an almost totally negative response. While some writers like Stockton argued that "undue importance has been placed in some quarters on inconsequential happenings," most condemned the very idea of an effort to bar Robinson. "There is a great lynch mob among us and they go unhooded and work without the rope," wrote Jimmy Cannon denouncing this "venomous conspiracy." John Lardner labelled the accused ringleaders as "athletes of great playing ability with mental batting averages of .030." The *Sporting News* alone voiced an opposite view. It reprinted its 1942 editorial that argued that blacks and whites alike favored segregation. This view, claimed the journal, which it still adhered to, "takes on a new interest in light of the stir caused by recent events."[24]

But even the *Sporting News* conceded that "the presence of Negroes in the major leagues is an accomplished fact." Sportswriters generally agreed that the legitimacy of baseball integration could no longer be questioned. "The universal opinion is that it is up to his admirers as well as Robinson himself whether he remains in the big leagues," wrote Edgar Brands. "What player feeling there is may be well repressed."[25]

May 9, 1947, marked perhaps the worst day of Jackie Robinson's baseball career. Threats on his life, torment from opposing players, discrimination at the team hotel, and rumors of a player strike simultaneously engulfed the black athlete. The following day, Jimmy Cannon, describing Robinson's relations with his teammates, reported, "He is the loneliest man I have ever seen in sports." And, if as the *Sporting News* argued, "It remains only to judge Robinson on his ability as a player,"[26] he appeared to many jurors to present a weak case. Although he had curtailed his 0 for 20 slump, his batting average still languished near the .250 mark. After one

month of regular season play the fate of the great experiment still seemed
uncertain.

I I

Amidst the swirl of controversy that followed the Dodgers on their first major road trip, the national interest in Jackie Robinson grew apparent. On
Sunday, May 11, the Dodgers faced the Phillies in a doubleheader before
the largest crowd in Philadelphia baseball history. Scalpers sold $2 tickets
for $6, "just like the World Series." Two days later in Cincinnati 27,164 fans
turned out despite an all-day rain "to size up Jackie Robinson."[27] Bad weather
diminished the crowds for two games in Pittsburgh, but when the skies
cleared, 34,814 fans appeared at Forbes Field for the May 18 series finale.
The following day the Dodgers met the Cubs in Chicago. Two hours before
game time Wrigley Field had almost filled. A total of 46,572 fans crammed
into the ball park, the largest attendance in stadium history. The tour concluded in St. Louis where the Dodgers and Cardinals played before the biggest weekday crowd of the National League season.

"Jackie's nimble/Jackie's quick/Jackie's making the turnstiles click,"
crowed Wendell Smith. Jimmy Cannon hailed him as "the most lucrative
draw since Babe Ruth." By May 23 when the Dodgers returned to Brooklyn, Robinson had emerged as a national phenomenon.[28]

Robinson had also erased all doubts about his playing abilities. At the
start of the road trip many still questioned whether Robinson belonged in
the big leagues. On May 13, the day of his first appearance in Cincinnati, a
writer in that city commented, "But for the fact that he is the first acknowledged Negro in major league history and so much attention has been focused on him, he would have been benched a week ago." The reaction to
these remarks by Brooklyn sportswriters, however, surprised the midwest-
erner. The next day he reported that despite Robinson's unimpressive statistics, eastern writers agreed that Robinson was "quite a ballplayer and a
cinch to stick with the Dodgers."[29] Dodger officials felt so confident of Robinson's abilities that during the past week they had eliminated his two primary first base competitors, sending Ed Stevens to Montreal and selling
Howard Schultz to the Phillies.

In city after city Robinson showed skeptical sportswriters and fans that
the Dodgers had not erred. He batted safely in the first ten games of the
May excursion, hitting .395 over that span. By June, Robinson had convinced even the most hardened opponents of integration of his exceptional
talents. "He is a major leaguer in every respect," allowed Ben Chapman.

Starting on June 14, Robinson hit safely in twenty-one consecutive games. At the end of June, he was batting .315, leading the league in stolen bases, and ranked second in runs scored. "Aside from getting up early in the morning, the thing a baseball writer dislikes most is to write about the same player day after day," complained Bill Roeder, "but there is no getting away from the fact that Jackie Robinson has been the headline man."[30]

Robinson's impressive statistics revealed only a portion of the tale. "Never have records meant so little in discussing a player's value as they do in the case of Jackie Robinson," wrote Tom Meany. "His presence alone was enough to light a fire under his own team and unsettle his opponents." Sportswriter John Crosby asserts, "He was the greatest opportunist on any kind of playing field, seeing openings before they opened, pulling off plays lesser players can't even imagine." Robinson's intense competitiveness provided the crucial ingredient. A seasoned athlete, even in his rookie year, Robinson seemed to thrive on challenges and flourished before large audiences. At Montreal the preceding year, Dink Carroll had observed, "Robinson seems to have that same sense of the dramatic that characterized such great athletes as Babe Ruth, Red Grange, Jack Dempsey, Bobby Jones, and others of that stamp. The bigger the occasion, the more they rose to it."[31] Robinson's drive not only inspired his own dramatic performances but intimidated and demoralized enemy players. Robinson "stirred up the situation both ways," recalls St. Louis sportswriter Bill Toomey. "He stirred up the Dodgers and Dodger fans in anticipation of victory and he stirred up the resentment of fans and players on other teams. To some degree because he was black, but most of all because he beat 'em." "This guy didn't just come to play," asserts Leo Durocher, "He came to beat ya. He came to stuff the goddamn bat right up your ass."[32]

At the plate and in the field, Robinson radiated dynamic intensity, but his true genius materialized on the base paths. Sportswriters struggled to capture the striking image of Robinson in motion. They called him "the black meteor," or an "Ebony Ty Cobb," and "the Bojangles of the Basepaths." "He looks awkward, but he isn't," recorded *Time*. "He steps and starts as though turned off and on with a toggle switch. . . . Once in motion he wobbles along, elbows flying, hips swaying, shoulders rocking—creating the illusion that he will fly to pieces with every stride."[33]

"He brought a new dimension into baseball," says Al Campanis. "He brought stealing back to the days of the twenties whereas up until that time baseball had become a long-ball hitting game." But the phenomenon went beyond base stealing. Robinson's twenty-nine steals in 1947 were actually less than the league leader of the preceding year. The style of play and the design of his baserunning antics better measure the magnitude of

Robinson's achievement. He revolutionized major league baseball by inject-
ing an element of "tricky baseball," so common in the Negro Leagues. In
an age in which managers bemoaned the lost art of bunting, Robinson, in
forty-six bunt attempts, registered fourteen hits and twenty-eight sacrifices,
a phenomenal .913 success rate. His tactics often went against the time-
worn conventional wisdom of baseball. He stole and advanced extra bases
when traditional logic dictated against it. Tom Meany told the tale of a
Dodger-Giant game in 1947 when Robinson doubled with one out in a tie
game and then tagged up on a routine fly ball to center field. A Giant executive sitting next to Meany angrily denounced Robinson as a "showboat."
"That's bush stuff," exclaimed the baseball man. "With two out he's just as
valuable on second as he is on third. What's he going to do now—steal home
I suppose?" On the next pitch, Robinson did just that, putting the Dodgers
in the lead.[34]

Nor did Robinson's effectiveness require the stolen base. "He dances
and prances off base keeping the enemy infield upset and off balance, and
worrying the pitcher," reported *Time*. In Donald Honig's *Baseball: Between
the Lines,* pitchers Gene Conley and Vic Raschi, both relate incidents not
of Robinson hitting or stealing, but of his talents of distraction. "Robinson
had broken my concentration," recalls Raschi of a game in the 1949 World
Series. "I was pitching more to Robinson [on first base] than I was to [Gil]
Hodges and as a result I threw one up into Gil's power and he got the base
hit that beat me." Conley tells an almost identical tale with Carl Furillo
getting the game-winning blow. "Carl Furillo got all the headlines," says
Conley, "but I knew it was Robinson who had distracted me just enough to
hang that curve."[35]

These attributes were much in evidence in 1947, though Branch Rickey
warned, "You haven't seen Robinson yet. Maybe you won't really see him
until next year. You'll see something when he gets to bunting and running
as freely as he should."[36] Rickey did not exaggerate. Robinson did not reach
his peak as a ballplayer for another two seasons.

Many National League players attributed Robinson's 1947 success to an
unwillingness of opponents to challenge him. "Some of the fellows may
be riding Jackie, but an even greater number are going out of their way
to avoid him," commented one unidentified athlete. "They just don't want to
get involved in a close play where Jackie might be accidentally spiked or
knocked around." Several pitchers complained privately that they feared
throwing tight to Robinson to move him away from the plate, giving him
an advantage in the batter's box.[37]

There is ample evidence, however, that the majority did not adhere to
this view. "Jackie Robinson can usually count on the first pitch being right

under his nostrils," reported the Cincinnati *Enquirer* in July. " 'They're giving him the smell of leather,' as the boys say." By the time the season was half over, pitchers had hit Robinson seven times, more than any National Leaguer in the entire preceding season. Tom Meany later wrote, "Often his great reflexes kept him from being hit more often than he was. He boasted early in his career that though he might be hit often, he would never be beaned. He never was." Robinson himself, often joked with reporters about his league leading hit-by-pitch statistics. After being struck twice during his early season slump he cracked, "Since I can't buy a hit these days, they're doing me a favor." Later in the season he suggested, "Guess I just haven't learned to duck major league pitching." But neither Robinson nor most other observers doubted that the black athlete reigned as the most popular target among the league's pitchers.[38]

Opponents also tested Robinson at his first base position. Playing second at Montreal, Robinson had offered an open target for runners barreling into second base trying to break up a double play. At first base fewer opportunities for physical contact existed, but the stretch required to tag the bag exposed Robinson's leg to the runner's spikes on close plays. A novice at the position, Robinson could not always protect himself. Several sympathetic players warned Robinson that he would "have to watch his tagging foot," a flaw he readily acknowledged. But some opponents deliberately attempted to spike him, making, according one account, "a pincushion out of Robinson."[39]

Only a scattering of overt racial incidents marred Robinson's first season. On June 22 after Eddie Stanky had shattered Cincinnati pitcher Ewell Blackwell's bid for a second consecutive no-hit game, Blackwell unleashed a stream of racial epithets at Robinson, the next batter. In May, against the Cubs, who proved one of the most troublesome clubs for Robinson, shortstop Len Merullo landed on top of Robinson on a pick-off play at second base. As they untangled from the pile, Merullo deliberately kicked the black man. Robinson started to swing at the shortstop but suddenly held back. "Plenty of times I wanted to haul off when somebody insulted me for the color of my skin," Robinson told a reporter. "But I had to hold to myself. I knew I was kind of an experiment. . . . The whole thing was bigger than me."[40]

In spring training Rickey had advised Robinson, "I want you to win the friendship of people everywhere. You must be personable, you must smile, and even if they are worrying you to death, make the public think you don't mind being bothered." Robinson created precisely this image. He publicly thanked opposing players, like Hank Greenberg and Frank Gustine, who welcomed him into the league. In his "Jackie Robinson Says" column,

Robinson also diplomatically praised the St. Louis Cardinals. Robinson's obvious intelligence, self-deprecating wit, and public willingness to forgive and understand his tormentors, made him an American hero. "Throughout it all," wrote Pittsburgh sportswriter Vince Johnson, "he has remained a gentleman and a credit to the game, as well as to his race."[41]

Robinson's exemplary demeanor won over his teammates as well. In early May when Jimmy Cannon described Robinson as the "loneliest man I have ever seen in sports," his comments were not inaccurate. But they came at a time when Robinson's isolation on the Dodger squad was receding. When Robinson had joined the Dodgers reporters had described the locker room scene as one of "cool aloofness" amidst a tense atmosphere. In dealing with his teammates Robinson continued the policy that he had pursued at Montreal. "Jackie wouldn't sit with any white player that first year unless he was asked to," recalls Bobby Bragan. In part, this was a facet of Robinson's personality. "I sort of keep to myself by habit," he explained. "Even in the colored leagues I was that way."[42] But, this behavior also reflected a decision to avoid forcing himself on those who objected to his presence.

Among northern teammates, playing alongside Robinson posed few problems. For southerners, on the other hand, it often required a significant adjustment. Several players feared repercussions at home for their involuntary role in baseball integration. "I didn't know if they would spit on me or not," recalled Dixie Walker of his Alabama neighbors. "It was no secret that I was worried about my business. I had a hardware and sporting goods store back home." Pee Wee Reese later said that in family discussions, "The subject always gets around to the fact that I'm a little southern boy playing shortstop next to a Negro second baseman and in danger of being contaminated." Both Walker and Kirby Higbe, before the Dodgers traded him, received insulting letters. "I got more than a thousand letters from people down South calling me 'nigger-lover,' " writes Higbe, "telling me I ought to quit playing baseball and come home rather than play with a nigger."[43]

Robinson's relationship with some of his teammates was unpredictable. Hugh Casey, the enigmatic pitcher from Atlanta, spent hours during the early season batting balls to Robinson to help him adjust to the first base position and gently chided Robinson about his fielding after the games. Casey rushed to Robinson's defense when an opposing player spiked him. In the pitcher's Brooklyn restaurant, he displayed a picture of his black teammate and he boasted, "I'm a southerner, but I enjoyed playing with him." But Casey, a heavy drinker, could also be tactless. During a mid-season card game with Robinson and others, he exclaimed, "Got to change my luck, Jackie. Tell you what I used to do down in Georgia when my poker luck got bad. I'd just go out and rub me the teat of the biggest, blackest nigger woman I could find." He then reached over and rubbed Robinson's head. Robinson required every ounce of his self-control to restrain his rage. When Roy Campanella joined the team the following season, Casey would rarely throw the type of pitch that the black catcher called for. Three years later, the alcoholic, erratic Casey committed suicide at the age of thirty-eight.[44]

The press carefully scrutinized the interplay between Dixie Walker and Robinson. On opening day, recalls then acting manager Clyde Sukeforth, photographers urged him to arrange a picture of Robinson and Walker together. Sukeforth refused, citing Walker's business concerns. Throughout the season, if Robinson happened to be on base when Walker hit a home run, he would refrain from the customary home plate handshake, not wishing to embarrass either Walker or himself. Walker, despite his distaste for integration, never went out of his way to be unpleasant to Robinson, who later described him as a man of "innate fairness." On one occasion, the southerner approached his black teammate in the locker room and offered several batting tips. This incident prompted sportswriter Vincent X. Flaherty to report, "[Robinson's] best friend and chief advisor among the Dodgers is Dixie Walker." This represented more than a mild exaggeration. (In Robinson's personal scrapbooks this item is accompanied by the hand-written comment, "Some sportswriters fall for anything.")[45] Nonetheless, Robinson and Walker maintained good relations throughout the season.

Rickey, recognizing the strain created by this unnatural pairing, persisted in his efforts to trade the Alabama outfielder. On June 4 he arranged a deal with the Pirates. That evening, however, Pete Reiser resumed his acquaintance with the Ebbets Field wall and Rickey, suddenly short an outfielder, cancelled the deal. After the season Walker rejected an offer from the Dodger president to manage one of Brooklyn's top farm clubs and Rickey traded him to Pittsburgh, bringing the awkward Walker-Robinson relationship to a close.[46]

During the course of the 1947 season and subsequent campaigns, Robinson developed his closest friendship with Pee Wee Reese, the shortstop from Kentucky. The alliance emerged out of mutual respect and Reese's unaffected acceptance of Robinson as a teammate. Two incidents typified the Robinson-Reese rapport. In June the Dodgers stopped in Danville, Illinois, to play an exhibition game with one of their farm teams. Reese joined a golf foursome with pitcher Rex Barney, Harold Parrott, and reporter Roscoe McGowan. Robinson and Wendell Smith played behind them. At the fourth hole, Reese halted the game and invited the two blacks to merge with his foursome. As the three teammates joked and kidded each other, wrote one observer, "Reese and Barney showed, without knowing it, during the golf game that they like Robinson and he is one of them." Early in the following season in Boston, Brave bench jockeys rode Reese mercilessly for playing alongside a black man. Reese strode over to Robinson, placed his arm around his teammate's shoulder, and prepared to discuss the upcoming game. The gesture silenced the Boston bench.[47]

Reese has frequently protested that people have exaggerated his role in the Robinson drama. "You know I didn't go out of my way to be nice to you," he once told Robinson. Jackie replied, "Pee Wee, maybe that's what I appreciated most."[48]

Dan Dodson, the sociologist who assisted Rickey in his preparations for the "noble experiment," drew two prescriptions from the Dodger experience. "Don't worry about the attitudes of people who are asked to accept new members," he advised. "When relationships are predicated on the basis of goals other than integration—in the Dodger case, winning the pennant—the people involved would adjust appropriately." But equally important, according to Dodson, was an absence of coercion in interpersonal contacts. "Don't meddle with relationships between members once integration starts," he admonished. "Let members work out their relationships. Forcing relationships makes for trouble."[49]

The Dodger clubhouse in 1947 aptly demonstrated the validity of these principles. With little outside interference from club management, the Brooklyn players gradually rallied to Robinson's side. Eddie Stanky, the second baseman from Alabama, became Robinson's leading defender against the taunts, brushbacks, and spikes of opposing players. Walker, explaining his unsolicited batting tips to Robinson, related, "I saw things in this light. When you're on a team, you got to pull together to win."[50]

Robinson's acceptance by the Dodger players occurred with surprising rapidity, even more so than at Montreal. Within six weeks, says Bragan, the barriers had fallen. Eating, talking, and playing cards with Robinson seemed natural. Reporters traveling with the Dodgers agreed. By the end of May, Smith could report "There is more warmth toward him these days in both the dugout and the clubhouse." Toward the end of the season, wrote white sportswriter Gordon Cobbledick, the Dodgers viewed Robinson with "something approaching genuine warmth and and affection."[51]

III

The evolution of Dodger attitudes toward Robinson reflected a process occurring throughout the nation. Robinson's aggressive play, his innate sense of dignity, and his outward composure under extreme duress captivated the

American people. Only Joe Louis, among black celebrities, had aroused the public imagination as Robinson did in the summer of 1947. Robinson's charismatic personality inspired not merely sympathy and acceptance, but sincere adulation from both whites and blacks alike.

To black America, Jackie Robinson appeared as a savior, a Moses leading his people out of the wilderness. "When times got really hard, really tough, He always send you somebody," said Ernest J. Gaines's fictional heroine Miss Jane Pittman. "In the Depression it was tough on everybody, but twice as hard on the colored, and He sent us Joe [Louis] . . . after the war, He sent us Jackie."[52]

Thousands of blacks thronged to the ball parks wherever he appeared. At games in the National League's southernmost cities blacks swelled attendance. Many traveled hundreds of miles to see their hero in action. The Philadelphia *Afro-American* reported that orders by blacks for tickets for the first Dodger-Phillies series had "poured in" from Baltimore, Washington, and other cities along the eastern seaboard. For games in Cincinnati, a "Jackie Robinson special" train ran from Norfolk, Virginia, stopping en route to pick up black fans.[53]

Throughout the season black newspapers continued to campaign for proper crowd behavior, and the deportment of the Afro-American spectators drew widespread praise. Blacks nonetheless found it difficult to restrain their enthusiasm. Robinson himself wrote that while the sight of so many blacks pleased him, their indiscriminate cheering sometimes proved embarrassing. "The colored fans applauded Jackie every time he wiggled his ears," complained one black sportswriter after a game in Cincinnati.[54]

As a boy, white columnist Mike Royko attended Robinson's first game at Wrigley Field in Chicago. Twenty-five years later he described the event:

> in 1947, few blacks were seen in downtown Chicago, much less up on the white North side at a Cub game.
>
> That day they came by the thousands, pouring off the north-bound ELS and out of their cars.
>
> They didn't wear baseball-game clothes. They had on church clothes and funeral clothes—suits, white shirts, ties, gleaming shoes, and straw hats. I've never seen so many straw hats.
>
> . . . The whites tried to look as if nothing unusual was happening, while the blacks tried to look casual and dignified. So everybody looked ill at ease.
>
> For the most part it was probably the first time they had been so close to each other in such large numbers.

When Robinson batted, recalls Royko, "They applauded, long, rolling applause. A tall middle-aged black man stood next to me, a smile of almost painful joy on his face, beating his palms together so hard they must have hurt." When Robinson struck out, "the low moan was genuine."[55]

The scenes at the ball parks represented only the surface level of black adulation of Robinson. "No matter what the nature of the gathering, a horse race, a church meeting, a ball game," explained Sam Lacy, "the universal question is: 'How'd Jackie make out today?' " In many cities pages of advertisements in the black press heralded Robinson's appearances as black businesses sought to identify themselves with the new hero. Clothing stores advised blacks to "Dress Sporty for the Jackie Robinson Game"; bars and nightclubs suggested they "Drop in after the game." Robinson's visit, reported the Philadelphia *Afro-American*, "will give the city something of a holiday setting and night spot owners were twirling their thumbs in happy anticipation of a boom in business."[56]

The idolatry even reached into regions where major league baseball remained an exercise in imagination. Bernice Franklin, a woman from Tyronza, Arkansas, an all-black town, wrote to Robinson: "I own and operate a rural general store and right now the farmers are gathering for your game this afternoon. . . . There is no greater thrill than a broadcast of a Dodgers' ball game. . . . We are so proud of you."[57] Black Americans affixed their loyalty not only to Robinson, but to the Brooklyn Dodgers as well. For many years, blacks throughout the nation would be Dodger fans, in honor of the team that had broken the color barrier.

Robinson's popularity was not confined to blacks; white fans also stormed baseball arenas to view the new sensation. At the start of the season the St. Louis edition of the Pittsburgh *Courier* warned its readers that tickets for the Dodger games were "going like hot cakes and it isn't the Sepia fans that are buying the bulk of them." In Brooklyn, the fans rallied behind Robinson "350 percent," recalls Joe Bostic. "They were with him, not just Jackie, they were with the idea. He became a state of mind in a community that was already baseball-oriented." After the games at Ebbets Field, fans waited for more than an hour for Jackie to appear. "Many wanted autographs and others simply wanted to touch him," reported Sam Lacy. "It was just as though [he] had suddenly been transformed into some kind of matinee idol."[58]

Awards flooded in from a wide variety of sources ranging from the Freedom Awards from the United Negro and Allied Veterans of America to the "Negro Father of the Year Award" presented by the National Father's Day Committee. Local writers composed poems in his honor. *Time* magazine published a lengthy story on the Dodger rookie sensation, highlighting his ebony face in a sea of white baseballs on the cover.[59]

As in Montreal the preceding season, Robinson found that his fame interfered with the normal processes of life. Wendell Smith reported, "He seldom gets a chance to eat a peaceful meal on the train. . . . He seldom has a moment to himself. He is the target of well-wishers, autograph hounds and indiscreet politicians who would bask in his glory to win prestige for themselves. They call him on the telephone at all hours of the morning or night."[60]

The volume of letters that Robinson received also reflected his popularity. From the day of his promotion to the Dodgers through the end of the World Series, each day brought "piles of mail."[61] The Dodgers hired a special secretary to handle his correspondence and Arthur Mann composed answers to all letters, both the inspirational and the insulting. Robinson reviewed, sometimes revised, and signed each response.

The Robinsons and the Dodgers disposed of most letters containing threats and insults, but a sample of the vitriolic language and personal attacks survive in letters to Branch Rickey. W. J. "Buck" Blankenship of Jackson, California, wrote criticizing the Durocher suspension, but added, "The blow that the commissioner dealt was not as severe as the one that the Brooklyn club handed itself when it signed Jackie Robinson." A Philadelphia writer told Rickey, "You should be ashamed of yourself. . . . If you want to do something for the negro, why not give some educated negro *your* job," and added, "The next time you take a shower get a negro to take one with you or does that just apply to some other man's son?" After asking Rickey if he would want his children to marry a Negro, the disgruntled critic concluded, "Well Good-Nite Dictator and Happy Dreams." Drew Linard Smith, an attorney from New Orleans, voiced similar sentiments:

> Your decision to break a big league tradition by playing a Negro on the Brooklyn team is indeed deplorable. In fact, it is inconceivable that any white man would force a Negro on other white men as you have done. . . . I tell you Rickey anything the Negro touches he ruins and your club will be no exception. . . . The first time Robinson steps out of line you will see what I mean. He will inevitably do this too because he will be egged on by a militant and aggressive Negro press forever propagandizing for the amalgamation of the races.

This type of mail also surfaced in other places. A Columbus, Ohio, newspaper reported that it had received a "surprisingly large" number of letters from people favoring the threatened player strike. Commissioner Chandler heard from well-known vaudeville comic Bert Wheeler. Wheeler wrote that although he was a cousin of Pee Wee Reese and used to attend many games, "Then along comes a nigger, so I wrote to Pee Wee and told him I would never come to another Dodger game as long as the Nigger was on the team."[62]

The opprobrium heaped upon the central actors in the integration drama reflects the stereotypes and the deep-seated prejudice of the era. But the torrent of sympathy and acclaim which Robinson inspired drowned out these negative sentiments. The surviving sampling of letters to Robinson reveals the thoughts of people from all sections of the country and in many walks of life: a deputy sheriff from Detroit, a black teenager from Johnson City, Tennessee, an accountant from Ontario, Canada, and a dry cleaner from Bellevue, Ohio. Robinson heard from doctors, ministers, lawyers, and college professors; from black and white students at every educational level; from a magazine editor in Rockford, Illinois and the president of a life insurance company in Durham, North Carolina. Twenty-four patients at the Oak Knoll Tuberculosis Sanitarium in Mackinaw, Illinois, wrote in support. Most letters, particularly after the early weeks of the season, contained words of advice and encouragement and reflected the impact of Robinson's ordeal upon the American public.

The letters often displayed a touching warmth, as people confessed, "This is the first fan letter I've written" or identified not only their names, but small facts about their lives. "I'm no autograph hunter, only an old doctor," wrote one man. "I am white, 76, played college football, but never baseball. I am a Methodist, ex-school teacher, ex-prison warden," revealed another. At times the letters could get too personal. A twenty-year-old winner of the Miss Akron beauty contest professed her love for Robinson and invited him to visit her. "I know that you are a married man and that you have a son," she admitted, "but you don't have to be an angel." Robinson's response, signed "yours in reproof," advised the woman, "When I married Mrs. Robinson, I exchanged vows to love, honor, and cherish her for the rest of my life. 'Honor' means just that to me and any sneaking, skulking escapade would destroy the very thing that enables me to hold my head up high."

Several correspondents described their own experiences when inserted into situations as the sole representative of their race. "I know what you are going through because I went through the same thing in a much smaller way," wrote G. Gilbert Smith of Jersey City. "I was the first Negro machinist in a big shop during the war. They did all the little dirty underhanded things to me that they must be doing to you." Matt Kirwan of Bellevue, Ohio, related his experiences as the only white employee at a dry-cleaning plant in Fort Lauderdale. "At first the colored boys didn't speak to me. I didn't know what was wrong," wrote Kirwan. "When we got acquainted and they found out I was from the north, I didn't have any better friends in Florida."

Robinson's early season difficulties brought numerous letters denouncing the Philadelphia players and the accused St. Louis strikers. "I happen to be a white southerner," wrote a man from Richmond on May 19, "but I just want you to know that not all us southerners are SOB's." A letter from Corpus Christi, Texas, dated May 11 advised him to "Stay in there and fight, Jackie. For there will be others to follow you in the Big Leagues if you are successful." A midshipman at Annapolis wrote of Robinson's tormentors, "personally, I'd like to paste them on the jaw. I think it's a shame that we have such people existing in *our* country."

Correspondents repeatedly reminded the black pioneer of his responsibilities to his race and to the United States. "Whether colored men are athletes, preachers, educators, or scientists," advised a city councilman from Grove, Kansas, "if they are leaders in their line they have moral responsibilities to their race." Harold MacDowell of Newark informed Robinson that "there are thousands of American youngsters of your complexion and my different complexion who are going to learn their first lesson in sociology from your experience. . . . Remember you are on a stage all the time. Your mistakes will be attributed to all Negroes."

Robinson's correspondence reflected the changes in racial attitudes that he inspired. His dynamic presence instilled a sense of pride in black Americans and led many whites to reassess their own feelings. The affection for Robinson grew so widespread that at the year's end voters in an annual public opinion poll named him the second most popular man in America. Only Bing Crosby registered more votes.[63]

IV

Toward the close of the 1947 season, the Philadelphia *Tribune,* a black newspaper, ran a playful story headlined, PAPERS PROVE JACKIE ROBINSON ISN'T WHITE. Sportswriters, noted the *Tribune,* repeatedly referred to Robinson as the "nimble Negro" or the "Negro flash" or myriad variations on that theme. John Drebinger of the New York *Times* referred to Robinson in this manner five times in one story. "It was so dark in the ninth inning," offered a Cleveland writer, "Jackie Robinson was only a blur."[64]

The *Tribune* story spotlighted a significant truth about Robinson's rookie season. Despite his growing acceptance, Robinson remained an oddity in organized baseball. Throughout the season, even after he had established himself as a bona fide major league player, Robinson confronted difficulties and challenges unknown to other athletes. The burdens of racial pioneering and the restrictions imposed on his behavior still rested heavily on his shoulders.

On the road, hotel accommodations remained problematical. Throughout the Jim Crow era the issue of housing black players had loomed as a major objection to integration. Even in many northern cities, the better hotels did not allow blacks. In border cities like St. Louis and Cincinnati segregation remained the rule. Rickey and his advisers had determined that the Dodgers would not challenge local customs. "The position was taken that the Brooklyn club could not assume the responsibility for discrimination in these places," explained Dodson.[65] Where objections to Robinson's presence were raised, other arrangements would be made. If another hotel would accept the entire team, the Dodgers would alter their future plans.

In Boston, Pittsburgh, and Chicago, Robinson had no problems. In Philadelphia and St. Louis, officials barred him and he stayed at Negro hotels. The Dodgers anticipated that Robinson would not be allowed to stay with the team in Cincinnati, but the Netherlands-Plaza Hotel accepted him under the provision that he eat his meals in his room so as not to offend other guests.

The Dodgers dared not tamper with one taboo—the prohibition on interracial roommates. One of the most common taunts that Brooklyn players heard from rival bench jockeys and fans was the charge that they were "sleeping with Robinson." In 1947 Robinson usually roomed with Wendell Smith, who traveled with the team as both a reporter and a Dodger employee.

While Jackie toured National League cities, Rachel Robinson unobtrusively learned the life of a baseball wife. She spent most of her days housecleaning, toting the considerable amount of laundry generated by Jackie, Jr., to the laundromat, and rushing off to the ball games which she never missed. "We were trying to make it as a family and that was as important and problematic as dealing with the baseball scene which was much more structured by other people," recalls Rachel. The threatening mail and crank letters unsettled them, she says, "But it wasn't in a period of kidnappings or things like that so we never worried about the baby being hurt, or our being accosted too much except by some crazy or irrational person who might shoot from the stands."[66]

Rachel's relationship with the Dodger wives paralleled Jackie's experience. For the first month of the season, she did not know any of them, as the players' wives did not sit in a single location. "One day a young girl asked if I was Mrs. Robinson," Rachel told a reporter. "When I said I was, she introduced herself as Mrs. Clyde King. After the game she took me down under the stands, showed me where the wives usually wait for their husbands and introduced me to the other girls." By early July, Rachel recounted, "When they gossip I join right in and gossip with them." The response of the Dodger fans also encouraged Rachel. "The fans don't realize I'm his wife," she explained, "So I hear what they really think. It's wonderful the way they're pulling for Jackie to make good."[67]

Throughout the first half of the season, the Robinsons lived on a tight budget. Despite his magnificent performance and ticket-selling feats, Robinson received only $5,000, the major league minimum. Baseball rules forbade any mid-season bonuses or salary increases. In addition, Rickey's protective prohibition on endorsements forced Robinson to turn down many lucrative offers. For the first month of the season, the family continued to live in the cramped confines of the McAlpin Hotel. In May they moved to Brooklyn where they shared a tenement apartment with a "widow courting." The tenement was filled with cockroaches and the widow and her suitor "occupied the living room all the time so Jack and I were stuck back in this little bedroom the whole season."[68]

While their living conditions remained poor, the Robinsons' financial position improved. Rickey lifted the ban on advertisements in mid-season and Robinson's smiling face began to appear in New York and national black newspapers promoting Bond Bread, Turfee Hats, and although he did not smoke, Old Gold cigarettes. On September 23, Rickey allowed the athlete's admirers to stage a Jackie Robinson Day at Ebbets Field. The chairman of the event vowed that the gifts would add up to "as much or more than any player has received on a similar occasion." Well-wishers bestowed an estimated $10,000 worth of goods on Jackie and Rachel, including a Cadillac, a television set, and a chest of silver. Contributions came from Harlem and other black communities throughout the nation.[69]

Robinson also received numerous money-making propositions for the winter and fall. He signed up for a theatrical tour of New York, Washington, and Chicago, traveling with three vaudeville acts. For each of his appearances Robinson would receive a minimum of $2,500. The articulate athlete became a popular radio guest and signed contracts to co-author an autobiography and to star in a Hollywood movie. Sources estimated that despite his low salary, Robinson's income for 1947 exceeded that of all major leaguers with the exception of Bob Feller and Hank Greenberg.[70]

On the field, meanwhile, Robinson had emerged as one of the crucial figures in the Dodger pennant drive. The Dodgers moved into first place in July, but in mid-August the Cardinals, recovered from their disastrous start, challenged for the league lead. The two clubs met at Ebbets Field on August 18 and Robinson again found himself surrounded by controversy. In the opening game of the series Cardinal outfielder Joe Medwick spiked

Robinson on the left foot, leaving a bloody gash. Two days later Robinson barely removed his leg in time to avoid Enos Slaughter's spikes on one occasion, but on another, Slaughter slashed Robinson on the left leg, dropping the injured athlete to the ground.

Observers disagreed as to whether the spiking was deliberate. Bill Corum of the New York *Journal-American* called it "as normal a play as anybody, whose imagination wasn't working too fast, ever saw." Robert Burnes, in the St. Louis *Gazette Democrat* argued, "If Slaughter had been trying to 'nail' Robinson, you can be sure Jackie wouldn't have been in condition to stay in the game." Slaughter, in a statement that must have surprised most National Leaguers, avowed, "I've never deliberately spiked anyone in my life. Anybody who does, don't belong in baseball." The incident, however, infuriated Robinson's teammates. Noting that the cut on his leg was located eight inches above the ankle on the outside of his leg, one player asserted, "How in the hell could Slaughter hit him way up on the side of the leg like that unless he meant to do it?"[71] Several Dodger players threatened "dire consequences" if the Cardinals continued their attacks on Robinson.

The Dodgers and Cardinals split their four-game series and Rickey, fearing his club might not withstand the St. Louis drive without pitching help, turned to the Negro Leagues for assistance. On August 23 he flew to Memphis to personally inspect right-handed pitcher Dan Bankhead of the Memphis Red Sox. After watching Bankhead strike out eleven men, Rickey purchased his contract from the Red Sox.[72]

One of five baseball-playing brothers (Sam, the oldest was one of the finest shortstops of the age), Bankhead came to the Dodgers touted as the "next Satchel Paige" and the "colored Feller." One report labelled him "the fastest pitcher in baseball, black or white." Bankhead also batted well and boasted a league-leading .385 average in the Negro American League. Despite these superlative notices, Rickey would have preferred to give Bankhead, like Robinson, some seasoning in the minors. But, explained the Mahatma, "I can't help myself. We need pitchers and we need them badly."[73]

Two days later Bankhead joined the Dodgers in Pittsburgh where he received "a terrific workout from photographers and newshounds." When the Pirates chased Dodger starter Hal Gregg from the mound in the second inning, manager Shotton decided to rush an admittedly nervous Bankhead into the fray. The Pirates, wrote Red Smith, "launched Bankhead by breaking a Louisville Slugger over his prow."[74] They pounded the first black pitcher in the major leagues for eight runs and ten hits in three innings. Bankhead's only solace came at the plate. He slammed a home run in his initial at bat, the first National League pitcher to accomplish that feat.

Bankhead did not prove the savior of the Dodger pitching staff. He appeared in only three more games with indifferent success and the Dodgers dispatched him to the minors for two years before recalling him in 1950.

Even without Bankhead's help the Dodgers continued to stave off the Cardinal pennant bid. When they arrived in St. Louis on September 11 for the final meetings between the two clubs, the Dodgers led the second-place Cardinals by four and a half games. The series marked the last opportunity for St. Louis to bring the Brooklyn club within striking distance.

As in the earlier series the first game was marred by a spiking incident. In the second inning Cardinal catcher Joe Garagiola caught Robinson on the heel. "I don't think Garagiola did it intentionally," Robinson said after the game, "but this makes three times in two games with the Cardinals that it's happened. He cut my shoe all to pieces." When Robinson came to the plate in the third inning he made a remark to Garagiola, who responded with a racial slur. For the first time during the long season, Robinson lost his temper. He and Garagiola "engaged in an angry teeth-to-teeth exchange" which brought coach Sukeforth out of the dugout to restrain Robinson, and required intervention by umpire Beans Reardon. *Time* magazine wrote of the episode, "That was the end of it; no fisticuffs on the field, no rioting in the stands. But it was a sign that Jackie had established himself as a big leaguer. He had earned what comes free to every other player; the right to squawk."[75]

Time's celebration of Robinson's acceptance was premature. It would be another year before Robinson could freely retaliate against his tormentors. The outburst against Garagiola merely underscores the pent-up anger and frustration that gathered within Robinson as he submerged his naturally combative instincts and channeled them into his performances. After the spiking Robinson powered a two-run home run to lead the Dodgers to a 4-3 victory. The following night Robinson had two hits and scored two runs in a losing cause and then stroked three hits in the series finale. "In the field," wrote Dan Daniel, "Robinson's tempo was a gradual crescendo which attained the truly spectacular in the eighth inning of the last game," when the rookie first baseman hurled himself into the Brooklyn dugout to make a "brilliant catch" of a foul pop-up.[76] The Dodgers won, 8-7, virtually assuring themselves the pennant.

"This week as the Dodgers raced toward the finish, seven games ahead," attested *Time* magazine in its cover story on Robinson, "it was at least arguable that Robinson had furnished the margin of victory." Dixie Walker agreed. "No other ballplayer on this club, with the possible exception of [catcher] Bruce Edwards, has done more to put the Dodgers up in the race than Robinson has," claimed the once recalcitrant Walker who, despite his own personal ordeal, delivered another .300 plus campaign. Another skeptic also surrendered when J. Taylor Spink and the *Sporting News* awarded Robinson the Rookie of the Year Award. The judges, wrote Spink, had "sifted only stark baseball values. . . . The sociological experiment that Robinson represented, the trail blazing that he did, the barriers he broke down, did not enter into the decision."[77] Spink personally flew to Brooklyn to present the award to Robinson at the pennant-clinching celebration at Borough Hall.

Throughout most of the season Robinson maintained his batting average over .300, but a late season slump after the Dodgers had clinched the pennant dropped him to .297. He finished second in the league in runs scored and first in stolen bases. Robinson also led the Dodgers in home runs with 12. Despite his reputation for being injury prone, Robinson appeared in 151 of the 154 contests, more games than anyone else on the club.

Robinson's performance also benefited other National League teams. Throughout the season fans continued to watch him in record numbers. At Pittsburgh in late July spectators overflowed the stands and lined up along the outfield wall. The grounds crew posted ropes to establish the boundaries of the playing field.[78] By the season's end Robinson had established new attendance marks in every city except Cincinnati. Thanks to Robinson, National League attendance in 1947 increased by more than three quarters of a million people above the all-time record set in 1946. Five teams set new season records, including the Dodgers, who attracted over 1.8 millon fans for the first, and last, time in the club's Brooklyn history.

In October the Dodgers met the New York Yankees in the World Series. The 1947 series ranks as one of the most thrilling in baseball history. Fans remember it for Bill Bevens's near no-hitter in the fourth game, Al Gionfriddo's spectacular catch of Joe Dimaggio's line drive in the sixth contest, and the tightly drawn struggles in five of the seven meetings. The Dodgers challenged the Yankees into the last game before succumbing to the effective relief pitching of Joe Page. For Robinson personally, the World Series marked an anticlimax. His presence in the Fall Classic seemed natural, rather than extraordinary. On the field he performed solidly, if not spectacularly. Robinson batted well, hitting .259 despite being robbed of three hits, and he drove in three runs. His baserunning bedeviled Yankee pitchers and catchers and his fielding was flawless. But even Wendell Smith concluded of the Series, "If we must get racial conscious about it in determining the wreath of heroism, we'll have to pass the laurels to the players of Italian extraction," noting the exploits of Dimaggio, Gionfriddo, and Cookie Lavagetto. "In short, it's been a great series," attested Smith, "No matter who your parents were."[79]

V

The saga of Robinson's first season has become a part of American mythology—sacrosanct in its memory, magnificent in its retelling. It remains a drama which thrills and fascinates, combining the central themes of the illusive Great American Novel: the undertones of Horatio Alger, the interracial comradery of nineteenth-century fiction, the sage advisor and his youthful apprentice, and the rugged and righteous individual confronting the angry mob. It is a tale of courage, heroics, and triumph. Epic in its proportions, the Robinson legend has persevered—and will continue to do so—because the myth, which rarely deviates from reality, fits our national perceptions of fair play and social progress. The emotional impact of Robinson's challenge requires no elaboration or enhancement. Few works of fiction could impart its power.

Indeed, so total was Robinson's triumph, so dominant his personality, that few people have questioned the strategies and values that underpinned Branch Rickey's "noble experiment." Rickey based his blueprint for integration both on his assessment of the racial realities of postwar America and his flair for the dramatic. He believed that the United States was ready for integrated baseball, but the balance remained so precarious that the breakthrough had to be carefully planned and cautiously advanced. Americans—both black and white, players and fans—needed time to accommodate themselves to the idea of blacks in baseball. The slightest false step, Rickey concluded, would delay the entry of nonwhites into the national pastime indefinitely. Rickey felt that the primary burden of this undertaking had to rest on the shoulders of a lone standard-bearer, upon whose success or failure the fate of the entire venture would be determined. The fact that this gradual process accrued publicity and added to the drama was never central to Rickey's thinking, but rather a natural component of his personality. Rickey conceived of schemes on the grand scale and enacted them accordingly.

Most accounts of the Robinson story unquestionably assimilate Rickey's reasoning, and several conclusions logically evolve from this: had Rickey not shattered the color line in 1945, the barrier would have remained erect for years to come; the success of integration depended upon the Mahatma's elaborate preparations and the selection of one central figure to spearhead the campaign; Robinson himself not only appears indispensable, but in most accounts emerges as the sole black athlete who could have withstood the pressures; and, had Robinson faltered, this setback would have delayed the cause of integration indefinitely. Most contemporary observers of these events shared these conceptions.

The credit for banishing Jim Crow from baseball belongs solely to Branch Rickey and the strategy that he pursued must be judged overwhelmingly effective. Yet the magnitude of his success has eradicated from memory the alternatives that existed. Rickey indeed was the only owner in 1945 with the courage and foresight to sign a black player. But with public pressure mounting, particularly in the New York area, it seems likely that political events would have forced the issue within the next few years. Rickey's action and his presentation of the Robinson case as an "experiment" actually relieved the pressure on other owners and allowed them to delay while awaiting the outcome of Rickey's gamble. It is also likely that if Rickey had not set the precedent, Bill Veeck would have. Veeck purchased the Cleveland Indians in 1946, and, given his background, he most likely would have tapped the Negro Leagues. The color line in baseball faced imminent extinction and probably would have collapsed by 1950, even if Rickey had not courageously engineered that collapse.

Rickey's preparations, in retrospect, also appear overelaborate and unnecessary. The Dodgers might have signed Robinson or another black player and immediately placed him on the Dodger roster with few adverse effects, or they might have launched wholesale signings of black players throughout the farm system and allowed the best to play their way to the major leagues. In subsequent years, the Indians pursued this strategy with great effect. Cleveland, of course, enjoyed the benefit of Robinson's prior success. Nonetheless, their less cautious tactics proved as successful as Rickey's maneuvers in the long run.

The Rickey blueprint placed tremendous pressure upon Robinson, his standard-bearer. Robinson's response to this challenge inspired a legend. His playing skills, intelligence, and competitive flair made Robinson the perfect path breaker. Still, did others exist who could have duplicated his feat? Unquestionably, many black athletes possessed major league talent, but could they have performed adequately under the intense pressure and retained their composure amidst insults? Former Negro League players differ on this matter. "I couldn't have done it," says Joe Black. "I might have taken it for a few days, or maybe a week, but then I'd have grabbed one of them in the dugout runway or outside the ballpark and popped him . . . and right there Mr. Rickey's whole program would have gone down the drain."[80] Other black players, however, argue that they could, and did, play in racially charged situations. Baseball was their profession, one which they plied under various conditions throughout the Americas. During the next decade, other blacks re-created Robinson's ordeal in different minor leagues; racial pressures chased few from the game.

Roy Campanella, following in Robinson's immediate wake, blazed an

alternate, but nonetheless effective trail. "Roy was a calm man," says Don
Newcombe. "He could withstand that kind of pressure. He was just dogged
enough to really stick with it."[81] Rickey might have introduced Robinson
and Campanella together, thereby relieving the pressures endured by a
lone pioneer and increasing the chances of success. It is interesting to specu-
late on what Rickey would have done had Robinson failed. Would he have
given up and cut Campanella, already acknowledged as one of baseball's
best catchers, adrift? Or, would Rickey have extended his experiment?

But Jackie Robinson did not fail and Campanella and the others who
followed benefited from his example. And in Robinson, Rickey had uncovered not only an outstanding baseball player, but a figure of charisma and
leadership. For blacks, Robinson became a symbol of pride and dignity; to
whites, he represented a type of black man far removed from prevailing
stereotypes, whom they could not help but respect. He would not fade into
obscurity after retirement as most athletes do. Robinson remained an active
advocate of civil rights causes and Afro-American interests. Other blacks
might have sufficed in his role, concedes Dick Young, who often feuded
with him, "But none, I believe, would have done it quite so well as Jackie
Robinson."[82]

The true significance of Jackie Robinson and his spectacular triumph in
1947 is reflected in the recollections of Dodger announcer Red Barber.
Robinson's arrival had posed a moral dilemma for Barber, but he accepted
the black man, "as a man, as a ballplayer. I didn't resent him and I didn't
crusade for him. I broadcast the ball." Both Robinson and Rickey expressed
their appreciation for Barber's tactful handling of the matter, but, writes
Barber in his autobiography, "I know that if I have achieved any understanding and tolerance in my life . . . if I have been able to follow a little
better the great second commandment, which is to love thy neighbor, it all
stems from this . . . I thank Jackie Robinson. He did far more for me than
I did for him."[83]

Jackie Robinson signs a contract to become the first black in organized baseball in the twentieth century, October 23, 1945. Looking on are (l to r): Hector Racine, president of the Montreal Royals; Branch Rickey, Jr., director of the Brooklyn Dodgers farm system; and Romeo Gavreau, vice-president of the Royals. (*Wide World Photos*)

Jackie and Rachel Robinson as newlyweds, 1946. Two weeks after their February 10 wedding in Los Angeles, they traveled to Florida to launch the "great experiment." (*Wide World Photos*)

Jackie Robinson touches home plate after hitting a three-run home run in his second at-bat in organized baseball, Opening Day, 1946. Montreal outfielder George Shuba shakes his hand. (*United Press International Photo*)

Robinson posed for this picture at the door of the Dodger clubhouse at Ebbets Field in April, 1947, shortly before his promotion to the Brooklyn club. (*United Press International Photo*)

Montreal Manager Clay Hopper bids farewell to Jackie Robinson, who has just been promoted to the Brooklyn Dodgers, April, 1947. (*United Press International Photo*)

Jackie Robinson and Philadelphia Phillies Manager Ben Chapman posed for this photograph after Chapman had been reprimanded by Commissioner Chandler for hurling racial insults at Robinson, May 9, 1947. (*United Press International Photo*)

A frequent target of brushback pitches, Robinson is sent to first base after being hit on the left arm in a game against the Pittsburgh Pirates in 1947. (*United Press International Photo*)

Willard Brown at Yankee Stadium in 1947 awaits his
turn at bat in the St. Louis Brown dugout. (*Keystone
Pictures Inc.*)

Cleveland Indian Manager Lou Boudreau congratulates Larry Doby
on his fifth home run of the 1948 season, May 10, 1948. (*United
Press International Photo*)

Cleveland Indian pitcher
Bob Feller welcomes his
old barnstorming rival
Satchel Paige to the ma-
jor leagues, July, 1948.
(*United Press Interna-
tional Photo*)

Shortstop Artie Wilson
in his Birmingham Black
Baron uniform. Wilson
later starred in the Pa-
cific Coast League and
appeared briefly with
the New York Giants in
1951. (*FPG*)

Jackie Robinson steals home against the Boston Braves, August 22, 1948. (*United Press International Photo*)

Montreal Royal outfielder Sam Jethroe connects for a home run against the Baltimore Orioles, 1949. (*Wide World Photos*)

Bob Thurman and Art Taborn joined the Newark Bears in the New York Yankee farm system in 1949. According to Thurman, Taborn's light complexion prompted teammates to ask, "Where's the other colored player?" (*FPG*)

Former Negro League great Ray Dandridge starred for the Minneapolis Millers from 1949-51, but the New York Giants never promoted him to the major leagues. (*FPG*)

Reunited on the Brooklyn Dodgers, pitcher Don Newcombe (right) and catcher Roy Campanella celebrate Newcombe's third consecutive shutout, September 2, 1949. (*United Press International Photo*)

Branch Rickey, in a characteristic pose, confers with (l to r): Gil Hodges, Gene Hermanski, and Jackie Robinson, before the 1949 World Series. (*United Press International Photos*)

NOTE
WE HAVE ALREADY
GOT RID
OF SEVERAL
LIKE YOU
ONE WAS FOUND IN RIVER
JUST RECENTLY

ROBINSON
WE ARE GOING
TO KILL YOU
IF YOU ATTEMP
TO ENTER A
BALL GAME AT
CROSLEY FIELD
THE 🏃🏃🏃 TRAVELERS

This letter, one of the many death threats received by Robinson, arrived before a doubleheader in Cincinnati on May 22, 1951. Robinson responded with a home run in the first game. (*United Press International Photo*)

Baseball's first all-black outfield—Monte Irvin, Willie Mays, and Hank Thompson—appeared in the 1951 World Series for the New York Giants. (*United Press International Photo*)

In a familiar scene, Robinson argues with umpire Al Barlick after being picked off second base in a 1952 game against the Giants. (*United Press International Photo*)

Luke Easter demonstrates his powerful swing in a 1952 Cleveland Indian intrasquad game in Tucson, Arizona. (*Wide World Photos*)

The Milwaukee Braves jubilantly carry Hank Aaron off the field after his eleventh-inning home run against the St. Louis Cardinals clinched the 1957 pennant. (*Wide World Photos*)

III

EXTRA INNINGS

II

Remember, All Our Boys
Can't Be a Robinson

*Just remember that they play with a lit-
tle white ball and a stick of wood up
here just like they did in your league.*

Cleveland Indian President Bill Veeck,
advising Larry Doby, the first black
player in the American League, 1947[1]

I

Surveying the success of his "noble experiment" in late June 1947, Branch
Rickey predicted, "In the near distant future I expect this thing to take its
natural course. The signing of a Negro will be no more than the news of a
white boy."[2] Twenty months had passed since Rickey had signed Jackie
Robinson, a period of undisputed success. During that span no other major
league owners had followed Rickey's lead. But the Mahatma's optimism was
not unfounded. He knew that within a matter of days, another team would
abandon racial restrictions and that both he and Robinson would be isolated no more.

On July 5 Bill Veeck, the ebullient owner of the Cleveland Indians,
announced that he had purchased the contract of Larry Doby from the
Newark Eagles, thus breaking the color barrier in the American League.
The source of this development came as no surprise to the baseball world.
Ever since Veeck had acquired the Indians the preceding year, observers
had considered him the most likely candidate to join Rickey in the hiring of
blacks. Few people in 1947 were aware of Veeck's wartime effort to buy
the Phillies and stock the club with Negro League players, but everyone
knew of his iconoclastic penchant for baseball promotion. "It seems that all
my life I have been fighting against the status quo, against the tyranny of
fossilized majority rule," Veeck wrote in his 1962 autobiography.[3] At the
age of twenty-seven he had taken over a bankrupt minor league franchise

in Milwaukee. Supplementing the traditional entertainment on the field with fireworks, clowns, acrobatics, and giveaways, Veeck resuscitated baseball in the city. Five years later in 1946, he unleashed the same innovative approach in Cleveland and attendance immediately skyrocketed. Through it all, Veeck never lost sight of the ultimate goal of a successful baseball franchise: fielding a winning team. This commitment impelled him to sign Doby. "I do not know Veeck's opinion about Negroes," Rickey later stated, "[but] he would be the first one in baseball to embrace any innovation, and therefore I would accept him as the one to hire a Negro quicker than anyone I can think of; not because of race, not because of grappling with a social problem. . . . He would not let any tradition interfere with his policy of winning a pennant for the Indians."[4]

"When I came to Cleveland, I was almost sure I was going to sign a Negro player," Veeck revealed in his autobiography. Veeck realized the potential box office appeal of black athletes but ranked that as a secondary consideration. "We were drawing better than Brooklyn," he argues. "That wasn't a factor. I simply couldn't find, at those prices, a ballplayer with similar talent."[5]

Nonetheless, admits Veeck, "I moved slowly, carefully, perhaps even timidly." Although the Cleveland Browns football team had integrated the preceding year with few problems, Veeck feared adverse reaction among local residents. "If Jackie Robinson was the ideal man to break the color line, Brooklyn was the ideal place," he explains. "I wasn't that sure about Cleveland."[6] As his first preparatory move, Veeck hired Lou Jones, a black public relations man, to work for the Indians. He assigned Jones to meet with black community leaders and lay the groundwork among Cleveland's black population. Jones also would serve as a "companion and buffer" for the athlete he selected.

Despite his reputation for boldness, Veeck felt reluctant to sign more than one player. "I felt I had to be in a position to extricate the club fairly easily in case we ran into too many problems," he wrote. To avert charges of signing a black man as a "publicity gimmick," Veeck determined to make his choice based on the long-run, rather than the short-term interests of the Indians. "I had informed the scouts that I wasn't necessarily looking for the best player in the Negro Leagues, but for the player with the best long-term potential."[7]

In Veeck's discussions with black sportswriters and other Negro League observers, they repeatedly mentioned Larry Doby as the top young prospect.[8] Cleveland scouts confirmed this opinion. The twenty-two-year-old Doby was a native of South Carolina. Following the death of his father, when Larry was only eight, he and his mother moved to Paterson, New

Jersey. At East Side High School, Doby became a spectacular four-letter athlete, good enough to earn a basketball scholarship at Long Island University under famed coach Clair Bee. Doby attended L.I.U. for three months before signing with the Newark Eagles in 1943. Shortly thereafter, he enlisted in the navy, where he batted .346 for the all-black Great Lakes Naval Station Training team, which often competed against squads of major leaguers. At the end of the war, he returned to the Eagles and quickly established himself as one of the top stars in black baseball. In July 1947, he was leading the Negro National League in batting with a .458 mark and in home runs with thirteen.

The Dodgers also expressed an interest in Doby. Brooklyn scouts rated him the best young Negro League player. "Oh, you had to like Doby," recalls Clyde Sukeforth. "He could run and he had real good power." The Dodgers almost signed the Eagle star, but news that the Indians also sought him changed their plans. "Wendell Smith called me and said that Doby was going to be signed by someone else, but he'd prefer Brooklyn," says Sukeforth. "So, I spoke to Mr. Rickey, but he said, 'By all means, let him go over to the other league. It will help the movement.' "[9] Rickey also expected that the acceptance of blacks on another team would ease the pressure on Robinson and the Dodgers.

When Rickey had signed Robinson, he had bypassed the owners of the Kansas City Monarchs. Veeck disagreed with Rickey's cavalier behavior. The ambiguity of Negro League contracts notwithstanding, Veeck was determined to buy Doby's contract from the Eagles. He contacted Effa Manley, who, along with her husband Abe, owned the Newark club. For two years Mrs. Manley, whose team rented playing facilities from the New York Yankees, had attempted to sell Doby to her landlords. The Yankees expressed no interest. The approach from Veeck therefore delighted her. Veeck offered the Eagles $10,000, an appallingly low figure in Mrs. Manley's judgment. She "couldn't resist" telling Veeck, "You know, if Larry Doby were white and a free agent, you'd give him $100,000 to sign as a bonus." Nonetheless, the Manleys, personally close to Doby and his wife, would not obstruct the athlete's opportunity to play in the major leagues. "I realize I'm in no position to be bargaining with you," she told Veeck. "If you feel you're being fair by offering us $10,000, I suppose we should accept." Veeck agreed that if Doby remained with the club for thirty days, he would pay the Eagles an additional $5,000.[10]

Veeck's integration strategy differed markedly from Rickey's. The Dodger president had, in the words of Cleveland's perceptive black sportswriter "Doc" Young, "planned Robinson's entrance as carefully as a man would plan building a house of matchsticks." Veeck felt that the cumulative publicity inherent in this approach had placed too much pressure on Robinson. "I'm not going to sign a Negro player and send him to a farm club. I'm going to get one I think can play with Cleveland," he advised a black reporter in April. "One afternoon when the team trots out on the field, a Negro player will be out there with them."[11] Veeck employed this precise strategy with Doby. As a result, neither Doby nor the Indian players received forewarning. Veeck formally announced the acquisition of Doby at a press conference in Chicago on July 5. That afternoon Doby joined the club for its game with the White Sox.

For the youthful Doby, the abrupt, unexpected transition came as a shock. In many ways he possessed a strikingly similar background to Robinson. Both had been born in the South and raised elsewhere; both had grown up in single-parent households supported by a mother who worked as a domestic; both had performed as talented all-around athletes and had attended integrated colleges; and both had served in the armed forces where they had faced military segregation. The common experiences they shared, however, had created two totally different men. Robinson was aggressive, outspoken, and audacious; Doby was shy, quiet, and unassuming. Robinson seemed relatively at ease with the press; Doby, wrote a Cleveland reporter, "submitted to the inevitable interviews with quiet politeness. But he was glad when they were over." He answered questions, according to a New York correspondent, "in the smallest voice in the world." Robinson, explains "Doc" Young, "dressed himself in a cloak of humility and made it a perfect fit through one of the greatest acting jobs in baseball history; Doby wore the cloak as a gift of nature."[12]

A comparison of their military careers reveals the divergent personalities of the two men. Robinson had experienced prejudice early in life and constructed defenses against it. Doby has said of his early years that he was "unconsicous of discrimination." When he entered the navy, he states, "For the first time I was conscious of discrimination and segregation as never before." Robinson, confronted with military Jim Crow, ignored personal risks and rebelled. Doby, by his own account, "just went into a shell. I thought: 'This is a crying shame when I'm here to protect my country.' But I couldn't do anything about it—I was under Navy rules and regulations and had to abide by them or face the consequences."[13]

The more combative Robinson also possessed the advantages of age and experience. Six years older than Doby, Robinson's long tenure as a national figure accustomed him to the pressures of the athletic spotlight. Doby's brief collegiate career did not give him this exposure and background in top-level interracial competition. Whereas Rickey had carefully groomed Robinson for his role as the first black in baseball, Doby received less than twenty-

four-hours notice before he found himself the sole representative of his race
in the American League.

Veeck attempted to prepare Doby for the ordeal ahead. "I couldn't put
myself in his spot," says Veeck, "because I had never been in his spot."
Nonetheless, the Indian owner counselled his new employee to expect a
more demanding trial than the average rookie and reminded him that black
players in the future would not have to duplicate his experiences. "Larry,
you are doing something that will be history some day," advised Veeck.
"There are thousands of black youngsters awaiting your footsteps."[14]

Veeck also met with the Cleveland players to give them a chance to
voice their opinions about their new teammate. "There were a couple of
grumbles," recalls Veeck. "It was only the fringe players who had objections. I think it represented an economic threat [to them]." Veeck informed
the dissenters that if they did not wish to accept Doby he would find other
locales in which they could play, "far away, with bus stops." This implied
threat of demotion to the minor leagues stifled further protest.[15]

Cleveland sportswriters described the atmosphere at the Indian locker
room as "tension charged" when Doby entered. But most of the players
greeted Doby cordially. Only Les Fleming, a first baseman from Texas evidenced his displeasure, turning his back as Doby approached to be introduced. In the dugout, two unidentified black men in street clothing appeared—detectives assigned by the Chicago police to guard Doby.[16]

In the seventh inning of the July 5 Indians-White Sox game, less than
three hours after he had signed a Cleveland contract, Doby made his American League debut as a pinch hitter. "I was so scared. I didn't even know
how many men were out," he told a reporter. He was greeted by a hearty
round of applause by the Chicago fans. With his "teeth chattering" Doby
swung wildly at the first pitch, missing it by a large margin. On the next
pitch he slammed a "scorching drive" that was foul by inches.[17] Three
pitches later, he returned to the dugout, a strikeout victim.

The Doby signing evoked a generally favorable response. Editorials in
Cleveland newspapers praised Veeck and welcomed Doby to the Tribe.
The Cleveland *Press* viewed the Doby signing as an appropriate message
for the Fourth of July. Although Veeck claims to have received around
20,000 letters of "violent" and "obscene" protest, fans interviewed at the ball
park took the matter in stride. "If Doby turns out good, I'll be all for it,"
was a typical reply. The *Sporting News* in an editorial entitled "Once Again,
That Negro Question," declared that now that a black had entered the
American League, the "race matter . . . no longer exists insofar as Organized Baseball administration is concerned."[18]

The only significant objections to be recorded emanated from players on other American League teams. Dan Daniel reported that "one outstanding American League player of Southern birth" had predicted a revival of the "Players' Fraternity" as a result of Doby's signing. A Yankee player, who professed resignation to the "influx of Negroes" protested that Doby's sudden appearance "discriminate[d] against the white player because he is white. I fought my way through the minors for five years. I rode buses all night . . . so I could get a chance at the majors . . . and Doby gets a job without any previous schooling in white baseball."[19] This argument contained minimal logic. Worse conditions existed in the Negro Leagues than in the minors and white players deemed ready for the majors also evaded minor league seasoning. Nonetheless, many sportswriters and players, including some of Doby's teammates, endorsed this view.

"You would have to be an idiot to overlook the animosity among the Indians toward Doby," wrote *Cleveland Press* columnist Guy Lewis on July 12. The use of Doby as a pinch hitter reportedly disgruntled some bypassed teammates. In the first game in Cleveland after Doby joined the Indians, pitcher Don Black hurled a no-hitter. Lewis described Doby as "a forlorn figure on the bench as Black came off the field to be mobbed by his teammates." Several weeks later Lewis reported resentment over the continuous presence of Lou Jones as a "private press agent and companion," asking, "Why does Doby, any more than Joe Blow, need a nurse?"[20]

No other sportswriter indicated a lack of acceptance by Doby's teammates and to some extent, Lewis's comments reflected his own reservations about the black man's presence. Nonetheless, some truth existed in his reports. Jim Hegan, the Indians catcher recalls, "At first there was a little bit of coolness. They didn't know how to take him. But, it didn't take long. This was their way of making a living and they weren't going to give it up for him."[21]

Doby found that while his teammates displayed no open hostility, few went out of their way to befriend him. Lou Boudreau and Joe Gordon were exceptions. Boudreau reigned as the team's manager and star shortstop—a leader in the dugout and on the field. When Doby joined the squad, Boudreau personally introduced him to each player and warmed up with him on the sidelines. "He imparted, by implication, his desires to the players," observed a Cleveland correspondent. Boudreau treated Doby as a typical rookie, neither pushing nor patronizing him. Gordon, the well-respected veteran second baseman, worked with Doby on his fielding and repeatedly gave him encouragement. In one of Doby's first games, the young black struck out after swinging wildly at three pitches. Disheartened, he returned to the dugout, walked past his teammates, and sat at the end of the bench, head in hands. Gordon, the next batter, facing a pitcher whom he normally hit well against, also flailed away at three straight pitches and returned to the bench following the same route as Doby. He sat down next to the black player and also placed his head in his hands. "I never asked Gordon then, and I wouldn't ask him today if he struck out deliberately," Veeck later recounted. The gesture was not lost on Doby. "After that, every time Doby went out on the field, he would pick up Gordon's glove and throw it to him," recalls Veeck. "It's as nice a thing as I ever saw or heard of in sports."[22]

Despite the efforts of Boudreau and Gordon, young Doby led a lonely existence. Initially, rumors circulated that the Indians would recruit a second black player as his companion and roommate on the road. This did not occur. Lou Jones filled this role during the first few weeks, but he soon returned to his normal public relations responsibilities, leaving Doby on his own. When the club traveled, Doby roomed alone. In some cities, hotels barred him. "I explained to the Negro community that I could not, and would not, discommode the entire team for one person," reveals Veeck. He promised to use "all due haste and what muscle we had" to force changes. But during the 1947 season, the Indians abided by hotel policies. In St. Louis and Chicago, Doby lodged in black hotels. In Washington, D.C., surprisingly, the previously restricted Hotel Statler accepted Doby as their first black guest.[23]

Doby could turn for solace and comfort to the black players who had preceded him. When the news of Doby's signing reached Montreal, Roy Campanella immediately wrote to Doby, telling him what he could expect from fans, teammates, and opponents. Robinson, in his *Courier* column, advised Doby not to "try so hard that he'll tighten up and lose some of his effectiveness" and counselled him to ignore those who would compare the two of them. "There's enough pressure on him without worrying if he's doing as good as I am," warned Robinson. The Dodger rookie confessed that the signing of Doby eased the pressure on him. "I no longer have the feeling that if I don't make good it will kill the chances of other Negro players," wrote Robinson. Throughout the season, the two men remained in regular contact, discussing their problems and frustrations. "Jackie and I talked often," recalls Doby. "Maybe we kept each other from giving up."[24]

Doby must have felt close to "giving up" on several occasions. From the start he held an uncertain status on the Indians. He had played second base for the Eagles, but most observers agreed that he lacked the attributes of a major league infielder. "As an infielder, Doby was all wrong," wrote Dan Daniel. "His pivot throw was bad. And his hands were too small."[25] In his first start on July 7 Doby played first base. He appeared four times as a second baseman and, on two occasions, replaced Manager Boudreau at shortstop. Most of his appearances came as a pinch hitter or pinch runner.

Doby remembers his early weeks with the Indians sadly. "Sitting on the bench day after day didn't help," he recalls. "No one seemed to know what I was supposed to do on the field. I struck out a lot because I tried too hard." Doby struck out six times in his first thirteen appearances and eleven times in his thirty trips to the plate in 1947. His problems, explained manager Boudreau, stemmed from a "tendency to swing viciously at low, bad balls. He was so hungry to succeed that he simply could not wait for the pitcher to throw the ball into the strike zone."[26] In his rare appearances, Doby stroked only five hits, compiling a puny .156 batting average.

"I used [Doby] sparingly," Boudreau later explained, "because the pressure on him was tremendous and I was unwilling to let half a year's playing under such terrific odds spoil his future." At a meeting in late July, Boudreau and his coaches agreed that the outfield best suited Doby's talents. In addition they felt that he should not be subjected to the pennant-race tempest. "We eliminated Doby from our 1947 plans and decided to concentrate on getting him ready for 1948," wrote Boudreau.[27] Doby remained with the Indians, working out regularly in the outfield, rather than at second base.

In light of Doby's poor performance, reporters and letter writers criticized Indian policies. After watching Doby play in one game, Gordon Cobbledick of the Cleveland *Plain Dealer* wrote that observers had concluded, "that the boy showed promise, that he might hit, might be an outfielder, that he definitely was not a shortstop or second baseman, and equally definitely was not ready for the big leagues." Lewis charged that "Doby is being exploited not because he is a rookie with a chance to make good but because he is a Negro." Lewis felt this unfair to Doby, who "got a worse rap than any rookie in baseball." On the other hand, at least one fan complained about Doby's lack of play, arguing, "No one ever became a star by warming the bench 99% of the time."[28]

By September, some described Doby as a "Class D ballplayer" and a "sandlot performer." Rumors spread that Veeck was trying to unload him to the minor leagues but could find no takers. "Doc" Young attributes Doby's rookie failure to the pressures of racial pioneering. "Doby for the first time was a symbol," writes Young. "For the first time he had been made aware of 'being different' by the initial coolness of the Indians' dressing room, by the teeming sportswriters who sought to grill him, and by the markedly accentuated cheering of the Negro fans." Bill Veeck admits that the sensitive, introverted Doby "was not the best man we could have picked for the first Negro player in the league. I don't say this from the club's point of view . . . but from his. . . . His inner turmoil was such a constant drain on him that he was never able to achieve his full potential."[29]

Nonetheless, at the close of the 1947 season Veeck and Boudreau had no

doubt that Doby was worth a second look. Coach Bill McKechnie, charged
with tutoring Doby on the intricacies of outfield play, advised the young
athlete that he would be considered for the Indians starting "pasture patrol"
in 1948. Observers commented on potential problems if Doby were sent to
the minors—the Indians top farm clubs were located in Baltimore and Oklahoma City, both in the Jim Crow belt—and speculated that Doby would be
loaned to the Dodger farm club at Montreal.[30] But based on his 1947 performance, few people expected to see Doby back in the majors for several
years—if at all.

I I

"In St. Louis they say that the fans would never stand for Negroes on the
Cardinals or the Browns," wrote Dan Daniel on July 16 in the wake of the
Doby signing. "St. Louis, they insist, 'is too much a Southern city.'" Events
quickly proved Daniel a poor prophet. On the following day the St. Louis
Browns defied conventional wisdom and custom by purchasing the contracts
of Hank Thompson and Willard Brown from the Kansas City Monarchs and
taking out a thirty-day option on the services of Piper Davis of the Birmingham Black Barons. In the Gateway City, where local officials had desegregated the stands at Sportsman's Park only three years earlier, citizens reacted with total surprise to what the local *Gazette-Democrat* described as
"an eyebrow-lifting experiment."[31]

The Browns signed the black players as an act of desperation. Firmly
entrenched in the American League cellar, the Browns languished twenty-
seven and one-half games out of first place. More significantly, Browns' attendance, never substantial even at its best, had plummeted precipitously.
Earlier that week an afternoon game had drawn only 478 people. "Mr.
[Richard] Muckerman, the new owner, hopes to jog up attendance," noted
the *Gazette-Democrat,* "and he certainly can't lose anything in league standing by signing three Negro players." Muckerman, stated the paper, "is obviously gambling for a bigger take at the gate . . . against the possibility that
resentment by some whites may reduce attendance." Browns' officials denied
that economic, rather than athletic, considerations were foremost in their
thinking, but they admitted that the large crowds drawn by Jackie Robinson in St. Louis had influenced their decision. "Naturally, we believe our
colored boys will help us at the gate, especially in our home city of St.
Louis," confessed general manager Bill DeWitt. His brother Charley added,
"It seems in order that this large Negro population should have some repre-
sentation on their city's ball team"[32]—a revolutionary concept amidst the
cobwebbed conservatism of the baseball hierarchy.

The completely unexpected St. Louis breakthrough left local opinion "evenly divided," according to the *Sporting News*. Many residents criticized the move. "Missouri is a border state," sportswriter Fred Lieb reminded his readers, "and many of its inhabitants are descendants of Confederate sympathizers. . . . They retain old prejudices." J. Roy Stockton charged that the Browns' had discriminated against white players. "Players should be brought up to the majors because they can help the club on the field, not as a shot in the arm for the box office," argued Stockton. The predominant reaction, however, was one of acceptance. "The national pastime has moved along with Negroes in the cast without incident, and St. Louis should not prove an exception," said the *Gazette-Democrat* in an editorial. "The die [has] been cast."[33]

The black athletes, suddenly thrust into the major leagues, reacted with unrestrained joy. "I've spent the last ten years playing baseball," enthused Brown. "I never thought I'd be this lucky." Thompson called it the "happiest day in my life," adding, "I've always wanted to play in the majors." According to Thompson, Monarch Manager Frank Duncan cried when he broke the news to the two players.[34]

Brown, Thompson, and Davis possessed undeniable talents. But, unlike the Dodgers and Indians, the Browns had not carefully scouted the Negro Leagues. Nor had they examined the character of the men that they had recruited. Willard Brown had long been regarded as one of the best players in the Negro Leagues. A powerful hitter, he had great speed and was an expert outfielder. Other Negro Leaguers dubbed him the "Big Bomb" and in the Winter Leagues fans called him *"Ese Hombre"* (That Man) for his home run hitting prowess. The Browns reported that Brown was twenty-six years old, but it was common knowledge that he had long ago passed his thirtieth birthday.[35] Some observers considered him on the downward slide. Thompson, on the other hand, ranked as a legitimate young prospect. A fine fielder, only twenty-one years old, Thompson batted .347 for Kansas City in 1947.

Nonetheless it seems surprising that the Browns would have taken a chance on Thompson. A product of reform school whom police had twice arrested, Thompson drank heavily and always carried a gun with him off the field. Describing his life, he later wrote, "Nothing ever was more serious than baseball. Yes, one thing. Drink."[36] It appears likely that the Browns had no knowledge of Thompson's problems, an indication of the haste and lack of planning characteristic of their plunge into integration.

Piper Davis was probably the most likely of the three recruits to succeed. A line-drive hitter adept at all infield and outfield positions, Davis had received strong consideration from the Dodgers in 1945. Many scouts felt that he would be a standout in the major leagues. Yet the Browns did not place Davis on their roster. He remained with the Black Barons while a St. Louis scout evaluated his performance. The Browns' option prohibited him from signing with another club. Brown and Thompson, on the other hand, were signed on a trial basis. The Browns paid the Monarchs $5,000 for their services; if either remained with St. Louis, the Monarchs would receive an additional sum.[37]

From the start the St. Louis experiment seemed destined for failure. A local newspaper described the Brown players as "none too happy over the addition of two Negro players." Alabama-born outfielder Paul Lehner reportedly delivered an ultimatum to club officials, threatening to quit the team if Brown and Thompson were retained. Lehner appeared late for the game the following day, triggering speculation that he had jumped the team. One sportswriter contended, "The gloom that pervaded the dressing room and bench of the Browns was thick enough to make one gasp for air" and that "tempers were taut." When Thompson and Brown joined the club, their teammates greeted them with silence. The two blacks warmed up together; no one else offered to throw with them.[38]

Thompson made his playing debut on the first day, failing to reach base in four-at-bats and committing an error as the Athletics battered the Browns, 16-2. Two days later Brown started in the outfield. In the first inning he came to the plate with the bases loaded and hit into a double play. In the fourth inning, with the bases filled again, he repeated this feat.

For the next month, Brown and Thompson led an unhappy existence as major leaguers. Their teammates ignored them as much as possible. "If Brown wasn't around and I asked another player to warm up with me, he'd just shake his head," Thompson later revealed. When he would walk into the dressing room to autograph souvenir baseballs, said Thompson, "Three guys—always the same three—would get up and one of them would say, "When you finish, we'll come back." Several players, notably Vern Stephens, attempted to befriend the two blacks and make them feel more comfortable. But they could not easily ignore the slights of the hostile Browns. During games the two blacks found themselves the targets of brushback pitches and racist taunts. "They ride the hell out of us," Thompson told Sam Lacy. "Call us all kinds of names, everything except Children of God. But it's part of the game. We're supposed to yell 'Dago' or 'Kike' or anything we think fits."[39]

Neither player performed impressively. An injury to the regular second baseman offered Thompson an opportunity to start for several weeks. He batted only .194 and Manager Muddy Ruel demoted him to pinch-hitting duty. Brown demonstrated awesome power in pregame practices, but in competition, his batting skills deserted him. He had an impressive outing at Yankee Stadium on July 23 when he stroked four singles and drove in three runs. Two weeks later he returned to the bench, like Thompson batting less than .200. Brown's only other moment of glory came on August 13, when as a pinch hitter, he smashed a drive off the 426-foot marker in center field at Sportsman's Park and raced around the bases for a two-run inside-the-park home run that tied the score. The Browns won the game as Thompson followed with a walk, a stolen base, moved to third on an out, and scored on a passed ball. Unfortunately, the two blacks rarely experienced such moments.

Brown and Thompson not only failed to lift the Browns from the cellar, they did little to boost home attendance either. On the road, black fans poured out to see them in New York, Philadelphia, and Washington. An eastern tour in late July attracted 250,000 fans on twelve dates, an unusually large turnout to see the last place club. But in St. Louis, where Jackie Robinson had packed Sportsman's Park, the presence of the two black players had no effect on attendance. The Browns, according to Vince Johnson, "continued to draw crowds like a two-bit carnival."[40]

The failure of the Browns' experiment soon became apparent to all. In mid-August Piper Davis declined an offer to play in the minor leagues and the Browns dropped their option on him. On August 23, barely a month after their signing, St. Louis released Brown and Thompson. Brown had batted only .179. Thompson, on the other hand, had earned a starting berth and improved his average to .256, one of the best marks on the weak-hitting Browns. Thompson asked General Manager DeWitt for an explanation. According to the young infielder, DeWitt looked uncomfortable and advised him, "There are things I can't discuss."[41] Brown and Thompson, the first black teammates in the major leagues, became the first blacks to be cut from a major league roster.

The response to the dismissal of the two athletes echoed none of the surprise that had accompanied their signing. Thompson, some argued, had displayed enough potential to merit a second chance or an opportunity to play in the minor leagues. Wendell Smith argued that had black fans supported the athletes more faithfully, the Browns might have retained Brown and Thompson long enough for them to have proven their abilities. Other black commentators expressed disappointment but remained philosophical. "Remember all our boys can't be a Robinson," advised a *Courier* columnist. "We've got to take our boys' setbacks just as gracefully as we glory in their triumphs."[42]

III

The appearance of five blacks in the major leagues in 1947 evoked predictions of a "general scramble" for Negro League players. "Why wait?" asked Bill Veeck after signing Doby. "I wanted to get the best of the available Negro boys for Cleveland while the grabbing was good." Branch Rickey predicted that within a year the bidding would be brisk as the color line was totally eliminated. Both Rickey and Veeck agreed that the great breakthrough would come, not in the major leagues, but in the farm systems. Dan Daniel expressed the views of most of the baseball establishment when he argued, "If there is going to be any progress in the Negroes-for-the-majors-movement it will have to start with the influx of young Negro players into the minors."[43]

For many years, baseball owners had cited the absence of blacks in the minor leagues as one of the reasons for segregation. This argument was always ingenuous. Most minor league clubs had affiliations with major league organizations who dictated their policies. In 1947 with integration a reality, no impetus for change emanated from above and the anticipated influx of blacks never materialized. In an empire that included more than fifty leagues and several hundred franchises, only a dozen blacks appeared on minor league rosters. Of these, four played in the Dodger chain and six with the independent Stamford club in the Colonial League. The St. Louis Browns were the only major league club other than Brooklyn to assign a black prospect to their farm system.

Catcher Roy Campanella of the Montreal Royals ranked as the premier black minor leaguer in 1947. "Campanella is the best catcher in the business—major or minor leagues," declared Buffalo Bison manager Paul Richards. When informed that Rickey had refused to promote Campanella, Richards commented, "If he doesn't bring that guy up, he may as well go out of the emancipation business."[44] At Montreal, Campanella demonstrated the varied talents for which he later became famous—powerful hitting, solid defense, ability to handle his all-white pitching staff, and an indefatigable enthusiasm for the game.

Following in Robinson's footsteps, Campanella experienced few problems. "Jackie made things easy for us," Campanella explained. "I'm just another guy playing baseball." Campanella's easygoing personality rendered him more readily acceptable to his Royal teammates than the intense Robinson had been. The stocky catcher frequently found himself in the middle of the traditional lighthearted locker room banter. "These were the same things that were missing in the same room last year," commented Sam Maltin. "They couldn't make fun of Robinson, not in front of him anyway."[45]

The Dodgers had returned Don Newcombe, their other top black prospect, for a second season at Nashua to develop a better curve ball. Newcombe briefly contemplated refusing the assignment and returning to the
Newark Eagles but finally bowed to Rickey's wishes. He became the outstanding pitcher in the New England League, posting a 19-6 record. The
sole black on the Nashua squad, Newcombe roomed with a white player on
the road, another first in organized baseball. In June, the Dodgers signed
Ramon Rodriguez, a black Cuban catcher and shipped him to Nashua. Rodriguez, injured for the entire month he was with Nashua, registered only
one at-bat before the club released him.[46]

Few other blacks appeared in the minor leagues. The St. Louis Browns
signed Chuck Harmon, a former basketball star at the University of Toledo,
and assigned him to their Gloversville farm club in the Canadian-American
League. He was joined in that circuit by eighteen-year-old Sammy Gee, "the
Wonder Boy of the Detroit scholastic athletic circles," signed by the Dodgers for their Three-Rivers club at the urging of Wendell Smith. The Stamford Bombers of the Colonial League, acting independently of any major
league club, signed six black players in August. The Bombers quickly
dropped two of them, but the remaining four players, none of whom advanced to the majors, helped Stamford win the league championship.[47]

The only other black in organized baseball toiled in obscurity in the
Class-C Sunset League in California. Nate Moreland, a veteran Negro League
pitcher who had accompanied Jackie Robinson to a Chicago White Sox tryout in 1942, pitched for the independent El Centro Imperials. Moreland
easily overmatched his younger opponents, winning twenty games. Moreland proved popular with both players and fans, though the league president complained that his presence had not stimulated black attendance as
anticipated. "I thought that many of his friends would attend the games
which he has pitched, but such has not been the case," lamented the executive. One baseball observer tabbed Moreland as "ready for anybody's
league,"[48] but the black hurler remained in the Sunset circuit for several
years, compiling extraordinary records but never getting a chance in a
higher classification.

Despite numerous rumors of the imminent signing of black players, only
the Dodgers, Indians, and Browns took the fateful step. In May the New
York Football Yankees, owned by Dan Topping, who also owned the baseball Yankees, signed black all-American Buddy Young. Dan Daniel, always
close to the Yankee front office, speculated that "the appearance of a Negro
among the Bombers cannot be farther off than 1948."[49] But Yankee general
manager Larry MacPhail claimed that New York scouts had failed to

uncover any Negro League players worth signing. Several baseball lords adopted this position to cover up their failure to scout the Negro Leagues.

More significantly, both Rickey and Veeck reinforced the opinion that few blacks were ready for the majors with statements that few qualified players remained in the Negro Leagues. The rationale for these proclamations remains unclear. Both the Dodgers and Indians had scouting reports that indicated otherwise. A conservative estimate would place at least ten Negro League players as worthy of major league trials; dozens more merited a gamble in the farm systems. In addition, young black prospects in the sandlots and high schools awaited recruitment. At a tryout camp in August, the Cardinals permitted blacks to participate for the first time but offered none serious consideration. Among the black youngsters who attended was Elston Howard. The Cardinals promised to contact him. "I'm still waiting," said the former Yankee catcher shortly before his death in 1980.[50]

The failure of organized baseball to follow Rickey's lead more actively sparked protests by radical groups in several cities. When Larry Doby appeared in Washington, representatives of "American Youth for Democracy" picketed the ball park and urged the Senators to hire blacks. In California the local Communist party applied pressure on Pacific Coast League clubs to recruit blacks. "The Dodgers and the Indians and Browns, too have a word for it—Democracy," read a Los Angeles handbill, "Why not the [Los Angeles] Angels and the [Hollywood] Stars?" In San Francisco where the Seals had entered "preliminary negotiations" to sign Sam Jethroe, the National Maritime Union passed a resolution in favor of this action. The Seals retreated, citing numerous letters of protest.[51]

The South also felt the impact of the integration breakthrough. Southern towns that hosted training camps or minor league teams began to reassess their racial policies. Several leagues and communities contemplated the adoption of formal rules preventing interracial play. In Greenville, South Carolina, where the Dodgers fielded a farm club, fans subjected Manager Frenchy Bordagaray to considerable abuse. "The fans were mad because Jackie Robinson was playing on the Brooklyn Dodger ball club," recalls Bordagaray. "They were calling me 'nigger lover' and everything else. They split my son's lip wide open, threw a pop bottle at him."[52]

To other southerners, however, the dangers of an arbitrary rejection of baseball integration grew apparent. "Major league club owners with Negro players will not look with favor upon a training site that prohibits these men from appearing in spring games," wrote Pete Norton of the Tampa *Tribune*. "It is entirely within the range of possibility that many major league clubs will move to . . . other states where there is no race segregation in sports." Many communities had already accepted Norton's reasoning. Dallas, Oklahoma City, Mobile, Atlanta, and other cities solicited Dodger exhibition appearances for the following spring, specifically requesting at Rickey's insistence, that Robinson perform.[53] The economic potential of a Robinson visit to these cities overshadowed racial considerations.

Assessing these 1947 developments, Dan Daniel concluded, "The Negro issue in the major leagues is fizzling out." To Daniel this represented "a good thing," because it indicated that blacks were no longer a "rarity." Pittsburgh columnist Vince Johnson found "a moral of sorts" in the ability of the St. Louis Browns to simply release black players. "The acceptance or rejection of Negro talent has become more or less a routine matter," he observed.[54] In reality, many years would pass before blacks in the major leagues would cease to be a "rarity" and transactions involving them would be "routine." Indeed the failures of Thompson, Brown, Doby, and Dodger pitcher Dan Bankhead in 1947 reinforced the caution and conservatism of baseball owners. The success of Jackie Robinson notwithstanding, baseball integration had reached a virtual standstill at the close of the 1947 season.

12

A Paul Bunyan in Technicolor

*Who ever heard of a rookie who has been
playing for 22 years?*

Satchel Paige, 1948[1]

I

On July 9, 1948, a legend strode through the bullpen gates at Cleveland
Municipal Stadium. From the moment that the tall, elongated figure appeared, the 34,780 people in the stands began to cheer and, as he slowly
"shuffled along" to the pitcher's mound, the roar grew louder with each
step. Photographers poured onto the field to record his warm-up pitches
and umpire Bill McGowan, "unwilling to interfere with history in the
making," allowed this breach of baseball protocol. The public address announcer, unsure of the pitcher's proper appelation proclaimed, "Now pitching for the Cleveland Indians, SATCHEL . . . LEROY . . . PAIGE."[2]

There is some debate as to Satchel Paige's age at that moment. He
claimed to be thirty-nine; the official record lists him as two days past his
forty-second birthday; his mother attested that he was forty-four; a detec-
tive hired by Bill Veeck, the man who signed him to a Cleveland contract,
concluded that Paige was at least forty-eight. Paige had pitched profession-
ally, by his own account, for twenty-two years. Throughout that period,
facing Negro League opponents, semiprofessional teams, Caribbean winter
players, and barnstorming major leaguers, he had established himself beyond doubt as a pitcher of championship caliber. At long last, replacing Bob
Lemon in the top of the fifth inning against the St. Louis Browns, Satchel
Paige advanced into the major leagues.

"I wasn't nervous exactly," Paige explained a few days later, "but I was
as close to that feeling as I could be. . . . I had been in many serious spots
before, but this was MOST serious." Chuck Stevens, the first batter to face
Paige, lined a single to center field. Cleveland shortstop/manager Lou Boudreau "picked up a few pebbles and kicked nervously at the dirt." "You
could hear the rustle sweep through the stands," he recalled. But, according

to Paige, the lead-off single "kind of woke me up." Suddenly, he related, "I was just as calm as could be. It was just another ball game, and home plate was where it always was."[3]

For the next two innings, Paige employed his entire repertoire of tricks to baffle the Browns' batters. "I used my single wind-up, my triple wind-up, my hesitation wind-up, and my no wind-up," he reported. "I used my step-and-pitch-it, my sidearm throw, and my bat dodger." He threw his hesitation pitch to Whitey Platt. Platt swung wildly, and the bat slipped out of his hands and rolled toward third base. When Paige essayed the pitch again, Browns' manager Zack Taylor dashed out of the dugout to protest unsuccessfully the legality of the delivery.[4]

In the sixth inning, Boudreau removed Paige for pinch hitter Larry Doby, the young black who preceded Paige on the Indians. In two innings, the ancient hurler had allowed no runs and only two hits. At an age at which most athletes had long since retired, competing against "guys who were in knee pants or weren't even born when I started pitching,"[5] Paige had successfully appeared as the first black pitcher in the American League.

When Jackie Robinson had signed a Montreal contract almost three years earlier, Paige had anticipated that he might also be given an opportunity in the major leagues. But the general consensus held that he was both too old and too expensive. "Some clubs talked to me," said Paige in his autobiography, "but my salary was more than they could pay." In 1947 he heard rumors that Bill Veeck had inquired if he was still good enough to pitch in the majors. When Veeck signed Doby, Paige wired, IS IT TIME FOR ME TO COME? Veeck responded: ALL THINGS IN DUE TIME.[6]

Paige had intrigued the adventurous young baseball executive for many years. In 1934 Veeck had witnessed a legendary thirteen-inning pitching duel between Paige and Dizzy Dean. Facing a squad of major league all-stars, Paige had topped Dean 1-0 in what Veeck described as "the greatest pitching battle I have ever seen." Thirteen years later Veeck was tempted to hire Paige to break the American League color line, but fears that he would be charged with signing the ageless Alabaman as a publicity stunt led him to opt for Doby. In 1948, however, the situation had changed. The Indians, engaged in a tight four-way pennant race, desperately needed a pitcher who could act as both a reliever and a spot starter. No available prospects could be found in the minor leagues and efforts to procure a pitcher before the June 15 trading deadline had failed. Scouting reports indicated Paige as the best player available. In addition, Cleveland had already established a record-breaking attendance pace. "I had foolishly believed that no one could accuse me of signing Paige as a gag," laments Veeck.[7]

Veeck first had to convince manager Boudreau that Paige represented more than a promotional gambit; in previous discussions the "boy-manager" had expressed no interest in hiring the elderly hurler. On the morning of July 7 Veeck secretly brought Paige to Cleveland and asked Boudreau to take some extra batting practice "against a young pitcher I thought might help us." "Where's the kid?" queried Boudreau when he arrived. Veeck pointed to Paige sitting in the dugout. "Lou almost dropped," recalls the impish baseball executive.[8]

Paige offered to run around the park "a few times" to loosen up. After jogging seventy-five yards, he trotted back, obviously winded. "Mighty big place you got here," he told Boudreau. "Guess that'll be enough running."

Boudreau caught Paige's warm-up pitches and later attested, "I couldn't help but be impressed by his uncanny ability to throw the ball where he wanted. Satch was in the strike zone four out of every five pitches." Boudreau then batted against the skinny hurler. At the time, the all-star short-stop was battling Ted Williams for the American League batting championship, his average near the .400 mark. In nineteen swings against Paige, Boudreau failed to connect solidly. The Indians signed Paige immediately.

Unlike other owners who had balked at Paige's high salary demands, the free-spending Veeck offered him a full year's pay to pitch the remaining three months of the season. "Paige was signed in accordance of our policy of getting the best available material, regardless of cost," proclaimed Veeck at a press conference the following day. "We signed Paige because we are convinced that he is the best available player who had a chance to help us win the pennant."

Nonetheless, the unexpected development created an uproar in baseball circles. Franklin Lewis, the sports editor of the Cleveland *Press* called the action "crude" and another local writer inferred that Paige was a comedian rather than a pitcher. Even some of Veeck's closest friends were critical. "Bill, you've gone too far. I think you're just trying to capitalize on the situation," protested Indians' publicist Bob Fishel.[9] The strongest critique emanated from J. Taylor Spink of the *Sporting News*. Avowing that his objections were "not based on Paige's color" and claiming, with no small amount of exaggeration, that the journal's editorial policy had previously supported "the striving of Negroes to gain a place in the major leagues," Spink protested that "Veeck has gone too far in his quest for publicity. . . . To sign a hurler at Paige's age is to demean the standards of baseball in the big circuits." Spink added his suspicion that "Were Satchel white, he would not have drawn a second thought from Veeck." (To this bit of sophistry, Veeck later responded, "If Satch were white, of course, he would have been in the majors twenty-five years earlier, and the question would not have been before the house.")[10] The *Sporting News* concluded that a refusal by American League President Will Harridge to approve Paige's contract would not have been unwarranted.

Spink and the *Sporting News* notwithstanding, Veeck and Paige had numerous supporters. Tom Meany called the event "far more interesting than was the news when Branch Rickey broke baseball's color line." Paige, wrote Meany, "has been a baseball legend for a long time, a Paul Bunyan in technicolor." In an editorial the Cleveland *Plain Dealer* commented, "We will take Bill Veeck at his word when he says the signing of Paige was not a publicity stunt, but an honest effort to strengthen the Indians." If Paige attracted a few thousand extra customers, noted the journal, "Veeck will somehow manage to make do with that aspect of the arrangement."[11]

Perhaps the most moving paean to Paige's unexpected ascension to the majors came from Wendell Smith, who penned an open letter to Tom Spink in response to the *Sporting News* editorial. To Smith, the signing of Paige was "a beautiful gesture—chock full of the mellow richness of the American ideology." Smith noted that Ty Cobb had been signed to a contract at the age of forty-one and Cy Young at forty-four. The reason for this, he wrote, was "because a venerable halo adorned their persons as, heroically, they approached the golden sunsets of glorious voyages." To be signed at such an advanced age, Smith advised Spink, "You have to be a Paige, a Cobb, or a Young. . . . They beat the scheme of baseball and the laws of average because, unlike you or I or the common run of humans, they are immortals."[12]

To most baseball fans, Paige had not yet achieved "immortality." He had not accomplished his fabled exploits in championship competition, and thus his fame was suspect. As Paige himself noted, testing his skills at his advanced age implied a considerable risk. "I had a pretty good thing with the Kansas City Monarchs and the barnstorming," explained Paige. "Now supposing I didn't make good in the big leagues. That would make me a poor draw if I went back to barnstorming." Even Paige admitted that his powers had diminished over the years. "I ain't as fast as I used to be," he allowed. "I used to overpower 'em; now I outcute 'em."[13]

Five days after his July 9 debut, Paige appeared in a charity exhibition game against the Brooklyn Dodgers. The contest provided a natural matchup. The Dodgers had recently promoted Roy Campanella to join Jackie Robinson and with Paige and Doby competing for Cleveland, all four black major leaguers were present. The promise of an appearance by Paige enhanced the attraction. Almost 65,000 fans jammed Cleveland Municipal Stadium, an estimated 40 percent of them blacks. Allowing for several thousand who had arrived from out of town for the game, "Doc" Young estimated that one out of every six blacks in Cleveland attended the game.[14] Paige did not disappoint them. He entered the fray in the seventh inning and struck out the side on twelve pitches. In the eighth, he again retired the Dodgers in order before Boudreau replaced him with a pinch hitter.

The following night the Indians journeyed to Philadelphia for a twi-night doubleheader. Fans began lining up at 10:00 A.M. hoping that Paige might appear in one of the games. By late afternoon the event had sold out and 20,000 fans had to be turned away.[15] Paige entered the competition in the sixth inning of the second game with the Indians ahead 5-3 and Athletic runners on first and third. He pitched out of the inning, only to surrender a two-run game-tying home run to Hank Majeski in the seventh. In the top of the eighth, the Indians scored three runs, two on a home run by Doby, and Paige retired the Athletics in the last two innings to record his first major league victory.

Within a week, Paige had emerged as the most discussed performer in baseball. On the mound he combined the skills of the consummate show-man and the consummate pitcher. "There is an electricity just in the sight of the Old Man walking lazily across the grass toward the pitching mound," explains Veeck. "He winds up in the old-fashioned, arm-cranking style that went out with the electric automobile," Ed McAuley added. "Sometimes he wound his arms in six revolutions, sometimes only in two. He threw over-hand, sidearm and underhand." The *Plain Dealer* sportswriter concluded, "Somehow you sense that of all the things Bill Veeck has done in entertain-ing the public, this was the best."[16]

Some argued that Paige's antics made a mockery of the game, but as Ed McAuley explained, Paige was "a serious workman who had discovered that a few idiosyncracies would sometimes fool the batter. Otherwise, he wouldn't use them." Nonetheless, not all of Paige's mannerisms adhered to major league standards. A furor erupted over the legality of his hesitation pitch. In his personal variation on the change-up, Paige would halt his motion briefly before planting his left foot forward. The delay disrupted a batter's timing. American League President Will Harridge ruled the pitch legal, though Paige's habit of wriggling his fingers at the top of the stretch con-stituted a balk when men were on base.[17]

By the end of July, Paige had appeared in eight games, allowing just four runs in eighteen innings. The Indians announced that on August 3 Paige would start his first major league contest against the Washington Senators. In a three-way tie for second place, only a game behind the league-leading Athletics, the Indians could move into a tie for first place if Paige won. A relatively minimal advance sale had accrued before the game and the concessionaire laid in supplies for 40,000 fans. Paige cau-tioned otherwise. "We'll do 70,000," he predicted. "Ol' Satch is pitching."[18]

Paige proved an able prophet. Seventy-two thousand fans poured into Municipal Stadium, the largest crowd for a night game in major league history. Paige started poorly, walking two batters in the first inning and surrendering a two-run triple to Ed Stewart. He then settled down to pitch seven solid innings. When he departed for a pinch hitter, the Indians led 4-3, and effective relief work gave Paige his second major league victory. An Athletics' loss propelled Cleveland into a four-way tie for first place.

The Paige pandemonium had now reached fever pitch. Ten days later he started his second game against the White Sox in Chicago. His appearance triggered, "one of the worst jams in the history of Comiskey Park." Streets leading to the stadium were described as "hopelessly entangled" and it took Veeck and Bob Fishel an hour and a half to make the normal fifteen-minute drive from downtown. "It was a frightening scene," recalls Fishel of their arrival at the park. "The turnstile broke just as I got there. . . . I was maybe twenty yards from it and I saw it fly in the air. It didn't hit anybody, but it could have killed me." Hundreds of people, whether ticket holders or not, poured through the broken gate into the ball park. "There was not a place in the park that was not covered by human, sweating flesh," writes Veeck. "I am not talking only about the seats and the aisles and the standing room in the back of the grandstand. There was not even loose standing room underneath the stands." Officials announced the attendance as 51,103, a new record for a night game in Chicago. But many more people had actually crowded into the arena, and an estimated 15,000 to 20,000 fans had been denied entry.[19]

As in his previous start, a Paige victory would elevate the Indians into first place. Before the game Veeck advised the hurler, "Leroy, this one is very important to me. Really give it to them tonight."[20] Paige rose to the occasion. He shut out the White Sox on only five hits, as the Indians won 5-0. Larry Doby supported Paige with a triple, two stolen bases, and two runs scored. In New York the Yankees beat the Athletics and Cleveland again shared the league lead.

On August 20 Paige faced the White Sox again, this time in Cleveland. Once again, high stakes prevailed. Indian pitchers had hurled three straight shutouts and had amassed a string of thirty innings without allowing a run. If Paige could sustain the streak, the Indians could challenge the record of forty-one consecutive scoreless innings. Two weeks earlier Paige had inspired a new major league attendance mark for a night game; this night, the crowd easily shattered that record. Over 78,000 people paid their way into the arena and the management welcomed an additional 2,000 as guests. In three consecutive starts, Paige had drawn over 200,000 spectators.

For four innings, Paige and his opponent hurled scoreless ball. In the fifth, a Doby single drove in an Indian run. Paige, backed by two splendid defensive plays by Doby, stingily protected this narrow margin. When Luke Appling made the final out of the game, writes Wendell Smith, "the entire press box stood and applauded Paige as he left the field," a tribute seldom accorded by the cynical sporting press.[21] Paige had hurled a three-hitter, his second consecutive shutout, and he extended the Cleveland scoreless streak to thirty-nine innings. (The following night, with Bob Lemon on the mound, the Indian staff established a new record of forty-seven consecutive innings without surrendering a run.) Paige now boasted a 5-1 record and a 1.33 earned run average.

The ebullient Veeck, whose gamble had paid off both in the standings and at the box office, wired the *Sporting News:* "Paige pitching—no runs, three hits. Definitely in line for the *Sporting News* Rookie of the Year Award." J. Taylor Spink was not amused. In a lengthy editorial, he defended his original position, complaining, "It is evident . . . that no matter what stand is taken on the signing of Negro players for major league service, some people will be displeased." Spink expressed "admiration for any pitcher—white or colored—who at Paige's age" could win in the majors. "But," he qualified, "it cannot express any admiration for the present day standard of major league ball that makes such a showing possible. Why not build up those standards instead of demeaning them further?" THREE OF FIVE PAIGE WINS OVER SECOND DIVISION TEAMS, hailed a *Sporting News* headline diminishing the pitcher's feats.[22]

Paige's success might have evoked scant pleasure from the *Sporting News,* but he clearly delighted most baseball fans. Even as his fortunes began to wane, people continued to turn out in large numbers to cheer Paige. In Boston on August 25 officials turned away thousands of disappointed fans from an overburdened Fenway Park. "The percentage of colored patrons in the stands was almost negligible," reported the *Sporting News.* "The white folks had come out to see this fabulous character—and they cheered him as loudly when he was knocked from the box as when he was introduced." Paige failed to last the third inning, though he received no decision. Against Washington on August 30 he experienced greater success. Despite "voluminous black clouds" and a "threatening electrical storm," another capacity crowd watched him hurl a 10-1 complete game victory over the Senators.[23]

In September the Paige aura dimmed. The St. Louis Browns twice chased him from the mound in the early innings. After September 20, as Cleveland struggled in a tight three-team pennant race, Paige did not appear on the mound. By the season's end, he had become—as much as Satchel Paige could ever be—a forgotten man.

Several elements account for the abrupt turnaround in Paige's fortunes.

Boudreau had obviously lost faith in the veteran rookie. "Every game during September was THE BIG ONE and I had to use a pitcher who was familiar with the batters," explained Boudreau. "Satch knew the weaknesses of only a few hitters. Often, he didn't know the batter's name." Veeck acquiesced to Boudreau's decision. "Lou's the manager," was his only comment.[24]

Rumors also circulated that Paige was in the Indians' "doghouse." Sportswriters in the Negro press grew harshly critical of Paige's off-the-field behavior. "It has been reported that Paige hasn't the willpower to give up his playboy antics," alleged Fay Young of the Chicago *Defender*. In late July Boudreau fined Paige for failure to report to the ball park on a rainy afternoon. The pitcher also frequently violated curfew and on more than one occasion his tardiness delayed train departures. Frank Gibbon of the Cleveland *Press* predicted that Paige would not rejoin the Indians in 1949. "Manager Boudreau's patience was tried too often by the eccentric veteran," wrote Gibbon.[25]

To both Young and Wendell Smith, Paige had violated a sacred trust. "If you were Satchel Paige would you represent your people admirably or would you remain Satchel Paige?" asked Smith, who feared that Paige's behavior could "have major repercussions and fatal effects on the future of the Negro player in the majors." Paige, wrote Young, "should not be allowed to jeopardize men like Larry Doby, Jackie Robinson, and Roy Campanella, all of whom have acquitted themselves as gentlemen on and off the field." Both writers agreed, however, that little chance existed that Paige would heed their warnings. "No one can change a leopard's spots and no one is going to change Paige," averred Young. "If nothing else, we hope he will at least be discreet," implored Smith. "For there are a lot of little Satchel Paiges on the way up."[26]

His late season fall from grace notwithstanding, Paige lost little of his lustre for American baseball fans. His spectacular August winning streak had confirmed his legendary reputation and whetted the appetite of the public to see other Negro League baseball stars. And, the thrilling American League pennant race overshadowed Paige's September disappearance, as the spotlight unexpectedly shifted to another black player—Paige's Cleveland roommate, Larry Doby.

II

Larry Doby, the talented, but personally lackluster young athlete who had broken the American League color line, suffered an ironic fate. His major league rites of passage were obscured first by the more dynamic Robinson and later by the more flamboyant Paige. Yet as Cleveland sportswriter Gordon Cobbledick asserted, "The story of Larry Doby's fight for a place in the Indian's starting line-up is one of the most remarkable stories of this or any other year."[27]

When the Indians opened their 1948 spring training camp in Tucson, Arizona, few people seriously considered Doby as a contender for a major league berth. The Indians introduced him as one of eight candidates for a starting job in the outfield; but following his poor showing in 1947 and given his inexperience as an outfielder, most experts judged him the least of the competitors. Manager Boudreau informed reporters that "I'll keep Doby only if I feel quite sure that he can play regularly. I won't have him sitting on the bench all year like he did last."[28] The only unresolved question seemed to be where in a minor league system dominated by southern franchises the Indians would find room for a black athlete.

Spring training began inauspiciously as Tucson's Santa Rita Hotel barred Doby from staying with his teammates. Owner Veeck had deliberately transferred the Cleveland preseason base to escape Florida Jim Crow. In Arizona he discovered that although the stands were not segregated, the hotels were.[29] Doby resided at the home of a local black family two miles from the ball park.

Whatever his feelings, the young, sensitive black man shielded his emotions. Doby had spent the winter contemplating his disappointing rookie season, playing professional basketball, and reading manuals on outfield play.[30] He arrived in Arizona determined to prove that his 1947 performance did not indicate his true talents. Segregated facilities would not deter him from this goal.

Reporters immediately noticed a transformation in Doby. He impressed them with his "quiet, earnest application" and eagerness to learn. Doby, recorded one reporter, "is a youngster so anxious to succeed, he eats advice." Coach Bill McKechnie worked closely with Doby to eliminate the wild swinging which had plagued him the preceding year and Hall of Fame center fielder Tris Speaker instructed him on the fine points of defensive play. By mid-March, a reporter described Doby as "one of the most impressive athletes in camp." By the end of the month the Cleveland *Plain Dealer* allowed, "If the boy keeps up his present pace at bat and in the field, there simply will be no sound reason for handing him a railroad ticket [to the minors]."[31]

His fine play notwithstanding, Doby endured a painful ordeal. "It's been a rough spring. Maybe rough isn't the right word, but its been lonely," Doby confessed to a black reporter. "The worst thing was not having anyone to communicate with and talk over the game with after it's over," he later added. When the Indians traveled, noted McAuley, Doby "stays with the club in some cities. In others, he quietly vanishes except for appearances at the parks." In Los Angeles, someone erroneously informed Doby that the Biltmore Hotel, where the Indians lodged, would not accept blacks. Rather than precipitate an incident, he registered at the Hotel Watkins, a black hotel, before learning of the error.[32]

Although he experienced little in the way of hostility from his team-mates or opposing players, Doby remained conscious of his unique status. In a game in Los Angeles a teammate hit a home run with Doby on base. Instead of waiting at home plate to award the customary handshake, Doby returned to "the semi-privacy of the dugout" before he warmly congratu-lated the batter. "He still has that vague, understandable dread of doing the wrong thing," explained McAuley. In that same contest, Doby uninten-tionally spiked Browns' shortstop Sam Dente on a play at second base. For years people had predicted that this type of incident would lead to racial violence. But no confrontation or retaliation ensued, prompting the *Sport-ing News* to headline: NEGRO SPIKES WHITE RIVAL—AND THAT'S THE WHOLE STORY.[33]

Doby's most trying moments occurred in Texas where the Indians and New York Giants played several exhibition games. Fearing that local au-thorities might try to block Doby's participation, Veeck booked a contin-gency schedule through New Mexico and Nevada. The Indians sold out the games in advance, but rumbles of cancellations should Doby appear echoed throughout the state. Veeck threatened to invoke his alternative itinerary and local officials retreated. "We found little disposition on the part of promoters to let their racial theories keep them from making a few dollars," observes Veeck.[34]

In some respects, Veeck still regrets forcing the young Doby to tour Texas in 1948. In Lubbock an attendant refused to let Doby into the park. In Houston he could not find a cab driver to deliver him to the stadium. Fans greeted him with boos and catcalls. "Larry was not a man to shake off those earlier slights and insults that easily," writes Veeck. Nonetheless, Doby continued to perform spectacularly. In Houston he responded to the boos by hitting the second pitch thrown to him for what Veeck describes "as the longest ball I have even seen hit in my life," one of two home runs Doby hit that day. Doby batted .354 in spring training and emerged from what Cobbledick described as "a competitive struggle as fierce as any I can remember" as the Cleveland right fielder on opening day. "He hustled the others right off the field," concluded Boudreau.[35]

"The kid rates a hand today," wrote Cobbledick at the season's start, "and he rates your patience and sympathy in the days and weeks ahead. He'll pay them back someday with interest compounded." Cobbledick's caveat proved

well founded. Peaks of excellence and valleys of despair characterized
Doby's early season play. On opening day, he struck out twice and dropped
an easy fly ball. In the next three games, he "murder[ed] practically everything tossed his way," registering five hits, including his first major league
home run.[36] On the first Sunday of the season, Doby struck out five times to
tie a major league record. Even this embarrassment failed to demoralize
him. In his next game, Doby slugged a home run and two singles.

Doby's unpredictability extended to his outfield play. He alternated
spectacular catches with errors on routine chances. A novice in right field,
Doby frequently misjudged fly balls, only to use his tremendous speed to
compensate. In one three-game stretch beginning May 3, he made five
errors, and the Cleveland fans, who had offered him nothing but encouragement since the first game, unleashed a cascade of boos. "Maybe it's a
healthy sign," offered Cobbledick. "At least they're treating the young Negro
now as they would treat any other whose work displeased them."[37] Boudreau
briefly banished Doby to the bench, so the athlete could regain his confidence.

Doby returned on May 9 against the Washington Senators. In the eighth
inning with two men on base, he launched what writers described as "the
second longest ball ever hit at Griffith Stadium." The ball hit the top of a
thirty-five-foot wall in center field. Not since a Babe Ruth clout had cleared
the fence in 1922 had anyone hit a ball farther in a major league game there.
The ball caromed back into play, and according to Boudreau, "Doby kept
circling the bases like a greyhound and hit the dirt in a long, twisting, slide
at the plate," safe on a three-run inside the park home run. Doby also hit
home runs in each of his next two games, one a 440-foot blow in Boston.
Doby's slugging feats merited a full page of commentary in the *Sporting
News*.[38]

Throughout May, Doby continued his erratic ways. Boudreau benched
him for a week in early June, but on June 17 the manager shifted his young
enigma to center field. Doby responded by batting over .400 for the next
two weeks before an ankle injury sidelined him. When he returned in July,
it was as the regular center fielder for the pennant-contending Indians.

The acquisition of Satchel Paige ended Doby's racial isolation. He now
had a black teammate and a roommate on the road. Doby performed particularly well when Paige took the mound, but hints of tension between the
two men repeatedly surfaced. "Satch was a fabulous name, he was confident,
and he was a proven success," observed "Doc" Young. "Doby was young,
was ambitious, and was fighting, as much as his nature allowed, for a place
in the sun." Bill Veeck sees Paige and Doby as "represent[ing] different
eras of American history." Doby always remained conscious of his role as a

standard-bearer for his race. Paige, argues Veeck, "never appeared to be
interested in fighting battles [or] changing social patterns." The intense
Doby found the nonchalance and disregard for rules by his legendary roommate distasteful. Nor did the older man, primarily engrossed in his own
eccentricities, provide either companionship or comfort for the struggling
young athlete. By the end of the season, according to Fay Young, Doby had
little to do with Paige.[39]

Neither racial obstacles nor personal disappointments deterred Doby,
however. He never allowed his disillusionment with Paige to interfere with
his performance. Nor did major embarrassments impair his resiliency. On
July 28 a routine fly ball bounced off the young outfielder's head. The resulting error allowed two runs to cross the plate and lost the game for the
Indians. Doby, reported the *Plain Dealer*, "couldn't be consoled." As Boudreau later wrote, "It is difficult for a major league outfielder to suffer a
greater blow to his pride than to be hit on the head by a fly ball. . . . He
might easily have cracked there and never been good again." Instead, attested Boudreau, Doby "took a new grip on his determination."[40]

In August Doby amassed a twenty-one game hitting streak. In several
crucial games in September, asserts Boudreau, "Larry Doby was the boy who
showed us the way." During one four-day stretch he stroked a grand slam
home run to win one game and a ninth-inning, two-run homer to win
another. On the next to last day of the season, he had a perfect four-for-four
day as the Indians clinched a tie for first place. The regular season ended
with Cleveland and Boston tied for the league lead. In the play-off game
to determine the pennant winner Doby slashed two doubles, as the Indians
prevailed 8-3. Overall, Doby batted .301 with fourteen home runs and sixty-
five runs batted in. "We all knew [Doby] had the markings of a great ballplayer," said Veeck in tribute, "but we didn't realize he could learn as
quickly or recover as quickly from setbacks as he did. He's a great competitor."[41]

"Every day was Mardi Gras and every fan a King," wrote Veeck of
Cleveland's fabulous 1948 season.[42] Veeck's entertaining promotions, the
presence of Paige, and, above all, the emergence of a pennant-winning team
combined to lure 2.7 million paid customers to Municipal Stadium, a major
league record. As with Robinson and the Dodgers the preceding year, the
Indians capped off the campaign with a journey to the World Series.

For Doby and Paige the World Series against the Boston Braves continued the patterns established during the September pennant drive. Doby
sparkled as the Cleveland center fielder, while Paige languished in the
bullpen, impatiently awaiting a call. After three games, Doby led all hitters
in the Series with a .363 batting average, as the Indians took a two games

to one advantage. In the fourth contest Doby hit the first home run of the Series, a 425-foot blast which proved to be the margin of victory in the Indians 2-1 win.

Paige finally appeared in the fifth game, his first outing since September 20. The Indians trailed 11-5 when Paige became the fourth Cleveland hurler of the seventh inning. With the outcome no longer in doubt, Paige retired the two batters he faced, sandwiching in a balk called on his hesitation pitch, to retire the side. Although Paige had become the first black man to pitch in the World Series, it marked an inauspicious conclusion to his triumphant season.

The following day, the Indians won the sixth and concluding game of the Fall Classic, with Doby contributing two singles in four at-bats. The young outfielder paced the World Champion Indians in batting with a .318 average and emerged as one of the standout performers of the series.

A widely distributed photograph encapsulated the significance of Doby's World Series heroics. The picture showed Doby and winning pitcher Steve Gromek grinning and hugging each other in the aftermath of the fourth game. "That picture of Gromek and Doby has unmistakable flesh and blood cheeks pressed close together, brawny arms tightly clasped, equally wide grins," wrote columnist Marjorie Mackenzie in the Pittsburgh *Courier*. "The chief message of the Doby-Gromek picture is acceptance." This image, asserted Mackenzie "is capable of washing away with equal skill, long pent-up hatred in the hearts of men and the beginnings of confusion in the minds of small boys."[43]

Other editorial writers read different implications into the continued success of the black ballplayers. The *Sporting News*, in an editorial entitled, "HIGH RESPONSIBILITY FOR LARRY DOBY," instructed the young black man on his new role. "Today, Doby occupies the position that just a year ago was filled by Robinson," advised the journal. "Doby must exercise extreme care and acute perspicacity. . . . He must realize that now he is the major league bellweather of the Negro race." The Cleveland *Plain Dealer* viewed the exploits of Doby and Paige as a "Triumph of Tolerance," but one which dictated against the civil rights legislation that would later prove essential to the eradication of Jim Crow. The acceptance of black athletes by white fans, argued the editorial was "more spectacular and noble than all the FEPC laws ever devised. . . . Talents and skills are above city ordinances and they don't need their specious support."[44]

To black newspapers, like the Chicago *Defender*, baseball represented "the strongest outpost for democracy" and the blueprint for the future. While segregationists hid in "dark corners," argued the *Defender*, "thousands upon thousands of white Americans are cheering. Someday these cheers will echo down through the badlands of the Deep South." Noting the increased attendance by whites, as well as blacks, at Dodger and Indian games, the *Defender* reminded its readers of earlier fears of baseball owners. "Their fears were founded on the same myths that are today supporting barriers in other fields," advocated the black journal, but the baseball experience illustrated "how flimsy and foolish the pattern of Jim Crowism and racism is in American life." Joseph Bibb, in the Pittsburgh *Courier* went a step further. "No one can gainsay the irrefutable fact that color pays off in sports," asserted Bibb. "When the recalcitrants awaken to the fact that color pays off, there will be a race to lower the color bars in business. The white man wants money and color pays off."[45]

III

As Larry Doby celebrated his major league success, the Newark Eagles, the team with which he had started his major league career, passed out of existence. Ever since Jackie Robinson had joined the Brooklyn Dodgers, attendance in the Negro Leagues, particularly in cities close to major league ball parks, had declined precipitously. "People started to go Brooklynites," recalls Monarch pitcher Hilton Smith. "Even if we were playing here in Kansas City, people wanted to go over to St. Louis to see Jackie." Newark Eagle attendance dropped from 120,000 in 1946 to 57,000 in 1947. "How long can any owner stand this?" complained Effa Manley.[46] At the end of the 1948 season, Manley and her husband Abe sold their franchise to a buyer from Houston and terminated their fifteen-year baseball association.

The departure of the Manleys was part of a broader reorganization of the troubled Negro Leagues. The Homestead Grays announced that they would continue solely as a barnstorming unit; the New York Black Yankees simply closed shop. Stripped of three of its major affiliates, the Negro National League disbanded after the 1948 season. The surviving black baseball franchises regrouped into a new ten-team Negro American League, hoping to withstand the onset of integration. "The livelihoods, the careers, the families of 400 Negro ballplayers are in jeopardy," warned Effa Manley, "because four players were successful in getting into the major leagues."[47]

Organized baseball, however, with the exception of the Brooklyn and Cleveland organizations, displayed scant inclination to accept the endangered Negro Leaguers. At the close of the 1948 season only Doby, Paige, Campanella, and Robinson were in the majors. Less than twenty others appeared in the lower classifications. "Why are the major leagues so stupid with respect to the Negro player?" wondered Effa Manley. "Why don't they get wise to the gold mine which lies in the Negro baseball talent?"[48]

The lack of black recruitment occurred against a backdrop of continued success wherever integration appeared. In the Dodger system black players reaffirmed Rickey's faith in his "noble experiment." Although Robinson had overindulged himself on the banquet circuit after his rookie season and reported overweight to spring training in 1948, by June he regained the form that had intimidated the National League in 1947. Relocated at second base, Robinson established himself as one of the outstanding performers in the national pastime by the season's end.

Roy Campanella joined Robinson on the Dodgers in April, but under peculiar circumstances. Branch Rickey had determined that Campy would be assigned to the Dodger farm club at St. Paul, where he would become the first black in the American Association. Despite Rickey's offer of a $1,500 bonus for his sacrifice, Campanella expressed reluctance. "I'm a ballplayer, not a pioneer," he protested. "If you want me to play at St. Paul, that's where I'll play. Because it's in my contract. For no other reason."[49]

Rickey launched another of his elaborate charades to obscure his intentions. He promoted Campanella to the Dodgers as an outfielder, rather than as a catcher, and forbade Leo Durocher, reinstated as the Dodger manager, from using Campanella behind the plate. Durocher was furious, but he complied with Rickey's directive. The Dodgers added Campanella to the squad, but he saw little action. On May 15 when the Dodgers cut their team to twenty-five players, they shipped Campanella to St. Paul, where Rickey anticipated he would spend the remainder of the season.

The transfer to St. Paul reunited Campanella with manager Walter Alston, who had piloted him at Nashua in 1946. Local sportswriters criticized Alston for using his new catcher "only because the Dodgers had sent Campanella to break the color line." The former Negro League star quickly dispelled these illusions. In thirty-five games, Campanella batted .325 with thirteen home runs and thirty-three runs batted in. He became, by one account, "the most popular player to join the team in many years." When the Dodgers recalled him on June 30, St. Paul fans responded by "arguing and cursing, on streetcars, in pool halls, on the street; everywhere they're moaning the loss of the stocky catcher."[50]

When he had ended baseball segregation three years earlier, Rickey had cited the quest for victory as his primary motivation. But by using Campanella as a pawn in the integration campaign, the Mahatma probably cost the Dodgers the 1948 pennant. Campanella rejoined the team on July 2 and immediately became the regular Dodger catcher. In each of his first three games he collected three hits. On July 4 his two home runs led Brooklyn to a 13–12 come-from-behind victory over the Giants. With Campanella behind the plate, the Dodgers, whose sluggish start had dropped them into the second division, came to life. Their belated surge, however, proved insufficient. The Dodgers finished in third place, behind the Cardinals and pennant-winning Braves. Campanella, meanwhile, had become acknowledged as the outstanding defensive catcher in baseball.

The performances of the black athletes in the Dodger farm system matched, and even exceeded, those in the major leagues. Following his abortive 1947 trial, the Dodgers dropped Dan Bankhead to the Class-B Nashua team to regain his confidence. Bankhead overwhelmed his younger, less experienced opponents, striking out 240 batters in only 202 innings, while becoming the first twenty-game winner in Nashua history. Late in the season Brooklyn promoted him to St. Paul, where he won four games without a loss. Don Newcombe continued his climb to the majors at Montreal, where he also won twenty games. In the league play-offs he hurled four complete games, winning three and losing one by a 1-0 score. Manager Clay Hopper described him as "the closest thing to Dizzy Dean in fifteen years."[51]

In July, Sam Jethroe, the fleet-footed center fielder who had accompanied Robinson to the Red Sox tryout sham in 1945, joined Newcombe at Montreal. The veteran Negro League performer easily ranked as the fastest man in the International League. The *Sporting News* described him as "an ebony ghost, drifting wraithlike all over center pasture for amazing catches."[52] In seventy-six games Jethroe batted .322, racing for eleven triples and eighteen stolen bases.

Cleveland also began stockpiling black prospects on their farm teams. In May, Veeck hired Abe Saperstein, a Negro League booking agent and the owner of basketball's Harlem Globetrotters, to recruit additional players for the Indians. Veeck instructed Saperstein to bypass established Negro League stars who had "passed the age of development" and to focus on young prospects. Since the Indians top farm clubs were located in the South, none of the players could be assigned higher than Class A. The Indians immediately gathered several of the outstanding young performers available. They assigned Al Smith to Wilkes-Barre in the Eastern League, where he batted .316. Dave Hoskins batted .393 in the Central League. And on September 1 the Indians signed the brightest of their prospects, Orestes "Minnie" Minoso, the "Cuban Comet." The twenty-three-year-old Spanish-speaking athlete played only eleven games for Dayton in the Central League, pounding Class-A pitching at a .515 pace. In the play-offs, Minoso improved, hitting .611 with three home runs and eight stolen bases.[53]

In retrospect, the scintillating successes of these pioneers should not be considered surprising. The Dodgers and Indians selected Negro talent in a noncompetitive market. Players were often assigned below their talent

level. In both organizations some athletes, particularly at the lower classifications, failed to make the grade. Overall, however, both clubs established
an extraordinary record in signing black talent. The large number of blacks
in the Cleveland organization by the spring of 1949 prompted a *Sporting
News* article featuring a picture of three players under the headline, TOILING
ON THE TRIBE PLANTATION, and photographs of "Emancipators" Lincoln, who
"freed the slaves," and Veeck, "who gives 'em baseball jobs."⁵⁴ To accommodate the influx of blacks into the Cleveland system, Veeck dropped Baltimore as the Cleveland Triple-A affiliate and added San Diego in the Pacific
Coast League. These efforts paid off dramatically as ten of the first twelve
blacks signed by the Indians above the Class-A level eventually reached the
majors.

In both the Brooklyn and Cleveland organizations, the introduction of
blacks had produced indisputable stars, championship teams, and a myriad
of attendance records. Yet through the end of the 1948 season, the anticipated scramble for Negro League players failed to materialize. When *Ebony*
magazine asked major league owners about the future of blacks in baseball,
it found, "Not a single one of the club owners polled . . . opposes Negro
players." A closer look at owner responses, however, reveals that very few
baseball lords expressed a willingness to sign blacks. The executives divided
between those like Bob Carpenter, Jr., of the Phillies who predicted "the
number of them in the major leagues will definitely increase," and others
like Red Sox General Manager Joe Cronin, who agreed that Robinson, Doby,
and Paige "certainly are a source of honor to their race."⁵⁵ For years baseball officials had cited an absence of qualified black players as a deterrent
to further integration. As late as 1949 Connie Mack improbably stated, "I
have been advised that there are not many Negro boys playing baseball."
Even after playing with Doby and Paige, Bob Feller reaffirmed this viewpoint, repeating his earlier assertions that "there are few Negro players who
can make the grade."⁵⁶

Doby's World Series heroics, however, influenced the thinking of at least
some baseball executives. "Although Robinson pioneered in the majors,"
reported *Ebony*, "probably Doby has been a more important factor in sending club owners into the chase for Negro talent." Some observers had viewed
Robinson, previously acknowledged as a masterful athlete, as an exceptional
case. But Doby, according to *Ebony*, "demonstrated convincingly that a
Negro player, given the right opportunity, encouragement, and direction,
can attain baseball heights." After watching Doby perform against his Boston Braves, owner Lou Perini, unlike most other owners, announced that
there would be a "delegation of Negro players" in his training camps.⁵⁷
Several teams dispatched scouts to the Latin American winter leagues.

With real, rather than imaginary scouts combing the Caribbean in the winter of 1948–49, major league teams found abundant talent awaiting them. Stoneham's Giants, long embattled by New York pressure groups, took the fateful step in January. The Giants signed Monte Irvin of the Newark Eagles and pitcher Ford Smith of the Kansas City Monarchs. Several weeks later they added Hank Thompson, the infielder who had appeared briefly with the Browns in 1947. The Giants assigned the trio to their Triple-A farm club at Jersey City.

With New York's other two teams recruiting black athletes, the pressure mounted on the Yankees to follow suit. Economic considerations also dictated the pursuit of black talent. Two of the Yankees' Negro League tenants, the Newark Eagles and the New York Black Yankees, had ceased operations due to poor attendance. By signing blacks, the Yankees could recoup rental losses and appeal to the abandoned fans in the two cities, particularly in Newark where fan interest had dwindled drastically.

The Yankees long had possessed an unmatched viaduct to Negro baseball. The Eagles, Black Yankees, and Kansas City Monarchs, all of whom rented facilities from the New York club, had repeatedly offered them their best players. Effa Manley had given the Yankees the first opportunity to purchase Doby and Irvin, while Tom Baird of the Monarchs notified the Yankees before selling Smith and Thompson to the Giants. "I feel as though I am a part of the Yankee organization and I want to give you first chance at any players that your organization might want," wrote Baird to Mac-Phail.[58]

Instead, the Yankees turned elsewhere. In February 1949, they announced the acquisition of shortstop Artie Wilson of the Birmingham Black Barons and outfielder Luis Angel Marquez of the Homestead Grays. When the deal for Wilson proved abortive, the Yankees replaced him with Frank Austin of the Philadelphia Stars. They assigned Marquez and Austin to Newark.

"Our three local baseball clubs are engaged in a carnival of acquisition of Negro players," wrote Dan Daniel.[59] The "carnival" atmosphere, however, did not spread far beyond New York. Several clubs sought to purchase Newcombe, Bankhead, or Jethroe from the Dodgers, but Rickey's high prices deterred them. The Cubs and Braves each signed a player for the lower minor leagues. During spring training, the Braves also added Negro League star George Crowe, who was sent to the Class-A Eastern League. Few other transactions occurred.

In stable periods keeping track of Negro League contracts was difficult; the chaotic conditions of 1948–49 made it impossible. With several teams now seeking black athletes, and with the Negro Leagues in organizational

disarray, disputes over the status of black players were inevitable and baseball executives, both black and white, contested signings. In December
1948, the Dodgers reached agreement with Monte Irvin, whom they believed was a free agent. When Effa Manley protested, Rickey immediately
withdrew from the deal. According to Dodger aide Fresco Thompson, the
Giants' interest in Irvin also influenced the decision. "Rickey felt certain that
Monte would make the Giants and he wanted Negro players on other ball
clubs," claimed Thompson. The Yankees ran into difficulties with each of
their first two signees. Cleveland also laid claim to both Artie Wilson and
Luis Angel Marquez. Wilson began the season in the Indians organization,
while Marquez played for the Yankees' Newark club. The dispute ultimately
reached Commissioner Chandler who illogically switched the players around.
And the Yankees, in disgust, dropped Wilson.[60]

The Wilson case illustrates the problems that these negotiations posed
for the players themselves. While black and white club owners bought and
sold their contracts for considerable amounts of money, the players had
little say in the matter. The Yankees offered Wilson a minor league contract, which would have required him to absorb a $250-a-month pay cut
from his Negro League salary. After accepting, Wilson reneged, demanding
a higher salary and a part of the purchase price. He then signed with Veeck,
who offered him a more lucrative major league contract.

Hank Thompson also objected to his sale to the Giants. "I didn't sign
right off," he recalled. "Not that I wasn't thrilled. I just didn't like the way
I was getting shuttled around, nobody asking my opinion. The big leagues
bought me, the big leagues fired me, the big leagues hired me again."
Thompson demanded a $5,000 bonus to sign with the Giants. They offered
half that amount, he remembers, "and I leaped for the pen."[61]

The flurry of activity in early 1949 notwithstanding, desegregation proceeded at a plodding pace. Only the Giants and Yankees, and to a lesser
extent the Braves and Cubs, had followed the leads of Brooklyn and Cleveland. None of the players signed during these months were assigned to
major league teams. Indeed, several years would pass before most American
and National League squads would add blacks. Throughout the late 1940s
and early 1950s the drama of baseball integration unfolded primarily in
baseball's shadow empire—the minor leagues.

13

The Only Thing I Wanted To Do Was Hit the Major Leagues

I was explaining the "situation" to Luke shortly after he joined our team. I told him that a few fans might not like him because of his race, that he must overlook their boos. But Luke explained the whole thing to me when he said, "Mister Starr, everybody likes me when I hit that ball!"

San Diego Padres President
William Starr, 1949[1]

I

Luscious Easter was a figure of Bunyanesque proportions. His massive six-foot, four-inch frame radiated awesome strength, yet he charmed people with his gentle manner and humor. Easter's tastes in fashion included "racy pinstripe suits" and a diamond ring that resembled "the headlight of the Santa Fe Chief."[2] His age was indeterminate; his background shrouded in mystery. The records list his birthdate as August 4, 1921, but Luke referred to that as his "baseball birthday" and hinted that he might be five, or perhaps ten years older. Despite his advanced age, Easter had not appeared in the Negro Leagues until 1947, when he materialized on the Homestead Grays as the power-hitting replacement for the late Josh Gibson.

Upon arrival in the Pacific Coast League two years later, Easter remained a relative unknown. Bill Veeck made a special excursion to Puerto Rico to sign the giant slugger during the winter and offered his services to the San Diego Padres. Veeck advised Padre President William Starr that his latest discovery "could hit the ball as hard and as far as Babe Ruth." "I thought he was kidding me," admitted the incredulous Starr.[3] In the Padres first six games Easter pounded two prodigious home runs and two blistering line-drive triples. Starr and the baseball fans of the western slope knew that Veeck had not exaggerated.

The arrival of Luke Easter in the Pacific Coast League in 1949 heralded the advent of widespread minor league integration. During the next few years Easter and other black athletes introduced interracial baseball to cities and towns throughout the nation, enduring regional variations of prejudice and discrimination while struggling to advance to the major leagues. To younger players the lower classifications represented the gateway to stardom. But for many Negro League veterans, trapped by the persistent racism of the newly integrated sport, the minor leagues at mid-century marked the final frustration of a lifetime of exclusion.

Easter was not the first black player in the Pacific Coast League. In 1948 the Padres had fielded John Ritchey, a promising young catcher who batted .300 as a part-time performer. Ritchey's debut had elicited minimal reaction in the West. The following season, the Padres signed a working agreement with the Cleveland Indians, who assigned Easter and shortstop Artie Wilson to join Ritchey on the roster.

Easter quickly captured the imagination of Coast League personnel and fans. In his first fifteen games the black first baseman batted .436 with five home runs and twenty-three runs batted in. Observers hailed him as the "greatest natural hitter the Coast League has seen since Ted Williams." "I've seen a lot of powerful hitters in my time," reflected Sacramento Manager Del Baker, "but for sheer ability to knock the ball great distances, I've never seen anybody better than Easter." Manager Fred Haney of Hollywood agreed. "I wish they'd get him out of here before he kills every infielder in the Coast League," exclaimed Haney.[4]

The prowess of the massive black athlete became legend on the West Coast. Scouts marvelled at Easter's "amazing fielding" and his speed, labelling him "the fastest big man in baseball." Writers compared his batting and drawing power to Babe Ruth. As early as March 23 the *Sporting News* reported, "fans are coming here from miles away to see him bust the apple." In a four-week tour of Oakland, San Francisco, Los Angeles, and Hollywood, the Padres attracted 240,000 customers, setting new records in Los Angeles and San Francisco. In the latter city, an estimated 1,000 fans stood atop automobiles to gaze over stadium walls at the conquering hero. When Easter came to bat, both blacks and whites in the crowd rose to their feet, tossing hats and seat cushions in the air when he hit safely. "When he takes his turn at batting practice," described sportswriter Frank Finch, noting the unusually early crowd arrival, "the other players, the sportswriters, the goober salesmen and fans rivet their eyes on the batting cage to watch Luke powder the ball."[5]

Easter's tape-measure home runs combined with his status as one of the few blacks in the Pacific Coast League to make him the frequent target of

brushback pitches. A month into the season, league President Clarence Rowland, in response to complaints about close pitches directed at Easter, issued
a memorandum cautioning against the use of the beanball. Easter seemed
unperturbed. Against Portland in April, pitchers "low-bridged" him twice.
The first time up Easter hit the next pitch for a home run and the second
time he "lashed a savage drive" right back at the pitcher.[6]

Remarkably, Easter performed his spectacular feats while playing with
a painful injury. During spring training, Easter had broken his kneecap in
a collision. Although surgery was required to repair the damage, doctors
advised Easter that he could continue to play without incurring irreparable
harm. Easter was determined to complete the season, but by late June the
pain had become unbearable. On July 1 Easter's career with the Padres
came to an end. He had played in eighty games and batted .363 with
twenty-five home runs and ninety-two runs-batted-in. To the chagrin of
Coast League owners attendance dropped to pre-Easter levels after his departure. Owners estimated that Easter's injury cost them $200,000 in gate
receipts.[7]

Luke Easter was the most spectacular of the wave of black athletes who
entered organized baseball in 1949. With major league teams signing nonwhites in greater numbers, blacks appeared in every Class-AAA and Class-A
minor league in 1949. (Both AA circuits, the Texas League and the Southern Association, were in the Jim Crow belt.) Major and minor league organizations, finally convinced that integration had become a reality, found
the cream of the Negro Leagues at their disposal. They purchased many
aging stars and young prospects from that dying institution. Generally un-
derestimating the quality of play in the Negro Leagues, baseball officials
placed most of the new recruits in classifications far beneath the players'
talents. As a result blacks compiled astounding statistics in the early years
of integration.

In the Pacific Coast League, "prompted by the record-breaking box-
office draw of Luke Easter," several clubs entered the hunt for black talent.[8]
In late May, Commissioner Chandler voided Artie Wilson's contract with
the Cleveland Indians who released him from their San Diego franchise.
The Oakland Oaks quickly signed the shortstop and the spindly, spray-
hitting Wilson immediately established himself as the outstanding infielder
in the Pacific Coast League. Wilson won the league batting championship
with a .349 average, also pacing the league in hits and stolen bases. The
Portland Beavers and Los Angeles also added blacks to their rosters during
the 1949 campaign. Within two years every Pacific Coast League club
fielded blacks.

Integration proceeded more slowly but no less successfully in the American Association. Roy Campanella had broken the league color line in 1948. At the start of the 1949 season, young Jim Pendleton, a fleet shortstop for the St. Paul Dodgers, was the sole black in the Association. His isolation ended on June 5 when the New York Giants assigned Negro League veterans Dave Barnhill, a pitcher, and Ray Dandridge, an infielder, to their Minneapolis Millers franchise. Barnhill met with indifferent success; Dandridge became the sensation of the American Association.

When he signed with the Giants, Dandridge stated that he was twenty-nine years old. He admits now that he actually was thirty-six. Many believe that even that figure stretches the truth. He had begun his playing career in 1933 with the Detroit Stars. One year later, he joined the Newark Eagles, where he played third base in the "black million dollar infield" alongside shortstop Willie Wells, second baseman Dick Seay, and first baseman Mule Suttles. Roy Campanella called it the greatest infield alignment he ever saw. In 1940 millionaire Jorge Pasquel lured Dandridge to the Mexican League, lavishing favors and bonuses on his star infielder for the next eight years. Mexican fans, recalls Dandridge, treated him like a king. While Jackie Robinson broke the color line in 1947, Dandridge was serving as player-manager of the Alamendares club in the Mexican League.[9]

Those who witnessed this short, stocky, strikingly bowlegged athlete in action agree that he may well have been the premier third baseman in baseball annals. Historian Richard Crepeau, who watched an almost forty-year-old Dandridge in the twilight of his career, calls him the greatest performer at the hot corner that he ever observed. Sam Lacy asserts that Dandridge's "quick hands would give the efforts of Billy Cox and Brooks Robinson the aspect of a replay in slow motion." Plus, adds Lacy, "He could hit far better than either of them." Monte Irvin concurs, "There's never been a third baseman who could play better than Dandridge. I don't care who it was—Brooks Robinson, Graig Nettles, Pie Traynor—nobody."[10] Yet in 1949 even the most knowledgeable of white baseball fans had never heard of Ray Dandridge.

Dandridge arrived in Minneapolis hoping that his play in the highest minor leagues would earn him an opportunity in the majors despite his advanced age. On June 5 he debuted against Warren McDermott, a young, fastballing, strikeout artist. "You know what he did to me," Dandridge states, rather than asks. "I had to eat dirt. He throwed at my head." The veteran rookie was undaunted. "I didn't pay it no mind. So I get back up. Next one, he came down the groove with it and I hit it right by his head, dead centerfield." Dandridge did not reach base on that play, robbed by an outstanding infield stop. The following night he began a twenty-eight-game hitting streak. He complemented his batting with the acrobatic fielding that had made him a legend among Negro and Mexican League patrons. Local reporters dubbed him "Old Bandy Legs the Dandy" and the "Black Honus Wagner." Minneapolis fans idolized him. Dandridge completed the season with a .364 batting average, just two points shy of the league lead. "Ol' Man Dandridge" finished second in the American Association balloting for Rookie of the Year.[11]

The third Triple-A minor league, the International League, had featured black players on the Montreal team since 1946. In 1949 league President Frank Shaughnessy boasted before the season, "We will have the most colorful league of all time."[12] Both the Jersey City franchise, affiliated with the Giants, and the Yankee farm team at Newark added blacks to their rosters. On all three clubs blacks approached the high standards set by Easter, Wilson, and Dandridge.

At Montreal the Dodger farm club which had already treated Canadian fans to Robinson, Campanella, and Newcombe offered Dan Bankhead and Sam Jethroe. Reporters labelled Bankhead, working his way back to the major leagues, "the wild man of the International League." Nonetheless, he posted a 20–6 record, while leading the circuit in strikeouts and walks. Jethroe, nicknamed "The Jet" and "Mercury Man," emerged as the foremost gate attraction in the league.[13] He batted .326 and scored 151 runs. His eighty-nine stolen bases established a new league record.

The Little Giants of Jersey City featured three black players: Monte Irvin, Hank Thompson, and pitcher Ford Smith. While Smith experienced a disappointing season, both Irvin and Thompson won promotion to the Giants in July. Irvin, the thirty-year-old former Newark Eagle, whom many had deemed the most likely prospect to break the color line before World War II, amply demonstrated his still considerable talents. In sixty-three games with the Little Giants, he batted .373 and drove in fifty-two runs. (In 1950 the parent club again asked Irvin to start the season at Jersey City. In eighteen games he batted .510 and drove in thirty-three runs, earning him the appellation of "Mr. Murder, Inc."[14] and a hurried call to the Polo Grounds.)

The Yankees had less success with their initial signees. Angel Marquez and Frank Austin began the season with the Newark Bears and both played well. In May when Chandler awarded Marquez's contract to the Indians, however, the Yankees also sold Austin, leaving their top farm team with no black players. The Bears, struggling at the box office, remained all-white until late July when the Yankees purchased outfielder Bob Thurman and catcher Earl Taborn from the Kansas City Monarchs. Thurman was the more impressive prospect of the two. The *Courier* described him as a "home run hitter deluxe," who, despite his powerful 6-foot, 1-inch, 210-pound frame, had "tootsies lined with mercury." The *Courier* added that Thurman, a former pitcher, "could throw with the best of them."[15]

Thurman immediately lived up to his advance billing. In his first game he hit two singles and then powered "one of the longest homers ever seen at the [Newark] ballpark." Thurman hit two more home runs in his first week of play, including a grand slam. Like Easter, his former Negro League teammate, Thurman astounded spectators with the sheer distance of his drives. All of his home runs traveled over 400 feet and at least one exceeded 500 feet.[16] After a month with Newark, Thurman was batting .371, though a hand injury dropped his average to .317 at the season's end.

At times, the black players in Triple-A baseball in 1949 appeared so unstoppable that rival managers devised unique strategies to thwart them. In the Pacific Coast League, where Artie Wilson's opposite-field swinging produced 211 hits, San Francisco Manager Lefty O'Doul applied a "reverse shift," bringing his center fielder in to play shortstop and placing all of his fielders except the first baseman to the left of second base. The strategy failed to significantly deter Wilson. At Buffalo, Manager Paul Richards defied conventional baseball logic and intentionally walked the pitcher when there were two outs and nobody on base to pitch to lead-off hitter Sam Jethroe. "If we get the pitcher out," explained Richards, "we have Jethroe leading off. . . . [If] he gets on base, he's going to steal second and very possibly third." On the other hand, argued Richards, if he walked the pitcher, even if Jethroe reached base, "He can't hurt us with his speed because he's got the pitcher in front of him."[17]

The black influx was not confined to the Triple-A level. Throughout the minor leagues in the north and west blacks appeared for the first time with comparable results. At Wilkes-Barre, Harry "Suitcase" Simpson established himself as "one of the greatest sluggers" ever to perform in the Class-A Eastern League, clouting "the longest drives hit in three of the loop's parks." His teammate Roy Welmaker, a veteran Negro League pitcher, registered twenty-two victories. Wilkes-Barre attendance increased dramatically.[18] In the New England League, George Crowe batted .365 and drove in over 100 runs.

Needless to say, not all of the black players active in 1949 attained these levels of performance. Many were given brief tryouts and then released; others displayed routine abilities. Nonetheless, given the relatively small numbers of black players in organized baseball, a high proportion produced not just good seasons, but spectacular ones. At the same time, the black standard-bearers in the majors continued their outstanding examples. Robinson, Doby, Campanella, and Newcombe all appeared in the All-Star Game. Robinson enjoyed his finest season as a professional. He batted .342 and won the National League Most Valuable Player Award, leading the Dodgers to the pennant. Newcombe became the Rookie of the Year. Paige alone among the five black major leaguers who played an entire season, fared poorly, registering only four wins in eleven decisions.

In the age of Jim Crow common stereotypes had depicted black ballplayers as road-show clowns, far inferior to their white counterparts. The high standards established by baseball's racial pioneers created a new, no less stereotypical, image of the black athlete. "They have an inborn advantage in natural speed and strength," concluded Boston Brave scout Jack Zeller, "and when they also possess high intelligence, they are better athletes, as a class, than whites."[19] The black ballplayer loomed as a "mercury-footed" daring baserunner, like Robinson, Jethroe, and Wilson; the author of gargantuan home runs, like Doby, Easter, and Thurman; a pitcher of blazing speed, tinged with a touch of wildness, like Newcombe and Bankhead. Americans readily assimilated the new image of blacks. As "natural" athletes, blacks depended on brawn and reflex rather than brain or reason; as entertainers they entered a domain in which they were already accepted. But these exacting standards raised the expectations for all blacks who entered baseball in the 1950s. Lesser performances provoked a chorus of boos and provided baseball executives with a rationale for keeping above-average, though not exceptional, black players in the minor leagues.

II

"I am a man of substance, of flesh and bone, fiber and liquids—and I might even be said to possess a mind," lamented the black protagonist in Ralph Ellison's novel *Invisible Man*. "I am invisible, understand, simply because people refuse to see me."[20] Ellison's portrayal of black America won the National Book Award in 1952. That same year eighteen-year-old John Roseboro began his professional baseball career in the Dodger farm system. For the next several seasons Roseboro played in cities like Pueblo, Colorado, Sheboygan, Wisconsin, and Danville, Illinois—a pioneer on a frontier that few realized existed, an invisible man in baseball's vast minor league domain.

Most Americans perceived racial prejudice as a southern problem, but hostility to blacks knew no regional boundaries. The introduction of black minor league athletes was an unwelcomed occurrence in many communities, particularly those in which few blacks resided or in which *de facto* segregation prevailed. "There isn't a Nigger in Sheboygan," Roseboro wrote his parents during his first season. "Send your clippers to me. The peckers don't know how to cut a Nigger's hair." In most towns, Roseboro and his black teammates lived in rundown boarding houses separate from their white colleagues. Restaurants often refused them service. In Salt Lake City, aware that most eating places would not welcome them, the black players on the Pueblo Dodgers tried a small Chinese restaurant. The waiters ignored them until, following a long wait, the Chinese owner asked them to leave. At rustic minor league ball parks, fans taunted Roseboro with cries of "Sambo," "Chocolate drop," and "Snowball."[21]

The Dodgers, states Roseboro, "have always been a first class organization." The team that had broken the color line, it remained throughout the 1950s more sensitive to the problems of black players than other clubs. Nonetheless, they offered little in the way of advice or assistance to the young black prospects in the farm system. "At the same time when they signed blacks and Latins," asserts Roseboro, "they should have made sure they would be welcome. If the black Dodgers weren't welcome in a motel, hotel, or theater, the white Dodgers should have fought for their rights and walked out." Instead, Roseboro discovered that "the Dodgers didn't care if I had race troubles to go with my growing up troubles and playing troubles."[22]

"You ache with the need to convince yourself that you do exist in the real world," asserted Ellison's invisible man. Recalling the indignities of his minor league career, Roseboro relates, "I'm sorry I didn't have the guts to do anything about it. . . . But what could I have done? Gotten locked up for disturbing the peace? I didn't know what to do about bigotry."[23]

Throughout the nation black athletes re-created Roseboro's experiences amidst the indifference of baseball officials. Minor league intermediaries rarely, if ever, relayed reports of race relations, and afraid to jeopardize their careers, the players themselves rarely complained. Major league executives remained blissfully unaware of conditions in their farm systems, an ignorance born of insensitivity and unfamiliarity rather than malice.

The reception accorded black athletes varied from region to region and city to city. Blacks who played in the Northern League in Wisconsin and Minnesota have fond memories of towns like Eau Claire and St. Cloud. Other areas were far less appealing. Piper Davis, the former player-manager of the Birmingham Black Barons entered organized baseball in 1950. During the next eight years he appeared in four different minor leagues. As a barnstormer in the Negro Leagues and as a basketball player with the Harlem Globetrotters, Davis had traveled extensively throughout the United States. When young players would ask him about conditions in the South, Davis would reply, "They love me in the South. They tell me where I can go. They got signs up that say, 'Negroes here and whites here.'" In the North, on the other hand, Davis explained, "You don't know where you can eat. You go into a restaurant in the lower part of Illinois and Indiana, the waitress pass you up ninety miles an hour. And finally, you come up and say, 'Can we get some service?' They say, 'We don't serve Negroes.' " Black players, alleged Davis, were refused service more in the West than in the South.[24]

Other athletes agreed with Davis's tongue-in-cheek observations. Pitcher Dave Hoskins, who later became the first black in the Texas League, experienced the harshest treatment of his career with Grand Rapids of the Central League. Former major leaguer Leon Wagner contends that "Conditions in southern Illinois were worse than I ran into in Tennessee." Syracuse, New York, ranked as one of the worst spots for blacks in the International League. Davis reports that in Pacific Coast League cities, where the large wartime and postwar migration of blacks had unleashed widespread racist sentiments, "I learned more names than I thought we had."[25]

Fans routinely hurled racial insults at black athletes, with certain spectators reappearing regularly to taunt them. Bob Thurman recalls an old man in Baltimore who always called him an "African Bohemian." An Oakland fan would sit behind the dugout with a bottle of Jim Beam and when an opposing black player would appear, he would howl at Davis, "Hey Piper, here comes your cousin." Artie Wilson had a personal heckler in Sacramento, who "called me all kinds of names." Most players rarely responded outwardly. "Every time I would hear a racial remark, I'd look straight ahead, and I'd just ignore it," says Davis. "I played mad a lot," laughs Thurman. "But I didn't let on. I was burning right in there, but I'd just take it out on the ball."[26]

Local displeasure at the appearance of black players also manifested itself outside of the ball parks. Piper Davis attended spring training in Oakland in 1951 and stayed with the local Oaks at the California Hotel. When the season began, the team stopped paying for players' housing and his welcome evaporated. Returning from his first road trip, Davis discovered that the hotel had not reserved a room for him. Teammate Hank Behrman arranged to have a rollaway bed placed in his room to temporarily accommodate Davis. "Checkout time was 2 o'clock Monday," recalls Davis. "I made it my business to be right over there at 2 o'clock for checkout. No room. Tuesday, no room." On Wednesday, hotel officials assigned Davis a room on the mezzanine right next to the elevator. "Looked like the elevator was in the room, it was so close," says Davis. When the team left for its next road trip, Davis attempted to reserve lodgings for his return. The clerk informed him that the hotel would no longer accommodate him.[27] In many cities black players regularly faced this type of treatment as they learned the limits of racial acceptance.

Minor league teams exacerbated this situation with their own segregation policies. Ball clubs rarely assigned blacks and whites as roommates. Where a team fielded more than one black, they always lived together. Where a solitary black appeared, he would normally have his own quarters. Only on rare occasions did teams violate this rule. In 1947 when Don Newcombe returned for a second season at Nashua without Roy Campanella, he roomed with his new catcher, Gus Gallipeau. At Olean in the Pony League, Chuck Harmon shared his lodgings with white teammate Paul Owens, who later became the general manager of the Philadelphia Phillies. In 1949 when shortstop Artie Wilson reported to Oakland, he relates, "I was supposed to room by myself, but I had one who chose to room with me, so I had no trouble at all." The "one" was Wilson's double-play partner, Billy Martin.[28]

These examples represent the exceptions. Throughout the 1950s and well into the next decade, most teams took precautions against interracial accommodations. "I played on four different Triple-A teams by myself and that was rough," recalls Bob Thurman. "I'd go to the movies by myself." Teammates rarely invited the genial Thurman to accompany them socially. An invitation by a new teammate on the San Francisco Seals to go to a movie so shocked Thurman, he "almost fainted." At the night's end, the two players returned to the hotel with "two blondes." Four days later the Seals traded away the white player. Thurman sorely felt the absence of social companionship. "If you had a bad day, you didn't have anybody to talk to. You'd talk to yourself," he remembers. "You had to be like a steel man to take being alone."[29]

Despite the absence of social contact and friendships, Thurman and most blacks who played in the 1950s have few complaints about their teammates. "I never had any trouble with any players," says Thurman, "because I respected the players and they always respected me." Wilson describes his white colleagues as "super." Piper Davis recalls only one instance of conflict with his teammates. After he swung at a pitch and fell off balance, he heard a voice from the dugout call, "Get up Uncle Remus." Davis sat down next to the culprit when he returned to the dugout and in his firm, quiet way, let it be known that he would not tolerate future remarks. No further taunts reached Davis.[30]

The racial tension inherent in the early years of integration notwithstanding, fights between black and white teammates proved rare. In 1949 in the Eastern League, pitcher Roy Welmaker and his white catcher squared off on the field following the catcher's refusal to support Welmaker's protests on close pitches. The pair exchanged several blows before teammates separated them. The following year, white pitcher Marino Pieretti and black shortstop Frank Austin of the Portland Beavers battled after a batting practice dispute. "It wasn't a racial fight, it was just a baseball fight," concluded reporters, none of whom wrote of the incident until several decades later.[31] Other minor flare-ups doubtless occurred, but contrary to the fears of integration opponents, little overt friction ever surfaced among blacks and whites involuntarily united on the same squad.

Nonetheless, every season after 1947 witnessed incidents of interracial conflict on the diamond. During the International League play-offs in 1948, "they came close to fighting the Civil War all over again," claimed Dink Carroll. Syracuse catcher Stan West attacked Montreal hurler Don Newcombe after the latter had brushed him back at the plate. Newcombe, not usually known for his even temper, ducked West's charge and refused to fight. "Had he tangled with West," reported Carroll, "there might have been a race riot in the stands that would have made a tornado look like a zephyr." The next season, Luis Angel Marquez engaged in two altercations with white players in the Pacific Coast League.[32]

These episodes, and others like them, were typical of baseball battles; despite enraged tempers, minimal combat ensued. The first true racial donnybrook occurred in Oakland in 1952. San Francisco Seals pitcher Bill Boemler regularly aimed fastballs at Piper Davis and Ray Noble, the Oaks' two black stars. In mid-July he hit Davis on the elbow, sidelining him for a week. On July 27 Boemler twice forced Davis to sprawl in the dirt. Davis responded with a two-base hit. On the next play, he attempted to score with Boemler covering home plate. "I said, 'Here's my chance,'" recalls Davis, "and I bowled him over." According to accounts of the game, Boemler attempted to tag Davis with a "vicious blow in the face." Davis "tore into the pitcher with both fists." Teammates and black and white fans soon joined the pair. Noble, according to a sportswriter, "knocked down San Francisco players as though they were ten pins." And Davis states, "Noble was hitting everything white coming towards him." One reporter described the battle as "one of the most slambang baseball fights ever witnessed." Several days later, a San Francisco-based "Group of 19" threatened violent retaliation against Davis and Noble when the pair appeared at Seals Stadium. The Oaks turned the matter over to the local police and F.B.I., and both men played as scheduled. They encountered no difficulties.[33]

The Coast League free-for-all constituted a rare event. It was triggered, however, by the most common weapon of anti-black hostility, the beanball. During the 1949 season when blacks first appeared in the minor leagues in significant numbers, a near epidemic of beanings resulted. Beanballs hospitalized one out of four black non-pitchers in Triple-A baseball in 1949. In June, Hank Thompson had to be carried off the field and hospitalized after being hit in the head by a pitch. Two weeks later Jim Pendleton in the American Association was rushed to the hospital, the victim of a Lew Burdette fastball. On July 26 an "errant" pitch knocked infielder Parnell Woods, recently acquired by the Oakland Oaks, unconscious and attendants removed him on a stretcher. "As soon as you walked up there, you'd get knocked down," recalls Thurman of his first year in organized baseball.[34]

The inordinate number of black victims did not decline as integration progressed. The 1951 season began with the beaning of Portland shortstop Frank Austin on March 31. Six weeks later, Bob Boyd of Sacramento received X rays at the hospital after a pitch struck him in the head. In the Western League, "errant" pitches found Denver second baseman Curt Roberts four times in one day. Roberts established a Western League record when pitchers struck him for the fifteenth time that season. The following year a beaning hospitalized the unfortunate Roberts.[35]

The fact that so many black players required hospitalization indicates that these were not always routine "brushback" pitches calculated to intimidate the batters, but included "beanballs" designed to injure them. Throughout the early years of baseball integration, and even beyond, black players, particularly those pioneering in a new league, faced greater dangers than the average performer. Where a black pitcher also appeared, the potential of retaliation offered a modicum of protection. On occasion blacks would protest and fight back. But most players accepted this harassment as part of the game. "I was knocked down in the Negro Leagues so much," asserts Thurman, "this didn't bother me." In one instance, Thurman shouted out to his opponent, "You got guts enough to knock me down, show the fans you got guts enough to throw some strikes now." Thurman hit the next pitch for a home run. "Boy, did I ever suck him in," he laughs. "Man that thing is still going out!"[36]

If a player hoped to ascend to the major leagues, he ignored the physical and verbal taunts tossed before him. "You just go out there and try to work harder and you end up having guys that are calling you names come up and shake your hand," says Chuck Harmon philosophically. "That meant more to me than wanting to punch them in the mouth."[37]

Harmon's minor league record reveals the success of his policy. During three seasons with Olean in the Pony League, Harmon batted .351, .374, and .375. Promoted to higher classifications, Harmon remained a .300 hitter. Nor was Harmon an exceptional case. Despite the adversity which confronted them and their relatively small numbers, blacks appeared regularly among the league leaders wherever they played. In 1952 and 1953 five blacks finished among the top ten American Association hitters. In the Pacific Coast League, Bob Boyd, Piper Davis, and Artie Wilson finished in the top three spots in batting in 1952. The following season, black hitters won the batting championship in both the American Association and the Pacific

Coast League, while for the second straight year, a black was named the most valuable player in the International League. Blacks duplicated these performances at many lower levels as well.

Jackie Robinson had endured his pioneering ordeal amidst considerable fanfare and publicity. In the aftermath of his accomplishment scores of other blacks performed in the unexposed corners of the United States, re-creating his trials and triumphs. Their remarkable achievements and con-tributions to the cause of racial equality rarely received acknowledgment. But, at a time when segregation remained an unyielding American reality, they, like Robinson, carved out and affirmed the black man's niche in the national pastime.

III

For Negro League veterans the minor leagues marked the final stepping-stone on a prolonged odyssey. Their careers had encompassed the Jim Crow circuits, the interracial barnstorming tours, and the international flavor of Caribbean baseball. Finally allowed into organized baseball, many hoped for one last opportunity to play in the major leagues. In most cases, how-ever, baseball officials continued to deny them. Philadelphia Athletics General Manager Art Ehlers confessed in 1953 that many Negro League players should have advanced rapidly in previous years. "The majors were reluc-tant," stated Ehlers, "and the men who were ready became over age and lost their opportunity."[38] While minor league spectators thrilled to the ex-ploits of Ray Dandridge, Piper Davis, Artie Wilson, and others, these great talents remained unknown to baseball's broader audience.

Among the greatest mysteries of the early 1950s were the ages of the Ne-gro League players flooding into the higher minor leagues. To enhance their possibilities for advancement, blacks routinely lied about their age, shearing off anywhere from two to ten years. Sug Cornelius recalls truthfully telling scouts who approached him that he was thirty-nine years old. "Then I read in the paper . . . out in San Diego, about eight or nine guys I had played with were playing," says Cornelius. "They were all 26, 28 years old. I could have kicked myself. I should have told him I was younger." Many players did just that. Pitcher Roy Welmaker walked into the Cleveland training camp in 1949 claiming to be twenty-seven. He won twenty-two games for the Class-A Wilkes-Barre team that season and the Indians promoted him to San Diego in 1950. Welmaker won eight of his first ten Pacific Coast League decisions and was hailed as "the best lefty to come down the pike in many moons." But, Welmaker "admitted he would never again see his

36th birthday," and the Cleveland management proclaimed him too old for a trial in the majors.[39]

The assumption that black players were older than the years they claimed sometimes worked to their detriment. "Why my Pappy isn't that old," exclaimed Dan Bankhead in response to rumors that he was thirty-nine. When Buzz Clarkson reported for a brief stint with the Boston Braves in 1952, a reporter described him as "a comparatively ancient colored shortstop," whose "indeterminable" age "was the only thing against him." Sam Jethroe charges that suspicions that he was older than his thirty-one years in 1953 may have shortened his major league career.[40]

The major league antipathy for aging players doomed most of the surviving stars of the Jim Crow era to the Triple-A arena. Only a handful played in the majors for any prolonged period of time. Satchel Paige fared better than most. Cleveland released Paige after he won only four games in 1949. It was not coincidental that Bill Veeck, Paige's patron, had relinquished control of the club. In 1951 Veeck purchased the hapless St. Louis Browns and he immediately returned Paige to the spotlight. At least forty-three years of age, Paige established himself as one of the outstanding relief pitchers in baseball during the next three seasons. In 1952, pitching for a team that won only sixty-four games, the great hurler won twelve games and saved ten more. Veeck sold the Browns after the 1953 season. The new owners proclaimed a youth movement and dropped Paige.

The indefatigable Paige spent two years on the barnstorming circuit before Veeck, operating the Triple-A Miami Marlins, beckoned again. Paige literally descended from the heavens on opening day, deposited by a helicopter. Marlin Manager Don Osborne believed Paige's appearance was another Veeck publicity stunt, but the "old man" hurled a four-hit shutout in his first start. Used primarily as a relief pitcher, Paige posted an 11-4 record with sixteen saves and a remarkable 1.86 earned run average. "He stood out on the mound and you could hear his stomach growl," recalls John Roseboro. "With all his windups and deliveries and soft stuff, it was a thrill just to bat against him."[41] Paige remained in the International League for three years. In his final season, he won 10, lost 10, and boasted a 2.95 earned run average.

Luke Easter's organized baseball career paralleled that of Paige. At the close of the 1949 season the Indians rushed Easter to Cleveland, amidst much fanfare, to help in their abortive pennant drive. Easter, overweight and still recuperating from his operation, batted only .222 with no home runs. The disappointed Indian fans made Easter "the most booed player in the history of Cleveland Stadium." The *Sporting News* quickly pointed out,

"There was no racial connotation. He was expected to hit and he didn't."[42]
In the spring of 1950 Easter started the season slowly, evoking more jeers.
In mid-May he finally uncoiled his power. At the season's end he had belted
28 home runs and driven in 107 runs. Over his first three seasons with the
Indians, Easter averaged 29 home runs and 100 runs-batted-in. Nearing the
age of forty and continually plagued by knee and ankle injuries, he appeared in only sixty-eight games in 1953. The following year, Easter returned to the minors.

Easter's playing career had not ended. For the next decade he reigned
as the toast of the International League, appearing first with the Buffalo Bisons and later for the Rochester Red Wings. As the years passed, Easter
could barely run and his defensive range grew more limited, but he remained a dangerous hitter, ever capable of launching one of his prodigious
projectiles. As late as 1957, Easter hit forty home runs. At Rochester fans
greeted his appearances with cries of "Luuuuuke, Luuuuuke, Luuuuuke,"
and waited through one-sided defeats in hopes that he might pinch-hit. He
became the most popular player in the league, particularly among the
younger fans. "In the early 1960's," writes sports columnist Bob Matthews,
who grew up in Rochester, "I was convinced Luke Easter was the greatest
man alive."[43] It was not until 1964, at the age of forty-three, or perhaps
forty-eight, or maybe fifty-three, that Luke took his last swing as a Red
Wing.

Several other Negro League stars also had relatively brief careers in the
major leagues. Sam Jethroe won the Rookie of the Year Award in 1950 as a
Boston Brave, but failing eyesight, poor defense, and an influx of younger
black players on the Braves, banished him to the International League in
1953. After wandering through the Triple-A maze for five years, Bob Thurman finally won promotion to the Cincinnati Reds in 1954. Already thirty-
three years old, Thurman served primarily as a pinch hitter for five seasons,
slugging sixteen home runs in only 190 at-bats in 1957. Pitcher Connie Johnson also amassed a five-year major league career, despite a belated start
while in his mid-thirties.

Baseball players refer to a brief tenure in the major leagues as "a cup of
coffee." Artie Wilson received his "cup" of big league life with the New
York Giants in 1951. The former Black Baron shortstop had batted .348 and
.312 in his two seasons in the Pacific Coast League. In spring training he
earned a place on the Giants with a .480 batting average. But Wilson engaged in little regular season action, registering only twenty-two at-bats. "I
was a rookie," he explains, "and a rookie does not get to break in with
a[n infield] combination like Eddie Stanky and Alvin Dark."[44] In late May
the Giants had to make room for another rookie—Wilson's former Black

Baron teammate, twenty-year-old Willie Mays. Wilson was dispatched to Minneapolis where he performed briefly before his former owners in Oakland requested his return to boost lagging ticket sales. He remained in the Pacific Coast League for the rest of his career. A consistent .300 hitter, Wilson never again received a major league offer.

Quincy Trouppe also received a brief taste of life in the big leagues. A powerfully built catcher, who prided himself on his defensive skills and general knowledge of baseball, Trouppe had been a player-manager on several Negro and Mexican League clubs. At the age of thirty-nine, he received an opportunity to play for the Cleveland Indians in 1952. "I guess no one who has ever broken into organized baseball could have felt any better than I did when I inked my name to that new Cleveland contract," writes Trouppe in his autobiography. But in two and a half months in the majors Trouppe batted only ten times. In June, Cleveland assigned him to Indianapolis. "The terrible disappointment nearly choked me," states Trouppe. He protested his demotion, but was advised, "You don't have a record to go on." The veteran catcher "thought about all the highs and lows that went into putting together 22 years of playing ball on two different continents and on islands in between."[45] Yet, according to organized baseball logic, he had no record. Trouppe reported to Indianapolis in the American Association, where he hit six home runs in his first two weeks, but the Indians never recalled him. At the season's end, Trouppe retired.

Although denied the full measure of fame and achievement that they deserved, players like Trouppe and Wilson at least had the satisfaction of playing in the major leagues. Other black stars, like Piper Davis and Ray Dandridge, were not as fortunate.

There is little doubt that Lorenzo "Piper" Davis possessed major league abilities. "If he'd had a chance when he was young," asserts Clyde Sukeforth, who scouted Davis for the Dodgers, "He'd have been outstanding."[46] The versatile, line-drive hitting Davis performed ably at all positions. In 1945 the Dodgers considered him in their initial search for black players. In 1947 the St. Louis Browns took out an option on his services. But when the Browns released Hank Thompson and Willard Brown, they also allowed the option on Davis to expire.

Three years later, the Boston Red Sox made their initial foray into the black player market when they purchased Davis from the Birmingham Black Barons. The Red Sox paid Barons' owner Tom Hayes $7,500 with the promise to double that figure if Davis remained in the Boston organization past May 15. Davis, the player-manager of the Barons, claimed to be twenty-nine years old, cutting two years off his real age. Red Sox General Manager Joe Cronin told reporters that he had obtained the "sleeper" of the season in the "26-year old" Davis. "He's a fine kid," boasted Cronin. "I'm going to try him out with the Scranton, Pa. club. If he makes good, I'm going to waste no time in moving him on to Boston."[47] Scranton, although only in the Class-A Eastern League, was Boston's highest affiliate above the Jim Crow region.

Davis reported to the Red Sox training camp in Cocoa, Florida, in the spring of 1950. On the first day of practice, he recalls, "I took the routine exercises, got ready to throw. I patted that ball around for a minute or more, but it felt like fifteen. Nobody spoke to me." Another player finally offered to toss the ball with Davis. Local custom forbade Davis from dressing, living, or eating with his teammates. "I lived in the city with one of the waiters," remembers Davis. "I'd eat in the waiters' quarters. The team ate out in the dining room. I had to dress in the visitors clubhouse." Davis did not start in the first exhibition game, but in the late innings he emerged from the dugout as a pinch hitter. "Well, I'll be damned," he heard a fan exclaim, "Boston done got a nigger." "That's one of the times I said my prayers in baseball," Davis relates. "I said 'Lord let me hit this ball please,' and I hit a screaming shot. If I'm not mistaken, I hit it over the boards."[48]

The Scranton farm team played several exhibition games in southern towns, but Red Sox officials dispatched Davis directly to Pennsylvania rather than challenge the Jim Crow laws. The veteran Negro League performer rejoined the club at the start of the regular season and proceeded to batter Class-A pitching. On May 13, two days before Boston was required to pay the second half of Davis's purchase price to the Black Barons, he led the team in batting, with a .333 average, home runs, runs batted in, and stolen bases. When the Scranton general manager summoned Davis to his office, the athlete anticipated a promotion to the Red Sox Triple-A farm club at Louisville. Instead, the general manager informed him that the Red Sox had released him for "economical reasons."[49]

The action infuriated Scranton field manager Jack Burns. Burns assured Davis that he had played no role in the decision. The manager escorted Davis to the locker room and advised him, "You just take anything in here you want." Davis declined the offer. "I just took my cap, because I knew they wouldn't want my cap anyway. They gave me my own brush and comb. They had all the combs up on the shelf. They gave me my own private brush and comb."[50]

The Scranton club did not even offer Davis a train ticket to return to Birmingham. Ironically, at Union Station in Washington, D.C., where law required all blacks to detrain and relocate to the blacks-only cars, Davis suddenly found himself face to face with Joe Cronin. Cronin awkwardly repeated the tale of "economic woe" that lead to Davis's dismissal before the two men went to their respective Jim Crow seats. Cronin later sent Davis first-class transportation and meal money to pay for his trip home.[51]

Davis never accepted the Red Sox explanation of "economical conditions." "I knew that was a joke," he asserts, "because [Red Sox owner] Tom Yawkey's one of the richest men in the East." Indeed, the financial fortunes of the Red Sox had reached a new peak. The club had shown a profit in four of its previous five seasons and the value of its assets had tripled during that period. In 1949 Boston attendance had surged to a record 1.6 million, a figure which would not be topped for eighteen years. Red Sox officials asserted that, "At 33, the Negro first baseman was not considered a major league prospect."[52] In the eyes of the Boston management, Davis, really thirty-one, had aged seven years in a few months. Four seasons passed before Yawkey's Red Sox signed another black player; not until 1959 did a black man even don a Boston uniform in spring training.

In 1951 Davis joined the Oakland Oaks. For the next six years he delighted Pacific Coast League fans as a utility infielder-outfielder, twice batting over .300. In 1956, ten years after the Dodgers had declined to sign him, Davis was traded to the Brooklyn farm team in Hollywood. The following season the Dodgers assigned him to their AA franchise at Fort Worth. "In the Texas League," recalls Davis, "I couldn't eat with [the team] anywhere and stay with them either. I couldn't even play in Shreveport." When the team arrived at a restaurant to eat, Davis waited in the bus until they brought him food. On one occasion when they forgot to bring him a meal, Davis advised his manager to ignore it. "I'm not worth waiting for anyway," he exclaimed bitterly. The following season, the Dodgers sent him a new contract, but Davis returned it unsigned.[53] A retired athlete at thirty-eight years of age, Davis had never played in a major league game.

Like Piper Davis, Ray Dandridge deserved a chance to perform at baseball's highest levels. A perennial all-star in the Negro and Mexican Leagues, Dandridge compiled three consecutive outstanding seasons with the Giants top farm club at Minneapolis. At third base, reported the *Sporting News*, "He astounded veteran observers with his plays. . . . The bowlegged Dandridge moves like a cat."[54] After batting .364 in 1949, he won the Most Valuable Player Award in the American Association in 1950, hitting .311 and leading his team to the pennant. In 1951 he continued to harass Triple-A pitchers with a .324 average, while pacing all third basemen in fielding. In May, Dandridge watched Willie Mays, his young black roommate ascend to the Giants, but the great black veteran remained behind.

"My biggest point in life was that I wanted to put my foot in major league ball," Dandridge asserts. Several stars on the Giants called for his elevation. Monte Irvin recalls that he and Hank Thompson urged Manager

Leo Durocher to promote Dandridge. White pitcher Sal Maglie, who had befriended the third baseman while both played in Mexico, snarled "Why the hell don't you bring that son-of-a-bitch out of Minneapolis?"[55] Durocher and the Giant front office steadfastly refused.

Ironically, the Giants were a pioneer club in baseball integration and seemed less conscious of a racial quota system than other teams of that era. Chub Feeney, then a Giant executive and now the president of the National League, explains, "Ray was considered several times and the strange thing about it was that [owner] Horace [Stoneham] loved him. Called him 'Dandy Dandridge.'" Age, not race, blocked Dandridge's chances according to Feeney. "Ray was probably in his early forties and by that time we had Henry Thompson and then Bobby Thomson at third base. There just never came a time when there was a real need." In retrospect, Feeney admits, "Probably we could have brought him up at the end of the season or something . . . if we'd recognized the fact that he had felt that need."[56]

Dandridge believes that his immense popularity in Minneapolis provided another reason for the failure of the Giants to promote him. Stoneham, he says, told him that the organization wanted him there because of his drawing power. Dandridge charges that the Giants turned down offers from other teams in order to keep him in the Twin Cities. Years later he rebuffed Stoneham at an old-timers game. "I said, 'Horace, I don't even want to talk to you,'" he heatedly recalls. "'You had the chance to sell my contract. You had the chance to bring me up and you wouldn't do it. The only thing I wanted to do was hit the major leagues. . . . You could have called me up for even one week! I could have said I hit the major leagues.'"[57]

"I loved baseball and everything in it. My life has been nothing but baseball," Dandridge told a reunion of Negro League players in 1980.[58] His audience remembered him as perhaps the finest third baseman to ever play the game. Most other baseball fans do not know him at all. Long the victim of racism, in the end, Dandridge fell victim to the universal experience of aging and the insensitivity characteristic of the newly integrated national pastime. For Ray Dandridge, Piper Davis, and countless others who ended their obscure, yet sparkling careers in the minor leagues, the demise of segregation occurred too late.

14

The Unwritten Law of the South

> There is no power in the world—not even
> all the mechanized armies of the earth,
> Allied and Axis—which could now force
> Southern white people to the abandon-
> ment of social segregation.
>
> Publisher Mark Ethridge,
> Louisville *Courier-Journal,* 1942[1]

I

The early weeks of 1949 found Dr. Samuel Green, the Grand Dragon of the
Ku Klux Klan, in an angry mood. Since the end of World War II the Atlanta obstetrician had labored arduously to rejuvenate his racist organization. He had registered his greatest success in his native Georgia, where
Klansmen included many law officers and city councilmen. In 1948 Klan intimidation campaigns composed of floggings, beatings, and gunfire had discouraged blacks from voting, assuring the election of arch-segregationist
Herman Talmadge as governor.[2] On the heels of this triumph, however, a
new threat to white supremacy had surfaced. In January 1949, the Brooklyn
Dodgers had announced that their next spring training junket, featuring
Jackie Robinson and Roy Campanella, would invade the dragon's personal
lair of Atlanta, as well as nearby Macon.

"You can bet your life I'll look up the segregation law and investigate
thoroughly," vowed Green. When state and city officials could unearth no
statute that banned integrated athletic competition, the Klansman invoked
his own edict. "There is no law against the game. But we have an unwritten
law in the South—the Jim Crow law," he proclaimed. "The Atlanta baseball
club is breaking down the traditions of the South and will have to pay for
it." Initiating a boycott of the Dodger game, Green warned that the local
Atlanta Crackers would lose "thousands of dollars in the end."[3]

The projected Dodger march through Georgia in 1949 marked the second consecutive year that Branch Rickey had extended his great experiment
into the segregated South. The previous year the Dodgers had traveled

north from their training camp in the Dominican Republic, stopping at Dallas, Fort Worth, Oklahoma City, Tulsa, and Asheville, North Carolina. Officials in all five cities, none of which had previously witnessed interracial competition, had submitted written invitations to Rickey, requesting not only a Dodger visit but Robinson's presence in the lineup. At each stop, the Brooklyn club shattered attendance records as thousands of southern fans, black and white alike, overflowed matchbox minor league arenas to watch baseball's most controversial performer.

Not since the days of Babe Ruth had spring training tours commanded so much attention. In Fort Worth over 15,000 fans jammed the stands and spilled into the far reaches of the outfield. In Dallas, where officials admitted blacks to the grandstand for the first time, they filled the reserved section and four bleachers, and lined the outfield six-deep to see their standard-bearer.[4]

In 1949 Rickey determined to take his precedent-setting and highly profitable tour to the "real South," adding several previously recalcitrant Florida and Georgia cities to the itinerary. The announcement of these plans evoked the outbursts by the Grand Dragon. The "Supreme Megoozelum," as the *Sporting News* dubbed Green, garnered little support. Although Governor Talmadge declined to comment on the issue, other state and local officials welcomed the Robinson visit. Newspapers in Atlanta and Macon denounced and ridiculed Dr. Green. "I'm glad to see that Old Doc Green has come charging to my rescue and is going to protect me from having to watch Jackie Robinson perform," commented acerbic Atlanta *Constitution* columnist Jack Tarver. "It sure would be a terrible thing for me, sitting there in the bleachers, to be contaminated by that darky out there playing second base." Polls taken by the *Constitution* and the Associated Press found support for the Dodger appearance running 4-1. "I'm just as much a southerner as anybody," wrote sportswriter John Bradberry, "but Providence willing, I'm going to see those three Dodger-Cracker games and am glad of the opportunity."[5]

Before their April 7 arrival in Macon, Robinson and Campanella had already pierced the color barrier in West Palm Beach and Miami, drawing record crowds in both Florida locales. In Miami, according to Bill Mardo, the two black athletes "forced the KKK to choke on its bedsheets," as Robinson hit the first pitch thrown to him for a home run and Campanella followed suit later in the game. In West Palm Beach black residents flooded the Jim-Crow section and "stretched themselves like a huge elastic band across the outfield."[6]

The true test lay in Macon and Atlanta. "I hated the thought of putting foot on Georgia soil," confessed Robinson as he deplaned in his native state.

From the private home in Macon where he and Campanella were quartered, they could see the charred remains of a Ku Klux Klan cross-burning across the street. But fears of a fan boycott were dispelled early. Sixty-four hundred people, the majority of them white, crammed into Macon's 4,000-seat arena. Robinson, wrote Wendell Smith, "was the center of every eye, every minute he was on the field."[7] His reception duplicated the pattern that characterized his appearances in the South. Enthusiastic cheers rolled in from the black sections in the outfield; a scattering of white fans responded with boos; finally, waves of applause from the majority of the white patrons drowned the catcalls.

The weekend contests in Atlanta re-created the Macon scene on a grander scale. Almost 50,000 fans attended the three games. In the climactic Sunday spectacle, over 25,000 people—almost double the seating capacity of the ball park—overflowed Ponce de Leon Stadium. Blacks made up more than half the crowd. They filled the Jim Crow bleachers, spread into hitherto restricted areas of the stadium, and "dangled on the four-tiered right-field wall and on the scoreboard, and even behind trees on the terraced centerfield." "They don't care to see the game," explained Robinson. "All they want is to be able to say that they were here."[8]

Characteristically, the black second baseman rose to the occasion. In the game at Macon, Robinson began nervously. "The first two pitches thrown at me were strikes," he related. "I wanted to swing at them, but I couldn't. I was actually paralyzed." Robinson loosened up enough to line the third pitch for a single, driving in the first Dodger run, one of three hits he recorded against the hometown Peaches. Facing the Atlanta Crackers, the Brooklyn star again drove in the initial run on Friday and on Sunday thrilled his supporters by stealing home in the first inning. In the four games, Robinson batted .412, reaffirming the faith of his worshippers and dispelling the doubts of his detractors. The admonitions of the Grand Dragon and all prior apprehension notwithstanding, the four games in Georgia passed without incident. "The only trouble the Dodgers had," quipped one sportswriter, "was in counting the money."[9]

Robinson's 1949 conquest of Atlanta reflected a subtle shift in race relations in the postwar South. Despite the sporadic violence and Klan growth, the rule of Jim Crow was softening. To a great extent these changes originated outside the region, but southerners also had contributed to the improved conditions. In July 1948, President Truman had initiated the desegregation of the armed forces, affecting military installations throughout the nation. A series of Supreme Court decisions in 1950 limited segregation on railway cars and in higher education. At the same time many southern communities rejected the most visible trappings of racial intimidation, passing anti-mask laws aimed at the Klan. In several states blacks returned to the polls and took their places on juries, school boards, and in colleges and universities. In the years before the Supreme Court's 1954 school desegregation decision, reports historian C. Vann Woodward, "The whites had 'moved over' in some degree to make room for colored southerners in various professional associations . . . in dining cars, and Pullman cars. Southern white draftees drilled, ate, and shared barracks with Negro draftees in all the military services."[10]

During this era of relative conciliation, baseball emerged as one of the most powerful agents of racial change below the Mason-Dixon line. "When the liberal forces in Atlanta, the stronghold of the Ku Klux Klan, defeated the white shirters who wanted to bar Robinson," wrote Dan Parker, "a powerful blow was struck against the color line in sports."[11] Spring training tours by the Dodgers, Indians, and other major and minor league teams integrated athletic facilities throughout the Jim Crow belt, as communities toppled like dominoes in their acceptance of interracial competition. In 1949 in addition to the Dodger breakthroughs, racial barriers fell in Norfolk, Virginia, Shreveport, Louisiana, and several Texas cities. In 1950 St. Petersburg, Florida, Columbia, South Carolina, and Mobile, Alabama, succumbed. In 1952 Chattanooga, Tennessee, New Orleans, and Montgomery, Alabama, accepted black players. Many smaller cities followed suit.

"We are swamped with offers," exclaimed Rickey in 1950. "And in booking us, the towns no longer say we can't play a Negro; they specify a Negro must appear." Economic considerations reinforced the more liberal attitudes which facilitated this change. The boundless enthusiasm of southern blacks for the pioneers of baseball integration guaranteed a capacity crowd for interracial contests. Rickey's southern tours, wrote Joe King, "were masterfully arranged to entice the Negro dollar."[12] Most minor league franchises, operating on precarious budgets, could not afford to pass up this attraction.

The fear of future consequences supplemented the lure of immediate profit. "If Dr. Green continues to press the issue," warned a Macon sportswriter during the 1949 controversy, "baseball in Georgia . . . stands to suffer a tremendous blow from which it may never recover." A major league appearance, noted the writer, "means money coming in and wonderful publicity for the city." Yet games could be scheduled elsewhere and Klan-inspired cancellations would simply force big league clubs to bypass the state.[13]

Florida's resort cities felt these pressures even more acutely. One observer attributed Miami's acceptance of black ballplayers in 1949 to "a desire to lure one or more clubs back here for spring training" because the city missed the accompanying nationwide publicity. In Mariana, Florida, where a notorious lynching had occurred several years earlier, the local chamber of commerce convinced the well-integrated Cleveland Indian organization to establish a minor league training camp.[14]

As the success of these ventures and the great popularity of baseball among southern blacks became apparent, widespread speculation emerged that minor league circuits in the Jim Crow belt might lower racial barriers in the near future. "I wonder, very cynically," wrote King after accompanying the Dodgers through the South in 1950, "how long the Texas League and Southern Association can hold out against the Negro dollar, since Rickey, the Great Emancipator, showed 'em the dark qualities of George Washington's eyes?"[15]

II

The itinerant extravaganzas of the Jackie Robinson Dodgers occurred at a critical moment in southern baseball history. By 1950 attendance, which had soared during the postwar sports bonanza, had begun to tail off. The burgeoning national production of consumer goods, absent in the immediate aftermath of World War II, now competed successfully for the sports and entertainment dollar. Among the newly marketed household items was television, which introduced major league baseball into the houses of Americans. Throughout the nation, and especially in the South, dwindling crowds forced the once flourishing minor leagues to suspend operations. In the smaller cities of the region, baseball's very survival was at stake. The emerging metropolitan centers, like Dallas and Houston, faced a different dilemma. When Texas oilman Dick Burnett purchased the Dallas Eagles in 1950, he spoke optimistically of luring a major league franchise to the city. "How does Burnett satisfy the big league teams he hopes to join?" asked Joe King. "He has to show population. And when he does," added King, proffering a solution to both the struggling and aspiring baseball cities throughout the South, "he includes Negroes."[16]

The triumphant tours of both the Dodgers and Indians clearly demonstrated the economic potential of integrated baseball. In 1950 and 1951 several clubs in the South and Southwest attempted to exploit this market. In May 1950, Phoenix in the Arizona-Texas League signed George Nicholson. Nicholson struck out in five of his first six at-bats earning a speedy release. The following season, the La Mesa team in the West Texas-New Mexico League held an "all-Negro" tryout for prospective athletes. Of the twenty blacks who appeared, La Mesa owner Jay Haney selected shortstop J. W. Wingate to pioneer in the southwestern circuit. Wingate hit safely in his first six games and became a fan favorite. The left-field Jim Crow section filled to capacity for every game. By June, however, Wingate's performance dropped off drastically and Haney released him.[17]

While Wingate toiled for La Mesa, pitcher Bob Bowman became the first black "to play for a team in Dixie," pitching for Middlesboro, Tennessee, in the Mountain States League. In August the Danville Leafs in the Carolina League signed Percy Miller, a local star. Although several fans threatened to cancel their season tickets, Miller's first appearance lured twice as many spectators as an ordinary contest; black attendance increased tenfold.[18]

These scattered breakthroughs and major league exhibition games notwithstanding, at the close of the 1952 season baseball in the South remained segregated. But unmistakable stirrings emanated from Texas. "You can't keep them out," argued Boston Brave scout Jack Zeller. "One Negro star would mean almost doubling the home attendance of several clubs in the Texas League." In 1951 the Dallas Eagles signed a working agreement with the Cleveland Indians, the team with the largest number of blacks in its minor league system, and Dallas Manager Lambert "Dutch" Meyer predicted both financial benefits and a minimum of friction should a black player be assigned to his squad.[19] At the same time, the sports color line in Texas seemed primed to fall, not in baseball, but on the gridiron. A Dallas syndicate purchased and relocated the New York Football Yankees, which unlike their baseball namesake, fielded several blacks.

It was therefore almost an anticlimax when in January 1952, Dallas Eagle owner Dick Burnett announced that his team desired a black athlete for the upcoming season. Six years earlier league President J. Alvin Gardner had predicted, "You will never see any Negro players on teams in Organized Ball in the South as long as the Jim Crow laws are in effect."[20] Now Gardner, along with most other Texas League owners, refrained from comment, silently accepting the inevitability of the Dallas action.

Like the Dodgers before them, the Eagles recognized the burdens that would be placed upon the Texas League pioneer. Burnett believed it essential to find "the right player." An all-Negro tryout for 200 players yielded no acceptable prospects. The Eagles auditioned second baseman Ray Neill of the Indianapolis Clowns but rejected him, according to one source, because "he didn't have the flash expected of a Negro player."[21] With the season drawing near, Dallas requested assistance from Cleveland. Hank Greenberg, the Indians' general manager, suggested Dave Hoskins.

Hoskins bore many of the earmarks of baseball's early black players. A veteran of the Homestead Grays, Hoskins claimed uncertainty about his age, guessing that he was twenty-seven but admitting that "another year or two either way" might be more accurate. Like many Negro League players,

Hoskins displayed great versatility, playing both the outfield and pitching. Sent to the Central League in 1948, the first black player in that circuit, Hoskins batted .393 in forty-six games as an outfielder. In 1950 a well-directed fastball to the head placed him on a hospital critical list for three days. When he rejoined the club he announced that henceforth he would be a pitcher. "I was tired of having pitches thrown at me," he explained. "I made up my mind I would start throwing at other guys."²² Recruited by Dallas as a hurler, Hoskins conferred with Burnett and Greenberg, and then agreed to become "the Jackie Robinson of the Texas League."

It is doubtful that even Robinson could have exceeded Hoskins's Texas League heroics. From his debut victory over Tulsa on April 13 to his two play-off triumphs in September, Hoskins stormed the Lone Star State. By mid-May, the right-handed curveball specialist had posted a 6-2 record, completing all of the games he had started. A left-handed hitter, Hoskins was batting close to .400. The combination established the black pitcher as one of the most popular gate attractions in the history of the Texas League. A tall, thin hurler, whose unusual mannerisms and delivery resembled those of Satchel Paige, Hoskins "continued to help spin the turnstiles"²³ wherever he pitched. In his first appearance at Houston, 11,000 spectators overflowed the stands. In his next start at Beaumont, a record crowd turned out. In both cases, blacks accounted for more than half the throng. Dallas discovered that even on days that Hoskins did not pitch, black attendance remained high. By the season's end, Hoskins had attracted sell-out crowds to every park in the circuit, no mean feat in a year in which overall Texas League attendance continued to decline.

Despite his status as the league's only black, Hoskins experienced relatively few problems. "Aside from the scattered jibes thrust at him by a few leather lunged fans," reported the Sporting News, "Hoskins' reception has been remarkably mild." Hoskins heard a minimum of jockeying from opposing benches and, as a pitcher, rarely found himself on the receiving end of brushback pitches. Throughout the league he drew accolades for his composure and deportment. For his part, Hoskins contended, "The only thing I care about is the way my teammates treat me. And they've been swell."²⁴

The only serious incident occurred in Shreveport, where Hoskins was scheduled to pitch on June 9. "I received three letters that morning, one at a time," he revealed the following year. "First one said I'd be shot if I sat in the dugout. Second one said I'd be shot if I went on the field, and the third one said I'd be shot if I took the mound." Afraid that he might be withheld from the game if he mentioned the threats, Hoskins remained silent. "I was a little scared when I took the mound," he related. "Later on I didn't even think about it and it was just another ball game."[25] With Shreveport's largest crowd of the season looking on, Hoskins hurled a 3-2 victory.

Hoskins's presence forestalled a potentially disastrous attendance year for several clubs, and by mid-season newspapers hailed him as the "Savior of the Texas League." Other blacks quickly followed him into the league. In early June, Dallas added pitcher Jose Santiago, "a pint sized Puerto Rican." In late July, Oklahoma City, managed by Tom Tatum, Robinson's former Montreal teammate, signed Bill Greason, yet another pitcher. Santiago and Greason reproduced the example established by Hoskins both on the field and at the gate. Greason's debut attracted the largest crowd of the year in Oklahoma City and on August 3, when Greason opposed Hoskins at Dallas in what promoters billed as "the first all-Negro duel," 11,000 fans crowded the Dallas park to watch the newcomer outpitch the hometown hero by a 3-2 score.[26]

At the season's end, the three black pitchers had compiled an astounding record. Hoskins won twenty-two games while losing ten. In 280 innings he registered a 2.12 earned run average. He also finished third in the league in batting with a .328 average. Hoskins's teammate, Santiago posted a 14-7 record in a little over half a season and Greason won nine of his ten decisions. Neither the performances nor the attendance figures were lost on other Texas League owners. The following year, Tulsa and San Antonio added blacks. By 1955 only Shreveport remained all-white. In the mid-1950s the Texas League was as thoroughly integrated as any minor league circuit in the nation.

Hoskins's spectacular Texas League breakthrough generated immediate repercussions. Throughout the South, minor league teams expressed an interest in signing blacks. General Manager Phil Howser of the Charlotte (North Carolina) Hornets spoke for many when he announced his intention to recruit a black prospect. Citing his club's poor early season attendance, Howser, in the words of the Sporting News, hoped that "a capable Negro player would give the stubborn turnstile a shot of oil." Defending his position, Howser added, "We pay to see Negroes sing, dance, and box. Baseball is entertainment and I see no reason why Negro players, provided they have the goods, can't play in our league."[27]

Howser's fellow owners in the Tri-State League did not accept his reasoning. When the Rock Hill (South Carolina) Chiefs inserted black twenty-two-year-old outfielder David Mobley into the lineup, league officials pressured the club to drop Mobley from the roster the following day. They claimed that his presence would "break up the league."[28] Two more years passed before another black appeared in the circuit.

In other sections of the Jim Crow belt, however, most notably in the

Southwest—Florida and the states of the upper South—racial barriers suddenly dropped. In the Florida International League, where black fans enthusiastically flocked to integrated major league exhibitions but ignored lilywhite minor league contests, four clubs introduced blacks at the start of the 1952 season. The Tampa club, managed by Robinson's erstwhile tormentor Ben Chapman, ranked among the converts. Blacks also appeared in the Gulf Coast League of Texas and Louisiana, the Sooner State League in Oklahoma, the Kitty League in Kentucky, the Coastal Plain League in North Carolina, and the Appalachian League in Virginia.[29]

In many instances teams blatantly exploited the black players, signing one at a time to attract fans and quickly releasing any who failed to excel on the field. At Rocky Mount, North Carolina, the home of Negro League great Buck Leonard, the local club signed three black pitchers in succession, none of whom lasted two games before his release.[30] A disproportionate number of these early signings involved pitchers as franchise owners sought to capitalize on and publicize a starting assignment to boost the crowd. In almost every instance, this strategy succeeded and attendance skyrocketed.

Several teams, in their avid pursuit of the "Negro dollar," held promotions to appeal to black fans. Crowley (Texas) in the Evangeline League held a special "Colored Night" to which the club admitted blacks for half-price. The all-star game in the Arizona-Texas League pitted an "All-American" squad against a "Mexican-Cuban" team, which featured native-born blacks as well as Hispanics. In 1953 Pampa in the West Texas-New Mexico League held the wedding of black infielder Ben Felder and a local black schoolteacher at home plate. Following the ceremony a "pair of Negro hurlers" opposed each other in the game. The promotion drew the largest crowd of the year.[31]

The trend continued in 1953. The biggest breakthrough occurred in the Class-A Sally League, which fielded clubs in Florida, Georgia, and Alabama. The Savannah Citizens fielded two black players and in Jacksonville, Florida, where several years earlier gates had been padlocked to exclude Jackie Robinson, local fans had the privilege of watching nineteen-year-old Henry Aaron pound his way to the Most Valuable Player Award. Attendance in Jacksonville increased by 135 percent.[32]

Given the unprecedented nature of these developments, the absence of active opposition is surprising. In only isolated incidents did local officials prevent clubs from using blacks. An interesting case occurred in Jacksonville Beach, Florida, where a local citizens' protest meeting prohibited the Class-D Sea-Birds from fielding blacks. "No race prejudice is involved," claimed the secretary of the chamber of commerce. "It's just that patrons of the team felt they would rather have an all-white team." The Sea-Birds' manager was Red Treadway. Years earlier Treadway had left the Newark Bears rather than play against Jackie Robinson. Now he supported the use of blacks by his team.[33]

A more serious controversy erupted in the Cotton States League in 1953 when the Hot Springs (Arkansas) Bathers signed Jim and Leander Tugerson, brothers who had pitched for the Indianapolis Clowns.[34] In Mississippi, the home of four Cotton States franchises, the state attorney general ruled that although no laws barred interracial competition, public policy forbade it. The Bathers' owners agreed to withhold the Tugerson brothers from games in Mississippi but asserted the right to play them in Hot Springs. League officials rejected this compromise and expelled the Hot Springs club.

The Bathers appealed their banishment to George M. Trautman, the president of the National Association of Professional Baseball Leagues. In a striking departure from the normal indifference of baseball's national hierarchy, Trautman overruled the league action. Trautman noted that the Cotton States League had ignored the rules for expulsion laid out in its own constitution. "Even if those procedures had been scrupulously followed," added Trautman decisively, "and it were found that . . . the real reason for the forfeiture of the franchise was the employment of Negro players, this office would be required to declare the forfeiture invalid." The right to employ any player, regardless of "race, color, or creed," concluded Trautman, lay with the individual club.

Trautman's unequivocal stance notwithstanding, the fate of the Hot Springs Bathers and the Tugerson brothers remained uncertain as the season approached. Finally on April 20, one day before the opening games, the Bathers surrendered to league pressure and optioned the Tugersons to Knoxville in the lower level Mountain States League. W. D. Rodenberry, the Hot Springs secretary, expressed regrets, adding, "It is our hope that other members of the league will reconsider the matter so we can recall these players." Rodenberry suggested that the newspapers in each of the localities poll their citizens on the issue. "Just let the baseball fans speak as they want," he implored, "since we think that all baseball fans want is good baseball."

Exactly one month later, when a series of injuries had depleted their pitching staff, the Bathers recalled Jim Tugerson. (Knoxville had released Leander after he developed a sore arm.) Tugerson was slated to pitch on May 20 and 1,700 fans, triple the normal attendance, turned out for the event. When Tugerson's name appeared in the starting lineup, however, the umpire, on orders from the league president, declared the contest a forfeit amidst a cascade of boos from the stands.[35]

Tugerson returned to Knoxville, where he won twenty-nine games, and filed a $50,000 suit against the president and owners of the Cotton States League. The suit charged the defendants with conspiring to prevent Tugerson from fulfilling his contract, pursuing his "lawful occupation of a baseball player," and enjoying the "equal protection of the law." In September a federal judged ruled that the rights Tugerson claimed had been violated "are not rights gauaranteed under the Constitution of the United States" and dismissed the case. Tugerson appealed the decision but ultimately dropped the suit when he signed to play in the Texas League in 1954.[36] The following season, the Cotton States League, on the brink of extinction due to poor attendance—partially due to a boycott by black fans—relented. Both the Bathers and the Meriden Millers fielded blacks during the 1954 season.

The handling of the Tugerson case did not necessarily reflect the popular will of the Cotton States region. A letter writer to the *Sporting News,* "a 100 per cent white native of Georgia" decried the action as a "disgraceful anti-democratic and anti-American episode" and wished "more power to the Tugersons and all kinds of ignominy to their benighted persecutors." Local newspapers also criticized the prohibition on the Tugersons. "We can't see that any social problem is involved here," argued an editorial in the Arkansas *Gazette* of Little Rock. "The fans are the final arbiters and the turnstiles will record their verdict." A column in Mississippi's *Delta Democrat Times* questioned whether a "third rate baseball league is any place to make a fight on equal rights because entertainment and not need is involved." The *Delta Democrat Times* saw the participation of blacks in baseball as "a good answer to the propaganda of our communist adversaries who say that the Negro has no chance in America."[37]

By the end of the 1953 season, only the Southern Association of the higher minor leagues continued to bar blacks. Speculation was rife, however, that the Double-A circuit would drop its color line in 1954. Blacks had already appeared with major league clubs in most Southern Association ball parks and as early as September 1952, the Arkansas *Gazette* reported that most league owners "are privately beginning to believe they are slashing their own economic throats by closing their eyes to the examples set in almost every other league."[38]

A Birmingham city ordinance which banned blacks and whites from engaging in athletic competition posed the major obstacle to the integration of the Southern Association. At the end of the 1953 season when it appeared that the Birmingham Barons might meet an integrated squad from the Texas League in the annual Dixie Series, Mayor James Morgan announced that he would seek repeal of the Jim Crow ordinance so that the games could be played. When Birmingham lost to Nashville in the Southern Association play-offs, Morgan dropped the matter. The following spring the Braves and Dodgers scheduled exhibition games in Birmingham and the threat of cancellation raised the possibility that the Barons and the city might lose thousands of dollars in gate revenues. In January 1954, the city commission repealed the ordinance forbidding interracial competition, and in April the Dodgers, Braves, White Sox, and Cardinals all fielded blacks in Birmingham exhibitions. The path appeared clear for the integration of the Southern Association.[39]

The player chosen to break the color barrier in the southern circuit was Nat Peeples, an outfielder with the Atlanta Crackers. Peeples, a twenty-seven-year-old veteran of the Negro Leagues, had batted .327 and .330 in his two seasons in the lower minors. When informed of his assignment to Atlanta, Peeples thought a mistake had been made. But the Crackers billed him as a legitimate contender for a spot on their 1954 squad and Peeples seemed to earn the position in spring training. In ten exhibition games he batted .467. Against Tulsa in his last appearance before his Atlanta debut, he hit two home runs. "I can't pass over a boy who has the kind of spring Nat has had," said Cracker manager Whitlow Wyatt. "Right now he's been the best outfielder I've got."[40]

Atlanta fans warmly greeted the black outfielder in his initial appearance at Ponce de Leon Stadium, rewarding him with the loudest ovation of any Cracker player. On April 9 when the season began, Peeples was on the roster, the first black in the history of the Southern Association. Despite Wyatt's lavish praise, Peeples did not appear in the starting lineup. Two weeks later, after only one pinch-hitting appearance and one starting assignment, Peeples was sent to Jacksonville. The Southern Association had regained its racial purity. Neither Atlanta, nor any other Southern Association team, fielded another black athlete before the league's dissolution in 1961.

The failure of the Southern Association to integrate reflected a shift in regional attitudes. The breakthrough in the late 1940s and early 1950s preceded the active stages of the civil rights movement and occurred amidst an atmosphere of moderation in race relations. Baseball integration represented one of the most significant manifestations of this change. Confronted by the influx of black athletes, whom they widely regarded as "entertainers," southern whites seemed wary, but unthreatened. To most, racial traditions did not hinge upon occurrences on a baseball diamond. On May 17, 1954, however, less than a month after the Crackers had released Peeples, the era of complacent acceptance came to an end. On that day the Supreme Court handed down its historic *Brown* v. *Board of Education* decision, declaring school segregation illegal. At the same time blacks began to agitate more forcefully for an end to Jim Crow. The South switched to the defensive.

Among the first concrete reactions to the *Brown* decision was the re-institution of the color line in Birmingham athletics. On June 1 the voters of Birmingham overruled the city commission, and by a three to one margin prohibited the competition between blacks and whites in "games of dice, dominoes, checkers, softball, basketball, baseball, football, golf, and track." Several weeks later, in Indianola, Mississippi, Robert Patterson, declaiming the dangers of "Communism and Mongrelism . . . hanging over the heads of our children," formed the first of the White Citizens' Councils which would lead the fight against integration.[41]

For the remainder of the decade, interracial baseball continued its expansion through the battle-scarred South, but its course no longer proceeded as smoothly as in earlier years. Local and state legislative bodies invoked the doctrine of "interposition," which asserted the right of the states to "interpose" themselves between the federal government and its citizens to prevent the advance of integration. By the end of 1956 Southern legislatures had approved over 100 new segregation statutes, including laws banning interracial competition.[42]

In Baton Rouge, Louisiana, for example, local officials in 1956 prohibited interracial contests at the city-owned ball park. The Baton Rouge Rebels competed in the Evangeline League which boasted two integrated squads, Lake Charles and Lafayette. Baton Rouge refused to allow these teams to field blacks. League directors initially took a hard line against the exclusion policy, forfeiting the first cancelled game in favor of the interracial squad. One official warned the Rebels that they must either forfeit all disputed home games, play them on the road, or drop out of the league. But the following week, the situation reversed. Under the threat of expulsion the Lafayette and Lake Charles franchises shipped their black players, including future major league star Felipe Alou, to more hospitable surroundings. A segregated peace returned to the Evangeline League.[43]

Toward the close of the 1956 season the Louisiana state legislature imposed fines and jail sentences on participants in interracial contests. This provoked concern over how Texas League clubs scheduled to appear in Shreveport in 1957 would be affected. Owners and officials struggled to resolve the problem. Several clubs suggested that they would withhold their black stars if Shreveport would bench a corresponding player. Shreveport owner Bonneau Peters refused to compromise. "If these clubs want to play at Shreveport, they'll just have to play under the law of Louisiana," he proclaimed.[44]

The final determination allowed Texas League clubs with black players to carry an extra man on the roster to compensate for their inability to field blacks in Shreveport. Throughout the 1957 season, blacks in the Texas

League, including Willie McCovey, Ruben Amaro, and Willard Brown, the former St. Louis Brown and a native of Shreveport, were left behind when their team journeyed to Louisiana.

The resolution of the Shreveport dilemma demonstrated the limits of black acceptance in the Texas League. For five years blacks had appeared in the circuit, excelling on the field and stimulating fan interest. Yet when confronted by the Louisiana segregation statute, league officials expressed more concern over the issue of competitive balance than with the rights and responses of the black athletes. Their short-sighted ingratitude did not go unanswered. In Shreveport and other Texas League cities black fans refused to attend games. By mid-season, Peters, denying that racial problems had caused his club's anemic attendance, placed the Shreveport franchise up for sale.[45] The following year the league dropped Shreveport, an action motivated more by economic than social enlightenment. In 1959 Shreveport found an appropriate home in the all-white Southern Association.

The boycott of Texas League clubs by black fans reflected the other side of the struggles rending the South in the 1950s. In late 1955 when blacks in Montgomery, Alabama (where the local Sally League franchise had employed blacks for two seasons), refused to board Jim Crow buses, launching the militant phase of the civil rights movement, boycotts already existed against many southern baseball franchises. Starting with the Cotton States controversy in 1953, black church, business, and community leaders wielded their economic power against segregated teams. In the Southern Association a protest movement had begun in New Orleans in the spring of 1955, when the local Pelicans dropped all five black players assigned to them by the Pittsburgh Pirates. "If the Pelicans are slapping you in the face, stay at home," advised local leaders. Black attendance in New Orleans, which normally exceeded 40,000, dropped to only 3,400 in 1956, jeopardizing the future of the franchise. "Give me the 40,000 Negro fans lost last year and we're out of trouble," admitted Pelican General Manager Vince Rizzo.[46]

The boycott spread to other Southern Association cities. The absence of black fans added to the general decline suffered by most minor league franchises and hastened the demise of the sixty-year-old league. In 1957 total attendance barely topped one million fans, a 50 percent decline from the pre-boycott years. By 1959 only 614,000 fans attended games. After the 1961 season, the league disbanded.[47]

The Southern Association did not fail solely because of the withdrawal of black support. Most leagues that had rushed to integrate to stave off financial disaster eventually succumbed in the face of competition from television and other entertainment media. The importation of black athletes usually provided a momentary attendance boost, but rarely a solution to the problems confronting minor league baseball. Yet during the late 1940s and early 1950s, developments on southern playing fields spearheaded the attack on segregation. The acceptance of blacks in interracial competition dented Jim Crow's armor, and in many instances, caused people, particularly business leaders, to re-evaluate the efficacy and wisdom of southern racial policies. Even as resistance to integration escalated, the baseball diamond remained an oasis of relative enlightenment amidst an increasingly hostile environment.

III

In the mid-1950s racial violence and intimidation became a hallmark of southern life. In 1955 at least four racially-motivated murders took place in Mississippi, including the well-publicized lynching of fourteen-year-old Emmett Till, who while visiting from Chicago had "wolf-whistled" a white woman. The Ku Klux Klan resurfaced throughout the South with parades, whippings, and bombings. From 1955 to 1958 forty-four persons were beaten and twenty-nine shot and wounded in racial incidents.[48]

Baseball integration in the South occurred against this backdrop. For dozens of blacks, thrust into the region at a time when racial tensions had dramatically escalated, the experience imposed a personal trial. "It was the first time I had been in the South," recalls Nebraska native Bob Gibson of his stint at Columbus, Georgia. "I spent a month there; it only seemed like a year. I thought Columbus was the worst place in the world." Other blacks described their experiences as "an ordeal" or a "sentence" and viewed the South as "enemy country" or a "hellhole."[49] Involuntary pioneers in an unplanned social experiment, these athletes, many of them teenagers, suffered adversity and discrimination. Yet they compiled remarkable records while blazing a trail for others.

Once the southern color line had yielded, most major league clubs gave little thought as to where they sent their young athletes. Baseball officials tried to judge black prospects impartially and assign them to the appropriate club, regardless of location. At times teams would make an effort to send more than one black to a southern community, but this did not always occur. In 1953 the Giants sent nineteen-year-old Bill White to play for the Danville, Virginia, team, where he would be the only black in the Carolina League. White asked to be demoted to a lower classification rather than play in the South, but the team denied his request. "Perhaps the Giants weren't sensitive to the problems I faced in the Carolina League," concluded

White when the club asked him to play in Texas two years later.[50] White became the first of a parade of blacks that the Giants sent to Danville and other southern affiliates.

Major league clubs rarely gave these youngsters special instructions or advice before their arrival in the South. For those raised in the North and the West, the shock of segregation was riveting. "I used to break into tears as soon as I reached the safety of my room," confesses Curt Flood. "I felt too young for the ordeal."[51]

Southern towns rarely welcomed these athletes. As the first black to play in Columbia, South Carolina, Frank Robinson found that "no one was quite sure how to handle the situation. I stayed in the room evenings because I couldn't go to the movie theaters in town. I just wouldn't sit in the last row of the balcony." Flood reached Savannah, Georgia, in 1956 amidst a battle over school desegregation. "I saw how uptight the black community was and how hostile the whites were," he recalls. Flood had to eat his meals at the Jim Crow lunch counter in the bus terminal. "It may have been the smelliest, greasiest, grimiest restaurant in the world," says Flood. "I went there assuming that indigestion was preferable to starvation."[52]

Black ballplayers encountered their most severe hardships when the team went on the road. "Of the many indignities to which I was subject," writes Flood, "few angered me more than the routine in [the] bus." The routine that Flood refers to stemmed from the inability of black players while on the road to stop at restaurants or restrooms with their teammates. "When we were in transit and the team made a dinner stop, I wasn't permitted in the dining room," reveals Flood. "I had to go to the back door of the restaurant, like a beggar." Often, the black athlete would remain in the bus while his teammates ate and the manager would send food out with a coach or another player. "They'd sit down and relax awhile and we had to wait until they brought us a sandwich or something out to the bus," recalls Frank Robinson. Toilet facilities were also off limits. "If I need to relieve myself, the bus would stop along the highway and I would hide from traffic as best I could while wetting a rear wheel," writes Flood bitterly.[53]

When the bus arrived at its destination, black and white teammates separated. "[We] would sit there watching them unload," recalls Hank Aaron of his season in the Sally League. "It was a silent kind of thing. The white players might have been joking and laughing when we drove into town, but when the unloading started they would get quiet."[54] Piper Davis describes a typical day on the road in the Texas League in 1957:

Go to the ballpark. Get in the bus and we go where we're going and we take them to their hotel and we take that great big old bus and drive me across over to the black hotel. In the evening we go to the ballpark. We drive that great old empty bus over to my hotel to pick me up . . . go back to the hotel where they're staying, and then go to the ball park. That was the routine.[55]

Teams occasionally instructed black players to use taxis to travel to and from the ball park, though this was easier said than done. Most cabs were not allowed to service nonwhites, and black taxi drivers feared being stranded at the ball park unable to attract a return fare. In one instance, when Chuck Harmon played for Tulsa, the team employed a fleet of white cabs to transport the team from the stadium to the railway station in Dallas. Harmon and his black teammate, Nino Escalera, boarded one of the cabs. Partway to the station, a police squad car intercepted them. The policeman, recalls Harmon "looks at the cab driver; and he looks at the cab, and then he looks at us, and then he does a [double-take]. Boy, that light went on." The policeman ordered, "You niggers get out of this cab!" and read the cab driver "the riot act" before handing him a ticket and allowing him to deposit his undesirable cargo at the train station.[56]

Hotel accommodations for blacks in the South also left something to be desired. If the athletes were lucky, they roomed in a private home. "Those people in private homes couldn't do enough for us," says Aaron, "and on top of it all, we were getting home cooking." More often, the blacks would end up in a cheap hotel or a YMCA. Robinson recalls sleeping "four to a room and no shower and we had to line up to get into the tub."[57] His white teammates, meanwhile, rested in an air-conditioned hotel.

The South's paranoia about its racial mores created problems for both light-skinned blacks and dark-skinned whites. Chuck Harmon recalls that when Don Mossi, a dark-skinned Italian, joined the Tulsa team, fans mistook him for one of the black players. "With that sun, the Texas sun, it really made him black," says Harmon. In Houston, a fan turned to his wife as Mossi took batting practice and howled, "Good God, Maude, they got three niggers now." When Puerto Rican Carlos Bonilla arrived in Florida one year for spring training, he was light-skinned enough to be allowed in the team hotel. After two weeks in the sun, his team ordered him to join the black players in a local boarding house.[58]

Harmon ran into difficulties when his wife joined him at Tulsa. A mixture of French, Irish, Indian, and black, Mrs. Harmon had blonde hair and a light complexion. On her first visit to the ball park a furor ensued at the pass gate. Tulsa officials could not decide which of the Jim Crow sections to seat her in. "If she's white, she can't sit in the black section," they told Harmon. "The black people over there will wonder what she's doing over here. And, if she sits in the white section, they'll want to know [what she's doing there]." The general manager called the parent Cincinnati team for advice, but the Reds, incredulous over the situation, simply advised them to work out a solution. Mrs. Harmon resolved the problem by avoiding most games, sitting in the black section on her rare appearances.[59]

Fan hostility further complicated the athlete's life. Hometown spectators rarely posed a problem, but southern fans unleashed an unending string of racial invective against visiting players. Frank Robinson heard cries of "Nigger go back to Africa," when he made a mistake. "One of my first and most enduring memories," adds Flood, "is of a large cracker who installed himself and his four little boys in a front-row box and started yelling 'black bastard' at me." Not all of the racial comments were negative. Chuck Harmon recalls playing in Shreveport when he and Escalera were "burning up" the Texas League. "When you gonna get yourself some niggers so we can win some ballgames?" shouted a fan to the Shreveport manager. "That tickled me" says Harmon. "He's gonna call you a nigger, but he appreciated how good you were."[60]

Fan animosity, however, also carried with it the threat of violence. Aaron and teammate Felix Mantilla received death threats in Montgomery, Alabama. In Macon, Georgia, Mantilla almost triggered a race riot when he charged a white pitcher who had hit him with a fastball. Both teams and many spectators poured onto the field and the police had to be brought in. "They stood out on that field with Tommy guns, announcing on the loudspeaker that if anyone came out on the field, they'd get shot," according to Aaron. Two years later at Columbia, South Carolina, Frank Robinson grabbed a bat and headed into the stands after some hecklers. Only the quick intercession by black teammate Marvin Williams prevented an ugly incident. Leon Wagner had the most frightening experience in Greensboro, North Carolina. "A guy hiding out behind the leftfield stands," related Wagner, "pointed a shotgun at me and yelled, 'Nigger, I'm going to fill you with shot if you catch one ball out there.'" Wagner, just nineteen years old, allowed his sole first inning chance to drop. When he reached the dugout he informed his manager and police arrested the gunman.[61]

Surrounded by racism and discrimination, black athletes had few external sources of support. Their managers and teammates displayed little sensitivity to the problems they faced. Curt Flood's Danville superior "made it clear to me that his life was sufficiently difficult without contributions from me." At Columbia, Ernie White, a native southerner, managed Robinson. Although generally fair, White once asked a team meeting about an opposing hitter, "How are we going to pitch to this big black nigger?" "A deathly quiet settled over the clubhouse," relates Robinson, "but White . . .

didn't realize what was going on." Hank Aaron, on the other hand, recalls his Jacksonville manager Ben Geraghty fondly. "I guess he was one reason I didn't realize I was crusading," claims Aaron, "because he crowded out a lot of stuff and never let it get close to me."[62]

Where more than one black played on a team, misery could be shared. But when the black athlete was isolated, he led a lonely, and often bitter, existence. For some, the inability to discuss the games and their off-field frustrations was the greatest lament. To others, the white players themselves were part of the problem. "For me, conventional team spirit was out of the question," asserts Flood in describing his season in the Carolina League. "My teammates despised and rejected me as subhuman. I would gladly have sent them all to hell."[63]

Flood's experience seems atypical. Southern social conventions prevented the development of off-field friendships, but minimal hostility surfaced among black and white teammates. At worst, most blacks found their white colleagues indifferent to their plight. Some of the white youngsters never even realized that segregation existed. "They never knew that we didn't stay in the same hotel they were," states Harmon. "They said 'Boy, you must have some nice stuff in this town, because we never see you around the hotel.'" When Earl Battey played in Louisville, his fellow Californians on the club would say, "'Come on, Earl, let's go somewhere tonight,' never thinking that there were places I couldn't go."[64]

These indignities evoked a wide variety of reactions. Older players had learned to accept segregation with a minimum of protest. Harmon says, "You know it hurts. But you just say, 'Well one of these days, things are going to get better.' But it puts a little scar on you." When asked if he was offended, Piper Davis would say, "No, I was born in the South. I was reared in the South. I know what's going on." Today, Davis admits, "I held back a lot of things I would have done something about, if it hadn't been for just trying to pave the way."[65]

Younger players born in the South also adjusted readily to the situation. "This was the way I was accustomed to seeing blacks treated," recalls Aaron, an Alabama native. Teenagers from the North, on the other hand, faced a rude awakening. Frank Robinson "couldn't figure out why I could do as I pleased in California and Utah, but not in South Carolina." Nineteen-year-old Bill White rebelled against his tormentors in the Carolina League, exchanging insults with abusive fans and casting obscene gestures in their direction. At times, he had to be escorted from the field, protected by his teammates.[66]

"What had started as a chance to test my baseball ability in a professional setting," writes Flood, "had become an obligation to measure myself as a man." For Flood, as for most of the black players who eventually climbed to the majors, "Pride was my resource. I solved my problem by playing my guts out." Most black athletes either ignored the provocations or channelled their frustrations into their performance. "Insults pushed me to play harder," says Leon Wagner. "I grew up. I grew aggressive. I tried harder to win every game." "The more the fans gave it to me, the harder I hit the ball," states White, who feels that the experience made him "a better man and a better player."[67]

White, Wagner, and the others, to paraphrase Flood, tore up those "peckerwood" leagues. Hank Aaron, according to a reporter, "led the [Sally] League in everything but hotel accommodations."[68] In 1953 White initiated an annual influx of black players who dominated the Carolina League. In 1955 Flood batted .340 and drove in 128 runs. Wagner exceeded these heroics the following year when he hit 52 home runs and amassed 166 runs-batted-in. Blacks regularly appeared among the league leaders in the Texas and Sally Leagues as well.

Other young blacks of lesser talents and resilience did not achieve this measure of success. But year after year and in league after league, black athletes defied local customs and antagonism by, as Bill White described it, "taking it out on the ball." Their performances often astounded their teammates. "I'll be goddamned," a white player summed up his impressions of the black experience in the Texas League to Chuck Harmon. "Hell, you don't know where you're gonna stay the next night; you don't know how you're gonna get to the ballpark; and you don't know where you're gonna eat. This game is hard enough. All I got to worry about is that damn curveball. You guys got to worry about all this other stuff, and still hit over .300." Harmon had one consolation. "One of these days," he anticipated, "I'm gonna move up to the major leagues and be someplace where it isn't like this."[69]

15

With All Deliberate Speed

> When the wrong is a deeply rooted state
> policy the court does its duty if it decrees
> measures that reverse the direction of the
> unconstitutional policy so as to uproot it
> "with all deliberate speed."
>
> Supreme Court Justice
> Felix Frankfurter, 1954[1]

I

"In the acceptance of black players," contended Ford Frick, who replaced Happy Chandler as baseball commissioner in 1951, "baseball showed a strength of purpose that will redound to the game's eternal credit." After the "original shock" of the Robinson signing, wrote Frick in his autobiography, "owners and players alike took up cudgels in defense of the move, not from any altruistic motive, but because they recognized . . . the competitive value of this new source of manpower." Confronted with integration, asserts Frick, baseball "met the challenge head on."[2]

In reality, major league baseball, like all American institutions, moved "with all deliberate speed" in its acceptance of widescale desegregation. In the late 1940s and early 1950s, as the Negro Leagues continued their rapid decline and black minor leaguers compiled impressive records, most major league teams failed to tap the newly available player pool. In 1949 the New York Giants promoted Monte Irvin and Hank Thompson. The following season the Braves purchased Sam Jethroe from the Dodgers. In 1951 the White Sox acquired Minnie Minoso in a trade with the Indians and Bill Veeck bought the St. Louis Browns and resurrected Satchel Paige. Although most clubs had begun to sign blacks for their farm systems, as late as September 1953, six years after Robinson had joined the Dodgers, only six of the sixteen major league clubs fielded blacks.

Baseball's failure to integrate more rapidly reflected not only a persistent hostility to blacks, but prevailing racial attitudes and assumptions, and widely shared player development strategies. Many teams stalwartly resisted desegregation. Others moved haltingly, bypassing established Negro League stars in favor of young prospects and demanding higher standards of performance and behavior from black players than white. Although doubts about the competitive abilities of blacks had disappeared and fears of box office repercussions had diminished, baseball executives continued to discriminate against black athletes.

"It is reasonably certain that there are some clubs in both major leagues which prefer to operate with all-white casts," concluded the *Sporting News* in 1952. At the time, the Cardinals, Phillies, Tigers, and Red Sox had only one black player among their organizations. Fred Saigh, who owned the Cardinals from 1947 to 1953, steadfastly refused to integrate. "I think we were thought of as a team for the South," he explained to interviewer Bill Marshall in 1979. Saigh claimed that the Cardinals sold over $200,000 worth of tickets in 1951, "largely because of the mail we'd get—'Well, we're glad you're not scumming.'" He also cited differences between midwestern and eastern writers, whom he described as "mostly Jewish boys" and very "minority-minded." Phillies officials reportedly told a scout in 1951, "If you keep talking about those Negro players you are going to find yourself working for Branch Rickey." Wendell Smith described Detroit Tiger owner Walter O. Briggs as "Oh so very prejudiced. He's the major league combination of Simon Legree and Adolf Hitler." The Tigers signed no blacks until after Briggs's death in 1952.[3]

Most major league owners cited a lack of qualified players, rather than discriminatory practices, as the reason for the absence of blacks on their teams. This argument received support from surprising sources. Several black sportswriters bemoaned the poor caliber of play in the Negro Leagues and the dearth of young black prospects. Even Jackie Robinson stated in 1951 that few additional blacks were available for immediate major league duty. "The cream has already been skimmed off the top of the Negro League," asserted Robinson, "and it will take time for the youngsters to develop."[4]

Robinson's comments notwithstanding, there appears to have been no shortage of talented blacks. By the end of the 1953 season blacks had won the National League Rookie of the Year Award five straight times and six out of seven years since Robinson's debut. Sportswriters had voted blacks the Most Valuable Player three times. In the American League, where integration had proceeded more slowly, official trophies eluded black athletes, although the *Sporting News* named Minoso Rookie of the Year in 1951 and Luke Easter Player of the Year in 1952. "Considering the small number of major league players of that race," wrote sports columnist Oscar Ruhl, "their showing is phenomenal."[5] Blacks also performed extraordinarily in the minor leagues. Furthermore, the clubs that had added black players had reaped substantial rewards. Starting in 1947 blacks appeared in every World Series, except for the 1950 Yankee-Phillie clash. Of the squads that included blacks, only the hapless St. Louis Browns and the 1952 Braves had finished out of the first division.

For some clubs the argument that qualified players were unavailable thinly camouflaged an unwillingness to recruit or promote blacks. For others the perception of a "Negro shortage" stemmed from the more stringent standards required for black players. Most teams routinely rejected older athletes who might have moved quickly into the majors, in favor of young prospects. "We'd rather take our chances with rookies, including Negroes, who could start from scratch in our minor league farm clubs and advance, year by year, in our organization until they mature into big leaguers," explained St. Louis Browns General Manager Bill DeWitt.[6] In 1951 when Branch Rickey and Bill Veeck took over new clubs—Rickey/the Pirates, and Veeck/the Browns—both signed numerous black youngsters for their farm systems. But with the exception of Satchel Paige, they ignored black veterans who might have helped their teams. This commitment to youth deprived many Negro Leaguers of the opportunity to play in the majors and delayed the integration of most clubs.

More significantly, teams generally considered only blacks of superior talents worthy of promotion. "Most are looking for sure-fire major leaguers," explained Philadelphia Athletics General Manager Art Ehlers in 1953. The average performer or potential bench warmer was ignored. The conviction persisted that the first black player on each team, as Senators' owner Clark Griffith asserted, "will have to be a great one." Yankee General Manager George Weiss announced, "The first Negro to appear in a Yankee uniform must be worth waiting for."[7] This reluctance to promote players with ordinary, or even slightly above average major league talent, condemned many blacks to the Triple-A level.

Baseball executives also demanded loftier standards of behavior from black athletes. "Never were free agents more carefully selected," boasted Ford Frick of the early years of integration. "Never before or since have scouts and general managers investigated the off-field habits, the social thinking, and the personalities of potential signees." In his initial selection of blacks Branch Rickey had stressed character as well as playing ability. In the eyes of many clubs this remained a prerequisite for black players long after integration became a reality. In 1949 Dodger Manager Burt Shotton dropped Don Newcombe from his squad because of the pitcher's temperament. "I think he can pitch in the majors, but he might undo everything these other fellows have accomplished," explained Shotton. A Boston Red

Sox scouting report on Earl Wilson, the first young black they signed, described him as a "well-mannered 'colored' boy, not too black, pleasant to talk to, well-educated, very good appearance, conducts himself as a gentleman." Articles described Elston Howard, the first black Yankee, as "an All-American boy" and "a clean-cut, religious young man who has his sizable feet planted firmly on the ground."[8] Club officials commonly described black prospects as "gentlemen," a characteristic rarely stressed about whites. In organizations that decided to actively pursue black players these demands naturally limited the number of qualified athletes.

The racism, conservatism, and indifference of baseball executives was supplemented by the absence of financial incentives. Although the experiences of the Dodgers and Indians had conclusively dispelled the argument that interracial competition posed an economic peril, by the early 1950s the presence of black athletes no longer guaranteed increased attendance. With the exception of Robinson, the drawing power of other black athletes depended more upon performance than race. "Any ball club that has a winning team will draw, regardless of whether there are Negro players on it or not," concluded Reds executive Gabe Paul. "The reverse of that is also true, a losing ball club will not draw."[9]

These factors combined to limit the spread of integration prior to the 1951 season. Even at the minor league level few teams had made a serious commitment to the development of black players. But in 1951 the search for blacks accelerated dramatically. The shift of Rickey and Veeck to the Pirates and Browns committed two more teams to integration. Other organizations that had merely dabbled in the hunt for nonwhite prospects suddenly reversed direction. In part, the continued excellence of Robinson, Campanella, Doby, Easter, and Newcombe stimulated their interest, as did the stellar rookie season of White Sox outfielder Minnie Minoso. And, Willie Mays had arrived in New York City.

Mays joined the Giants on May 25, 1951. One year earlier he had patrolled the outfield for the Birmingham Black Barons at home games while he attended high school. Several teams heard rumors of his prowess and inquired about purchasing his contract from Barons owner Tom Hayes. But Giants scout Eddie Montague discovered that the teenager had never formally signed with the Barons. Montague negotiated directly with Mays and his father and the Giants garnered the prize. (The New York organization subsequently agreed to pay Hayes $10,000 as a gesture of goodwill—and insurance against a law suit.)[10] The Giants assigned Mays to Trenton in the Class-B Interstate League where he batted .353. At the start of the 1951 season Mays joined the top New York farm club at Minneapolis.

The Triple-A franchise at Minneapolis dated from 1902, yet local fans had never viewed the likes of Willie Mays. In the Millers' first home stand Mays batted .607 over fourteen games. Dispatches described his fielding and throwing as "amazing" and "sensational." The premier gate attraction in the American Association, Mays compiled a .477 batting average over the first thirty-five games. His popularity achieved such heights that Giants owner Horace Stoneham felt obligated to place the following four-column advertisement in the Minneapolis Sunday *Tribune* in late May:

> We feel that the Minneapolis fans, who have so enthusiastically supported the Minneapolis club are entitled to an explanation for the player deal that on Friday transferred outfielder Willie Mays from the Millers to the New York Giants. We appreciate his worth to the Millers, but in all fairness, Mays himself must be a factor in these considerations. On the record of his performance since the American Association season started, Mays is entitled to his promotion and the chance to prove he can play major league baseball.[11]

As a Giant, Mays experienced less than immediate success. He failed to hit in his first twelve at-bats before drilling a home run off Warren Spahn, the great Braves left-hander. Through seven games that remained his sole hit. Yet Giants manager Leo Durocher, his players, the press, and the fans immediately sensed the presence of greatness. Mays's fielding and ebullient enthusiasm sparked and inspired his teammates. In a short time his hitting also improved. The Giants charged from thirteen and a half games out of first place in mid-August to tie the Dodgers for first place, setting the stage for the single most famous moment in baseball history, Bobby Thomson's "shot heard round the world," which won the pennant. At the season's end Mays had batted .274, slugged twenty home runs, and earned the Rookie of the Year Award.

Raw statistics cannot capture the significance of the young Mays. Charles Einstein, in *Willie's Time*, a paean to a baseball legend, argues that while Jackie Robinson "established that a Negro can make it," Mays "established that a young Negro could make it." Einstein also attributes the final demise of the old Negro Leagues to Mays's success. Einstein exaggerates on both counts. Young black players like Larry Doby and Don Newcombe were already established stars when Mays arrived and the collapse of the Negro Leagues was a foregone conclusion long before he deserted the Barons. Mays added, instead, a certain intangible element. "Willie gave the respectability to all of us because of his outstanding play and skills," asserts Giant teammate Monte Irvin. After watching Mays perform, Dan Daniel mused, "We wonder how the magnates kept the Negro out so long."[12] Mays contributed not only with his abilities, but with his youthful exuberance and his innocent, yet infectious love for the national pastime. He quickly established himself as the most exciting player in baseball, with the possible exception of Jackie Robinson. For the next two decades Mays attracted more fans, both black and white, than any of his contemporaries.

Grantland Rice called Mays "the kid everybody likes." The phrase is significant. Robinson was a great player, but his pioneering role and continuing outspokenness alienated many. Mays provided the skills and excitement without the controversy. "I think just about all the Negro players who came up to the majors before I did had the same scouting report," explained Mays in the autobiography he co-authored with Einstein. "First they said the player was a Negro and then they said he was great. With me they said great, then they said Negro." When Mays joined the Giants in May 1951, people predicted that he would "prove to be the greatest Negro player in the history of baseball." By the close of the season this appraisal had changed. "Mays is going to be the greatest ever to lace on a pair of spiked shoes," crowed Leo Durocher.[13] And few who had witnessed Mays in action disagreed.

Ironically, Mays's initial stay with the Giants proved short-lived. In May 1952, the army hoped Mays could somehow turn back the Communist tide in Korea by playing baseball at Fort Eustis, Virginia. He did not return to the Giants until 1954. Nonetheless, his example triggered a widespread talent hunt by all but a few major league clubs. In 1952 and 1953 every team except the Phillies, Tigers, Red Sox, and Cardinals began to sign greater numbers of black prospects.

In earlier years, efforts to discover promising young blacks had focused primarily on the Negro Leagues. By 1952 the rapid decline of these circuits required major league teams to adjust their scouting operations. Several teams employed Negro League veterans to scout black communities and engaged full-time talent hunters in the Caribbean. Most clubs, however, relied on their regular scouting staffs, often with disastrous results.

Lee MacPhail, the Yankee farm director in the early 1950s contends, "It didn't seem that [the scouts] really believed we wanted to sign black players." Despite his repeated urgings, says MacPhail, Yankee "bird-dogs" failed to sign black prospects. On one occasion a scout from the Gulf States region finally signed a black player, who, it developed, had minimal ability. "Well he wanted us to sign them, so I signed one," MacPhail later learned the scout had boasted. "Now we'll see what he thinks of him."[14]

The Boston Red Sox also found their scouts recalcitrant in the recruitment of blacks. According to one unconfirmed tale, a prejudiced scout cost the Red Sox an opportunity to sign Mays. The Birmingham Black Barons rented facilities from the local Red Sox affiliate. The Red Sox therefore knew of Mays's abilities and dispatched scout Larry Woodall to observe him in action. Bad weather forced postponement of the scheduled games and the Texas-born Woodall abandoned the quest. "Woodall resented having to hang around town waiting for the rain to stop," contends sportswriter Al Hirschberg, "because he was being inconvenienced by a black."[15]

On another occasion, a Red Sox "superscout," who made the final evaluation on promising players was advised of a Negro tournament in the Southwest. "How long is this nigger tournament going to last?" he asked. "I'm not hanging around here three days to watch a bunch of black kids." The scout agreed to spend an afternoon at the tournament, but after driving two thirds of the hundred-mile trip, he abruptly turned back. "I'm not going to sit through this thing," he announced. He reported to the Red Sox, with brazen honesty, that he had not noticed anyone worth signing. Other clubs recruited perhaps a dozen prospects at the tournament.[16]

But the Red Sox could not blame their belated entry into interracial baseball on the biases of individual scouts. The Boston organization assigned no scouts to the Caribbean in the 1950s, nor did they employ any black talent hunters.[17] The enlistment of black athletes required new personnel and scouting strategies. The Red Sox and other teams either failed to recognize this or declined to make the necessary adjustments.

The continuing absence of integration on most clubs inspired protests by fans, reporters, and political action groups in many cities. Pickets appeared sporadically at Yankee and Senator home games. "How CAN WE GET GREATER DEMOCRACY ON THE YANKEES?" read a flyer handed out in April 1953 by the Bronx County Labor Youth League. "While the Yankees are World Champs, they still fall behind many other ball clubs who are the real representatives of Democracy in baseball!"[18]

Major league owners usually dismissed these demonstrations as the machinations of, as Senators owner Clark Griffith described them, "a committee of Commies." Nonetheless, less radical groups joined in the agitation. In St. Louis in 1952 NAACP threats to picket all Cardinal home games produced a vague promise to sign a black player "in the near future." The following season daily newspapers in Detroit, Chicago, and Washington questioned the racial policies of the local teams. When Philadelphia's mayor described the city as "a training ground of human understanding" where "there is no discrimination," a sportswriter challenged, "Maybe the Mayor can explain how come neither Philadelphia club has hired a Negro."[19]

In the face of these critics major league owners often portrayed the vice of exclusion as a virtue. "Nobody is going to stampede me into signing Negro players merely for the sake of satisfying certain pressure groups," proclaimed Griffith in response to the protestors. Yankee General Manager George Weiss likewise took a "principled" stand. The Yankees, he stated, "are averse to settling on a Negro player merely to meet the wishes of the people who insist they must have a Negro player." Weiss claimed that this "fair stand" had been endorsed "by thrice as many letter writers as have condemned us for alleged discrimination."[20]

These defenses, however, could not hide the fact that while a handful of teams had benefited dramatically from the use of black players, ten out of sixteen teams remained segregated in 1953. Indeed, not since 1951 had a new team joined the interracial ranks. But the growing appreciation of black players and the post-1951 recruiting efforts left several teams poised on the brink of integration. In the waning weeks of the 1953 season and at the start of the 1954 campaign, all but a few teams would silence their critics and make integration a reality.

II

During the second week of September 1953, the Philadelphia Athletics and the Chicago Cubs fielded black players for the first time. On Opening Day 1954, the Pittsburgh Pirates, Cincinnati Reds, Washington Senators, and St. Louis Cardinals followed suit. Over the span of a few months the number of interracial teams had doubled, yet racial controversy continued to haunt baseball. Set against a growing national concern about civil rights, the upsurge of integration served not to defuse the integration issue but to focus attention on the most prominent remaining holdout: the perennial World Champion New York Yankees.

The Philadelphia Athletics launched the new desegregation drive with the promotion of pitcher Bob Trice. At the outset of integration in 1945, Connie Mack, the octogenarian owner of the Athletics, had adamantly opposed black entry into organized baseball. But the "Tall Tactician" proved far more malleable than his detractors allowed. In 1950 the Athletics employed Judy Johnson, a former Negro League star, to scout black prospects. Like other teams the Athletics increased their efforts in 1951. Their belated harvest included Trice.[21] A veteran of the Homestead Grays, the twenty-seven-year-old pitcher compiled a 21-10 record for Ottawa in the International League in 1953, earning a late season call. He appeared in three games for the Athletics in 1953, winning two.

In Chicago the Cubs ended a long siege of criticism and controversy when they acquired their first black athletes. For two years critics had demanded to know why black shortstop Gene Baker remained in the Pacific Coast League, while white players of lesser abilities inadequately manned that key position for the parent club. Baker, a twenty-eight-year-old veteran of the Kansas City Monarchs, had reigned as a fixture on the top Cub farm club at Los Angeles since 1950. From the start Coast League observers hailed him as the best fielding shortstop in the circuit, if not the minor leagues. Yet during his first three seasons Baker received minimal attention from the Cub hierarchy.

In the spring of 1953 Baker seemed ready to take over at shortstop for the Cubs, but the club used him sparingly in exhibitions before returning him to Los Angeles. Baker's demotion drew cries of outrage and charges of discrimination. Sam Lacy called the situation, "the prize stinkeroo of the 1953 spring training season" and "one of the scurviest deals in baseball." Baker, by virtue of his absence became, "the most controversial figure in Chicago baseball circles."[22] While incumbent shortstop Roy Smalley reestablished his mediocrity, Baker enjoyed his finest season in Los Angeles, exacerbating the debate.

On September 8 Baker finally received his summons to Chicago. But destiny did not intend him to become the first black Cub. Instead, that honor fell to another former Kansas City Monarch shortstop, Ernie Banks. Though only twenty-two, Banks glided smoothly from the Monarchs to the majors, the last of the great players produced in the Negro Leagues. The Cubs outbid several clubs for his services, paying $35,000 for Banks and eighteen-year-old Monarch pitcher Bill Dickey and thus acquired the man who was to become the most popular player in the history of the Chicago franchise. The Cubs ordered Banks to report immediately to Wrigley Field and sent for Baker so that their young prize would not be isolated. Ironically, the durable Baker, who earlier had played in 420 consecutive Pacific Coast League games, had just suffered an injury which temporarily barred his participation. Banks therefore appeared first, batting .314 over the Cubs' final ten games. In 1954 the Cubs shifted Baker to second base and the pair became one of the best keystone combinations in the National League.

Four more teams presented blacks for the 1954 season. Clark Griffith's Senators promoted outfielder Carlos Paula, one of the many Cubans in the Washington organization. ("Mr. Griffith would give Washington fans dark players from other lands," charged Shirley Povich, "but never an American Negro."[23]) Cincinnati elevated Chuck Harmon, a minor leaguer since 1947, and outfielder Nino Escalera. Branch Rickey and the Pirates rescued second baseman Curt Roberts from the head-hunting pitchers of the Western League and also offered Sam Jethroe, dropped by the Braves, a brief chance for redemption. Jethroe batted only once before the Pirates returned him to the International League. In St. Louis beer baron August Busch purchased the Cardinals from Fred Saigh in 1953, inheriting an all-white organization. Busch immediately proclaimed "a new policy with regard to Negro ballplayers."[24] He added Quincy Trouppe to the Cardinal scouting staff and purchased fancy-fielding first baseman Tom Alston from the San Diego Padres for $100,000. Alston became the first black in Cardinal history.

The rhetoric of the owners notwithstanding, with the exception of Banks and Baker, the first blacks on the newly integrated clubs proved a mediocre lot. Despite the influx of blacks on many teams, a black player failed to win the Rookie of the Year Award for the first time since 1948. Nonetheless, the 1954 season introduced several black stars. On June 24 the Cardinals elevated pitcher Brooks Lawrence to the varsity. The "Big Bull," performing in both starting and relieving roles, won fifteen games and lost six. The campaign also produced two future Hall of Famers in Banks and Braves rookie outfielder Henry Aaron. In addition, 1954 marked the return of Willie Mays. Still only twenty-four, Mays fulfilled the promise of 1951. He led the National League in batting, pacing the Giants to the World Championship, and won the Most Valuable Player Award.

Twelve of the sixteen major league teams fielded blacks in 1954. The major controversy, however, involved not one of the new entrants into interracial competition, but the most notorious of the holdouts—the New York Yankees. Since 1949 the Yankees alone among the three New York teams fielded an all-white squad. "Jackie and the Dodgers was for the colored people," commented Ernest Gaines's fictional heroine, Jane Pittman. "The Yankees was for the white folks."[25]

Stories circulating in the nation's media center attributed the absence of blacks to an undercurrent of racism which permeated the Yankee organization. According to Roger Kahn, there was a high-ranking club executive, who assisted by several martinis, confessed that a black man would never be allowed to wear a Yankee uniform. "We don't want that sort of crowd," he slurred. "It would offend boxholders from Westchester to have to sit with niggers." In 1953 traveling secretary Bill McCorry growled, "No nigger will ever have a berth on any train I'm running," and received no public reprimand from the front office. Yankee Manager Casey Stengel commonly referred to blacks as "niggers" and "jungle bunnies." The Yankees, concluded Wendell Smith, were a "ruthless, vindictive lot."[26]

Yankee officials bristled at the charges that they discriminated against blacks. "Jim Crow, my eye," exclaimed owner Dan Topping, noting that he had signed Buddy Young as the first black in the All-America (football) Conference. "How can anybody accuse any organization of which I am the head of Jim Crowism?" General Manager George Weiss, in charge of player development, repeatedly denied any bias. "We have been looking for a Negro player for some years," asserted Weiss in 1952, adding that the Yankees "will have a Negro player as soon as we are able to find a Negro player among the availables."[27]

Both the charges against the Yankees and the adamant denials of club officials possessed elements of truth. In 1949 the New York club had been among the first to follow the lead of the Dodgers and Indians in signing blacks. Weiss recruited Artie Wilson, Luis Angel Marquez, and Frank Austin. The subsequent disputes regarding the contracts of Wilson and Marquez unravelled these early efforts. The Yankees then purchased the contracts of Bob Thurman and Earl Taborn from the Kansas City Monarchs. Thurman performed impressively for the Triple-A Newark Bears in 1949. The Yankees, recalls Thurman, "said something about taking me to spring training, but at the end of the year they sold the Newark franchise to the Cubs and somehow I went in the deal."[28] The transfer also included Taborn and once again the Yankees had no blacks under contract.

In 1950 the Yankees again tapped the Monarchs, their Kansas City tenants, and acquired outfielder Elston Howard and pitcher Frank Barnes. The club assigned both to a Class-B affiliate. In August the Yankees acquired Vic Power, the nineteen-year-old Puerto Rican sensation of the independent Provincial League. Over the next three years, Power and Howard emerged as the leading candidates to break the color barrier on the Yankees.

The Yankees had thus followed the same begrudging path toward integration as the majority of other clubs. In the early stages of the great experiment, they had exceeded the efforts of most clubs. In the post-1951 era, however, Yankee efforts lagged, as they recruited few additional prospects. Located in New York with a large black population and an active sporting press, the Yankee situation came under more stringent scrutiny than other clubs. As the years passed with no blacks added to the squad, even Dan Daniel, a devoted defender often accused of being on the Yankee payroll, admitted "If the Yankees weren't guilty as charged, they were certainly going out of their way looking for trouble."[29]

Trouble emerged on November 30, 1952, in the figure of Jackie Robinson. Robinson appeared on the television show "Youth Wants to Know." Toward the end of the program one of the teenage questioners unexpectedly asked, "Mr. Robinson, do you think the Yankees are prejudiced against Negro players?" By one account, Robinson gasped audibly and then forthrightly replied, "I think the Yankee management is prejudiced. There isn't a single Negro on the team now and very few in the entire Yankee farm system." Robinson's remark ignited a storm of outrage. Weiss described Robinson's comments as "silly" and added "If Robinson can get me a free agent who is capable of taking the job of any Yankee regular, I would be only too glad to establish a Negro player on our club."[30] Robinson steadfastly defended his allegations.

In 1953 the Yankees faced further embarrassment when black pitcher

Ruben Gomez joined the crosstown Giants and won thirteen games. Gomez had played in the Yankee farm system but concluded that he would never be promoted to the parent club. In an unusual move, Gomez purchased his own contract from the Yankees and then signed for a $10,000 bonus with the Giants who placed him on the major league roster. The Gomez incident fanned the flaming rhetoric of Yankee critics. "How did these saintly gentlemen ever let a good pitcher like [Gomez] of the Giants get away?" asked Wendell Smith.[31]

Amidst these controversies young Vic Power advanced a strong case for a major league position. "I've been in baseball 40 years," said minor league manager Bruno Betzel, "and Vic Power is the greatest young prospect I've ever seen."[32] In 1952 as the first black in the history of the Kansas City Blues, Power batted .331 and drove in 109 runs. Returned to Kansas City in 1953 Power accelerated his production. At the end of July he led the American Association in batting, hits, doubles, and runs batted in. Yet when the Yankees recalled four minor leaguers on July 31, Power was not among them. Critics again scored the Yankees for their racial policies.

The perennial World Champions denied all allegations of discrimination, but at the same time the club began to circulate stories disparaging Power's abilities. Power, stated Dan Topping, "is a good hitter, but a poor fielder." Daniel reported that "Power is major material right up to his Adam's apple. North of that location, he is not extraordinary. He is said to be not too quick on the trigger mentally." Other releases charged that Power did not hustle and that "he was hard to handle."[33] In short, according to the Yankee organization, Power did not possess the "right attitude" to join the Yankee family.

Power's subsequent career belies these assertions. Baseball experts rank him as one of the outstanding defensive first basemen in history. An exuberant, exciting player who always exerted the utmost effort, Power also demonstrated a sharp wit and mental alertness, which made him a favorite of fans and sportswriters.

Equally questionable were the allegations that Power did not fit the Yankee image. "Since when is it necessary for a member of the Yankees to conduct himself according to the dictates of Emily Post?" wondered Wendell Smith. Smith described the 1953 Yankees as "the derelicts of the major leagues, the most brazen incorrigibles in the game today." This characterization was exaggerated but not far off the mark. Off the field young Yankee superstars Whitey Ford and Mickey Mantle playfully cavorted through the nightclubs of New York with their favorite companion, Billy Martin. Martin had already established his reputation as a two-fisted brawler. "If there is anyone who wears his feelings on his shoulder with more defiance," stated Smith, "we'd like to know who it is."[34]

The charges, Power later admitted, gave him "a crawly feeling on his spine." "I say, 'Why? What I do?'" Power explained. Objections arose, recalls former Yankee Farm Director Lee MacPhail, "not because he was black, but just because he was Vic Power." To some extent the problem lay in Power's flamboyant style of play. "I am the original showboat hot dog," he would later boast. His one-handed catches offended Yankee traditionalists. More significantly, Power rarely retreated from physical challenges, racial or otherwise. In 1953 he engaged in a fistfight with an opposing player. "He is a rough, tough customer. He refuses to scare easily," wrote Smith. "If you start punching, he'll punch back." Perhaps most important, rumors reached New York that Power dated white women.[35] For any or all of these reasons, the Yankees decided that Power did not fit the requirements for their first black player.

Throughout the fall of 1953 the Yankees continued to denigrate Power and instead extolled the virtues of their second black prospect, Elston Howard. Howard batted only .286 for Kansas City, some fifty points lower than Power. Nonetheless, Yankee officials touted Howard as a more likely prospect to break the color line. Howard, reported Daniel, "is faster of foot, and a quicker thinker as well. He has a better educational background."[36] Unlike Power, implied team spokesmen, the likable, easygoing Howard was the Yankee type of player.

At the close of the 1953 season the Yankees placed both Power and Howard on their major league roster. Critics greeted this maneuver with skepticism. Several writers noted that had the Yankees not named the two players to their roster, both would have become eligible for the major league draft and the Yankees might have lost them for a small fraction of their market value. Sam Lacy predicted that it was "quite likely" that neither athlete would appear with the Yankees, whose "preference would be to work out a trade that will send either, or both, elsewhere."[37]

In December the Yankees transformed their detractors into prophets by trading Power to the Philadelphia Athletics for veteran slugger Eddie Robinson and promising pitcher Harry Byrd. "Why should we be criticized?" asked Weiss in response to the resulting uproar. "We could not have made the deal if we had not consented to let Power go. When you trade you don't examine colors." Even Lacy concluded that "the deal sending Vic away was a plausible one."[38] Nonetheless, the trade reaffirmed suspicions of prejudice in the Yankee front office.

In spring training the focus shifted from Power to Howard. The twenty-four-year-old Howard represented the antithesis of his former teammate. A shy, retiring, workmanlike ballplayer, Howard attempted to avoid controversy or confrontations. To Lacy, Howard was "a lad . . . so young, so

trusting, so naive as to still have faith in human nature, Yankee version."
Throughout his minor league career Howard had played the outfield. Upon
his arrival in Florida, Manager Stengel informed him that he would be converted into a catcher. "As an outfielder he would never be more than a minor leaguer," commented Stengel. "In order to play up here, he'd best turn
his efforts to catching." To many observers, the position switch constituted
another ploy by the Yankees to avoid integration. In Yogi Berra the Yankees
possessed the best catcher in the American League. Furthermore, argued
Lacy, "If Howard is not a major leaguer as an outfielder . . . it stands to
reason he is not a major leaguer as a catcher." The Yankees, alleged Lacy
and others, were giving Howard the "runaround" before dispatching him to
the minors.[39]

The Yankees returned Howard to the minors, as predicted, exposing
themselves to further attacks. "All up and down Seventh Ave. [in Harlem],"
reported the Chicago *Defender*, "all you can hear is 'I told you so.' " A correspondent to the *Sporting News* wrote, "For years I defended the Yankees.
After watching developments this spring, however, I am convinced that
they don't want a Negro player; they want a Negro superman." Another
letter asked, "Who do the Yankees think they are fooling? The double talk
and hypocrisy they are trying to foist on the public is just too much."[40]

Yet whatever the Yankees past sins, the allegations regarding the treatment of Howard in 1954 appear unjustified. Howard's minor league record
did not merit promotion and although the durable Berra remained the regular Yankee catcher for several more years, the transfer of Howard from the
outfield proved beneficial to both him and the Yankees. The following
spring after a banner season at Kansas City, Howard joined the New York
club with whom he played or coached for all but two seasons until his
death in 1980.

Current American League President Lee MacPhail, then the Yankee
farm director, states today, "I will agree that the Yankees may have perhaps dragged their feet a little bit." But, adds MacPhail, "I can't agree there
was any racial bias there at all. The Yankees were very anxious that the
first black player that they brought up would be somebody with the right
type of character whom they felt was ideal. Elston was ideal."[41] The major
phase of the Yankee controversy ended with the addition of Howard. But
throughout the 1950s, the Yankees fielded few blacks and the productive
Yankee farm system yielded no other black stars for the parent club. To
those who never forgave the Yankees for their belated entry into the integrated ranks, the club's efforts smacked of tokenism.

It had required seven seasons for a majority of major league clubs to
integrate, a painfully slow pace by modern standards. To contemporary ob-

servers, however, a remarkable transition had occurred. "I didn't think the Negro ballplayer would be accepted all over so soon. Neither did Mr. Rickey," commented Robinson in 1952, even before the major influx of the following seasons. For American society as a whole the years 1954-55 represented a new departure in the struggle for civil rights. The Supreme Court's school desegregation decision marked the beginning of a frontal assault against Jim Crow. In baseball the battle for desegregation, if not racial equality, was entering its concluding stages. To sportswriter Harold Rosenthal, an "athletic revolution" had transpired. Recalling the early opposition to Robinson's presence, Rosenthal wrote, "From open rebellion to universal acceptance in just seven seasons is a staggering thought."[42] But acceptance was not yet universal. The Philadelphia Phillies, Detroit Tigers, and Boston Red Sox remained as vestiges of the Jim Crow era.

III

The rapid expansion of integration after 1953 simultaneously contributed to and obscured the death throes of an American institution. "Every colored player who makes his way up to the majors," observed Bill Roeder, "taps another nail into the coffin of the Negro Leagues."[43] By 1951 the demise of black baseball seemed imminent. The Negro National League had folded, and the Negro American League, optimistically reconstituted with ten teams in 1949, fielded only six squads. In 1953 only four teams remained: The Birmingham Barons, the Memphis Red Sox, the Kansas City Monarchs, and the Indianapolis Clowns. In 1955 the Detroit Stars replaced the Clowns. These four teams survived the decade. But as interracial play became more commonplace and the ideology of the civil rights movement engulfed black Americans, interest in Jim Crow competition vanished, and the Negro Leagues dissolved.

Initially, many observers had viewed the rapid dissolution of black baseball with alarm. "How will major league scouts be able to look over Negro material if there are no Negro teams playing?" asked *Courier* columnist Jack Saunders. Black writer Alvin Moses feared that without the Negro Leagues, "colored youths will no longer attain promise as being of sufficient caliber to even interest scouts for white clubs." Saunders predicted that once the Negro Leagues had disappeared and the first wave of black pioneers had retired, "major league baseball will revert to the national pastime of those Americans with white skins." These commentators could not conceive of a baseball universe devoid of discrimination. Branch Rickey disagreed. The Negro Leagues, he argued in 1951, had existed due to "necessity and prejudice," but blacks no longer required apprenticeship in their own circuits.[44]

The most dire jeremiads of Negro League defenders never came to pass; yet Rickey's assessment remained premature. Throughout the early 1950s most blacks recruited by the major leagues continued to come from the Negro Leagues. "If I had waited in Mobile for a white scout to find me," commented Henry Aaron, who began his career with the Indianapolis Clowns, "I don't know if I'd ever have been discovered for the big leagues or not."[45] The delayed entry of major league scouts into black communities, coupled with the decline of the Negro Leagues, doubtless curtailed the careers of many black hopefuls.

Negro League President J. B. Martin, always a staunch advocate of integration, repeatedly justified the continued existence of his operation on these grounds. "Colored players are far from being fully integrated into baseball," he explained in 1952. "Until I see colored players accepted just as are other players in both the South and the majors and not considered as a novelty, I say there will be a need for organized colored baseball." Martin also clung to the hope that with the "curiosity" of blacks in the major leagues wearing off, "our old fans are now going to start coming back." As late as 1954 he optimistically told Wendell Smith that "with the excitement over Negro players in organized baseball apparently dying down," black baseball "anticipates a renaissance."[46]

With olders stars retiring or entering the minor leagues, and young prospects quickly sold to the majors, however, black teams boasted few attractions to lure back their patrons. In addition, the same economic difficulties unravelling the minor leagues hampered the black circuit. Negro League entrepreneurs tried desperately to rejunvenate their franchises. Clubs slashed salaries and invited back stars who had defected to the Mexican League. Ernie Wright, whose Cleveland Buckeyes competed with the integrated Indians, introduced simultaneous radio and television broadcasts in the 1940s to stimulate interest. The experiment failed and the Buckeyes succumbed in 1949. Some clubs signed white players. The Indianapolis Clowns boosted attendance in 1953 when they signed Toni Stone, a black woman, to play second base. The Clowns issued rave notices about Stone's smalltown appearances, but she always seemed to perform briefly and ineffectively when observed by urban reporters.[47]

With gate receipts declining, black teams experienced increasing difficulties renting facilities in their hometowns. Yankee Stadium and the Polo Grounds evicted their Negro League tenants after the 1948 season. By 1950 the Clowns, although bearing the name of Indianapolis, could not play in that city because of contract difficulties with stadium owners. Even more than in the past black teams relied on barnstorming to locate audiences. "They were cutting salaries and bus riding like mad," recalls Quincy

Trouppe. As minor leagues collapsed, available ball parks also became scarce, rendering scheduling more difficult.[48]

"Now Negro baseball must develop talent and sell it to the majors to survive," observed Wendell Smith as early as 1950. Increasingly, the livelihood of black franchises depended not on gate receipts, but on the newly created market for black players. Owners found themselves in an extremely precarious position. Major league teams offered startlingly low prices for black athletes, but the economic vulnerability of the Negro League clubs and their fear of fan disapproval dictated acceptance. When owners attempted to withhold players to procure higher prices, the Chicago *Defender* reported that fans "became infuriated," charging the teams with blocking the advancement of black players.[49]

Effa Manley has described the transactions between the major and Negro Leagues as a "bargain basement rush." The case of Sam Jethroe illustrates the one-sided nature of these deals. In 1948 Cleveland Buckeye owner Ernie Wright, desperately in need of operating capital, sold Jethroe, his leading attraction, to Branch Rickey's Dodgers for $5,000. Two years later Rickey received a figure in excess of $100,000 for Jethroe from the Boston Braves.[50] Yet the moneys offered and accepted for black players remained low. In an age in which teams offered six-figure bonuses for untried prospects, like pitcher Paul Petit, and top minor league players, like Jethroe, the going rate for a good Negro Leaguer ranged from $5,000 to $15,000. Only Ernie Banks, who moved directly from the Kansas City Monarchs to the Chicago Cubs, brought a figure as high as $20,000. Nonetheless, the sale of a player or two each year meant the difference between profit and loss for the surviving Negro League clubs.

The Kansas City Monarchs reigned as the most productive outlet for prospective stars. More than a dozen major league players, including Robinson, Paige, Banks, and Howard emerged from the Monarch roster. For some major league clubs scouting black players meant scouting the Monarchs. But by 1955 even the Monarchs could no longer sustain a profitable operation. Major league baseball had arrived in Kansas City in 1954, distracting attention from the black club. Furthermore the transplanted Athletics proved inhospitable landlords. The Athletics increased their percentage of the gate receipts of Monarch games and added incidental charges for the use of the tarpaulin, public address system, and "office overhead." "There is a charge for everything except the flagpole," complained Monarchs owner Tom Baird. Syd Pollock of the Clowns described the expenses as "the stiffest I've ever seen." "They're murdering you," he told Baird. Even a brief return by Satchel Paige provided minimal relief. At the close of the 1955 season Baird sold twelve of the clubs' eighteen players, including future major leaguers George Altman and Lou Johnson, and prepared to dissolve the franchise. Black sports entrepreneur Ted Rasberry, who already owned the Detroit Stars, bought the remnants of Baird's club, allowing a temporary reprieve.[51]

Most white fans were unaware of the continued existence of the Negro American League, but Rasberry and league President J. B. Martin struggled to keep the ghost of black baseball alive. Martin, a wealthy Chicago businessman, donated his services and provided an office and league staff at no cost. On several occasions he appealed to Commissioner Frick with minimal success for help for the struggling league. In 1957 the Negro American League actually added teams in Mobile and New Orleans, but neither squad survived a full season. Two years later the Los Angeles Dodgers, believing that the black clubs might still uncover talent, offered to subsidize the circuit in exchange for a first chance at all prospects. Martin rejected the offer in favor of an "open market" in player sales. That year the 27th Annual East-West Game at Comiskey Park, once the best showcase and income supplement of the league, netted only $5,000 to be divided among the four clubs. After 1960 the Negro American League simply ceased operations. By 1965 all that remained was a barnstorming club capitalizing on the name, Indianapolis Clowns. "We are all show now," said their owner, "We clown, clown, clown . . . like the Harlem Globetrotters in basketball."[52]

The side effects of integration included the destruction of a significant cultural entity and way of life. At one time the Negro Leagues had constituted one of the largest primarily black-owned and operated enterprises in the nation. With its demise, as Charles Einstein notes, "The possibility is strong that fewer blacks make their living from professional baseball than at any previous time in this century." The abandonment of the black leagues strikingly demonstrates the black commitment to an integrated society in the 1950s. "Nothing was killing Negro baseball but Democracy," concluded Wendell Smith. "The big league doors suddenly opened one day and when Negro players walked in, Negro baseball walked out." And, most blacks, added "Doc" Young, "far from being sorry . . . are glad."[53]

16

They've Just Got To Forget They're Black

> Baseball has been wonderful for my people. Where else could a Negro shake a stick at a white man and 50,000 people cheer.
>
> A Black comic in the 1960s[1]

> I am pleased that God made my skin black, but I wish He had made it thicker.
>
> Curt Flood, 1972[2]

I

Cincinnati Reds pitcher Herschel Freeman worked as a sheriff in his native Alabama during the off-season. In his lifetime he had dealt with blacks only in the authoritarian context of the Jim Crow South. Playing in the mid-1950s for the Reds, a team which included seven blacks at one point, Freeman worked in an unfamiliar racial environment. Impressed by the nonwhite players, he concluded that his black teammates were somehow different from his Alabama neighbors. Joe Black, the former Dodger pitcher, corrected him. "No way. There's no difference," explained Black. "You just don't know those people down South. You don't socialize with those people down South. But here we're all equals, so it's a different ballgame."[3]

The locker room lesson of the Cincinnati Reds reflected the changing racial perspectives of the United States in the 1950s. Greater interracial familiarity and enlightenment through education, according to the liberal creed, would eliminate prejudice and discrimination. The *Brown* decision rested largely on these assumptions; the baseball experience seemed to affirm them. On the surface the spread of integration in baseball proceeded with a surprising absence of friction. But the early years marked a difficult period of adjustment for players, managers, fans, and sportswriters, a process which would be repeated as blacks entered other industries and institutions in subsequent years. Confronted by lingering prejudice on the playing field, in their private lives, and in Florida and Arizona training camps, black athletes, led once again by Jackie Robinson, changed from stoic pioneers, grateful to be accepted, to militant protesters, demanding equal treatment—foreshadowing the evolution of the civil rights movement.

Contrary to the predictions of integration opponents, the addition of blacks rarely precipitated resentment from home fans or created significant problems on any major league club. The Cincinnati experience was an illustrative example. Crosley Field, the home of the Reds, attracted crowds from the racially-charged border states of Kentucky and West Virginia and most facilities in Cincinnati remained segregated into the late 1950s. "The worst fans were in Cincinnati," recalled Hank Thompson. "Whenever there was a lull, some loudmouth would yell: 'Nigger' or 'black unprintable' and you could hear it all over the place." In 1952 a death threat against Jackie Robinson necessitated armed body guards during his stay in the city.[4] Southern ballplayers like Freeman, Johnny Temple, Ed Bailey, and Roy McMillan predominated on the Reds' roster. Yet when Chuck Harmon and Nino Escalera joined the Reds in 1954, they experienced few difficulties.

"You know how cozy Crosley Field was," states Harmon. You're right there next to the people. You can hear anybody talk. But I can't remember anybody saying anything offensive to me." Harmon's reception from his teammates also pleased him. "The southern ballplayers were more friendly to me than the northern ballplayers," remembers Harmon. "We'd eat together, and go to the movies. They would come looking for me to play cards. And I wasn't a pigeon either." Bob Thurman, who joined the Reds in 1955, experienced the same phenomenon. "You talk about a family," he exclaims. "That's the greatest set of guys you ever wanted to be around. They didn't think nothing about any color."[5]

Most blacks who entered the major leagues in the 1950s have similar recollections. Despite the problems that Jackie Robinson had with the southern-born Dodgers, once integration was a reality, southern whites, who normally had more experience dealing with blacks than did northerners, often seemed more adaptable to the new situation. On the Giants, Hank Thompson felt most comfortable with fellow infielders, Alabaman Eddie Stanky and Louisianan Alvin Dark. Brooks Lawrence, who played for both the Cardinals and the Reds, asserts, "The white ballplayers from the South had a much better handle on things than the white players from the North." One or two players, who resented the intrusion of blacks, "stayed out of your way," states Lawrence, but most "did start to accept you as a person."[6]

Integration also raised the issue of racial attitudes among managers and coaches. When southerners assumed managerial jobs many questioned their ability to handle an interracial team. Commenting on the prospect of Rogers Hornsby returning to the managerial ranks, Wendell Smith asked, "Now that the color bars have been dropped in the majors, we wonder if Hornsby is qualified to hold such a responsibility." Frequent accusations depicted Casey Stengel as a racist, an image enhanced by the Yankees' well-publicized delay in using blacks. Stengel did not dispel this image when he commented about Howard, "When I finally get a nigger, I get the only one that can't run."[7]

On occasion, embarrassing racial attitudes slipped to the surface. Sam Jethroe complains that one manager repeatedly called him "Sambo." At a Yankee team meeting, scout Rudy York, a Georgian, told the team how to detect opponent Connie Johnson's pitches according to how he held his hand. "You know niggers have white palms, lighter than the backs of their hands," advised York. Whitey Ford recalls, "It was so quiet in the room, you could hear a pin drop. We were so embarrassed, with Elston sitting there and listening."[8] The most publicized instance of a manager's racial prejudice occurred in 1964 when Giants pilot Alvin Dark told a Long Island *Newsday* reporter that black and Latin players lacked "mental alertness" and "pride."

Yet few players in their recollections complain about discriminatory treatment by managers. Howard said of Stengel, "I never felt any prejudice around Casey. He treated me the same as he did any other player." This appears to have held true in most cases. Amidst the furor over Dark's comments, Willie Mays told his teammates, "Regardless of his philosophy, Dark did not discriminate when it came to fielding the best possible line-up." Henry Aaron praised managers Chuck Dressen and Bobby Bragan for empathizing with the problems peculiar to the black player. But among most managers, Aaron discovered, "Their attitude was 'Let 'em live. Keep 'em satisfied.'"[9]

Blacks more commonly confronted racial stereotyping and prejudice in their treatment by the press. West Coast reporters in 1949 delighted in depicting Luke Easter with what the Pittsburgh *Courier* described as a "Deep South dialect" and a "Stepin Fetchit manner." The *Sporting News* quoted Easter saying things like, "I shore likes to play and I likes the money I'm making." A 1950 cartoon in the same journal depicted Easter as "The Kingfish Clouter." A fat-lipped caricature of Easter approached a former major league star, asking, "Mistah Peppah Mahtin! May Ah have yo' autograff?" Willie Mays fared little better. A 1951 cartoon figure of Mays proclaimed, "Ah gives base runners the heave ho!" and "Ah aims to go up in the world."[10] In the World Series that year, in which the Giants fielded the first all-black outfield, a Chicago writer composed the following unpublished doggerel:

> Willie Mays is in a daze
> And Thompson's lost his vigor,
> But Irvin whacks for all the blacks—
> It's great to be a nigger.[11]

These images recurred throughout the early years of integration, but by the mid-1950s, the most blatant examples of racial stereotyping had disappeared. In addition, newspapers no longer felt compelled to repeatedly define a player's race. Overall, the desegregation of baseball received highly sympathetic coverage. Even the *Sporting News,* whose editorials at best revealed a patronizing attitude toward blacks and whose illustrations could be tasteless, generally covered the integration saga with exceptional thoroughness and objectivity.

The most highly publicized instances of racial discord occurred, ironically, on the Brooklyn Dodgers. The Dodger difficulties, all relatively minor, surfaced primarily because the Dodgers represented both baseball's most intensely integrated team and the most closely watched. As each season delivered additional blacks to the Dodger squad, sportswriters speculated about a "saturation point"—the number of blacks on a team, or in the lineup, beyond which a franchise, for either reasons of economics or player morale, dared not go. In 1950 with Robinson, Campanella, and Newcombe all established stars and Bankhead and Jethroe meriting promotion, reporters predicted that the Dodgers dared not increase the number of black players to five. The Dodgers sold Jethroe to the Braves and Rickey later admitted, "Ownership thought there was a surfeit of colored boys on the Brooklyn club. . . . [If] a fifth one would tend to lose a pennant, then the reason for hiring Robinson was the identical reason for not hiring Jethroe."[12]

Each subsequent year, as black prospects in the Dodger chain matured into major leaguers, the issue reappeared. "The thought has been advanced," reported the *Sporting News* in 1954, that to have too many blacks on a team "would not be good business." Dick Young attempted to justify the controversy. "Suppose you own a ball club and it represents $3,000,000," reasoned Young. "Everything you do in connection with the club must be done with an eye toward protecting your investment." Playing too many blacks, he argued "would be taking a chance—and no man takes a chance with $3,000,000 if he doesn't have to." By Young's reckoning in 1955, five blacks on a twenty-five-man squad was not excessive. Regarding the prospect of eight blacks on the Dodger roster, however, Young concluded, "I honestly don't believe baseball is ready for that step right now."[13]

The racial cauldron almost boiled over in the spring of 1953 when Dodger manager Chuck Dressen announced that black rookie second baseman Jim Gilliam would replace Robinson, who would transfer to third base, supplanting veteran Billy Cox. Cox and his roommate, Preacher Roe, resented the projected maneuvers. "How would you like a nigger to take your job?" Cox drunkenly asked reporter Roger Kahn. Others on the team passed offhand remarks about the growing number of blacks. "I don't mind them in the game but now they're really taking over," confessed one Dodger.[14]

The attitude of the players appalled reporters covering the Dodgers. "Why and how could this have happened on a team which served as the classic demonstration that whites and Negroes can work side by side, not with tolerance, but with respect?" asked Milton Gross. "What an infinitely barren ending for the Robinson experience," reacted Kahn. The Dodger front office rushed to conciliate both black and white players. The reports embarrassed Roe and Cox, who had played alongside Robinson for several seasons. "For five years I've broken my back for you and for five years you've broken your back for me," Roe apologized to Robinson. "No matter what you've heard or what you think, that's all I want you to remember." Robinson downplayed the incident. "What a better world this would be if there were no more racial discrimination than there is on this ball club," he advised reporters.[15]

The Cox-Gilliam controversy quickly passed, but the "saturation" issue persisted. In 1954 yet another black prospect entered the Dodger picture. Sandy Amoros, a fleet black Cuban who had batted .353 for Montreal in 1953, greatly impressed the Dodger management in spring training. Nonetheless, reported Bill Roeder, there existed "an undercurrent of suspicion" that the Dodgers "were reluctant to add another Negro to the squad." Amoros's presence raised the spectre of a lineup, including him, Robinson, Campanella, Newcombe, and Gilliam, in which blacks would outnumber whites on the playing field. When Manager Walter Alston consigned Amoros, who was probably not ready to start, to the bench, Roeder wondered, "Are the Dodgers going out of their way to avoid having more than four Negroes in the line-up at the same time?"[16] Through the first three months of the season, though probably not by design, the four-player barrier remained intact. Finally, on July 17 Alston named a lineup which included all of the black Dodgers, except pitcher Joe Black.

Since few other teams included many black players at this time, the "saturation point" argument rarely surfaced. Only the Indians experienced similar speculation. As the number of black Indians rose, some observers blamed the team's failure to repeat its pennant success of 1948 to an excess of blacks. "We have five of them," the Pittsburgh *Courier* repeated 1953

Cleveland gossip, "and that's at least three too many." Indian General Manager Hank Greenberg admitted receiving mail on this subject, but added, "The only time the fans complain is when the Negroes aren't delivering."[17] The controversy evaporated when the Indians topped the American League in 1954.

If interracial conflict rarely surfaced among teammates during the early 1950s, a different pattern emerged between opposing teams. When an integrated club faced an all-white squad, race baiting frequently entered the repertoire of the bench jockeys. "Sometimes players would yell from the dugout, 'Nigger, what are you doing up here?'" wrote Hank Thompson of his early years in the majors. In 1952 when Joe Black joined the Dodgers, the Cincinnati bench greeted him with a chorus of "Old Black Joe." Black responded by aiming a fastball at the heads of each of the next seven Cincinnati batters. "Musta been some crooners in the lot," said Black. "That stopped the music."[18] For the most part black players ignored the taunts, or let their teammates respond.

On occasion, race baiting erupted into controversy. In 1952 the St. Louis Cardinals unleashed a barrage of racial insults at Robinson and his Dodger teammates. Shouts of "Nigger," "black bastard," and "Porter, get my bag" emanated from the dugout. At one point a Cardinal player held up a pair of baseball shoes and shouted, "Here boy, shine." Robinson reacted with fury. "I've been in the league six years," he told Roger Kahn, "and I don't think I have to put up with it anymore." Cardinal Manager Eddie Stanky, Robinson's former teammate, denied any wrongdoing. "I heard nothing out of line," he reported. The following day he added, "I heard 'black bastard!' I don't consider that out of line." To Stanky, this represented "just routine bench-jockeying." Cardinal owner Fred Saigh advised, "Negro players shouldn't be touchy about those things. They've just got to forget they're black."[19]

After 1954 as more teams fielded blacks, racial bench jockeying declined. But another form of racial antagonism continued unabated. Virtually all black players in the early 1950s agreed that major league pitchers, like those in the minors, made them targets of a disproportionate number of brushback pitches and beanballs. "No question about it," states Monte Irvin, "They threw at us like we were something good to eat." His teammate Hank Thompson contended, "I was Negro which meant certain pitchers knocked me down regularly. I don't mean brushback stuff. I mean knockdown pitches thrown at my skull."[20]

Major league moundsmen had always directed close pitches at successful batters and the high level of performance by blacks accounts in part for their target status. Nonetheless, statistics reveal that pitchers hit blacks with startling frequency. Robinson continually ranked among the league leaders in the hit-by-pitch category. In 1947 he set a National League record for rookies when pitchers found him nine times, seven during the first half of the season. The following year Robinson led the league. In 1952 he established a new Dodger record with twelve "hits." The next season he broke the record. Through the 1954 campaign pitchers had victimized Robinson sixty-five times. "Some pitchers just can't resist the Coney Island urge to throw at Robinson's head," concluded one writer. Roger Kahn noted that Robinson's teammate Carl Furillo, often cited as a frequent beanball target and less agile than Robinson, had been struck only thirty-one times over a longer span of time.[21]

The controversial, aggressive Robinson did not represent a special case. In 1950, Luke Easter's first full season in the majors, pitchers hit him ten times, tying him for the league lead with Al Rosen, one of the few Jewish players in the majors. The following year rookie Minnie Minoso surpassed both Easter and Rosen. With less than a third of the season gone, Minoso had been struck ten times, and many were "deliberate beanballs." At the season's end he totalled sixteen, one less than the rookie record. At one point Minoso suggested that he could end the barrage with "a bucket of white paint." Later in the season he complained, as depicted in dialect by a *Sporting News* writer, "You know it get so bad, I theenk I wear a headguard even in bed. Maybe somebody throw at me when I sleep too. I don't know whatta kind of baseball this is. Yes, you try to get a man out. You brush back. But you not try to keel him." During his first four seasons, pitchers hit Minoso sixty-five times, eight in the head.[22]

Other players received similar treatment. In mid-July 1955, Al Smith established a new Cleveland Indian record when he was hit for the fifteenth time. Frank Robinson joined the Reds in 1956 and immediately became a popular target, absorbing twenty poundings in his rookie year. Robinson, unlike other blacks, did not feel that pitchers singled him out because of his race. "Those guys were just trying to test me," he writes. "They were trying to see what I was made of. . . . It had nothing to do with what color I was." Ernie Banks agrees. "I just thought that was part of the game," he explains. "I felt they were basically paying me a compliment because they thought I was a threat to win the game."[23] Players like both Robinsons and Minoso crowded the plate and many commentators attributed their unusual hit-by-pitch statistics to their batting stances. Nonetheless, the persistent appearance of black players among league leaders and record setters in this category indicates otherwise.

More than any other incident, brushback pitches triggered racial confrontations. In 1953 the normally mild-mannered Roy Campanella exploded after Lew Burdette twice knocked him down. Campanella glared at Burdette, who hollered, "Nigger, get up and hit."[24] The Dodger catcher struck out on the next pitch and then charged the mound. The Dodger bench poured onto the field and Joe Black had to be restrained from attacking Burdette.

In the American League Larry Doby retaliated several times against pitchers who threw at him. "If a guy wants to brush you back, that's baseball," he contended. "But headhunting for a Negro isn't baseball." In 1950 he faced off with Dizzy Trout after a close pitch and an insult, though umpires quickly stepped in. In 1953 Doby charged St. Louis Brown pitcher Bob Cain after being hit. In 1957, in his tenth year in the majors, Doby punched Art Ditmar, who had just decked him with a fastball. According to Shirley Povich, this marked "the complete emancipation of the American Negro in America's national game," the first time "a Negro [had] thrown the first punch in a player argument."[25]

The absence of earlier incidents reflected, in part, a conscious effort by black players to avoid confrontations. Well into the 1950s black players, particularly the older ones, remained acutely aware of what they saw as the responsibilities inherent in their pioneer status. "Jackie may have broken the barrier to playing," says Sam Jethroe, who debuted with the Braves in 1950. "[But] I knew when I arrived there was more required for me to do than a white player. It still was a hard thing to go through." Bob Thurman, who arrived five years later, recalls, "We always felt that we were the first coming along and that we had to set an example so that the whites could see what the blacks were really like."[26]

Black players, accepting the liberal credo of education and assimilation as the keys to tolerance, viewed their relations with white teammates as both a learning and a teaching opportunity. "It was a totally new experience for the [white players] too," states pitcher Brooks Lawrence. "It was a two-way street." On many occasions, black players took responsibility for awkward situations. "We had been involved in more of society than they had," explains Lawrence, and "and because of the ways most blacks had been brought up, we learned to adjust to things."[27]

As the numbers of blacks on a given team grew, they consciously adopted strategies to facilitate the integration experiment. On the Dodgers, Robinson ordered the blacks to "spread out" at team meals and in the locker room. Blacks on other clubs adopted this policy as well. On the Reds they steadfastly resisted the temptation to congregate together. "We were dead against that," asserts Thurman. "That was a no-no, to put our lockers together." According to Lawrence, intermixing in the locker room "was a good move because if you keep huddled up, you're like a bunch of crabs in a barrel; we're not gonna learn anything, and the people around us are not going to learn anything." On the Cleveland Indians, on the other hand, the *Courier* criticized a "Negro corner in the dressing room," which prevented the emergence of "better harmony" on the club.[28]

This sense of responsibility continued away from the ball parks as well. "Each new black kid who came up, we took him under our wing," recalls Lawrence. "We'd teach him the ropes. We'd set up a screen around him and say, 'No, you can't do this type of thing. You can't go into these kinds of bars.'" In each city, black players hosted visiting black opponents after the games, usually in local taverns in the Afro-American section of town. To some this represented simple comradery, but to others the gesture had more significance. "You were taking care of me in your town, seeing that I did not do anything that might jeopardize the situation in baseball," explains Lawrence. "We didn't necessarily always like each other. But the situation was bigger than our personality conflicts."[29]

In retrospect one might question the necessity of these precautions. Certainly by 1954 minimal danger existed that baseball would return to its pre-Jackie Robinson ways. Yet with the civil rights movement gaining momentum, black athletes found themselves showcased as examples of integration in action. In addition, if a measure of equality had been achieved on the playing field, black players remained aware of the restricted nature of their acceptance. Lest they forget, life on the road and during spring training repeatedly reminded them.

II

When Ernie Banks played for the Kansas City Monarchs, the team always stopped at the Olive Hotel in St. Louis. After joining the Cubs in 1953, St. Louis was the first city he visited. "Now I was traveling with the big boys," thought Banks, accommodations would improve. Major league teams boarded their players at the fashionable Chase Hotel. But the Chase, like all other leading St. Louis hotels, barred blacks. In his first stop on the big league tour, Banks found himself back at the Olive.[30]

The situation in St. Louis represented a constant irritant for black players. The Chase had air-conditioning; black hotels did not. "Summers used to boil in St. Louis," recalls Don Newcombe, "and the air hung so heavy in our rooms at night we could hardly breathe. We used to soak our sheets in cold-water." But major league executives were reluctant to challenge the color line. Browns owner Bill Veeck complained to the local chamber of commerce, "Baseball players are not coming to [the] St. Louis [Browns] if they cannot get meals and hotel lodgings like all the other ballplayers in the downtown hotels and restaurants."[31] But except for a rare moment in 1952, when Chase officials allowed Satchel Paige to attend a team dinner, Veeck's plea went unheeded.

In Cincinnati the Netherlands-Plaza Hotel offered accommodations to blacks, but players ate their meals in their rooms, a tradition begun by Dodger officials who feared offending other guests. After several seasons Robinson, accompanied by his wife, decided to defy this convention. The maître d' greeted the Robinsons at the door, led them to a table, and then disappeared. He immediately returned with a baseball and a pen in his hand. "I've been waiting all season for you to come in here, Jackie," he explained. "I've got every other Dodger's autograph. Will you please sign this ball for me?"[32]

Robinson also triggered a breakthrough at the Chase in 1954. The St. Louis hotel announced that blacks could room there, but forbade them from using the dining room and swimming pool or loitering in the lobby. Dodger pitcher and player representative Carl Erskine recalls, "Now, looking back, I want to say to myself, 'Why wasn't I outraged at that?' and say 'Are you kidding, these guys are our teammates. If they don't eat with us, we don't eat there either.' " But, adds Erskine, "What you don't get is the feeling of the time and the fact that instead of being received as an affront, it was received as a fantastic step for these guys."[33]

Robinson agreed with Erskine. He viewed the limited Chase concessions as a wedge, swallowed his pride, and accepted the conditions. Other black Dodgers refused to follow his lead. "I'm not going to stay there," stated Campanella. "If they didn't want us before, they won't get my business now." Unlike Robinson, to whom the extension of integration outweighed all other considerations, Campanella expressed loyalty to the black hotel that had treated them royally for years. Players on other teams also objected to the Chase offer. One player told Wendell Smith that when presented with the new arrangement he told his club's traveling secretary, "If we couldn't live there like other players, sit in the lobby, and eat our meals like the others, then the management of the Chase could go to hell." Another athlete responded, "I don't mind breaking down barriers, but I wasn't going to be treated like cattle." The Brooklyn management, said these players, should have insisted that the black Dodgers receive equal treatment or transferred their lodgings elsewhere.[34]

Robinson's logic ultimately prevailed. Other blacks accepted the hotel's offer and the restrictions gradually fell. However, discriminatory practices persisted. When the Reds stopped here in 1955, black entertainer Nat King Cole was appearing in the night club. Hotel rules nonetheless forbade blacks from patronizing lounges or eating places. Thurman and Harmon protested the arrangement to Cole, who threatened to cancel the concert if the two blacks could not attend, and the hotel surrendered. As late as 1964, long after the Chase had officially removed all restrictions on blacks, Hank Aaron complained, "We never get a room in St. Louis hotels on the outside or over the swimming pool. We're always in a blind spot looking out at some old building or some green pastures, or a blank wall, so nobody can see us through a window."[35]

By the time the Chase Hotel accepted black guests the American League no longer fielded a franchise in St. Louis. The Browns had relocated to Baltimore, another Jim Crow city. Blacks had never played for the Baltimore Orioles franchise in the International League, and the NAACP objected to the presence of a major league team in Baltimore, citing "the city's rigid pattern of segregation, including the exclusion of Negroes from hotels and restaurants," and "the racist nature of the city." These protests notwithstanding, the American League approved the transfer of the Browns, who adopted the traditional Oriole nickname. The new Orioles fielded blacks from their inception in 1954, but visiting players faced unrelenting segregation. On his first road trip with the Yankees in 1955 Elston Howard had to separate from his teammates not only in Baltimore, but in Chicago and Kansas City as well. On the next tour Stengel demanded that Howard accompany the team to all hotels. Barriers abruptly fell in Chicago and Kansas City, but Baltimore hotels remained off limits for blacks for many years.[36]

Regardless of where black players lodged, one unwritten rule remained sacrosanct: blacks and whites could not room together. No one questioned this assumption. In 1950 when the Braves purchased Sam Jethroe, sportswriters and baseball officials openly discussed the need to find him a black roommate. The Braves chose Luis Angel Marquez in the next minor league draft, to provide "a Negro roommate for Jethroe." Five years later Dan Daniel reported that Elston Howard "rooms alone. Not that there aren't Yankees who would be ready and willing to room with him on the road. But Elston likes it the way it is." In the aftermath of the 1955 season the Yankees toured Japan. Traveling secretary Bob Fishel assigned Howard to room with first baseman Bill Skowron. Neither man saw anything unusual in the arrangement, yet when the team returned for the 1956 campaign, Howard again roomed alone. Even in the 1960s few teams breached the prohibition on interracial roommates.[37]

As discriminatory practices in major league cities receded, the annual ordeal of Florida spring training emerged as the primary grievance among virtually all black ballplayers. By the early 1950s most Florida communities, fearful of losing their lucrative status as training sites, had accepted the presence of blacks. Nonetheless, off the playing field, nonwhite athletes were still subjected to the vagaries of southern segregation. Problems of housing, transportation, recreation, and eating places remained as acute in Florida as in other areas of the South. Most major league clubs did little to ameliorate the situation or to wield their considerable economic power to force changes until the end of the decade.

A chilly reception at the team hotel constituted the inaugural experience for many young blacks in Florida. The St. Louis Cardinals instructed Bob Gibson, arriving at his first training camp in 1958, to report to the Bainbridge Hotel in St. Petersburg, as did all other prospects. The taxi driver deposited Gibson at an alley exit rather than the front entrance. The hotel clerk immediately instructed the driver to deliver Gibson to another address. "We drove across the railroad tracks to the other side of town," recalls Gibson. "I didn't have to see the people in the street to know we were in the Negro district." The driver delivered Gibson to a private house where six or seven other black ballplayers were lodged. "It was a terrible shame and disappointment," writes Gibson. " 'So this,' I said to myself, 'is the major leagues.' "[38]

"Until it happens you literally cannot believe it," says Curt Flood of this same experience. "After it happens, you need time to absorb it." Yet many of the older players did not mind living in the boarding houses. "To tell you the truth," states Harmon, "I liked it better than I did staying at the hotel because oh, she [the housekeeper] could cook and she washed our clothes for us and did everything. Of course, it would have been nice having a swimming pool." Since low rates prevailed at these boarding houses, players could actually save money from their expense allowances. But if blacks found day-to-day conditions acceptable, some balked at the reasons underlying their isolation. "The whole set-up is wrong," protested Jackie Robinson during his tenth season in the majors. "There is no reason why we shouldn't be able to live with our teammates."[39]

Discontent escalated when the team visited other Florida cities or traveled northward. Each club had a traveling secretary who arranged accommodations, but these officials seldom familiarized themselves with facilities for blacks. "We had to go around and make inquiries as to where the black ballplayers stayed when they came through here with other clubs," recalls Bob Thurman. "The white players would usually be all checked into their hotels. But they didn't know that we would be having some problems trying to find a decent place." Thurman was the "traveling secretary" for the blacks on the Cincinnati Reds, responsible for housing arrangements. On the Milwaukee Braves Bill Bruton served as "senior officer." "When we would arrive in a town," explains Aaron, "Duffy Lewis, the traveling secretary, would appoint Bruton to handle the money for cab fares and tips and other things we might need, and Bruton would be in charge of our group until we joined up with the rest of the team again."[40]

Major league players, like their minor league counterparts, endured the "routine on the bus." Nothing humiliated veteran stars like Robinson and Campanella more than waiting on a bus while their teammates ate in a restaurant. Even breakthroughs could be degrading. Dodger catcher John Roseboro recalls that when a restaurant in one small Florida town admitted blacks, the proprietors hid them behind a screen while the white players ate in the main room.[41] These situations embarrassed many of the white Dodgers, but most felt that they could do little to provoke change.

Even at the ball parks discrimination plagued black athletes. Though the playing fields were integrated, the stands were not. This rule sometimes applied to athletes as well as spectators. In 1955 local officials ordered blacks on the Pirates who did not suit up for the first exhibition game to sit in the colored section. Thereafter, the Pirates instructed all players to appear in uniform even if they were not scheduled to play. In Tampa, relates Reds pitcher Brooks Lawrence, after being removed from a game he and catcher Ed Bailey entered the stands to watch the remainder of the contest. A rope separated the black and white sections and while Bailey sat on the white side, Lawrence sat next to him on the black. "Boy, this is stupid," exclaimed Bailey, a Tennessean. "I'm gonna change this." The catcher removed the rope and, according to Lawrence, no one ever reattached it.[42]

Black players often responded to these incidents with bemused acceptance. "I think humor was the saving grace in the whole thing," asserts Lawrence. "We learned to laugh at that and we learned to laugh at ourselves." When a waitress in Little Rock told Vic Power that the restaurant did not serve Negroes, the effervescent Puerto Rican replied, "That's all right, I don't eat them." On another occasion, Power avoided a fine for jaywalking by explaining to the judge that he thought the Don't Walk sign referred to "whites only."[43]

Power, however, had no jokes when a sheriff almost arrested him on a bus ride from Fort Meyers to West Palm Beach when he played with Kansas City in the mid-1950s. The team stopped at a gas station and, like the other players, Power, the only black, used the rest room. He then bought a Coca-Cola from a machine and returned to the bus. The gas station attendant boarded the vehicle and demanded that Power return the soft drink. Power cursed the man and the other players chased the attendant from the bus. Ten minutes later the local sheriff intercepted the team and attempted to arrest Power "for using obscene language." His teammates refused to allow Power's removal and posted a $500 bond. The Athletics later advised

316 EXTRA INNINGS

Power to forfeit the bond and not return to face trial. "They told me that was the best way, because if I go back they might kill me back there," explained Power. Nonetheless, the club repaid the players who had contributed to Power's bail—and then took the money out of his salary! "I lose $500 for buying a bottle of coke," lamented Power.[44]

Some clubs made an effort to ameliorate these conditions, avoiding segregated hotels and restaurants by traveling in special railway cars where the team slept and ate. The Cardinals ultimately provided box lunches for the players on the buses or served food at the clubhouse.[45] Several teams abandoned Florida and pitched camp in Arizona. While the race issue did not constitute the sole determinant in this decision, it was a significant factor. In 1953 five out of seven teams with blacks on their rosters trained in the West. In Arizona, however, segregated housing remained the rule. Not until 1952 did the Indians house all of their players under one roof in Tucson. Even after the Giants desegregated the Adams Hotel in Phoenix, black players remained unwelcome in the dining room and swimming pool. Segregation also persisted in most off-base recreational facilities.

Branch Rickey and the Dodgers adopted the most ambitious scheme to counteract spring training problems. After the unpleasant incidents during Robinson's debut appearance in 1946, Rickey leased a former naval station, complete with an air strip which enabled the club to avoid transportation problems, at Vero Beach. The new "Dodgertown" base, opened in 1948, fulfilled Rickey's dream of a "college of baseball" and provided a haven from southern segregation. Black and white players could room together, eat together, and train together without interference from outside authorities. "You were segregated by ability, not color," asserts John Roseboro.[46]

According to Sam Lacy, however, "Dodgertown was an anachronism in Vero Beach." The surrounding community, wrote Lacy in 1948, "fairly seethes with prejudice. . . . Even native Floridians, hardened to the indignities of 'Jim Crowism' shun Vero Beach." Blacks did not even live within the city limits. They huddled together in the tiny adjoining town of Gifford, which consisted of a movie house, a drugstore, a barber shop, and a pool hall.[47]

Racial incidents repeatedly marred the inaugural training session at Vero Beach in 1948. Dodger officials reprimanded a canteen operator who refused to serve Roy Campanella. Local police, according to Lacy, "busied themselves herding the colored fans into a roped off area . . . sweating, cussing, and fuming in the process."[48] More significantly, an argument between Don Newcombe and Philadelphia Athletics' catcher Mike Guerra launched rumors of a lynching on the base. Guerra, a light-skinned Cuban, had managed Newcombe in Havana during the winter season and had cut him from the squad. The hot-headed Newcombe confronted Guerra at Dodgertown and their shouting match attracted a crowd. A fan ripped a picket from a fence and tossed it to Guerra. "Kill that Nigger," he shouted. "He can't do that down in Florida to a white man." Embarrassed, the two ballplayers ended their argument. Rumors spread that Newcombe had attacked a white man and rumblings of a lynching spread through the town. The following morning at 5:00 A.M. Rickey gathered the five blacks in the Dodger camp at his house where they met with Vero Beach public officials. Only Rickey's persuasiveness and a pledge to keep Newcombe confined to the training camp allowed the pitcher to remain.[49]

Despite these shaky beginnings, Dodgertown became a haven of tolerance. Yet no amount of effort could totally shield the black Dodgers from the realities of life beyond Dodgertown. "We always felt like we were walking on eggshells when we had to be in the town," remembers Roseboro. White players could visit beaches, go on fishing trips, play golf at the country clubs and shop in the better stores of Vero Beach. Blacks could do none of these things. While white Dodgers saw first-run movies at the local theater, blacks, according to Roseboro, "had to go to a dump in Gifford to see some of the first movies ever made, like Buck Jones Westerns and Buck Rogers serials." A theater at nearby Fort Pierce allowed blacks, but to gain entry they had to "go around back, climb up to a fire escape to a door leading to a balcony." The Dodgers compensated by showing movies on the base and even building a nine-hole golf course for the players.[50]

These efforts notwithstanding, some of the blacks on the Dodgers felt that the club had not done enough. "They did not always protect their black players the way they should have," states Roseboro, who suggests that the team should have abandoned Florida in favor of a friendlier locale.[51] Yet no other team made the concentrated effort that the Dodgers did to shield their players from local customs. For blacks living in the boarding houses, there was no respite from residential and recreational segregation.

The hardships confronted by the black players often paled in comparison with those endured by their ardent fans. In almost every stadium during the early years, particularly when Robinson and the Dodgers appeared, blacks overflowed the traditional Jim Crow seating areas to cheer their standard bearers. In some towns, like Haines City, Florida, where custom forbade black attendance at baseball games, workmen hurriedly constructed "colored stands." In other communities the grounds crew extended ropes across the outfield to accommodate the crowds. Often, local officials allowed the black throngs into previously restricted seating areas amid shouts of joy and celebration. In Atlanta in 1950 black fans jammed the Jim Crow section and "bulged the restraining ropes in the outfield." Finally, Cracker president Earl Mann opened the bleachers to blacks for the first time, triggering, according to Joe King, "The Charge of the Dark Brigade." People fell, wrote King, "not from cannon to the right and left but from overeagerness to gain a position in the bleachers where no Negro had even been permitted to sit."[52]

The cruel exploitation of black fans tempered the celebratory atmosphere. Rachel Robinson describes their treatment in some communities as "outrageous." In West Palm Beach, she asserts, blacks "came through a hole in the fence and not a turnstile. . . . Black fans were so eager to come in and so excited about what was happening that they just kept pouring in. It was like seeing cattle come through a hole in that fence." In Haines City, Sam Lacy, seeking a "colored" rest room, was "directed to a tree about 35 yards off where the right field foul line ended." "I finally got so I couldn't go to the ballpark," says Rachel. "I just couldn't stand to see my people treated like animals."[53]

Jackie Robinson and other blacks on the Dodgers greeted the fan enthusiasm with mixed emotions. Many white patrons booed, Robinson believed, only in retaliation to the black exuberance. Robinson objected even more stridently to the jubilant outbursts when officials allowed blacks into restricted seats. "Don't cheer those goddamn bastards," he shouted in New Orleans. "Keep your fucking mouths shut. You got it coming. You only get what's coming. . . . Don't cheer."[54]

For the first generation of black players conditions in the South seemed irremediable. "[It was] degrading as hell," recalls Monte Irvin, "but what the hell else could we do? We wanted to play so badly, that it didn't bother us that much." According to Harmon, players feared that protests would lead to dismissal. "Anytime you dispute with the management, whether you're white, black, or indifferent, you're gone, back then," says Harmon.[55]

Blacks entering baseball in the mid-1950s, who had not been raised in a Jim Crow environment and who expected to find baseball thoroughly integrated, displayed less patience and understanding. In the late 1950s as the civil rights movement gathered momentum, black baseball players became more vocal in their protests against conditions in Florida. "After ten years of traveling in the South," charged Jackie Robinson in 1956, "I don't think the advances there have been fast enough. It's my belief that baseball itself hasn't done all it can to help remedy the problems faced by those playing in O.B." Major league teams, noted Robinson, spent millions of dollars in the South each year. Baseball could therefore exert economic pressure to "help remedy a lot of the prejudice that surrounds the game as it's played below the Mason-Dixon line."[56]

A growing number of ballplayers joined the protest in the late 1950s and early 1960s. Bill White, Curt Flood, and Bob Gibson, the talented Cardinal trio, called for an end to segregation in St. Petersburg, where both St. Louis and the Yankees trained. In 1961 players on the Braves voiced objections to the situation in Bradenton. That year the Major League Baseball Players Association took up the issue and demanded that ball clubs make greater efforts to integrate facilities at their training camps. Under this pressure racial barriers began to fall. Some clubs bought their own hotels to house their entire squads. The Yankees, previously accused of "putting up a luke-warm fight for their Negro players," moved from St. Petersburg to Fort Lauderdale, where officials promised integrated housing. At the same time, St. Petersburg dropped its restrictions for the Cardinals and the recently created New York Mets. In Bradenton, black Braves won a partial victory. They received permission to stay at the team hotel but had to sit behind partitions when they ate in the dining room.[57]

Despite these improvements, black major leaguers remained embittered over their treatment in the South. In 1963 when Jackie Robinson interviewed black players for his book *Baseball Has Done It,* almost every player complained about conditions in Florida. While virtually all teams provided integrated facilities for the athletes, off-base discrimination remained a constant irritant. Unlike their white counterparts, blacks, unable to locate decent housing for their wives and children and unwilling to expose their offspring to the humiliations of segregation, rarely brought their families to spring training. Surveying these complaints, Robinson reiterated the demands he had made seven years earlier. Baseball, he wrote, "should bring pressure on Southern towns to end all forms of discrimination, on the penalty of cutting bait and letting local bigots swim for other dollars than theirs. . . . The league should enact a rule demanding that local authorities provide equal accommodations and services to all players at all times."[58]

Gradually, baseball accomplished these goals. Economic coercion and federal civil rights legislation ended the worst abuses of southern segregation during the next decade. Nonetheless, occasional episodes of overt discrimination persisted into the 1970s. But, if baseball moved slowly to protect its black athletes, its sins were at least partially understandable. No other agency in the 1950s destroyed as many racial barriers without the aid of mass protests and federal intervention. Although organized baseball did not utilize its maximum economic potential to eliminate Jim Crow practices, the very existence of interracial competition in the South established a compelling precedent. Integration, baseball demonstrated, was feasible and, at times, profitable. By the same token, the economic pitfalls of continued segregation grew apparent. These lessons were not lost on the modern prophets of a New South.

III

In the training camp controversy black players displayed a new militancy characteristic of the rising age of protest. Fittingly, their leading spokesman was not one of the bold young stars of the late 1950s, but the trailblazer himself. During the decade that he played and for many years thereafter, Jackie Robinson personified blacks in baseball. Ardent, tempestuous, and controversial, he continually probed and expanded the boundaries of the "noble experiment." "Robinson did not merely play at center stage," explains Roger Kahn, "He was center stage; and wherever he walked, center stage walked with him."[59] In the process, Robinson came to symbolize not only the black athlete, but the "New Negro" of the civil rights era.

Writing several years before Robinson's debut, Gunnar Myrdal had observed "the popular glamour and potential" that accrued to the first black in a business or profession, particularly when he had "achieved something extraordinary . . . in competition with whites." The accomplishments of "the first," wrote Myrdal, "offer every Negro a gloating consolation in his lowly status and a ray of hope."[60]

Robinson exemplified this phenomenon for blacks of all ages. "I'll never forget the day the Dodgers brought Jackie Robinson to St. Pete," recalls Ed Charles of his Florida boyhood. "There were so many people the stadium couldn't hold them." After the game Charles and his friends followed Robinson to the railroad station and gazed through the train windows at the black athlete playing cards with his white teammates. "It was a great, great day," states Charles, who later played eight years in the major leagues, "because for the first time we realized that it could really happen."[61]

Black writer John Head captures Robinson's charismatic appeal for an older generation of black Americans:

> "Ain't that Jackie Robinson?"
> Grandaddy would ask the same question everytime a black player was shown during the television baseball game of the week. And if he had forgotten his glasses again or if the television picture was a bit fuzzy, he would ask it for the white players too. Grandaddy asked the question long after Robinson . . . had retired and was going blind.
> It was the same with almost all the old black men who came to watch us play in the youth league. . . . Whenever one of us made a good play in the field, the old men would whoop and holler, and invariably would yell, "Just like Jackie Robinson!" The cry would build into a chorus and the old men would be yelling, "Yes suh! Just like ol' Jackie Robinson!"[62]

"To the old men," writes Head, "baseball began and lived through one person: Jackie Robinson. He was the game incarnate." And to white America Robinson represented integration incarnate. The combination of popularity and controversy which followed in his wake reflected the national ambivalence to advances by blacks. Unlike other black athletes, Robinson could supplement his income with advertisements and endorsements. Entrepreneurs marketed Jackie Robinson dolls, caps, jackets, and other clothing. Robinson broadcast his own weekly radio show in New York and regularly appeared as a guest on many television and radio programs. In 1951 a poll of boys' athletic leagues in twenty-seven states named Robinson and Joe Dimaggio as their favorite athletes.[63]

Although Robinson's pioneer status accounted for a large measure of his appeal, his defiant excellence on the diamond enhanced his charismatic image. From 1949 to 1954, Robinson ranked, along with Stan Musial, as the dominant player in the National League. Over those six seasons Robinson batted .327. Yet observers measured his true value in his ability to influence the outcome of a game. "Robinson is the difference. The squeezer. The fellow who twists the screws in the pressure cooker that cooks the other team's goose," wrote Bill Corum. Many sportswriters labelled him, "the most dangerous man in baseball today."[64] Even added years and excess weight failed to decrease his ardor. In 1955 and 1956, though his statistical performance declined, Robinson remained the spirit of the pennant-winning Dodger teams.

Robinson's dynamic performances notwithstanding, from 1949 on he appeared in the newspapers as often in controversy as in glory. During his first two years in organized baseball the mercurial Robinson had curbed his natural aggressiveness in the interests of the "great experiment." As late as June 1948, he told *Ebony* magazine, "Until the time comes when a Negro player can go out and argue his point as well as any other ball player, I hope that all of us are able to bite our tongues and just play ball." For Robinson himself this task became increasingly difficult. He grew restive under the restraints that he and Rickey had agreed upon and less certain of their necessity. In September 1948, umpire Butch Henline threw Robinson out of a game for protesting a call. Robinson and many others hailed the event as evidence of his arrival as a major league player.[65] He could argue just like any white athlete—and be ejected when he tread beyond established boundaries.

By the close of the 1948 season Robinson had, for all intents and purposes, declared his independence from Rickey's initial restrictions. Before the following season Rickey advised him that the experiment had reached a successful conclusion and that he could now behave naturally. "All along I had known that the point would come when my almost filial relationship with Jackie would break with ill-feeling if I did not issue an emancipation proclamation for him," Rickey later explained.[66] In reality, Robinson had removed the matter from Rickey's hands; the Mahatma simply recognized and approved the change.

Robinson arrived at Vero Beach in 1949 and announced, "They better be prepared to be rough this year, because I'm going to be rough on them." From another player the comment would have represented innocuous pre-season bravado. When Robinson and Southern rookie pitcher Chris Van Cuyk engaged in a "genuinely nasty, name-calling, beanballing spat" in the Dodger camp, observers read racial overtones into his statement. Commissioner Chandler called Robinson "on the carpet" to explain his new persona.[67] The unnecessary meeting marked the first of a series of clashes between Robinson and the baseball hierarchy which would characterize the remainder of his career.

No season went by without at least one major dispute surrounding Robinson. His relationship with umpires declined steadily. "He was the most difficult ballplayer I had to deal with as an umpire," wrote Jocko Conlan in his autobiography. "Jackie was one of those players who could never accept a decision." Robinson, on his part, charged "I have no doubt that there are some umpires in the National League who are 'on' me."[68] Robinson also tangled repeatedly with opposing players and managers, exchanging verbal taunts and accusations. His acid confrontations with the similarly tempered Leo Durocher achieved legendary proportions. His 1952 denunciation of the Yankees as prejudiced provoked widespread reprimands. After Walter O'Malley squeezed Branch Rickey out of the Dodger presidency in 1950, Robinson's relations with his employers deteriorated. When the new owners fired manager Charlie Dressen and replaced him with Walter Alston in 1954, Robinson emerged as one of the most outspoken critics of the move. During the next three seasons Robinson's strident personality frequently clashed with the stolid, colorless Alston. Even the story of Robinson's retirement, which he sold to *Life* magazine for a $50,000 fee, became complicated by an unexpected trade to the Giants, triggering one final controversy.

Many reporters did not appreciate the "new" Robinson. At the close of the 1949 season, Dick Young reported, "Robinson has reached the stage where he says what he believes and says it without reservation, which is a trait unfortunately frowned on in most social circles." After Robinson's charges against the Yankees, Cleveland writer Ed McAuley questioned his motives and implied that Robinson had become a "rabble rouser" and a "soap box" orator. Annually, the *Sporting News* composed an editorial calling Robinson to task under headlines reading, THE JACKIE ROBINSON SITUATION; A PROBLEM GROWS IN BROOKLYN; ROBINSON SHOULD BE A PLAYER, NOT A CRUSADER; A WORD TO JACKIE SHOULD BE SUFFICIENT, and others.[69]

Even black reporters began to question Robinson's behavior. W. Rollo Wilson of the Pittsburgh *Courier* reported that the Dodger star "is becoming increasingly obsessed with his own importance" and advised Robinson "to mend his manners." Wendell Smith noted that Robinson "isn't as popular in the press box as he once was" and concluded, "Robinson had better take inventory." When the American commander in Korea defied President Truman in 1951, one unidentified black quipped, "Who does General MacArthur think he is—Jackie Robinson?"[70]

The constant controversy evoked widespread analysis from contemporary observers. "He was hot-tempered in my opinion only because he was martyred," stated teammate Carl Erskine, echoing a common sentiment among Robinson's defenders. Robinson's tempestuous nature, according to this interpretation, emerged from the unreleased pressures of his early seasons. "I had too much stored up inside me," Robinson admitted. "I blamed it on the fact that I wasn't able to squawk when I thought I had a squawk coming." The unnatural restraints contributed to, but did not determine, Robinson's behavior. His aggressive outspokeness had been evident during his earlier collegiate and army careers. Indeed, as Roger Kahn explained, "It was this fury of Robinson's that enabled him to do the great and immensely difficult thing that he did."[71]

Robinson often blamed his troubles and his image on the racial stereotypes commonly held in white America. "I learned that as long as I appeared to ignore insult and injury, I was a martyred hero to a lot of people who had sympathy for the underdog," he later wrote. "But the minute I began to sound-off—I became a swell-head, wise guy, an 'uppity' nigger." The same behavior in a white player, argued Robinson, would be seen as "spirited." Robinson charged that baseball officials, umpires, and sportswriters objected not to his actions but to behavior deemed "inappropriate to a black man." In a 1955 *Look* magazine article entitled "Now I Know Why They Boo ME," Robinson wrote that he was "resented not just because I am a Negro, but because I was the NEGRO who broke the color line in baseball."[72]

On the other hand, Robinson often appeared in the headlines for reasons that superceded race. Far more articulate, intelligent, and outspoken than the average person, Robinson represented "good copy" to the press. He answered questions honestly, forthrightly, and with a measure of naïveté. "He has the tact of a child, because he has the moral purity of a child," explained Dick Young. Robinson repeatedly pledged, "That's the last time I'm opening my mouth," but his silence always proved short-lived. Within days, an incident would trigger a long tirade, which Robinson would punctuate with a resounding, "You're damn right you can quote me." Unlike other ballplayers, he never avoided adverse repercussions by denying a controversial statement. "It was almost ridiculous the way reporters made for Robinson's cubicle after the critical games," noted sportswriter John Hanlon. "Others may have starred, but Robinson, all knew, was the one who talked."[73]

Robinson readily acknowledged his shortcomings and excesses. "You know me," he told reporters. "When I get hot, I pop off and say a lot of things I shouldn't say." But Robinson bristled with defiance when he considered the attacks of others unfair or biased. The baseball hierarchy frowned upon outspoken employees, black or white, but Robinson refused to be silenced and heretically reserved the right to respond to perceived injustices. When Ford Frick demanded that Robinson explain his remarks about Yankee prejudice, the black athlete informed the commissioner that despite his gratitude to baseball for the opportunities and material possessions it had offered him, "All this I would have to give up gladly if baseball attempted to muzzle me to the extent that whenever I saw evil or wrong I could not speak out about it."[74]

Frick disavowed any intent to censor Robinson, but the player's repeated protests on a wide variety of issues rankled baseball officials. In 1952 when National League President Warren Giles fined Robinson $75 for arguing with an umpire, Robinson refused to pay until Giles granted him a hearing on the matter. In an age before a players' union existed the demand seemed outrageous. "You can't tell the president of the league what to do," admonished Dodger General Manager Buzzie Bavasi. "You can tell us you want [a hearing] and we can request it."[75] But to Robinson, even a baseball player possessed the basic right to a fair hearing. It is not surprising that twenty years later, when Curt Flood courageously challenged baseball's reserve clause in the courts, Robinson was one of the few former players to testify on Flood's behalf.

Robinson's actions unquestionably exceeded the bounds of the accepted posture for all athletes. Nonetheless, according to sportswriter Milton Gross, many people felt that Robinson "interpreted any criticism of himself as a Negro, never as a ballplayer when it was intended as such." Red Smith recalled, "I felt he was fiercely racist. I thought he saw racism and prejudice under the bed and I'd get out of patience with things he'd say and do."[76]

Robinson's critics hinted at an element of paranoia in his personality. Even Wendell Smith, rebutting Robinson's charges that newsmen were prejudiced, cautioned, "The press has been especially fair to him throughout his career. . . . Mr. Robinson's memory it seems, is getting shorter and shorter." Yet the Dodger star had ample evidence to support his suspicions. "Anybody else may say anything and its completely disregarded," commented Gross. "Jackie opens his mouth and everybody rushes to put their feet into it."[77] Exaggerations, false stories, and unwarranted controversy repeatedly marred press reports.

If Robinson experienced difficulty separating his image as an athlete from his role as the nation's most visible black figure, he shared a common problem. To most Americans the two Robinsons were indistinguishable. "It might help Jackie Robinson if he remembered he came into the majors as a ballplayer, not a symbol," remarked sportswriter Joe Williams. In reality, Robinson always had been both "ballplayer" and "symbol." The record-breaking pace at which pitchers hit him with fastballs attested to this. Nor could Robinson, despite his good-natured jesting about the matter, completely ignore the repeated threats on his life. On September 16, 1953, a St. Louis letter warned, "You die, no use crying for the cops. You'll be executed gangland style in Busch Stadium." This marked the tenth reported death threat in seven years, doubtless another baseball record. Reporters might pretend that Robinson was only another baseball player, but as Kahn noted, "The ordinary standards don't apply to Robinson. He is larger than life size."[78]

Often the same critics who called upon Robinson to limit his energies to the playing field reminded him of his dual role. To the *Sporting News*, Robinson had lost his sense of perspective and abandoned his responsibilities as the symbol of integration. "Robinson has forgotten his color and his mission," argued the journal after his initial reprimand from Chandler in 1949. "There are definite restraints under which Jackie must place himself, and definite obligations which, as the first Negro in the modern history of the majors, he owes to his race." The *Sporting News* hammered this message home repeatedly in their annual *Jackie Robinson* editorial, an "honor" accorded no other player. "Jackie must be beyond reproach," commented the "Baseball Bible" in a 1951 column, STOP, LOOK, AND LISTEN, JACKIE. "He is still on a pedestal, not only with his race, but with all fans." In 1954 the weekly reminded Robinson that he had "become a symbol of emancipation for his race—a symbol that extends far beyond baseball."[79]

The *Sporting News* and other commentators, including several black players, viewed Robinson's outspokenness as evidence of ingratitude to the game that had given him fame and fortune. "You owe a great deal to the game," admonished the journal in an "open letter" in 1955. It urged Robinson to "Put down your hammer, Jackie, and pick up a horn," to repay base-ball "by words of goodwill instead of any bitterness." Teammate Roy Cam-panella agreed. "Instead of being grateful to baseball, he's criticizing it," complained Campanella. "Everything he has he owes to baseball."[80]

Robinson refused to accept this argument. The role of submissive grati-tude, he believed, stereotyped blacks and reinforced images of inferiority. Baseball—or at least Branch Rickey—had simply offered him the opportu-nity that he rightly deserved; his own courage and skills had produced suc-cess. Robinson recognized the financial security that his baseball career had provided, but, he reasoned, in an economic sense he had offered an ample return. Although he reigned as the greatest drawing card in the game, Rob-inson's salary never exceeded $42,500, less than that of several white stars. In a broader sense his contributions on the playing field and to baseball mythology loomed immeasurably large. "The way I figured it," Robinson later wrote, "I was even with baseball and baseball was even with me." Others judged this assessment far too charitable. "If there is an unfulfilled obligation in the case of Baseball vs. Jackie Robinson," asserted New York reporter Harold Weissman, "the debt belongs to baseball, which can never pay off in full."[81]

Robinson agreed with the *Sporting News* that his celebrity and status imposed "definite obligations"; he differed, however, in his interpretation of what these responsibilities entailed. Many commentators implored Rob-inson to emulate the deportment of Joe Louis; in particular Vincent X. Flaherty advised him to "follow the example of Joe Louis, who steered away from anything that got him involved throughout his career," and "be-came the greatest goodwill ambassador his race ever had." But to Robin-son, Louis, whom he liked and respected, did not project the appropriate image of black America. Black leaders, argued Robinson, should be de-manding and outspoken. "Think of me as the kind of Negro who's come to the conclusion that he isn't going to beg for anything," he told Dick Young. "That he is reasonable, but he is damn well tired of being patient." Robin-son cherished the image accorded him by young black journalist Carl Rowan. "Future generations will remember him," concluded Rowan in Rob-inson's authorized biography, "as the proud crusader against pompous bigots and timid sentinels of the status quo—as a symbol of the new Negro American."[82]

On the Brooklyn squad the divergent personalities of Robinson and catcher Roy Campanella embodied the differences between the "new" and "old" Negro. Campanella displayed the attributes of gratitude, stoic pa-tience, and philosophical complacency expected of blacks in America. He had risen from poverty in Philadelphia, through nine grueling seasons of year-round Jim Crow baseball and two and a half years in the minors, to his lifelong dream of starring in the majors. When young black Dodgers would complain about discrimination, Campanella would call them aside and explain, "You're in the big league now. It's nice up here. You're getting an opportunity to show what you can do—don't louse it up for everyone else." Confronted by the growing militancy of the civil rights movement, Campanella could respond, "I'm a colored man. I know there are things I can do and things I can't do without stirring up some people. But a few years ago there were many more things I couldn't do than I can today. I'm willing to wait. All this came by waiting."[83] Campanella disapproved of Robinson's outbursts and militancy; Robinson grew irritated by Campanella's uncritical acceptance of existing conditions. Sportswriters emphasized their differences and the relationship between the two men deteriorated.

Many writers, baseball officials, and contemporaries preferred the easygoing Campanella to the truculent Robinson. Campanella "seems to have realized that inborn prejudices cannot be eradicated overnight," praised Roscoe McGowen. Dick Young told Robinson, "When I talk to Campy I almost never think of him as a Negro. Any time I talk to you, I'm acutely aware of the fact that you're a Negro." To Robinson, this line of thinking represented hypocrisy. "People thought of [Campanella] as a Negro when he was Jim Crowed at the Adams Hotel down in St. Louis," he countered. "They think of him as a Negro when he goes to spring training in the South. . . . They think about him as a Negro when he goes to buy a house." What Young meant, asserted Robinson, was "that he didn't think of [Campanella] as a *certain kind* of Negro."[84] Robinson sought to imbed the image of this "kind of Negro"—proud, defiant, and combative—on the minds of a new generation of Americans.

Critics condemned Robinson as a crusader; he bore that cross willingly. Robinson recognized that acceptance in organized baseball marked the beginning, not the conclusion, of the struggle for equality. To those who predicted that his strident militancy might jeopardize the gains that he had made possible, Robinson responded that as long as discrimination continued on the playing field, in spring training, and in major league communities, his achievement remained incomplete. Others viewed the integration of baseball as an end in itself; Robinson envisioned the baseball experience as the stepping stone to more significant advances. To Robinson, the aggressive expansion of the beachhead that he had established, through the constant assertion of equal rights, represented the obligation of the successful black person. This obligation extended beyond the realm of sport and into the broader society. In an age of rising protest, Robinson, more than any other athlete, articulated and advanced this vision.

17

Baseball Has Done It

> *Integration in baseball has already proved that all Americans can live together in peaceful competition.*
>
> Jackie Robinson, 1964[1]

> *There is one irrefutable fact of my life which has determined much of what happened to me: I was a black man in a white world. I never had it made.*
>
> Jackie Robinson, 1972[2]

I

In January 1957, after ten tempestuous years with the Brooklyn Dodgers, Jackie Robinson announced his retirement. "If 13 major league teams can come up with colored players," he asked in parting, "why can't the other three?"[3] Two years had passed since Elston Howard had joined the Yankees and three teams—the Philadelphia Phillies, the Detroit Tigers, and the Boston Red Sox—continued to perform with all-white casts. Although each employed blacks in their minor league systems, none appeared close to adding a black player to their roster.

Within months of Robinson's comments the Phillies reached outside of their organization to integrate.[4] The Philadelphia club purchased shortstop John Kennedy from the Kansas City Monarchs and his spring performance unexpectedly earned Kennedy, the last player to jump directly from the Negro Leagues to the majors, a slot on the 1957 Phillies roster. Shortly before opening day the Phillies also acquired Chico Fernandez, another shortstop, from the Dodgers and thus started the season with two blacks. On April 22 Kennedy became the first black Phillie. After only two at-bats he injured his shoulder and never again appeared in the majors. Fernandez claimed the starting shortstop position.

The Detroit Tigers, like the Phillies, displayed no evidence of imminent integration. Before 1953 the Briggs-owned Tigers signed no blacks. Following his death and the sale of the club the new owners claimed to have spent $75,000 in four years to develop black players. By 1958 seventeen blacks performed in the Detroit farm system. Most, however, languished in the lower classifications. In April 1958, an *ad hoc* civil rights group, the Briggs Stadium Boycott Committee, threatened a fan boycott of Tiger games unless the club desegregated. Club officials delayed the protest action with pledges to end its all-white policies as soon as possible.[5] On June 6 the Tigers fulfilled this promise when they called up black third baseman Ossie Virgil, obtained in a preseason trade with the Giants, from their Charleston farm team.

Fifteen teams had now integrated. Only the Red Sox remained and pressures mounted on the Boston club. In early 1959 longtime Red Sox General Manager Joe Cronin became the president of the American League. Cronin faced embarrassing questions about Red Sox racial policies. Critics recalled that Boston might have initiated desegregation in April 1945, when Jackie Robinson, Sam Jethroe, and Marvin Williams had auditioned at Fenway Park. Robinson, speaking in Boston, labelled the Red Sox prejudiced. One familiar voice of protest went unheard. Dave Egan, the Boston sportswriter who campaigned on behalf of black athletes for two decades, had died in May 1958, never having seen a black man in a Red Sox uniform.[6]

Many observers placed the blame for Boston's recalcitrance on owner Tom Yawkey. "The Red Sox will never have a regular colored player as long as Yawkey is the owner," predicted Sam Lacy. The scion of a wealthy Detroit family, Yawkey purchased the Red Sox in 1933. In Boston his charitable enterprises and passionate devotion to his club earned him immense popularity. Yet in his two and a half decades at the Red Sox helm, Yawkey's club recorded only one American League championship. "Maybe if he had a good Negro player he might have won [more] pennants," suggested Robinson, among others. Yawkey rarely, if ever, publicly discussed integration. This task fell to Cronin, Yawkey's handpicked top assistant. "The Red Sox care nothing about a man's color," Cronin annually refrained, "they only want good ballplayers."[7]

Al Hirschberg, a longtime Boston sportswriter, absolved both Yawkey and Cronin of guilt in the Red Sox failure to desegregate in his 1972 book, *What's the Matter With the Red Sox?* Hirschberg admitted that the Boston organization had not "taken a bum rap on dragging [its] feet." But, he argued, the blame lay "not at the top, but in the middle and lower echelons of the scouting system." Thus, the worst charge that could be levelled at Yawkey was that he placed "too much trust in his department heads and the men under them."[8]

The Red Sox doubtless experienced problems with individual scouts, as did other clubs. Nonetheless, had they wished, Yawkey and Cronin might easily have eliminated these obstacles. As Hirschberg notes, the Red Sox did not assign a scout to the Caribbean until 1960. No blacks joined the scouting staff until 1964. Whether by conscious design, indifference, or benign neglect, the Red Sox racial policies emanated from the top of the organization. The team's laggard position in the integration procession eloquently describes management attitudes.

Yet the Red Sox might not have suffered the dubious distinction of fielding the last all-white team if it had not been for the United States Marine Corps. In 1953 Boston signed catcher Earl Wilson, their first black recruit since Piper Davis, to a minor league contract. Converted into a pitcher, Wilson joined the Red Sox Triple-A affiliate in the spring of 1957 and defeated the parent club in a preseason exhibition game. The black pitcher seemed likely to make the majors the following year. Unfortunately, the marines drafted Wilson for two years, derailing his progress.[9]

The loss of Wilson elevated infielder Elijah "Pumpsie" Green to the forefront of the integration campaign. Green, a California native who had long since forgotten the childhood origins of his unusual nickname, had entered the Red Sox organization in 1955. In his youth, states Green, the advent of blacks in the Pacific Coast League "was the greatest thing I'd ever seen." Oakland Oaks star Piper Davis ranked among his boyhood heroes.[10] In 1953 Green signed with the Oaks, who placed him with a Class-B affiliate. Toward the close of the second season the Oaks sold his contract to the Red Sox.

Boston demonstrated no apparent discrimination in its treatment of Green. A good fielder, but a relatively light hitter, Green steadily ascended the minor league ladder, moving from the Class-A Eastern League to the Triple-A American Association in just three seasons. In 1959 despite the fact that he had batted only .253 at Minneapolis the preceding year, the Red Sox placed him on their major league roster.

"I never felt I was one of the early black players," recalls Green. "I never even thought of it." Nonetheless his presence in the Red Sox Arizona camp in 1959 made him a *cause célèbre*. A black leader hailed his arrival as "a shot in the arm for baseball in Boston," but nonetheless warned, "We are not totally satisfied yet. We want to see him out there at Fenway Park." Green discovered that, "People keep asking me time and again whether I think the Red Sox are prejudiced. I can only judge by the way I was treated and at the moment, I have no complaints."[11]

Controversy immediately engulfed the young infielder when officials in Scottsdale, Arizona, barred him from staying at the team hotel. The Red Sox initially denied the existence of segregation, citing insufficient space as the reason for Green's exclusion. When they lodged Green fifteen miles away in Phoenix, however, the truth became apparent. After a few days Green moved in with the San Francisco Giants, who trained in Phoenix.[12]

Based on his minor league statistics, Green seemed unlikely to qualify for the Red Sox in 1959. But he began the preseason with an impressive batting streak. "Every once in a while you get hot," he remembers. "In spring training, I was hot." In his first eleven games, Green batted .444 and hit three home runs. Boston sportswriters voted him the "Red Sox Rookie of the Year."[13] When the team departed Scottsdale, Green accompanied the squad for a Texas barnstorming tour against the Chicago Cubs.

Green's Arizona performances had not deluded him. "I knew myself," he admits today. "I knew that I wasn't that good." In Texas his fortunes waned. In his last nineteen at-bats he registered only two hits. His fielding also grew erratic. A two-run throwing error on April 6 dimmed his prospects. Nonetheless, when General Manager Bucky Harris announced on April 9, "We now have 30 men and can carry that many. We don't have to cut anyone from our squad for 30 days," it appeared that Green had made the team. The following day, Manager Mike Higgins surprised everyone by cutting Green and returning him to Minneapolis for "more seasoning."[14]

Higgins dictated the decision to demote Green, not the Red Sox front office. A Texas-born former major league third baseman, Higgins had once told a reporter, "There'll be no niggers on this ball club as long as I have anything to say about it." Yet Green liked Higgins and describes their relations as "fine." Indeed, from a baseball standpoint the decision made sense. Based on Green's minor league record and his late spring slump, he required more preparation. In addition the Red Sox had decided to convert him into a second baseman. Green tactfully declined immediate comment, but several months later he admitted, "I wasn't ready. I played very poor defensive ball in Arizona [and] I was in a daze all the time."[15]

Nonetheless, the Red Sox failure to integrate provoked a chorus of protest. "The mealy-mouthed words of the Red Sox management notwithstanding," wrote Lacy, "it is rather easy to conclude that the club has no desire to employ a colored ballplayer." Harold Kaese of the Boston *Globe* called the action wise in baseball terms but added, "From every other point of view, they undoubtedly have pulled a colossal blunder." A lone picket appeared at Fenway Park bearing placards charging, "Race Hate is Killing Baseball in Boston" and "We Want a Pennant, Not a White Team." Inside the stadium, fans booed Don Buddin, the regular shortstop. The Boston chapter of the NAACP and the Ministerial Alliance of Greater Boston called for an investigation of the Red Sox by the Massachusetts Commission Against Discrimination (MCAD).[16]

The attack on the Red Sox, as even their critics noted, stemmed not from their treatment of Green, but rather their segregated history. Lacy pointed out that other clubs had sent down black prospects without repercussions. But, he argued, "The Red Sox are suspect. Their past record makes them vulnerable to the charges hurled at them." Herbert F. Tucker, head of the local NAACP, called the cutting of Green "just one facet of our relations with the Red Sox." Tucker cited their rejection of Robinson and Jethroe, their failure to sign Willie Mays in 1950, and the absence of black employees in any capacity at Fenway Park.[17]

The following week, the MCAD opened hearings on the matter. Neither Yawkey, who was out of town, nor his new general manager, Bucky Harris, attended. Instead, Business Manager Richard O'Connell defended the club. O'Connell denied all charges and described the uproar as "exploitation of a cause which is not just," which "is turning into prejudice against whites." The Red Sox, he argued, had seven blacks in their minor league system and although only one black worked at Fenway Park, only three had applied for positions in seventeen years. "For some reason they are not interested in working for us," explained O'Connell innocently. One month later the MCAD cleared the Red Sox of charges of racial bias, accepting as "evidence of good faith" a letter from the club promising to "make every effort" to end segregation.[18]

In Minneapolis, Pumpsie Green divorced the entire controversy from his mind. "To me," he explains, "baseball was a tough enough game to play itself. I can't think about racial things and try to get a jump on a curve ball." Green enjoyed his finest season, batting .320 in the early months. His teammate, Earl Wilson, recently released from the marines, compiled a 10-1 record. The *Sporting News* described the two as "racing" for the distinction of becoming the first black on the Red Sox.[19]

Green won the "race." On July 21 the Red Sox, residing in last place in the American League, promoted the infielder. One week later Wilson also received the call. On Green's first evening with the club on July 21 at Chicago's Comiskey Park he appeared as a pinch runner and played an inning at shortstop. Thirteen years and nine months had passed since Branch Rickey had announced the signing of Jackie Robinson. More than twelve years had transpired since Robinson's debut at Ebbets Field. The formal desegregation of baseball was at last complete.

I I

As the gates at Fenway Park swung open to welcome Pumpsie Green, the doors to the public high schools in Little Rock, Arkansas, stood shut. Gov-

ernor Orville Faubus had ordered the schools closed after federal troops
had forced the desegregation of Central High School in 1957. "I will never
open the public schools as integrated institutions," vowed Faubus. The
defiance at Little Rock reflected the reactionary tenor of the era. Five years
after the *Brown* decision, school desegregation throughout the South had
virtually halted; the integration of public accommodations had barely begun. In Congress debates raged over the passage of new civil rights legislation, but parliamentary maneuvers, filibusters, and a lack of widespread
political support doomed the adoption of a strong measure. The final product, commented Senator Paul Douglas of Illinois, could "only by courtesy
be called a civil rights bill." In September 1959, two months after Green
crossed baseball's last color barrier, Clyde Kennard, another twenty-five-
year-old black man, attempted to enroll at the University of Mississippi.
Police arrested the former paratrooper shortly thereafter and charged him
with the theft of three bags of chicken feed worth $25. His alleged accom-
plice and accuser faced no charges, but Kennard was sentenced to seven
years in jail. Four years later, denied adequate treatment for cancer, Kennard died in prison.[20]

Amidst this atmosphere of stiffening southern resistance, contemporary
observers asserted great pride in baseball's achievement. "I guess most good
citizens of Arkansas and Virginia and other states as well refrained from
tuning in their TV to the lately completed World Series for fear of scarring
their eyeballs before a flagrant act of interracial fraternizing," wrote Robert
Ruark in 1958. Baseball no longer symbolized the inequities of racial segregation, but instead, in the view of the *Sporting News,* "the democratic
spirit of the National Game." During the mid-1950s, the Baseball Bible annually reprinted Ernie Harwell's psalm, "The Game for All America." "In
baseball, democracy shines its clearest," intoned Harwell. "Here the only
race is the race to the bag. The creed is the rule book. Color is something
to distinguish one teams' uniform from another."[21]

To many commentators baseball's "great experiment" offered a model
for the nation and the world. "Anybody who watched this World Series,"
concluded Ruark, "knows that integration comes as swiftly and surely as
the people involved recognize its inevitability." Jackie Robinson, in his
bluntly titled book, *Baseball Has Done It,* sought to demonstrate "how integration has come to baseball and how it can be achieved in every corner
of the land." Sociologist Dan Dodson, writing of his role as Branch Rickey's
co-conspirator, viewed the baseball experience as having "considerable significance" for educators and community workers in the impending integration of schools and other agencies.[22]

The adherents of "moderation," however, drew alternative lessons. An editorial in the Mobile *Press* in 1956 could express pride in the achievements of native son Henry Aaron in interracial competition because Aaron did not "take advantage of his peculiar position as a famous Negro player to further any bitterness over race or other questions," unlike other black ballplayers, "notably the ones in Brooklyn." The *Sporting News*, celebrating the tenth anniversary of integration, cited baseball's record of "gradual, voluntary, and peaceful advance," an obvious contrast to the growing militance and calls for government action by civil rights advocates.[23]

In the international arena, America's most visible example of interracial harmony had quickly become a weapon of Cold War politics. As early as 1949, when actor Paul Robeson, a former all-American football player, had told a Paris audience that American blacks would not bear arms against the Soviet Union, the House Un-American Activities Committee had invited Jackie Robinson "to give lie" to Robeson's statements. At Rickey's urging, Robinson agreed. Seated before the House committee, the Dodger star strongly denounced American racial policies. "I'm not fooled because I've had a chance open to very few Negro Americans," stated Robinson. He vowed to continue fighting racial discrimination in sports and other areas. At the same time Robinson rejected Robeson's assertion that blacks would not fight for the United States. "I've got too much invested for my wife and child and myself in the future of this country, and I and other Americans of many races and faiths have too much invested in our country's welfare, for any of us to throw it away for a siren song sung in bass," the Dodger star testified.[24]

Newspapers lavished praise on Robinson, emphasizing his denunciation of Robeson and the Communists and downplaying other parts of his speech. The episode greatly enhanced Robinson's popularity. Nonetheless it remains one of the more embarrassing moments of his career. Robinson's attack on Robeson contributed to the pillorying and banishment of one of the most talented figures in American history. Shortly before his death Robinson defended the contents of his 1949 speech but added, "I have grown wiser and closer to the painful truth about America's destructiveness. And, I do have an increased respect for Paul Robeson, who . . . sacrificed himself, his career, and the wealth and comfort he once enjoyed because, I believe, he was sincerely trying to help his people."[25]

In subsequent years other people also attempted to use baseball integration as a pro-American, anti-Communist propaganda message. Reports from the Gold Coast of Africa related that copies of the *Sporting News* with pictures of black players "have done much to make the missionary work of the Catholic missions easier." In 1952 patriotic promoters planned a world tour by the Brooklyn Dodgers and Cleveland Indians, an idea heartily endorsed by the *Sporting News*. "Doby and Robinson are considered all but essential to the success of the proposed tour," the journal reported. The sponsors considered it "most important that the Negro race be well represented, as living evidence of the opportunity to reach the top which America's No. 1 sport gives all participants regardless of race."[26] Plans for the world tour collapsed, however, aborting the international civics lesson.

Baseball's boosters also pointed proudly to the game's influence on other sports.[27] Desegregation in professional football and basketball had advanced rapidly. After the Cleveland Browns and Los Angeles Rams had abandoned racial restrictions in 1946, most football teams promptly recruited black players. Only the Washington Redskins, whose owner George Preston Marshall openly resisted the introduction of blacks, continued to field an all-white team throughout the 1950s. Since the formation of the National Basketball Association in 1949 black college stars had entered the professional ranks with relative ease. Barriers also fell in the more "aristocratic" sports. In 1955 the Supreme Court ordered the desegregation of public golf courses. Most country clubs continued to bar black members, but golfer Charlie Sifford waged a largely unpublicized battle against discrimination on the Professional Golfers' Association tour. In 1957 he won the Long Beach Open, the first black to win a major PGA event. That same year Althea Gibson won the women's tennis championships at Wimbledon and Forest Hills.

The national pastime itself underwent a dramatic transformation, unforeseen by even the most optimistic postwar observers. "Right now, colored players dominate the National Baseball League," boasted a Baltimore *Afro-American* editorial in August 1959.[28] Blacks constituted one out of every five National League players, but they occupied seven out of the top ten positions among batters. In home runs, runs batted in, and stolen bases, blacks held four out of the first five spots. Since 1949, blacks had won the Most Valuable Player Award in nine of eleven years.

Blacks not only excelled, they changed the way in which baseball was played. Black athletes reintroduced speed and baserunning into a game which for three decades had been dominated by power hitters. As early as 1949 Dan Daniel noted that Jethroe, Doby, and Robinson were the fastest men in baseball. "As you will note, all are Negroes," added Daniel. "If that race has contributed nothing else to the game . . . it has brought the consummate speed of a quality rarely demonstrated since the Ty Cobb heyday."[29] Since Robinson's debut blacks have led the National in stolen bases every year except two; in the American League blacks and Latins have topped this category in all but two seasons since 1951. In 1962 black shortstop Maury Wills stole 104 bases shattering the seemingly impregnable record of 96 thefts established by Cobb in 1915. During the next two decades two other black speedsters, Lou Brock and Rickey Henderson, surpassed Wills's mark.

The injection of speed did not imply the sacrifice of power. The contrasting images of the ponderous, slow-legged home run hitter and the willowy, spray-hitting speed merchant lost their validity. Willie Mays, Hank Aaron, and Frank Robinson, the greatest power hitters of the modern age, were highly proficient base stealers. Mays alone registered more stolen bases in his career than the combined totals of Babe Ruth, Jimmy Foxx, Ted Williams, and Mel Ott, the leading home run hitters before 1960. By the 1960s baseball, in this respect, more closely resembled the well-balanced offensive structure of the Negro Leagues than the power-oriented attack of the all-white majors.

These changes occurred far earlier in the National League than in the American. In 1959 more than twice as many blacks played in the National circuit. Concurrently, the quality of play in the older league far outstripped that in the American. Between 1954 and 1969 National League teams won ten out of sixteen World Series. Since 1950 the National League has won twenty-eight out of thirty-five All-Star games. "You want to know why the National League is the stronger league?" asks Bobby Bragan. "Branch Rickey, he's the answer. . . . He signed Robinson. Then he signed Campanella and Newcombe. Then the other teams in the National League got the message. . . . The American League was left holding the sack for a long, long time." Even American League President Lee MacPhail admitted that the late entry of blacks hurt the quality of play in his circuit.[30]

The racial imbalance of the two leagues reflects the persistence of discrimination in baseball, a situation that has provoked repeated attacks by players and the press. As sportswriter Robert Lipsyte has noted, "The integration of baseball was a great deal more public and spectacular than the integration of almost any other aspects of American life, and so baseball has been made to feel particularly defensive about its segregated years." The same comment might be made with regard to the lingering discrimination in the game. Other sports, equally guilty of racial bias, rarely receive the criticism levelled at baseball. "Probably because people believe the myth that baseball is the national pastime," explains black sports publisher Allan P. Barron, "baseball is constantly raked over the coals for its mistakes."[31]

During the 1960s black athletes, freed from the insecurity of the early years of integration, grew increasingly outspoken about inequitable conditions. What stands out in Jackie Robinson's *Baseball Has Done It* is not only a message of achievement, but a litany of complaints attesting to continued inequality. Players related tales of mistreatment in the minor leagues, the hated spring training rituals, and recurring problems in hotels. Furthermore, many noted that their hard-won success on the playing field did not bring the rewards accorded white players. "I don't think I make as much as I'm worth," asserted Frank Robinson. "No Negro does, except Willie Mays. White stars with records poorer than mine are paid more than I am." Several black stars protested the lack of opportunities to supplement their income with commercial endorsements. "National advertisers of such things as cigarettes, shaving creams, and foods, Gillette and tobacco companies, do not use Negroes enough," contended catcher Earl Battey. Others noted that despite relatively high salaries and fame, they still experienced discrimination when they attempted to purchase homes in the cities in which they performed. "Baseball has done a lot for me," concluded Hank Aaron. "It has taught me that regardless of who you are and regardless of how much money you make, you are still a Negro."[32]

Economists studying the game later confirmed many of these charges. Anthony Pascal and Leonard Rapping discovered that although desegregation coincided with the age of lucrative bonuses for young prospects, black players rarely shared in this bonanza. Pascal and Rapping found that in 1968 one out of five white major leaguers who had signed before 1959 had accepted bonuses in excess of $20,000. None of the thirty blacks playing in 1968 who had signed in the 1950s had received this inducement. From 1959 to 1961 more than a third of the white athletes had been "bonus babies." Only three of twenty-two blacks qualified. As late as 1964 the proportion of whites receiving bonuses remained twice as high as that for blacks.[33]

On the other hand, Pascal and Rapping employed a complex set of econometric calculations to argue that in 1968 "there was no salary discrimination against black baseball players who have achieved major league status." Players of equal abilities received equal compensation. Economist Gerald Scully disagreed. Studying the same period he found that although blacks ranked as the highest paid players in baseball and blacks earned a higher average salary at each position, "Among experienced ballplayers, blacks, on the average, earn less than whites of equal ability" and "pay differentials between whites and blacks of equal ability persist throughout the observed performance levels of experienced players." As performance improved, added Scully, the salary imbalance widened.[34]

Although these researchers differed in their analysis of income distribution, both agreed with a 1967 study by Aaron Rosenblatt that, "The Negro ballplayer may have to be better qualified than a white player to win the same position." Rosenblatt found that from 1953-65, black batters averaged approximately twenty points higher than their white counterparts. Among players with lower batting averages the proportion of blacks steadily declined. The outstanding player thus suffered minimally from discrimination, but, argued Rosenblatt, "The undistinguished Negro player is less likely to play in the major leagues than the equally undistinguished white player." Scully added that a "retention barrier" also existed. Black players not only had to be better than whites to reach the majors, "but they must consistently outperform them to stay in baseball." As late as 1982, almost 70 percent of black non-pitchers in the majors were everyday starters.[35]

All three studies uncovered another, more subtle pattern of discrimination. Although blacks in the major leagues outperformed whites at every position, teams disproportionately relegated them to specific slots. Blacks dominated outfield play but rarely could be found in the infield or as pitchers and catchers. In 1968 blacks constituted more than half of the major league outfielders, but they accounted for one out of five other players. Although black pitchers won an average of 2.7 more games a year, only 9 percent of all pitchers were black. One possible explanation for the imbalance was that the inequality of training facilities in black communities and inferior attention from white coaches and managers in the minors effectively limited opportunities for blacks in positions which required special instruction. Other commentators argued that longstanding stereotypes barred blacks from positions thought to require more thinking, intellect, and leadership qualities. Scully suggests that infield and battery spots are more central to the action and that they are located closer to the fans in the higher-priced seats. At these showcase positions teams preferred to place light-skinned players. Scully discovered that among black players, those judged "very light" or "light brown" could be found more often as infielders, pitchers, and catchers, while "dark brown" and "very dark" players were likely to be outfielders.[36]

Far more blatant discrimination manifested itself in baseball dugouts and front offices. "We bring dollars into club treasuries when we play," protested Doby in *Baseball Has Done It*, but "when we stop playing our dollars stop." Since the advent of integration, baseball executives have displayed minimal interest in hiring blacks in nonplaying capacities. In 1964 when Doby made his comment, no blacks had managed in the major leagues and only two had served as full-time coaches. The minor leagues also offered few opportunities. During the early 1950s several independent teams hired former Negro League stars to pilot primarily black teams, allowing Sam Bankhead, Nate Moreland, Marvin Williams, and Chet Brewer to experience brief terms as managers. In 1961 Gene Baker became the first black to manage a major league affiliate when he assumed the helm of the Batavia Pirates.[37] In the 1980s black minor league managers remain rare.

The black major league manager has been even more unusual. In 1960 Bill Veeck outlined the qualities that he saw as essential for the first black pilot. "A man will have to have more stability to be a Negro coach or a manager and be slower to anger than if he were white," he asserted. "The first major league manager will have to be a fellow who has been playing extremely well for a dozen years or so so that he becomes a byword for excellence."[38] Veeck stated that these qualifications were unfair but necessary. Veeck left baseball in 1961 and no other owners during that decade seriously considered hiring a black manager. Not until 1975 when the Cleveland Indians hired Frank Robinson, who embodied Veeck's requirements, did a black manager appear in the majors. Since that time only two other blacks, Larry Doby, hired by Veeck, and Maury Wills, have managed major league teams. The combined tenure of the latter pair amounts to less than a full season.

Blacks have found limited opportunities in other nonplaying capacities as well. The first black umpire did not reach the major leagues until 1966 when Emmett Ashford joined the American League after a sixteen-year apprenticeship in the minors. Few teams employ blacks in front-office positions. A 1982 survey of 24 major league clubs (with the Yankees and the Red Sox refusing to cooperate) discovered that blacks held only 32 of the 913 available white-collar baseball jobs, including secretarial positions. Of the 568 full-time major league scouts, only 15 were black. Despite the widespread use of former athletes in the announcers' booth, few teams hired blacks to fill these slots.[39]

The absence of blacks in managerial and executive roles and the stereotyping and tracking of players into specific positions mirrors conditions in the vast majority of American corporations. Studies of other industries would doubtless reveal similar and even more pronounced histories of discrimination and bias. Yet, if baseball's guilt is relative, so is its innocence, and after four decades of integration the persistence of discrimination clouds baseball's proudest achievement.

No one understood these shortcomings and the paradox of baseball integration better than Jackie Robinson. After his 1956 retirement Robinson remained an outspoken civil rights advocate, but the magnitude of his accomplishment often overshadowed his protests. To most Americans the saga of Jackie Robinson not only dramatized the injustices of discrimination, but reaffirmed the openness of American society. Amidst the reality of inequality Robinson stood as confirmation that the American Dream encompassed all, regardless of race.

Although he recognized its limitations, Robinson shared this perspective throughout most of his life. A personification of the rags-to-riches myth, he believed that true integration could be achieved not solely through legislation, but by individual effort. Robinson advocated "black capitalism" and called upon blacks to "become producers, manufacturers, developers and creators of businesses, providers of jobs." Upon retirement from baseball he became an executive in the Chock Full O' Nuts restaurant chain. Robinson later participated in several black-owned, community-oriented business ventures, including the Freedom Bank in Harlem and the Jackie Robinson Construction Corporation.[40]

Controversy stalked the outspoken Robinson in his post-baseball life, much as it had during his playing career. Although most blacks identified with the Democratic Party, Robinson's economic beliefs allied him with the Republicans. Black and white liberals were shocked by his support of Richard Nixon's presidential candidacy in 1960, an endorsement which Robinson soon regretted. He became a close advisor to New York Governor Nelson Rockefeller, who appointed him his Special Assistant for Community Affairs in 1966 and dispatched Robinson to Harlem to defend unpopular state policies. In 1967 Robinson angered the black establishment when he resigned from the NAACP. Long one of the NAACP's most effective spokesmen and fund raisers, Robinson objected to the organization's domination by a "clique of the Old Guard" and its failure to include "younger, more progressive voices." Ironically, at the same time the former firebrand of baseball came under increasing attack by young black militants, who derided him as an "Uncle Tom," created by white people, for his pro-business, pro-Rockefeller allegiances.[41]

Personal tragedy also kept Robinson in the public eye. His son Jackie, Jr., became a drug addict, which led to two well-publicized arrests. After successful treatment at Daytop Village, a drug rehabilitation center, Jackie, Jr., died in a car accident in 1971 at the age of twenty-four.

By the early 1970s Robinson, though still a staunch advocate of integration, had grown increasingly skeptical of what he viewed as a waning national commitment to equality. "There was a time I deeply believed in America. I have become bitterly disillusioned," he wrote in his 1972 autobiography, revealingly entitled *I Never Had It Made*. He also continued his sharp criticism of the baseball establishment for its failure to hire blacks in nonplaying capacities. In 1969 he refused an invitation to a Yankee old-timers' game because, "my pride in my blackness and my disappointment in baseball's attitudes requires that until I see genuine interest in breaking the barriers that deny access to managerial and front office positions, I will say no to such requests."[42]

Three years later, although baseball had made no significant strides to remedy these conditions, Robinson ended his personal boycott in order to participate in events commemorating the twenty-fifth anniversary of his major league debut. In June he attended ceremonies at Dodger Stadium in Los Angeles, just a few miles from his childhood home in Pasadena. His appearance shocked those who saw him. For years he had been battling diabetes and heart disease. Although he was only fifty-three years old, his hair had grown snow white. He walked slowly and hesitantly and his eyesight was rapidly failing. As the Dodgers retired number 42, which he had worn throughout his career, Robinson fondly recalled Branch Rickey, his friend and mentor, who had died seven years earlier at the age of eighty-three. On October 15 Robinson appeared at Riverfront Stadium in Cincinnati to throw out the first ball at a World Series game. Despite his poor health, he retained his pioneering fervor. "I'd like to live to see a black manager," he told a national television audience.[43] Nine days later Robinson died of a heart attack at his Connecticut home.

Robinson's well-founded disillusionment notwithstanding, his legacy grew even more apparent in the years immediately following his death. During the early 1970s the first generation of black stars whose careers had not been foreshortened by Jim Crow launched an assault on baseball's most cherished lifetime records. Before integration only Babe Ruth had hit more than 534 home runs. His legendary total of 714 seemed unapproachable. In 1969, however, Willie Mays, formerly of the Birmingham Black Barons, hit his 600th home run, placing him within reach of Ruth's record. Over the next four seasons Mays, who had missed two years of play due to military service in 1952-53, added 60 more home runs before retiring short of Ruth's mark. Henry Aaron, the sole remaining Negro League veteran in the majors, picked up the fallen baton.

Aaron's challenge to Ruth surprised most baseball observers. The stolid, workmanlike Braves outfielder had long lingered in the shadows of the more flamboyant Mays. Spending his career in Milwaukee and Atlanta, on teams which after 1958 never reached the World Series, Aaron performed beyond the spotlight of the national media, steadily, but unobtrusively, amassing record-threatening statistics. At the start of the 1971 season the thirty-seven-year-old Aaron had hit 592 home runs, still far distant from Ruth's standard. That year Aaron stroked 47 home runs, the most of his career. In 1972 he hit 34 more home runs, surpassing Mays and raising his own total to 673, only 41 shy of Ruth. The record seemed within imminent reach.

Aaron's pursuit of the legendary white baseball hero reawakened the latent racism in the national pastime. As he neared Ruth's record, Aaron received "Dear Nigger" letters from both North and South. "You can hit all dem homeruns over dem short fences," mocked one letter writer, "but yo' can't take that black off yo' face." The mail included threats against Aaron and his family. His daughter Gaile, a college student, received abusive telephone calls. On one occasion Aaron engaged in a shouting match with racist fans in Atlanta.[44]

The race-baiting incidents, however, obscured the broader significance of Aaron's quest. The overwhelming majority of his mail, particularly after news of his difficulties became public, expressed support and encouragement. Aaron's assault on Ruth's record, his calm, unassuming dignity under pressure, and his good-natured acceptance of the media circus which followed in his wake, captured the public imagination, much as Jackie Robinson had a quarter of a century earlier. For most Americans the race issue proved insignificant. They rooted for Aaron, the athlete and the man, to break the record.

Aaron responded in heroic fashion. Throughout the 1973 season the Braves outfielder relentlessly chased Ruth. In the next to last game he hit home run number 713. On the final day of the season he stroked three hits, all singles, leaving him one short of Ruth's record. Aaron's forty home runs in 1973 marked the only time in baseball history that this plateau had been reached by a player over the age of thirty-nine.

As the 1974 season approached the nation avidly awaited the grand finale. Aaron did not prolong the anticipation. On his first swing of the new season Aaron tied the record with a three-run, first-inning home run. Three days later, on April 8, 1974, before a nationwide television audience, Aaron hit home run number 715. Babe Ruth's record, long a symbol of unattainable standards, thus fell to a man whose baseball career had begun as an infielder with the Indianapolis Clowns.

The excitement of Aaron's Ruthian pursuit obscured his many other achievements. By the time that he retired in 1976 Aaron ranked first in baseball history in games played, at-bats, runs batted in, and extra-base hits, as well as home runs. He ranked second to Ty Cobb in both hits and runs scored. Other black players had also rewritten the record books, challenging or shattering other previously thought unattainable marks. Frank Robinson accumulated 586 home runs, moving him into fourth place on the all-time list behind Aaron, Ruth, and Mays. In 1977 Lou Brock established a new lifetime stolen-base record, surpassing Ty Cobb's fifty-year-old mark. When pitcher Bob Gibson retired in 1975 he had struck out more batters than any other pitcher except Walter Johnson. Between 1976 and 1982 five of the ten players elected to the Hall of Fame were black. "I'm proud to be standing where Jackie Robinson, Roy Campanella and others made it possible for players like Frank Robinson and myself to prove that a man's ability is limited only by his lack of opportunity," stated Aaron as he and Frank Robinson were inducted into the Hall of Fame in 1982.[45]

Reflecting on baseball's experiment in race relations, Jackie Robinson once asserted, "I really believe that in breaking down the color barrier in baseball, our 'national game,' [Branch Rickey] did more for the Negroes than any white man since Abraham Lincoln." Robinson may be forgiven his hyperbole. Nonetheless, the events unleashed by the historic alliance between Robinson and Rickey significantly altered American society. Within the realm of sports, opportunities hitherto closed to black athletes expanded. "When I first see Jackie Robinson play in my country," said his Cuban teammate Sandy Amoros, "I say if he can do it, I can do it too." Joe Black, now an executive with the Greyhound Corporation stated, "When I look at my house and when I look at the grass around my house, I say, 'Thank God for Jackie Robinson.' "[46]

Rickey and Robinson, however, did not simply end baseball segregation. Their tours through the South, later emulated by other teams, challenged deeply entrenched Jim Crow traditions. Racial exclusion in most southern baseball leagues terminated before the onset of the major civil rights agitation. Furthermore, as Rickey noted, "Integration in baseball started public integration on trains, in Pullmans, in dining cars, in restaurants in the South, long before the issue of public accommodations became daily news." In 1952 a Boston University professor introduced Rickey as a man who "can take ball clubs with Negro players to a hotel where a Negro bishop can't stay." Within two decades, most barriers had fallen for ballplayer, bishop, or bellhop. Federal legislation, court actions, and moral pressures precipitated most of these advances. But throughout the nation, black athletes represented both the harbingers and the agents of change. "We were paying our dues long before the civil rights marches," states Don Newcombe proudly. "Martin Luther King told me, in my home one night, 'You'll never know what you and Jackie and Roy did to make it possible to do my job.' "[47]

In 1944 Gunnar Myrdal had viewed the indifference of northern whites as the greatest obstacle to race progress. "To get publicity," he concluded, "is of the highest strategic importance to the Negro people." The Robinson experience fulfilled this requirement. "By applauding Robinson," writes

Roger Kahn, "a man did not feel that he was taking a stand on school integration, or on open housing. . . . But . . . to disregard color even for an
instant is to step away from old prejudices."[48] Thus, the pioneering efforts
of Robinson and those who followed him, their poise under pressure, and
their skilled performances demonstrated the possibilities of interracial cooperation and dramatized the plight of black Americans.

Sportswriter Leonard Koppett, in a perceptive eulogy of Robinson, assessed the impact that his triumph had on Americans. "Millions of people,
and especially children, found nothing wrong with the fact that there were
no black players," recalled Koppett. "These decent people weren't against
blacks. . . . They simply never questioned a system that excluded them."
By challenging the caste system in baseball, the pre-eminent pastime of the
age which was lavishly chronicled in newspapers and on radio, the Robinson drama, writes Koppett, "compelled millions of decent white people to
confront the fact of race prejudice—a fact they had been able to ignore for
generations before." As a result, asserts Koppett, Robinson accomplished
more than any other individual to focus attention on the inequities of
American society. "The consequences of the waves his appearance made
spread far beyond baseball, far beyond sports, far beyond politics, even to
the very substance of a culture."[49]

In the three and a half decades since Robinson and Rickey eliminated
baseball's color line, the elements that contributed to the desegregation of
baseball—direct confrontation and personal courage, economic pressures,
and moral persuasion by the mass media—have been re-created in many
other areas of American life. The concept of a Negro League or an all-white
team has become alien; black drinking fountains and seating sections have
become obsolete. Legislated segregation has disappeared not merely in fact,
but from the national consciousness. And if the vision of an integrated and
equal society, free from racism and discrimination, which impelled Rickey
and Robinson to launch their "great experiment," remains unfulfilled, their
efforts have brought it closer to reality.

Notes

CHAPTER 1. THE CRUCIBLE OF WHITE HOT COMPETITION

1. Montreal *Gazette*, April 19, 1946.
2. Baz O'Meara in the Montreal *Daily Star*, April 19, 1946; Wendell Smith in the Pittsburgh *Courier*, April 27, 1946; Jackie Robinson in Carl Rowan with Jackie Robinson, *Wait Till Next Year* (New York, 1960), p. 150.
3. Jim Semler and Willie Wells in the Pittsburgh *Courier*, April 20, 1946.
4. Wendell Smith in the Pittsburgh *Courier*, April 27, 1946; interview with Rachel Robinson; Jackie Robinson in Rowan, *Next Year*, p. 150.
5. Rowan, *Next Year*, p. 150.
6. Pittsburgh *Courier*, April 27, 1946.
7. Marvin Rackley in Rowan, *Next Year*, p. 152; reaction of John Wright and Wendell Smith in Pittsburgh *Courier*, April 27, 1946; Montreal *Gazette*, April 19, 1946.
8. New York *Times*, April 19, 1946; Rowan, *Next Year*, p. 50.
9. Crowd reaction in Rowan, *Next Year*, p. 154.
10. New York *Times*, April 19, 1946.
11. Pittsburgh *Courier*, April 27, 1946.
12. Ibid.; Joe Bostic in the *People's Voice*, April 27, 1946; New York *Times*, April 19, 1946.
13. New York *Times*, April 19, 1946; Bostic in the *People's Voice*, April 27, 1946.
14. Gunnar Myrdal, *An American Dilemma: The Negro Problem and Modern Democracy* (New York, 1962), p. lxi; C. Vann Woodward, *The Strange Career of Jim Crow*, 3rd rev. ed. (New York, 1974), pp. 118, 102; Myrdal, *American Dilemma*, p. 41.
15. See Thomas Brooks, *Walls Come Tumbling Down* (Englewood Cliffs, N.J., 1974), pp. 24-25; Woodward, *Strange Career*, pp. 119-20.
16. Myrdal, *American Dilemma*, pp. 1002-4, 1009.
17. Ibid., p. lxxvi.

CHAPTER 2. TWILIGHT ERE THE NOON

1. Quoted in John Holway, *Voices from the Great Black Baseball Leagues* (New York, 1975), p. 353.

2. Biographical information on Bud Fowler from Robert Peterson, *Only the Ball Was White* (Englewood Cliffs, N.J., 1970), pp. 18-49.

3. On the rise of segregation, see Woodward, *Strange Career*, Chs. 1-3.

4. For the development of baseball in the late nineteenth century, see Harold Seymour, *Baseball: The Early Years* (New York, 1960) and David Voigt, *American Baseball: From Gentleman's Sport to the Commissioner's System* (Norman, 1966).

5. On the National Association of Base Ball Players, see Peterson, *Only the Ball*, pp. 16-17.

6. On the Walker Brothers and George Stovey, ibid., pp. 21-31.

7. On the League of Colored Base Ball Clubs, ibid., pp. 26-27.

8. On the Syracuse Stars and Bob Higgins, ibid., p. 28.

9. For the Stovey-Anson incident, ibid., pp. 28-29.

10. For the rise of the "culture of professionalism" emerging during the late nineteenth century, see Barton Bledstein, *The Culture of Professionalism: The Middle Class and the Development of Higher Education in America* (New York, 1972).

11. On the experiences of blacks in the International League, see Peterson, *Only the Ball*, p. 28.

12. Ibid., p. 41; Tony Mullane cited in Long Island *Newsday*, August 17, 1980.

13. On blacks in baseball in the 1890s, see Peterson, *Only the Ball*, pp. 46-51.

14. On the Cuban Giants, see Holway, *Voices*, p. 1.

15. Peterson, *Only the Ball*, pp. 59-60.

16. Art Rust, Jr., *"Get That Nigger Off the Field"* (New York, 1976), p. 16.

17. Holway, *Voices*, p. 276.

18. Cited in William Brashler, *Josh Gibson: A Life in the Negro Leagues* (New York, 1978), pp. 73-74.

19. Roy Campanella, *It's Good to Be Alive* (New York, 1959), p. 65; on night baseball, see Holway, *Voices*, pp. 8, 262 and Peterson, *Only the Ball*, p. 124.

20. Holway, *Voices*, p. 50; Campanella, *It's Good*, p. 65.

21. Quincy Trouppe, *20 Years Too Soon* (Los Angeles, 1977), p. 66.

22. Ibid., p. 67; Holway, *Voices*, p. 317.

23. On clowning in the Negro Leagues, see ibid., p. 346 and Peterson, *Only the Ball*, pp. 70, 151.

24. Quoted in Theodore Rosengarten, "Reading the Hops: Recollections of Lorenzo Piper Davis and the Negro Baseball League," *Southern Exposure* 5 (1977): 79.

25. Harold Seymour, *Baseball: The Golden Age* (New York, 1971), p. 85; Peterson, *Only the Ball*, pp. 74-75.

26. On salaries in the Negro Leagues, see Peterson, *Only the Ball*, 220-21.

27. Bill Yancey in ibid., p. 5; Ted Radcliffe in Holway, *Voices*, p. 186.

28. Hilton Smith in Holway, *Voices*, p. 295; Buck Leonard in Peterson, *Only the Ball*, p. 81.

29. Peterson, *Only the Ball*, pp. 126-27; Campanella, *It's Good*, p. 74; Jackie Robinson in *Ebony*, June 1949.

30. Brashler, *Josh Gibson,* p. 59.

31. Interview with Quincy Trouppe; Holway, *Voices,* p. 96.

32. Campanella, *It's Good,* p. 65; Holway, *Voices,* p. 14.

33. Peterson, *Only the Ball,* pp. 64, 88.

34. Ibid., p. 93.

35. Ibid., p. 95.

36. On Yankee rentals to Negro League clubs, see "Report of Major League Steering Committee," in Study of Monopoly Power, Pt. 6, *Organized Baseball,* Hearings Before the Subcommittee on the Study of Monopoly Power, House of Representatives, 82d. Cong., 1st sess., 1951, p. 484.

37. On booking agents, see Arthur Mann, *The Jackie Robinson Story* (New York, 1951), p. 17.

38. Brashler, *Josh Gibson,* p. 83; Campanella, *It's Good,* pp. 108-9; Peterson, *Only the Ball,* p. 138.

39. Holway, *Voices,* p. 321.

40. On the career of Gus Greenlee see Brashler, *Josh Gibson,* pp. 58-59, 101-15, and Peterson, *Only the Ball,* pp. 91-92.

41. Buck Leonard in Holway, *Voices,* p. 260; Leroy "Satchel" Paige and David Lipman, *Maybe I'll Pitch Forever* (Garden City, N.Y., 1962), p. 159.

42. On the East-West All-Star Game, see Brashler, *Josh Gibson,* p. 90.

43. Baltimore *Afro-American,* November 10, 1945.

44. Joe Williams in the *Sporting News,* November 1, 1945; Holway, *Voices,* p. 2.

45. See David Voigt, *America Through Baseball* (Chicago, 1976), p. 225 and Seymour, *The Golden Age,* p. 84.

46. Seymour, *The Golden Age,* pp. 84-85; Daniel C. Frio and Marc Onigman, " 'Good Field, No Hit:' The Image of Latin American Baseball Players in the American Press, 1871-1946," *Revista/Review InterAmericana* 9 (Summer, 1979): 199-208.

47. Red Smith in the Pittsburgh *Courier,* November 3, 1945; Seymour, *The Golden Age,* p. 85.

48. On games between blacks and major leaguers see, Holway, *Voices,* xvi-xvii, 3; Ban Johnson cited in Seymour, *The Golden Age,* p. 85.

49. Newt Allen in Holway, *Voices,* p. 103; Paige, *I'll Pitch,* pp. 47, 29.

50. Paige, *I'll Pitch,* p. 93.

51. Speech by Judy Johnson, Negro League Reunion, Ashland, Ohio, June, 1980; Holway, *Voices,* p. 10.

52. Interview with Gene Benson; Jake Stephens in Holway, *Voices,* p. 166.

53. Interview with Sam Lacy; Buck Leonard in Holway, *Voices,* p. 268.

54. Holway, *Voices,* p. 202; interview with Gene Benson.

55. Ted Page in Holway, *Voices,* p. 166; Campanella, *It's Good,* p. 82; Trouppe, *20 Years,* p. 11.

CHAPTER 3. THE CONSPIRACY OF SILENCE

1. *Sporting News,* March 3, 1948.

2. On the Career of Judge Landis, see Seymour, *The Golden Years,* pp. 368-71.

3. George Moriarty to A. B. Chandler, April 19, 1947 (Chandler Papers, Uni-

versity of Kentucky); Ford C. Frick, *Games, Asterisks, and People: Memoirs of a Lucky Fan* (New York, 1973), p. 94; Judge Landis in Peterson, *Only the Ball*, p. 178; *Sporting News*, March 3, 1948.

4. *Sporting News*, November 1, 1945; Alva Bradley in New York *Times*, February 18, 1948.

5. Peterson, *Only the Ball*, p. 176; Holway, *Voices*, p. 10; Peterson, *Only the Ball*, p. 10; Holway, *Voices*, pp. 86, 235.

6. Fred Lieb, *Baseball As I Have Known It* (New York, 1977), pp. 57-58; on Jake Powell, see Richard Crepeau, "The Jake Powell Incident and the Press: A Study in Black and White," unpublished manuscript.

7. Dizzy Dean cited in Paige, *I'll Pitch*, p. 93.

8. Interview with Sam Lacy.

9. Interview with Bill Veeck; Frick, *Games*, p. 94.

10. Press comments are cited in Crepeau, "Jake Powell," pp. 3-5.

11. Westbrook Pegler and Jimmy Powers in Peterson, *Only the Ball*, p. 175; Jimmy Powers in the New York *Daily News*, August 27, 1939; Shirley Povich in Peterson, *Only the Ball*, p. 176.

12. For a brief biography of Wendell Smith, see *Sporting News*, June 22, 1974.

13. Interview with Joe Bostic.

14. Undated clippings, Baseball Hall of Fame, Cooperstown, New York; *Daily Worker*, May 25, 1942.

15. Richard Goldstein, *Spartan Seasons: How Baseball Survived the Second World War* (New York, 1980), p. 265.

16. Pittsburgh *Courier*, August 23, 1947.

17. Pittsburgh *Courier*, July 8, 1944; Jackie Robinson, *Baseball Has Done It* (New York, 1964), p. 37.

18. Goldstein, *Spartan Seasons*, pp. 19-20.

19. On Quinn-Ives Act, see *Sporting News*, November 8, 1945.

20. *Sporting News*, August 6, 1942.

21. Holway, *Voices*, p. 12.

22. *Sporting News*, January 11, 1950.

23. Wendell Smith in Pittsburgh *Courier*, January 26, 1950; William Benswanger in Peterson, *Only the Ball*, p. 177; Holway, *Voices*, p. 12.

24. Campanella, *It's Good*, p. 95.

25. Brashler, *Josh Gibson*, p. 132.

26. On the proposed Pacific Coast League tryouts, see Peterson, *Only the Ball*, p. 179.

27. On Veeck's effort to buy the Phillies see Bill Veeck with Ed Linn, *Veeck As In Wreck: The Autobiography of Bill Veeck* (New York, 1962), pp. 170-71.

28. Interview with Bill Veeck.

29. Interview with Sam Lacy; Paul Robeson in Goldstein, *Spartan Seasons*, p. 265.

30. Baltimore *Afro-American*, February 28, 1948; interview with Sam Lacy.

31. Joe Bostic in undated clipping, Chandler Papers; Bat Masterson, Jr., in undated clipping, Jackie Robinson Scrapbooks, Jackie Robinson Foundation, Brooklyn, New York.

32. Tom Spink to A. B. Chandler, June 5, 1945, Chandler Papers; Larry MacPhail to A. B. Chandler, April 27, 1945, Chandler Papers.

33. Holway, *Voices*, p. 14; undated clipping, Baseball Hall of Fame.

34. Boston *Daily Record*, April 16, 1945.

35. Ibid.

36. Interview with Sam Jethroe; Boston *Globe*, July 22, 1979.

37. Jackie Robinson in ibid.; Eddie Collins in the Pittsburgh *Courier*, April 25, 1959.

38. Boston *Globe*, July 22, 1979.

39. On the Bear Mountain tryout, interview with Joe Bostic.

40. Bill Roeder, *Jackie Robinson* (New York, 1950), p. 10.

CHAPTER 4. OH, THEY WERE A PAIR!

1. Donald Honig, *Baseball: When the Grass Was Real* (New York, 1975), p. 189.

2. On Rickey's press conference, see Rowan, *Next Year*, p. 104.

3. Lee Lowenfish, "Sport, Race, and the Baseball Business," in *Arena Review* (Spring, 1978), p. 2; Ludlow Werner in the New York *Age*, November 3, 1945.

4. *Look*, March 19, 1946; *Time*, September 22, 1947; interview with Red Smith by Bill Marshall, Chandler Papers.

5. Interview with Rachel Robinson.

6. New York *Times*, February 17, 1946.

7. Harvey Frommer, *New York City Baseball: The Last Golden Age, 1947-1957* (New York, 1980), p. 57.

8. Interview with Rachel Robinson.

9. On Rickey dictating letters, interview with Red Smith, Chandler Papers; on Rickey's theories of baseball, see the *New Yorker*, May 26, 1950 and David Lipman, *Mr. Baseball: The Story of Branch Rickey* (New York, 1966), p. 56.

10. On the farm system, see the *New Yorker*, May 26, 1950.

11. Harold Parrott, *The Lords of Baseball* (New York, 1976), p. 143; Arthur Mann, *Branch Rickey: American in Action* (Boston, 1957), pp. 226-27.

12. Parrott, *Lords*, pp. 142-43; Jimmy Powers cited in Mann, *Branch Rickey*, pp. 238-39.

13. Mann, *Branch Rickey*, p. 226.

14. On Charlie Thomas, see undated clipping, Baseball Hall of Fame and Rowan, *Next Year*, p. 106.

15. Branch Rickey to Arthur Mann, October 7, 1945, Arthur Mann Papers, Library of Congress, Washington, D.C.; *Sporting News*, July 24, 1976.

16. Bob Addie in undated clipping, Robinson Scrapbooks; *Look*, March 19, 1946.

17. *Sporting News*, August 7, 1957.

18. *New Yorker*, June 2, 1950.

19. Mann, *Branch Rickey*, p. 217.

20. Branch Rickey in the *Sporting News*, November 1, 1945; Dan Dodson, "The Integration of Negroes in Baseball," in *The Journal of Educational Sociology* (October, 1954), p. 78.

21. Red Barber with Robert Creamer, *Rhubarb in the Catbird Seat* (Garden City, N.Y., 1968), pp. 265-73.

22. On Rickey and Tannenbaum, see Roeder, *Jackie Robinson;* for Tannen-

baum's views, see Frank Tannenbaum, *Slave and Citizen: The Negro in the Americas* (New York, 1946.)

23. Mann, *Branch Rickey*, p. 212.

24. *Sporting News*, July 24, 1976.

25. On Scouting in the Caribbean, see Mann, *Branch Rickey*, p. 217; interview with Clyde Sukeforth.

26. Interview with Clyde Sukeforth.

27. See Mann, *Robinson Story*, p. 19 and Arthur Mann, "The Negro and Baseball: The National Game Faces a Racial Challenge Long Ignored," unpublished manuscript, Mann Papers.

28. On Rickey and Dodson, see Dodson, "Integration of Negroes," pp. 76-77.

29. Undated speech, Mann Papers.

30. On Rickey's selection process, see Mann, *Robinson Story*, pp. 24-25.

31. On Wendell Smith and Rickey, see *Sporting News*, June 22, 1974; Mann, *Robinson Story*, p. 219.

32. For details of Robinson's court-martial, see Jules Tygiel, "The Court-Martial of Jackie Robinson," in *American Heritage* (forthcoming).

33. All quotes on Robinson's collegiate career come from undated clippings in the Jackie Robinson Scrapbooks.

34. Jackie Robinson, *I Never Had It Made* (New York, 1972), p. 16.

35. Robinson, *Baseball*, p. 29; on 1936 Pasadena pool incident, see Mann, *Robinson Story*, p. 41.

36. Undated clippings, Robinson Scrapbooks.

37. Ibid.

38. On Robinson's army career, see Tygiel, "Court-Martial."

39. Honig, *Grass*, p. 310.

40. Rowan, *Next Year*, p. 73.

41. Interview with Don Newcombe; Rowan, *Next Year*, p. 109; Will Connolly in undated clipping, Robinson Scrapbooks; Branch Rickey in Rowan, *Next Year*, pp. 109-10.

42. Interview with Othello Renfroe.

43. Trouppe, *20 Years*, p. 149.

44. *Negro Baseball*, April 1945.

45. Interview with Clyde Sukeforth.

46. Honig, *Grass*, p. 185.

47. Ibid., p. 186.

48. Ibid., p. 188.

49. Ibid.

50. Clyde Sukeforth in ibid., p. 189; Jackie Robinson in *Readers Digest*, October, 1961.

51. *Sporting News*, March 20, 1971; John Crosby in the Syracuse *Herald*, November 12, 1972.

52. Pittsburgh *Courier*, November 3, 1945; *Readers Digest*, October, 1961.

53. Rowan, *Next Year*, p. 117.

54. Ibid., p. 118.

55. Clyde Sukeforth in the Mann Papers; Honig, *Grass*, p. 191.

56. Interview with Rachel Robinson.

57. Dodson, "Integration of Negroes," p. 78; Branch Rickey to Arthur Mann, October 7, 1945, Mann Papers.

58. Branch Rickey to Arthur Mann, October 7, 1945, Mann Papers.

59. Interview with Roy Campanella; interview with Clyde Sukeforth.

60. Pittsburgh *Courier,* May 18, 1946.

61. Interview with Don Newcombe.

62. Campanella, *It's Good,* p. 109; interview with Roy Campanella.

63. Mann, *Robinson Story,* pp. 23, 122.

64. Parrott, *Lords,* p. 114; MacPhail cited in Holway, *Voices,* p. 13 and "Report of the Major League Steering Committee."

65. Rowan, *Next Year,* pp. 119-20.

66. Campanella, *It's Good,* pp. 109-11.

CHAPTER 5. IT WON'T WORK OUT!

1. Pittsburgh *Courier,* November 10, 1945.

2. Montreal *Daily Star,* October 23, 1945.

3. On reaction to Royals' announcement, see the Montreal *Daily Star,* October 24, 1945 and *Sporting News,* November 1, 1945.

4. Hector Racine in the Montreal *Daily Star,* October 24, 1945; Branch Rickey, Jr., in New York *Times,* October 24, 1945.

5. Al Parsley in the *Sporting News,* November 1, 1945; Jackie Robinson and Wendell Smith, *Jackie Robinson: My Own Story* (New York, 1948), p. 28.

6. *Sporting News,* November 1, 1945.

7. Ibid.

8. Ibid.

9. Ibid.

10. Ibid.

11. Dan Parker in the *Sporting News,* March 28, 1946; Sam Maltin in the Pittsburgh *Courier,* November 10, 1945; Jimmy Powers in the New York *Daily News,* March 12, 1946; interview with Joe Bostic.

12. Ed Danforth, George White, and Bud Seifert cited in the Chicago *Defender,* November 3, 1945.

13. Elmer Ferguson in the Pittsburgh *Courier,* November 3, 1945; Adam Claton Powell in the New York *Times,* October 25, 1945; Lee Dunbar in the Pittsburgh *Courier,* November 3, 1945.

14. Montreal *Gazette,* October 25, 1945; Dan Parker in the *Sporting News,* March 28, 1948.

15. Hugh Germinio in the Deland *Sun News,* October 25, 1945; W. N. Cox in the *Sporting News,* November 1, 1945; Fred Maley in the Chicago *Defender,* November 3, 1945.

16. Ludlow Werner in the *Sporting News,* November 1, 1945; Sam Lacy in the Baltimore *Afro-American,* May 11, 1946; Wendell Smith in the Pittsburgh *Courier,* December 29, 1945.

17. Pittsburgh *Courier,* November 3, 1945.

19. Cited in Rowan, *Next Year,* pp. 122-23.

18. Undated clipping, Jackie Robinson Scrapbooks.

20. *Sporting News*, November 1, 1945.

21. Pittsburgh *Courier*, November 3, 10, 1945.

22. Undated clipping, Robinson Scrapbooks.

23. Brooklyn *Eagle*, October 24, 1945.

24. Rudy York in the Brooklyn *Eagle*, October 25, 1945; NAACP letter, Baltimore *Afro-American*, November 10, 1945.

25. See Roger Kahn, *The Boys of Summer* (New York, 1971), pp. 287-88; *Sporting News*, November 22, 1945.

26. *Sporting News*, November 1, 1945; on cotton mill owners, see Rowan, *Next Year*, p. 122.

27. Undated clipping, Robinson Scrapbooks; Paige, *I'll Pitch*, pp. 172-73.

28. Baltimore *Afro-American*, November 10, 1945; interview with Effa Manley by Bill Marshall, Chandler Papers; Buck Leonard in Rust, *Off the Field*, pp. 30-31.

29. *Sporting News*, August 16, 1961.

30. *Sporting News*, November 22, 1945; New York *Age*, November 10, 1945.

31. Joseph Brown in the *Sporting News*, November 1, 1945; Herb Armstrong in the Baltimore *Afro-American*, November 3, 1945; telegram, Thomas Richardson to A. B. Chandler, October 24, 1945, Chandler Papers.

32. *Sporting News*, November 1, 1945.

33. Daytona Beach *Evening News*, October 24, 1945; Alva Bradley in the New York *World Telegram*, October 24, 1945; Eddie Collins in the Daytona Beach *Evening News*, October 24, 1945; Horace Stoneham in the *Sporting News*, November 1, 1945.

34. New York *Times*, February 18, 1948.

35. *Sporting News*, February 25, 1948.

36. Ibid.

37. Washington *Star and News*, October 27, 1972.

38. Ibid.

39. New York *Post*, October 25, 1945.

40. Copies of the "Report of the Major League Steering Committee" may be found in the Chandler Papers and U.S. Congress, *Organized Baseball*. For background on the Major League Steering Committee, see Lee Lowenfish, *The Imperfect Diamond: The Story of Baseball's Reserve System and the Men Who Fought to Change It* (New York, 1980), pp. 147-52.

41. U.S. Congress, *Organized Baseball*, pp. 504-7.

42. Montreal *Gazette*, October 25, 1945.

43. Daytona Beach *Evening News*, October 24, 1945.

44. New York *World Telegram*, October 24, 1945.

45. Clark Griffith in the New York *Times*, October 25, 1945; Larry MacPhail in the *Sporting News*, November 29, 1945.

46. New York *Post*, October 25, 1945.

47. Interview with Effa Manley, Chandler Papers.

48. Pittsburgh *Courier*, November 3, 1945.

49. Ibid.; Chicago *Defender*, November 10, 1945; Pittsburgh *Courier*, November 24, 1945.

50. Pittsburgh *Courier*, November 3, 1945.

51. Chicago *Defender*, November 10, 1945.

52. Chicago *Defender*, November 17, 1945.

53. Chicago *Defender*, January 26, 1946.

54. *Sporting News*, January 31, 1946.

55. Ibid.; Sam Lacy in the Baltimore *Afro-American*, March 30, 1946; Wendell Smith in the Pittsburgh *Courier*, January 26, 1946.

56. Ibid.; Chicago *Defender*, February 9, 1946.

57. Lee Dunbar in the Pittsburgh *Courier*, January 26, 1946; Sam Adams in the Montreal *Daily Star*, December 7, 1945.

58. National Baseball Congress, Chicago *Defender*, December 15, 1945; on the American Bowling Congress, see the Brooklyn *Eagle*, March 15, 17, 1946.

59. On the integration of professional football, see the Baltimore *Afro-American*, March 3, 1946 and Jack Orr, *The Black Athlete: His Story in American History* (New York, 1970), p. 112.

60. On the Big Six conference, see the New York *Times*, May 19, 1946; on Levi Jackson, see the Baltimore *Afro-American*, August 3, 1946.

61. On Jesse Brooks, see the Sporting News, March 18, 1946; on the Florida State League, see the Pittsburgh *Courier*, April 6, 1946; on Eddie Klepp, see the Pittsburgh *Courier*, April 6, 1946 and Peterson, *Only the Ball*, p. 197.

62. New York *World Telegram and Sun*, February 2, 1957.

63. New York *Times*, February 4, 1946.

64. *Sporting News*, February 14, 1946; New York *Times*, February 4, 1946; Wendell Smith in the Pittsburgh *Courier*, February 13, 1946.

65. On Rickey's illness, see Mann, *Branch Rickey*, pp. 230-32.

66. *Sporting News*, February 24, 1946; Baltimore *Afro-American*, March 16, 1948.

67. Gene Benson Scrapbooks, Philadelphia, Pennsylvania.

68. Interview with Rachel Robinson.

69. Ibid.

70. Ibid.

CHAPTER 6. IF THEY COME HERE, THEY CAN'T PLAY

1. Rowan, *Next Year*, p. 131.

2. On violence in the postwar South see, Brooks, *Walls*, pp. 53-58 and Geoffrey Perrett, *A Dream of Greatness: The American People, 1945-63* (New York, 1979), p. 80.

3. Robinson, *Had It Made*, p. 47; Rowan, *Next Year*, p. 132.

4. Robinson, *Had It Made*, p. 48; Rowan, *Next Year*, p. 134.

5. Rowan, *Next Year*, p. 136; Pittsburgh *Courier*, March 9, 1946.

6. New York *Times*, March 17, 1946.

7. Sam Lacy in the Baltimore *Afro-American*, January 26, 1946; Harold Burr in the *Sporting News*, November 29, 1945.

8. Deland *Sun News*, October 25, 27, 1945.

9. Brooklyn *Eagle*, March 13, 1946; Jim Titus quoted in the Chicago *Defender*, November 3, 1945; Red Smith in the *Sporting News*, March 14, 1946.

10. Branch Rickey in the Pittsburgh *Courier*, November 3, 1945; Jackie Robinson in ibid. and Pittsburgh *Courier*, January 12, 1946.

11. On the crowded conditions at the 1946 training camps, see *Sporting News*, February 7, 1946 and Montreal *Gazette*, April 15, 1946.

12. Rowan, *Next Year*, p. 136.

13. Harold Burr in the *Sporting News*, November 8, 1945; Wright's biography from the Baltimore *Afro-American*, February 9, 1946; New York *Times*, January 30, 1946; Chicago *Defender*, July 15, 1944; *Sporting News*, February 7, 1946.

14. Sam Lacy in the Baltimore *Afro-American*, March 16, 1946; John Wright in the Montreal *Daily Star*, March 15, 1946.

15. Interview with Clyde Sukeforth; evaluations of Wright appeared in the Daytona Beach *Evening News*, March 10, 1946, Pittsburgh *Courier*, February 26, 1946, and Montreal *Gazette*, March 6, 1946; Alex Pompez in the *Sporting News*, March 7, 1946.

16. Montreal *Daily Star*, December 10, 1945; Baltimore *Afro-American*, December 15, 1945.

17. Rowan, *Next Year*, pp. 139, 145.

18. Hopper's biography from *Sporting News*, October 16, 1946 and Montreal *Gazette*, December 6, 18, 1945.

19. Baltimore *Afro-American*, March 16, 1946.

20. Pittsburgh *Courier*, April 6, 1946.

21. Pittsburgh *Courier*, March 9, 1946.

22. Ibid.

23. Ibid.; Robinson, *Had It Made*, p. 51; Bob Finch in the Pittsburgh *Courier*, March 9, 1946.

24. Brooklyn *Eagle*, March 1, 1946.

25. Clay Hopper in Barber, *Rhubarb*, p. 274; Jackie Robinson in Rowan, *Next Year*, p. 139.

26. New York *Times*, March 5, 1946.

27. Robinson and Smith, *My Own Story*, p. 97.

28. On press coverage of the trip to Florida see Brooklyn *Eagle*, March 1-3, 1946, New York *Times*, March 2, 3, 1946, Chicago *Defender*, March 9, 1946, and Pittsburgh *Courier*, March 9, 1946; Wendell Smith in the Pittsburgh *Courier*, April 13, 1946.

29. Interview with Rachel Robinson.

30. New York *Times*, March 17, 1946; Pittsburgh *Courier*, March 23, 1946; Robinson, *Had It Made*, p. 51; Bill Corum in undated clipping, Baseball Hall of Fame.

31. Jackie Robinson in the New York *Times*, March 19, 1946; Buster Miller in the New York *Age*, March 24, 1946.

32. Florida *Times Union*, March 20, 1946.

33. New York *Times*, March 22, 1946.

34. Ibid.; Pittsburgh *Courier*, March 30, 1946.

35. Wendell Smith in ibid.; Chicago *Defender*, April 6, 1946; Brooklyn *Eagle*, March 25, 1946; Baz O'Meara in the Montreal *Daily Star*, March 25, 1946.

36. Deland *Sun News*, March 26, 1946; Brooklyn *Eagle*, March 26, 1946; interview with Red Smith, Chandler Papers.

37. Wendell Smith in the Pittsburgh *Courier*, April 6, 1946; Baltimore *Afro-American*, April 20, 1946.

38. Rowan, *Next Year*, pp. 148-49.

39. Pittsburgh *Courier*, April 13, 1946.

40. Mel Jones in the Baltimore *Afro-American*, April 6, 1946; Hector Racine in the Baltimore *Afro-American*, April 20, 1946.

41. Daytona Beach *Evening News*, March 21, 1946.

42. Daytona Beach *Evening News*, March 15, 1946.

43. Daytona Beach *Evening News*, March 21, 1946.

44. Daytona Beach *Evening News*, October 25, 30, 1946, and December 17, 30, 1945.

45. On efforts to get the Dodgers to return to Daytona Beach, see Daytona Beach *Evening News*, February 1, 1946, *Sporting News*, April 11, 1946, and Pittsburgh *Courier*, April 13, 1946; on the advertisements, see Daytona Beach *Evening News*, March 30, 1946; Ministerial Association in the Daytona Beach *Evening News*, April 4, 1946.

46. Deland *Sun News*, April 3, 1946.

47. Baltimore *Afro-American*, April 6, 1946; Pittsburgh *Courier*, March 16-30, 1946; on increased *Courier* circulation, see Harvey Frommer, *Rickey and Robinson: The Men Who Broke Baseball's Color Barrier* (New York, 1982), p. 115.

48. On Jacksonville cancellation, see Florida *Times Union*, March 23, 27, 29, 1946.

49. Deland *Sun News*, March 26, 1946.

50. Deland *Sun News*, April 7, 1946.

51. Dan Parker in the *Sporting News*, March 28, 1946; Jimmy Powers cited in the Pittsburgh *Courier*, March 23, 1946 and New York *Age*, March 23, 1946.

52. Pittsburgh *Courier*, March 23, 1946.

53. Brooklyn *Eagle*, March 1, 1946.

54. Robinson and Smith, *My Own Story*, p. 37; Buster Miller in the New York *Age*, March 17, 1946.

55. On attendance at exhibition games, see the Chicago *Defender*, March 23, 1946; on black fans from West Palm Beach, Pittsburgh *Courier*, April 6, 1946.

56. Brooklyn *Eagle*, April 2, 1946.

57. Baltimore *Afro-American*, March 16, 1946.

58. Pittsburgh *Courier*, April 20, 1946.

59. Deland *Sun News*, April 9, 1946.

60. Sam Lacy in the Baltimore *Afro-American*, April 6, 1946; Jackie Robinson in ibid.

61. Jackie Robinson in the *Sporting News*, March 14, 1946; Sam Lacy in the Baltimore *Afro-American*, April 6, 1946; on Robinson and Breard, see Baltimore *Afro-American*, March 16, 23, 1946; on Lou Rochelli, see the Pittsburgh *Courier*, March 16, 1946 and Robinson, *Had It Made*, pp. 50-51.

62. Rowan, *Next Year*, pp. 146-48; Clay Hopper in the Montreal *Gazette*, April 20, 1946.

63. Montreal *Daily Star*, April 19, 1946; on the opening day picture layout, see the Montreal *Daily Star*, April 19, May 2, 1946.

64. Interview with Rachel Robinson; Pittsburgh *Courier*, April 13, 1946.

65. On Robinson's batting problems, see the Pittsburgh *Courier*, March 16, 23, 1946; Brooklyn *Eagle*, March 1, 1946; Montreal *Daily Star*, April 2, 1946; Rowan, *Next Year*, p. 44.

66. Rachel Robinson in Rust, *Off the Field*, p. 79; Clay Hopper in the Montreal *Gazette*, April 20, 1946.

67. Montreal *Daily Star*, April 2, 1946; Pittsburgh *Courier*, April 13, 1946.

68. Baltimore *Afro-American*, March 16, 1946; Jackie Robinson in Peterson, *Only the Ball*, p. 196; on Wright's performances, see *Sporting News*, March 28, 1946, Pittsburgh *Courier*, March 23, 30, 1946, and April 13, 1946; Wendell Smith in the Pittsburgh *Courier*, April 13, 1946.

69. Branch Rickey in the Brooklyn *Eagle*, March 29, 1946; Campanella, *It's Good*, pp. 115-16; on game cancellations, New York *Times*, April 6, 1946.

70. Rachel Robinson in Rowan, *Next Year*, p. 131 and Rust, *Off the Field*, p. 77.

71. Chicago *Defender*, April 13, 1946.

CHAPTER 7. IL A GAGNÉ SES EPAULETTES

1. Undated clipping, Robinson Scrapbooks.

2. On the Treadway desertion, see the Newark *Star Ledger*, April 21, 1946, and Montreal *Daily Star*, April 24, 1946.

3. Rowan, *Next Year*, p. 60.

4. Wendell Smith in the Pittsburgh *Courier*, May 11, 1946; Montreal *Daily Star*, April 25, 1946.

5. Rowan, *Next Year*, pp. 155-56.

6. Ibid.

7. Jackie Robinson in the Baltimore *Sun*, April 29, 1946; Rowan, *Next Year*, p. 156; interview with Rachel Robinson; *Sporting News*, September 11, 1946.

8. Robin Winks, *The Blacks in Canada* (New Haven, 1971), p. 471; Dink Carroll in the Montreal *Gazette*, October 25, 1945.

9. Winks, *Canada*, pp. 420, 481-82.

10. For a description of Delormier Downs, see the Louisville *Courier-Journal*, October 3, 1946.

11. Interview with Rachel Robinson.

12. Jackie Robinson in *Black Sports*, March, 1972; Winks, *Canada*, p. 481.

13. *Black Sports*, March, 1972.

14. Montreal *Daily Star*, May 16, 1946.

15. Montreal *Daily Star*, May 28, 16, 1946.

16. Interview with Al Campanis; Montreal *Gazette*, October 7, 1946.

17. Pittsburgh *Courier*, July 20, 1946; on hospital visit, see Pittsburgh *Courier*, June 29, 1946 and Montreal *Daily Star*, June 18, 1946.

18. Pittsburgh *Courier*, May 4, 11, 1946.

19. Baltimore *Afro-American*, May 25, 1946.

20. Interview with Don Newcombe; Jackie Robinson in Peterson, *Only the Ball*, p. 196.

21. Sam Lacy in the Baltimore *Afro-American*, May 25, 1946; biography of Roy Partlow is from *Sporting News*, May 23, 1946, Baltimore *Afro-American*, May 25, 1946 and Peterson, *Only the Ball*, p. 170; interview with Don Newcombe.

22. On the purchase of Partlow, see Roy Partlow to Branch Rickey, August 12, 1946 and Ed Bolden to Branch Rickey, April 26, 1946, Mann Papers.

23. Baltimore *Afro-American*, June 8, 1946.

24. *Sporting News*, July 3, 1946; Clay Hopper in the Montreal *Daily Star*, June 25, 1946.

25. Buffalo *Evening News*, May 20, June 20, 1946.

26. Montreal *Gazette*, September 24, 1946.

27. Interview with John Jorgenson.

28. Sam Lacy in the Baltimore *Afro-American*, August 3, 1946; Tommy Thomas quoted in an interview with John Jorgenson; on Baltimore riot, see the *Sporting News*, August 7, 1946.

29. Sam Lacy in the Baltimore *Afro-American*, August 3, 1946; J. Taylor Spink in the *Sporting News*, September 11, 1946; on International League attendance, see the *Sporting News*, September 11, 18, 1946.

30. Pittsburgh *Courier*, July 28, 1946.

31. Montreal *Gazette*, August 16, 1946.

32. On Frank Ellis, see the Pittsburgh *Courier*, May 4, 11, 1946; on John R. Williams, Pittsburgh *Courier*, May 4, 1946; on the Frederick Douglass Non-Partisan Civic League, see the Montreal *Daily Star*, August 17-20, 1946.

33. W. L. Gibson in the Baltimore *Afro-American*, April 27, 1946; undated clipping, *Chicago Defender*.

34. Baltimore *Afro-American*, May 11, 1946.

35. Baltimore *Afro-American*, May 4, 18, 1946.

36. Sam Lacy in the Baltimore *Afro-American*, May 18, 1946; Montreal *Daily Star*, June 9, 1946; Lula Jones Garrett in the Baltimore *Afro-American*, May 11, 1946.

37. Curt Davis in the *Sporting News*, September 11, 1946; on MacPhail, see the Pittsburgh *Courier*, September 13, 1947; *Sporting News*, September 11, 1946.

38. Joe Page in the *Sporting News*, October 23, 1945; Pittsburgh *Courier*, August 24, 1946.

39. Curt Davis in *Sporting News*, September 11, 1946; Joe Page in *Sporting News*, October 23, 1946; anonymous manager and Jackie Robinson in *Sporting News*, September 11, 1946.

40. Interview with Tom Tatum; Jackie Robinson in the *Sporting News*, September 11, 1946.

41. Interview with Tom Tatum; Jackie Robinson in the Pittsburgh *Courier*, July 13, 1946.

42. Interview with Tom Tatum; interview with Al Campanis; Baltimore *Sun*, June 29, 1946.

43. Montreal *Daily Star*, June 8, 1946.

44. Clay Hopper in the Buffalo *Evening News*, July 15, 1946; Abe Saperstein in the Montreal *Daily Star*, June 7, 1946; interview with Red Smith, Chandler Papers.

45. Pittsburgh *Courier*, June 29, 15, 1946.

46. Interview with Tom Tatum; Jackie Robinson in the *Sporting News*, September 11, 1946; Dink Carroll in the Montreal *Gazette*, April 20, 1946.

47. *Sporting News*, September 11, 1946.

48. Interview with John Jorgenson; interview with Al Campanis; interview with Tom Tatum.

49. Interview with Tom Tatum.

50. Dink Carroll in the Montreal *Gazette*, April 20, 1946; interview with John Jorgenson; interview with Tom Tatum.

51. Interview with Al Campanis; interview with Rachel Robinson.

52. Pittsburgh *Courier*, May 4, 1946; Montreal *Daily Star*, October 5, 1946.

53. Bruno Betzel in the *Sporting News*, September 11, 1946; Ted Reeves in an

undated newspaper clipping, Robinson scrapbooks; Sam Lacy in the Baltimore *Afro-American*, September 7, 1946.

54. Montreal *Gazette*, August 16, 1946.

55. Sam Lacy in the Baltimore *Afro-American*, September 7, 1946; Joe Page in the *Sporting News*, September 11, 1946.

56. Bruno Betzel in the *Sporting News*, September 11, 1946; Clay Hopper and Lloyd McGowan in the *Sporting News*, August 20, 1946.

57. Montreal *Daily Star*, July 27, 1946; Pittsburgh Courier, August 10, 1946; Mel Jones in the *Sporting News*, August 20, 1946.

58. Montreal *Gazette*, August 29, 1946.

59. Jimmy Cannon in the Pittsburgh *Courier*, August 31, 1946; Jackie Robinson in the *Sporting News*, October 16, 1946; interview with Rachel Robinson; Mel Jones in the Montreal *Gazette*, October 7, 1946.

60. Rowan, *Next Year*, pp. 162-63.

61. Interview with Rachel Robinson.

62. On segregation in Louisville, see Montreal *Gazette*, September 30, 1946; Sam Lacy in the Baltimore *Afro-American*, October 5, 1946.

63. Baltimore *Afro-American*, September 28, 1946.

64. Louisville *Courier-Journal*, October 10, 1946; Sam Lacy in the Baltimore *Afro-American*, October 5, 1946.

65. Ibid.

66. Ibid.

67. Interview with John Welaj; Jackie Robinson in the Montreal *Gazette*, October 7, 1946.

68. Louisville *Courier-Journal*, September 29, 1946.

69. Louisville *Courier-Journal*, October 6, 7, 1946.

70. Montreal *Daily Star*, October 5, 1946.

71. Louisville *Courier-Journal*, October 3, 1946.

72. Louisville *Courier-Journal*, October 4, 1946.

73. Rowan, *Next Year*, pp. 10-12; Sam Maltin in the Pittsburgh *Courier*, October 12, 1946.

CHAPTER 8. THEY DON'T WANT ME?

1. Interview with Roy Campanella.

2. Campanella, *It's Good*, p. 114.

3. Trouppe, *20 Years*, p. 155.

4. On the United States All-Stars, see Holway, *Voices*, p. 267; Campanella, *It's Good*, p. 114; Trouppe, *20 Years*, p. 155.

5. Campanella, *It's Good*, p. 115; interview with Don Newcombe.

6. Roy Campanella and Dick Young, *The Roy Campanella Story* (New York, 1954), p. 26.

7. Fred Dobens in the New York *Times*, April 5, 1946; Brooklyn *Eagle*, April 5, 1946.

8. Pittsburgh *Courier*, April 13, 1946; Sam Lacy in the Baltimore *Afro-American*, April 13, 1946.

9. Holway, *Voices*, p. 317; *Sporting News*, July 17, 1946; interview with Effa Manley, Chandler Papers.

10. Kahn, *Boys*, p. 327; interview with Don Newcombe.

11. Baltimore *Afro-American*, April 13, 1946.

12. Campanella, *It's Good*, p. 119; interview with Don Newcombe.

13. Pittsburgh *Courier*, May 18, 1946; interview with Don Newcombe.

14. Interview with Walter Alston.

15. Ibid.

16. Pittsburgh *Courier*, May 18, 1946.

17. Baltimore *Afro-American*, June 29, 1946.

18. Campanella, *It's Good*, p. 119; Baltimore *Afro-American*, August 3, 1946.

19. Interview with Don Newcombe; interview with Walter Alston.

20. Ibid.; Campanella, *It's Good*, p. 119; Baltimore *Afro-American*, August 30, 1946.

21. Campanella, *It's Good*, p. 120.

22. Ibid., pp. 120-21.

23. Interview with Don Newcombe; interview with Walter Alston.

24. Campanella, *It's Good*, p. 120.

25. Kahn, *Boys*, p. 339.

26. *Sporting News*, September 18, 11, 1946.

27. Interview with Walter Alston.

28. Interview with Frenchy Bordagaray.

29. Ibid.

30. Ibid.

31. Pittsburgh *Courier*, July 20, 1946.

32. Baltimore *Afro-American*, July 20, 1946.

33. Interview with Frenchy Bordagaray.

34. Ibid.; Pittsburgh *Courier*, June 29, 1946; interview with Frenchy Bordagaray.

35. Ibid.

36. Ibid.

37. Ibid.

38. Interview with Don Newcombe; interview with Frenchy Bordagaray.

39. *Sporting News*, September 11, 1946.

40. Interview with Frenchy Bordagaray; John Wright in the Pittsburgh *Courier*, October 9, 1946.

CHAPTER 9. THE MOST COSTLY TRIAL EVER GIVEN A PLAYER

1. Alexander Pope, *Selected Works* (New York, 1951), p. 113.

2. On Truman and Civil Rights, see Barton Bernstein, ed., *The Politics and Policies of the Truman Administration* (Chicago, 1970), pp. 269-76.

3. *Sporting News*, January 22, 1947.

4. *Sporting News*, January 8, 1947.

5. *Sporting News*, October 30, 1946.

6. Pittsburgh *Courier*, February 15, 1947.

7. Pittsburgh *Courier*, December 14, 1946; on Bill Veeck, see Pittsburgh *Courier*, February 15, 1947; Wendell Smith in the Pittsburgh *Courier*, October 12, 1946.

8. Baltimore *Afro-American*, January 18, 1947.

9. For an account of the YMCA meeting, see Mann, *Robinson Story*, pp. 160-65.

10. Interview with Joe Bostic.

11. Mann, *Robinson Story*, p. 164.

12. William G. Nunn in the Pittsburgh *Courier*, April 19, 1947; Dan Burley in an undated clipping, Robinson Scrapbooks.

13. On barnstorming tour, see the Baltimore *Afro-American*, October 19, 1946; on the Los Angeles Red Devils, see the Pittsburgh *Courier*, November 6, 1946.

14. Interview with Rachel Robinson.

15. On the death of Josh Gibson, see Brashler, *Josh Gibson*, pp. 145-46.

16. *Sporting News*, April 16, 1947; Baltimore *Afro-American*, March 8, 1947.

17. On Rickey's Cuban strategy, see Dodson, "Integration of Negroes," pp. 78-79; Pittsburgh *Courier*, February 1, 1947; *Sporting News*, March 1, 1947; Jackie Robinson in Rowan, *Next Year*, pp. 172-73.

18. Wendell Smith in the Pittsburgh *Courier*, October 18, 1947; on the Cuban diet see the Baltimore *Afro-American*, April 15, 1947; interview with Don Newcombe; Sam Lacy in the Baltimore *Afro-American*, April 5, 1947.

19. *Sporting News*, March 26, 1947; Baltimore *Afro-American*, March 15, 22, 1947.

20. Parrott, *Lords*, p. 159; Baz O'Meara in the Montreal *Daily Star*, October 4, 1946.

21. Baltimore *Afro-American*, April 12, 1947; Branch Rickey in Leo Durocher with Ed Linn, *Nice Guys Finish Last* (New York, 1975), p. 4.

22. Robinson and Smith, *Jackie Robinson*, p. 119.

23. New York *Times*, October 26, 1972.

24. *Sporting News*, April 2, 1947; Robinson and Smith, *Jackie Robinson*, p. 120.

25. Parrott, *Lords*, p. 208.

26. *Sporting News*, January 22, 1947.

27. Interview with Pee Wee Reese.

28. Kirby Higbe, *The High Hard One* (New York, 1967), pp. 104, 111.

29. Baltimore *Afro-American*, March 8, 1947; on Bobby Avila tryout, see the Baltimore *Afro-American*, March 15, 1947, the Pittsburgh Courier, March 15, 1947, and Dodson, "Integration of Negroes," p. 79.

30. Higbe, *Hard One*, p. 104.

31. Rowan, *Next Year*, p. 176.

32. Parrott, *Lords*, p. 208, and Durocher and Linn, *Nice Guys*, pp. 177-79.

33. Rowan, *Next Year*, p. 175; Mann, *Robinson Story*, p. 169.

34. Higbe, *Hard One*, p. 177.

35. Interview with Bobby Bragan; see also Mann, *Robinson Story*, pp. 169-70.

36. Honig, *Grass*, p. 312.

37. New York *Times*, July 17, 1977.

38. Dixie Walker to Branch Rickey, March 26, 1947, Mann Papers.

39. Mann, *Robinson Story*, pp. 173-74.

40. Bobby Bragan in Donald Honig, *The Man in the Dugout: Fifteen Big League Managers Speak Their Mind* (Chicago, 1977), pp. 7-8; Branch Rickey in Robinson, *Baseball*, p. 45.

41. Honig, *Man in the Dugout*, p. 78.

42. Rowan, *Next Year*, p. 175.

43. On black players in Panama, see the *Sporting News*, March 26, 1947 and Pittsburgh *Courier*, March 29, 1947.

44. *Sporting News*, March 26, 1947.

45. Pittsburgh *Courier*, March 29, 1947; Roy Campanella in Kahn, *Boys*, p. 339; interview with John Jorgenson.

46. New York *Times*, April 1-4, 1947; Branch Rickey in the New York *Times*, April 2, 1947; *Sporting News*, April 16, 1947.

47. New York *Post*, April 5, 1947; Sam Lacy in the Baltimore *Afro-American*, April 12, 1947; Mike Gaven in the *Sporting News*, April 16, 1947.

48. *Sporting News*, April 16, 1947.

49. Campanella, *It's Good*, p. 127; interview with Don Newcombe.

50. Pittsburgh *Courier*, March 15, 1947; Jackie Robinson in the Pittsburgh *Courier*, March 22, 1947; Pittsburgh *Courier*, April 5, 1947.

51. *Sporting News*, April 9, 1947.

52. On the Durocher suspension, see Durocher and Linn, *Nice Guys*, pp. 229-36, Parrott, *Lords*, p. 204, and Mann, *Branch Rickey*, pp. 250-51.

53. Dodson, "Integration of Baseball," p. 76; Parrott, *Lords*, p. 204.

54. New York *Times*, April 12, 1947; Dave Egan in the Pittsburgh *Courier*, May 3, 1947.

55. Baltimore *Afro-American*, April 19, 1947.

56. Boston *Chronicle*, April 19, 1947; on the reception of Dixie Walker, see the Pittsburgh *Courier*, April 19, 1947; Dan Burley in an undated clipping, Robinson Scrapbooks.

57. Baltimore *Afro-American*, April 9, 1947.

58. *Sporting News*, September 17, 1947.

59. New York *Times*, April 23, 1947; see also the *Sporting News*, April 30, 1947.

60. Interview with Rachel Robinson.

61. Ibid.

CHAPTER 10. A LONE NEGRO IN THE GAME

1. Peterson, *Only the Ball*, p. 176.

2. Barber, *Rhubarb*, p. 290.

3. Tom Spink in the *Sporting News*, April 16, 1947; Parrott, *Lords*, p. 204.

4. Undated clipping, Robinson Scrapbooks.

5. On Ben Chapman's playing career, see Rowan, *Next Year*, p. 181; Ben Chapman in the Pittsburgh *Post-Gazette*, May 15, 1947; Parrott, *Lords*, p. 194.

6. J. Roy Stockton in the St. Louis *Post Dispatch*, May 11, 1947; George Moriarty to A. B. Chandler, April 19, 1945, Chandler Papers.

7. *Sporting News*, May 14, 1947.

8. *Sporting News*, May 7, 1947; J. Roy Stockton in the St. Louis *Post Dispatch*, May 11, 1947; Baltimore *Afro-American*, May 10, 1947.

9. Branch Rickey in Rowan, *Next Year*, pp. 181-84.

10. Pittsburgh *Courier*, May 3, 10, 1947; Robinson, *Had It Made*, p. 64.

11. New York *Daily News*, April 7, 1947.

12. New York *Post*, May 10, 1947; on the Dodgers and Robinson's mail, see Mann, *Robinson Story*, pp. 186-88.

13. Parrott, *Lords*, p. 192.

14. Ibid.; Baltimore *Afro-American*, May 15, 1947.

15. Ben Chapman in the *Sporting News*, March 24, 1973; Jackie Robinson in Rowan, *Next Year*, p. 184.

16. Robinson, *Had It Made*, p. 68.

17. New York *Herald Tribune*, May 9, 1947.

18. St. Louis *Post Dispatch*, May 9, 1947; interview with Red Schoendienst; interview with Marty Marion by Bill Marshall, Chandler Papers.

19. New York *Herald Tribune*, May 9, 10, 1947.

20. Terry Moore in the St. Louis *Post-Dispatch*, May 9, 1947; interview with Dick Sisler.

21. Interview with Marty Marion, Chandler Papers.

22. Frick, *Games*, pp. 97-99.

23. Pittsburgh *Courier*, May 17, 1947.

24. J. Roy Stockton in the St. Louis *Post-Dispatch*, May 11, 1947; Jimmy Cannon in the New York *Post*, May 10, 1947; John Lardner in the Chicago *Daily News*, May 17, 1947; *Sporting News*, May 21, 1947.

25. *Sporting News*, May 21, 1947.

26. New York *Post*, May 10, 1947; *Sporting News*, May 21, 1947.

27. Baltimore *Afro-American*, May 17, 1947; *Sporting News*, May 21, 1947.

28. Wendell Smith in the Pittsburgh *Courier*, May 31, 1947; Jimmy Cannon in an undated clipping, Robinson Scrapbooks.

29. Cincinnati *Enquirer*, May 13, 14, 1947.

30. Ben Chapman in the Pittsburgh *Courier*, June 28, 1947; Bill Roeder in the New York *World Telegram*, June 25, 1947.

31. Tom Meany in an undated clipping, Baseball Hall of Fame; John Crosby in the Syracuse *Herald*, November 12, 1972; Dink Carroll in the Montreal *Gazette*, April 20, 1946.

32. Interview with Bill Toomey by Bill Marshall, Chandler Papers; Leo Durocher in Kahn, *Boys*, p. 358.

33. *Sporting News*, September 17, 1947; St. Louis *Post-Dispatch*, August 14, 1947; *Time*, September 22, 1947.

34. Interview with Al Campanis; *Sporting News*, September 17, 1947; a Giant executive in an undated clipping, Baseball Hall of Fame.

35. *Time*, September 22, 1947; Vic Rashi and Gene Conley in Donald Honig, *Baseball: Between the Lines* (New York, 1976), pp. 173, 197.

36. New York *World Telegram*, June 25, 1947.

37. *Sporting News*, May 21, 1947; on pitcher complaints, see *Sporting News*, August 20, 1947.

38. Cincinnati *Enquirer*, July 15, 1947; Tom Meany in an undated clipping, Baseball Hall of Fame; Jackie Robinson in the Baltimore *Afro-American*, May 10, 1947 and in an undated clipping, Robinson Scrapbooks.

39. Pittsburgh *Courier*, April 26, 1947; Leo Durocher, *The Dodgers and Me* (New York, 1948), p. 282.

40. On Blackwell and Merullo incidents, see Robinson and Smith, *Jackie Robinson*, pp. 159-60; Jackie Robinson in an undated clipping, Robinson Papers.

41. Branch Rickey in the Pittsburgh *Courier*, April 26, 1947; Vince Johnson in the Pittsburgh *Post-Gazette*, August 25, 1947.

42. Cleveland *Plain Dealer*, September 19, 1947; interview with Bobby Bragan; Jackie Robinson in an undated clipping, Robinson Scrapbooks.

43. Dixie Walker in the Springfield *Republican*, May 7, 1972; Pee Wee Reese in Rowan, *Next Year*, p. 228; Higbe, *Hard One*, p. 106.

44. New York *Daily News*, April 17, 1947; Pittsburgh *Courier*, May 31, 1947;

Sporting News, December 24, 1947; Rowan, *Next Year,* p. 188; on Campanella and Casey, see Kahn, *Boys,* p. 334.

45. Clyde Sukeforth in Mann Papers; Kahn, *Boys,* p. 59; Dixie Walker in Robinson, *Baseball,* p. 46; Vincent X. Flaherty in an undated clipping, Robinson Scrapbooks.

46. Mann, *Branch Rickey,* pp. 257-58.

47. Pittsburgh *Courier,* June 28, 1947; Rowan, *Next Year,* pp. 227-28.

48. New York *Times,* July 17, 1977.

49. Dodson, "Integration of Negroes," p. 81.

50. Springfield *Republican,* May 7, 1972.

51. Wendell Smith in the Pittsburgh *Courier,* May 21, 1947; Gordon Cobbledick in the Cleveland *Plain Dealer,* September 19, 1947.

52. Ernest Gaines, *The Autobiography of Miss Jane Pittman* (New York, 1972), pp. 203-4.

53. Philadelphia *Afro-American,* May 17, 1947; *Sporting News,* August 13, 1947.

54. Baltimore *Afro-American,* September 27, 1947.

55. Chicago *Daily News,* October 26, 1972.

56. Baltimore *Afro-American,* May 3, 1947; Pittsburgh *Courier,* May 10, 1947; Philadelphia *Afro-American,* May 10, 1947.

57. Bernice Franklin to Jackie Robinson, August 20, 1947, Mann Papers.

58. Pittsburgh *Courier,* April 26, 1947; interview with Joe Bostic; Sam Lacy in the Baltimore *Afro-American,* April 19, 1947.

59. On awards to Robinson, see the *Sporting News,* June 12, 1947 and Pittsburgh *Courier,* June 14, 1947; *Time,* September 22, 1947.

60. Undated clipping, Robinson Scrapbooks.

61. Unless otherwise noted, all letters quoted on pp. 198-200 may be found in the Arthur Mann Papers, Library of Congress, Washington, D.C.

62. Columbus *Citizen,* May 29, 1947; Bert Wheeler to A. B. Chandler, Chandler Papers.

63. Pittsburgh *Courier,* November 22, 1947.

64. Philadelphia *Tribune,* October 11, 1947; Cleveland *Plain Dealer,* October 6, 1947.

65. Dodson, "Integration of Negroes," p. 80.

66. Interview with Rachel Robinson.

67. *Sporting News,* September 7, 1947.

68. Interview with Rachel Robinson.

69. Pittsburgh *Courier,* September 27, 1947, and *Sporting News,* October 1, 1947.

70. *Sporting News,* October 1, 22, 1947.

71. Bill Corum in an undated clipping, Robinson Scrapbooks; Robert Burnes in the St. Louis *Gazette Democrat,* August 23, 1947; Enos Slaughter in ibid.; teammate in the Baltimore *Afro-American,* August 30, 1947.

72. St. Louis *Post-Dispatch,* August 25, 1947.

73. Cleveland *Plain Dealer,* August 26, 1947.

74. Baltimore *Afro-American,* September 7, 1947; Red Smith in the Baltimore *Afro-American,* September 7, 1947.

75. St. Louis *Post-Dispatch,* September 12, 1947; New York *Daily Mirror,* September 12, 1947; *Time,* September 22, 1947.

76. *Sporting News,* September 24, 1947.
77. *Time,* September 22, 1947; *Sporting News,* September 17, 1947.
78. Undated clipping, Robinson Scrapbooks.
79. Pittsburgh *Courier,* October 11, 1947.
80. *Sporting News,* February 3, 1973.
81. Interview with Don Newcombe.
82. *Sporting News,* January 13, 1957.
83. Barber, *Rhubarb,* p. 274.

CHAPTER 11. REMEMBER, ALL OUR BOYS CAN'T BE A ROBINSON

1. Cleveland *Plain Dealer,* July 6, 1947.
2. *Sporting News,* July 2, 1947.
3. Veeck, *Veeck,* p. 171.
4. Robinson, *Baseball,* p. 57.
5. Veeck, *Veeck,* p. 171; interview with Bill Veeck.
6. Veeck, *Veeck,* p. 175.
7. Ibid.
8. For Doby biography, see Robinson, *Baseball,* pp. 58-65, and A. S. "Doc" Young, *Great Negro Baseball Stars and How They Made the Major Leagues* (New York, 1953), pp. 50-56.
9. Interview with Clyde Sukeforth.
10. For two versions of the Veeck-Manley negotiations, see Veeck, *Veeck,* p. 176 and Effa Manley and Leon Herbert Hardwick, *Negro Baseball . . . Before Integration* (Chicago, 1976), pp. 174-75.
11. Young, *Baseball Stars,* p. 51; Bill Veeck in the Pittsburgh *Courier,* April 16, 1947.
12. A Cleveland reporter in the *Sporting News,* July 16, 1947; A New York correspondent in the Cleveland *Press,* July 7, 1947; Young, *Baseball Stars,* p. 56.
13. Robinson, *Baseball,* p. 58.
14. Interview with Bill Veeck; undated clipping in Baseball Hall of Fame.
15. Interview with Bill Veeck.
16. Robinson, *Baseball,* p. 60; Cleveland *Plain Dealer,* July 7, 1947.
17. Larry Doby in the Cleveland *Plain Dealer,* July 9, 1947; *Sporting News,* November 12, 1947; New York *Times,* July 6, 1947.
18. Veeck, *Veeck,* p. 170; Cleveland *Press,* July 6, 1947; *Sporting News,* July 16, 1947.
19. New York *World Telegram,* July 5, 1947; *Sporting News,* July 16, 1947.
20. Cleveland *Press,* July 12, 24, 1947.
21. Interview with Jim Hegan by Bill Marshall, Chandler Papers.
22. Cleveland *Press,* July 7, 1947; on Doby and Gordon, see *Sports Illustrated,* December 4, 1961.
23. Interview with Bill Veeck; Cleveland *Plain Dealer,* July 13, 1947; Pittsburgh *Courier,* August 2, 1947.
24. On Campanella and Doby, see the Pittsburgh *Courier,* July 19, 1947; Jackie Robinson in ibid.; Larry Doby in undated clipping, Baseball Hall of Fame.
25. New York *World Telegram,* September 8, 1948.
26. Robinson, *Baseball,* pp. 60-61; Lou Boudreau with Ed Fitzgerald, *Player-Manager* (Boston, 1952), p. 108.

27. Boudreau, *Manager*, pp. 106-7.

28. Cleveland *Plain Dealer*, July 10, 1947; Guy Lewis in the Cleveland *Press*, July 12, 1947; Cleveland *Plain Dealer*, July 30, 1947.

29. Young, *Baseball Stars*, p. 51; Sporting News, September 17, 1947; Pittsburgh *Courier*, July 20, 1947; Young, *Baseball Stars*, p. 57; Veeck, *Veeck*, pp. 177, 180.

30. Pittsburgh *Courier*, November 15, 1947; Cleveland *Press*, October 15, 1947.

31. *Sporting News*, July 16, 1947; St. Louis *Gazette Democrat*, July 19, 1947.

32. St. Louis *Gazette Democrat*, July 19, 1947; *Sporting News*, July 23, 1947.

33. Fred Lieb in the *Sporting News*, July 30, 1947; J. Roy Stockton in the St. Louis *Post-Dispatch*, July 20, 1947; St. Louis *Gazette Democrat*, July 19, 1947.

34. Willard Brown in the Pittsburgh *Courier*, July 26, 1947; Hank Thompson with Arnold Hano, "How I Wrecked My Life—How I Hope to Save It," *Sport* (December, 1965), p. 95.

35. Holway, *Voices*, p. 334; *Sporting News*, July 23, 1947.

36. Thompson, "Wrecked My Life," p. 95.

37. *Sporting News*, July 30, 1947.

38. St. Louis *Post-Dispatch*, July 21, 1947; on warming up, see New York *World Telegram*, April 18, 1950.

39. Thompson, "Wrecked My Life," p. 95; Baltimore *Afro-American*, August 9, 1948.

40. On Browns' attendance, see the *Sporting News*, August 6, 1947; Vince Johnson in the Pittsburgh *Post Gazette*, August 25, 1947.

41. Interview with Piper Davis; Thompson, "Wrecked My Life," p. 96.

42. Wendell Smith in the Pittsburgh *Courier*, August 30, 1947; Pittsburgh *Courier*, August 9, 1947.

43. Bill Veeck in the Cleveland *Press*, July 6, 1947; Branch Rickey in the *Sporting News*, July 16, 1947; Dan Daniel in the *Sporting News*, August 20, 1947.

44. Pittsburgh *Courier*, July 12, 1947.

45. Roy Campanella in the Pittsburgh *Courier*, May 24, 1947; Sam Maltin in the Pittsburgh *Courier*, July 19, 1947.

46. On Ramon Rodriguez, see Baltimore *Afro-American*, May 17, 1947 and Pittsburgh *Courier*, July 5, 1947.

47. On Sammy Gee, see *Pittsburgh Courier*, July 5, 1947; on the Stamford Bombers, see *Sporting News*, August 6-20, 1947.

48. Pittsburgh *Courier*, July 19, December 20, 1947.

49. New York *World Telegram*, July 16, 1947; *Sporting News*, August 6, 1947.

50. New York *World Telegram*, July 18, 1947; *Sporting News*, July 16, 1947; on Elston Howard, Pittsburgh *Courier*, August 23, 1947 and interview with Elston Howard.

51. Cleveland *Plain Dealer*, July 28, 1946; handbill cited in the *Sporting News*, August 13, 1947; on Sam Jethroe and the Seals, see the Cleveland *Plain Dealer*, July 30, 1947, Pittsburgh *Courier*, August 23, 1947, and *Sporting News*, August 27, 1947.

52. *Sporting News*, July 16, 1947; interview with Frenchy Bordagaray.

53. Pete Norton in the *Sporting News*, July 16, 1947; on spring training, see *Sporting News*, December 10, 17, 1947.

54. Dan Daniel in the *Sporting News*, August 20, 1947; Vince Johnson in the Pittsburgh *Post Gazette*, August 25, 1947.

CHAPTER 12. A PAUL BUNYAN IN TECHNICOLOR

1. Pittsburgh *Courier*, August 28, 1948.
2. Paige, *I'll Pitch*, p. 200; *Sporting News*, July 21, 1948; Young, *Baseball Stars*, p. 79.
3. Cleveland *News*, July 23, 1948; Boudreau, *Manager*, p. 164.
4. Cleveland *News*, July 23, 1948; Pittsburgh *Courier*, July 17, 1948.
5. Paige, *I'll Pitch*, p. 205.
6. Ibid., p. 181; Veeck, *Veeck*, p. 183.
7. Veeck, *Veeck*, pp. 183-4.
8. Ibid., and Boudreau, *Manager*, pp. 162-63.
9. Undated clipping, Baseball Hall of Fame; Franklin Lewis in the Pittsburgh *Courier*, July 24, 1948; interview with Bib Fishel.
10. Tom Spink in the *Sporting News*, July 14, 1948; Veeck, *Veeck*, p. 185.
11. Tom Meany in the *Sporting News*, July 21, 1948; Cleveland Plain *Dealer*, July 8, 1948.
12. Pittsburgh *Courier*, July 24, 1948.
13. Cleveland *News*, July 23, 1948; Cleveland *Plain Dealer*, July 8, 1948.
14. Young, *Baseball Stars*, p. 63.
15. *Sporting News*, July 28, 1948.
16. Veeck, *Veeck*, p. 186; Cleveland *Plain Dealer*, July 12, 1948.
17. Ed McAuley in the *Sporting News*, September 22, 1948; on the hesitation pitch, see the *Sporting News*, September 29, 1948.
18. Baltimore *Afro-American*, August 14, 1948.
19. *Sporting News*, August 25, 1948; interview with Bob Fishel; Veeck, *Veeck*, p. 187.
20. Veeck, *Veeck*, p. 187.
21. Pittsburgh *Courier*, August 28, 1948.
22. *Sporting News*, September 22, 1948.
23. Ibid.; Baltimore *Afro-American*, September 11, 1948.
24. *Sporting News*, September 22, 1948.
25. Fay Young in the Chicago *Defender*, October 16, 1948; Frank Gibbon in the *Sporting News*, October 27, 1948.
26. Wendell Smith in the Pittsburgh *Courier*, November 20, 1948; Fay Young in the Chicago *Defender*, October 23, 1948; Wendell Smith in the Pittsburgh *Courier*, October 16, 1948.
27. Cleveland *Plain Dealer*, April 20, 1948.
28. Cleveland *Plain Dealer*, March 24, 1948.
29. Veeck, *Veeck*, p. 178.
30. *Sporting News*, October 27, 1948.
31. For reporters reactions to Doby, see the Cleveland *Plain Dealer*, March 24, April 20, 1948 and the *Sporting News*, December 29, 1948.
32. Larry Doby in the Pittsburgh *Courier*, April 24, 1948; Robinson, *Baseball*, p. 61; Ed McAuley in the *Sporting News*, March 31, 1948; on the Biltmore Hotel incident, see Young, *Baseball Stars*, p. 59.
33. *Sporting News*, March 31, 1948.
34. Interview with Bill Veeck.
35. Young, *Baseball Stars*, p. 59; Veeck, *Veeck*, p. 178; Gordon Cobbledick and Lou Boudreau in the Cleveland *Plain Dealer*, April 20, 1948.

36. Gordon Cobbledick in the Cleveland *Plain Dealer*, April 20, 1948; *Sporting News*, May 4, 1948.

37. Cleveland *Plain Dealer*, May 6, 1948.

38. Boudreau, *Manager*, p. 122; *Sporting News*, May 18, 1948.

39. Young, *Baseball Stars*, p. 80; Veeck, *Veeck*, p. 181; Fay Young in the Chicago *Defender*, October 16, 1948.

40. Cleveland *Plain Dealer*, July 29, 1948; Boudreau, *Manager*, p. 177.

41. Boudreau, *Manager*, p. 199; Bill Veeck in the Pittsburgh *Courier*, October 19, 1948.

42. Veeck, *Veeck*, pp. 104, 118.

43. Pittsburgh *Courier*, October 23, 1948.

44. *Sporting News*, October 27, 1948; Cleveland *Plain Dealer*, August 22, 1948.

45. Chicago *Defender*, May 22, August 28, 1948; Joseph Bibb in the Pittsburgh *Courier*, September 7, 1948.

46. Hilton Smith in Holway, *Voices*, p. 294; Effa Manley in the New York *Mirror*, January 6, 1948.

47. On the reorganization of the Negro Leagues, see the Baltimore *Afro-American*, January 31, 1948; Effa Manley in the *Sporting News*, October 20, 1948.

48. *Sporting News*, October 20, 1948.

49. Campanella, *It's Good*, p. 135.

50. Ibid., p. 136; Baltimore *Afro-American*, July 10, 1948.

51. *Sporting News*, October 20, 1948.

52. *Sporting News*, September 1, 1948.

53. Chicago *Defender*, May 15, 1948; on Minoso, see *Sporting News*, January 12, 1949.

54. *Sporting News*, March 23, 1948.

55. *Ebony*, May, 1949.

56. Ibid.

57. Ibid.

58. Tom Baird to Lee MacPhail, January 17, 1949, Baseball Hall of Fame.

59. *Sporting News*, February 9, 1949.

60. New York *World Telegram*, October 6, 1951; on the Wilson-Marquez decision, see commissioner's decision, May 13, 1949, Chandler Papers.

61. Thompson, "Wrecked My Life," p. 96.

CHAPTER 13. THE ONLY THING I WANTED TO DO WAS HIT THE MAJOR LEAGUES

1. Young, *Baseball Stars*, p. 226.

2. *Sporting News*, March 23, 1949.

3. Pittsburgh *Courier*, May 28, 1949.

4. *Sporting News*, April 20, 1949; Del Baker in *Sporting News*, October 12, 1949; Fred Haney in undated clipping, Baseball Hall of Fame.

5. *Sporting News*, June 1, March 23, 1949; Young, *Baseball Stars*, p. 201.

6. *Sporting News*, May 4, April 27, 1949.

7. *Sporting News*, August 2, 1949.

8. *Sporting News*, June 1, 1949.

9. Dandridge's biography is drawn from an interview with Ray Dandridge by Bill Marshall and Donn Rogosin, Chandler Papers; Campanella in Holway, *Voices*, p. 318.

10. Interview with Dick Crepeau; interview with Sam Lacy; interview with Monte Irvin.

11. Interview with Ray Dandridge, Chandler Papers; *Sporting News*, July 20, September 7, 1949; Pittsburgh *Courier*, September 3, 1949.

12. *Sporting News*, February 16, 1949.

13. *Sporting News*, July 20, 1949.

14. *Sporting News*, May 17, 1950.

15. Pittsburgh *Courier*, August 6, 1949.

16. Ibid.; *Sporting News*, August 31, 1949.

17. *Sporting News*, May 25, 1949; Paul Richards in Honig, *Man in Dugout*, pp. 136-37.

18. *Sporting News*, July 27, August 3, 1949.

19. *Sporting News*, February 13, 1952.

20. Ralph Ellison, *Invisible Man* (New York, 1952), p. 1.

21. John Roseboro with Bill Libby, *Glory Days With the Dodgers and Other Days With Others* (New York, 1978), pp. 54-55, 72-74.

22. Ibid., pp. 73-79.

23. Ellison, *Invisible Man*, p. 1; Roseboro, *Glory Days*, p. 74.

24. Interview with Piper Davis.

25. On Dave Hoskins see the *Sporting News*, May 4, 1953; Leon Wagner in Robinson, *Baseball*, p. 195; interview with Piper Davis.

26. Interview with Bob Thurman; interview with Piper Davis; interview with Artie Wilson by Bob Barnett.

27. Interview with Piper Davis.

28. Interview with Don Newcombe; interview with Chuck Harmon; interview with Artie Wilson by Bob Barnett.

29. Interview with Bob Thurman.

30. Ibid.; interview with Artie Wilson by Bob Barnett; interview with Piper Davis.

31. On Roy Welmaker, see the *Sporting News*, July 27, 1949; on the Austin-Pieretti fight, see the San Francisco *Chronicle*, October 23, 1980.

32. Dink Carroll in the Pittsburgh *Courier*, October 9, 1948; on Marquez, see the *Sporting News*, June 15, August 24, 1949.

33. On the donnybrook at Oakland, see the Baltimore *Afro-American*, August 23, 1952, *Sporting News*, August 13, 1952, and interview with Piper Davis.

34. *Sporting News*, June 8, 19, July 20 and August 10, 1949; interview with Bob Thurman.

35. *Sporting News*, April 11, May 23, June 13, August 22, 1951 and August 27, 1952.

36. Interview with Bob Thurman.

37. Interview with Chuck Harmon.

38. Pittsburgh *Courier*, March 7, 1953.

39. Holway, *Voices*, p. 247.

40. Dan Bankhead in the *Sporting News*, May 10, 1950; *Sporting News*, May 7, 1952; interview with Sam Jethroe.

41. Miami *Herald*, April 22, 1979; Roseboro, *Glory Days*, p. 92.

42. *Sporting News*, April 26, 1950.

43. Undated clippings, Baseball Hall of Fame.

44. Interview with Artie Wilson by Bob Barnett.

45. Trouppe, *20 Years,* p. 202.

46. Interview with Clyde Sukeforth.

47. Interview with Piper Davis; Joe Cronin in the Pittsburgh *Courier,* December 17, 1949.

48. Interview with Piper Davis.

49. Ibid.

50. Ibid.

51. Ibid.

52. On the Red Sox finances, see the *Sporting News,* June 7, 1950; *Sporting News,* May 24, 1950.

53. Interview with Piper Davis.

54. *Sporting News,* September 13, 1950.

55. Speech by Ray Dandridge at Negro League Reunion, June, 1980; Sal Maglie quoted in an interview with Ray Dandridge, Chandler Papers.

56. Interview with Chub Feeney.

57. Interview with Ray Dandridge, Chandler Papers.

58. Speech by Ray Dandridge, Negro League Reunion, June, 1980.

CHAPTER 14. THE UNWRITTEN LAW OF THE SOUTH

1. Woodward, *Strange Career,* p. 120.

2. David M. Chalmers, *Hooded Americanism: The History of the Ku Klux Klan* (New York, 1981), pp. 325-34.

3. Atlanta *Constitution,* January 15, 1949; undated clipping, Robinson Scrapbooks.

4. *Sporting News,* April 14, 1948.

5. *Sporting News,* February 9, 1949; Atlanta *Constitution,* January 15, 17, 1949; *Sporting News,* January 26, 1949.

6. Bill Mardo in an undated clipping, Robinson Scrapbooks; Baltimore *Afro-American,* March 26, 1949.

7. Jackie Robinson in the Pittsburgh *Courier,* April 16, 1949; Baltimore *Afro-American,* April 16, 1949; Wendell Smith in the Pittsburgh *Courier,* April 16, 1949.

8. *Sporting News,* April 20, 1949.

9. Ibid.; undated clipping, Robinson Scrapbooks.

10. Woodward, *Strange Career,* p. 51.

11. *Sporting News,* February 22, 1950.

12. Branch Rickey in the New York *Daily News,* January 25, 1950; Joe King in the *Sporting News,* April 19, 1950.

13. Macon *Telegraph and News,* January 16, 1949.

14. *Sporting News,* January 19, March 2, 1949.

15. *Sporting News,* April 19, 1950.

16. Ibid.

17. On the events in the Arizona-Texas League and the West Texas-New Mexico League, see the *Sporting News,* March 7-June 6, 1951.

18. On Bob Bowman, see the *Sporting News,* May 23, 1951; on Percy Miller, see *Sporting News,* August 22, 1951.

19. *Sporting News,* February 13, 1952; Pittsburgh *Courier,* April 14, 1951.

20. *Sporting News,* November 1, 1945.

21. Pittsburgh *Courier,* April 19, 1952; *Sporting News,* March 26, 1952.

22. *Sporting News,* March 4, 1953, May 14, 1952.

23. *Sporting News,* May 14, 1952.

24. Ibid.

25. *Sporting News,* March 4, 1953.

26. *Sporting News,* June 11, July 2, August 6, 13, 1952.

27. *Sporting News,* May 14, 1952; Pittsburgh *Courier,* September 6, 1952.

28. *Sporting News,* September 3, 1952; Pittsburgh *Courier,* September 6, 1952.

29. On Florida International League, see the *Sporting News,* April 2, 1952; on the spread of integration, see the *Sporting News,* June 18-August 6, 1952.

30. *Sporting News,* June 25-July 26, 1952.

31. *Sporting News,* May 14, July 9, 1952, August 19, 1953.

32. *Sporting News,* November 11, 1953; Daytona Beach *Evening News,* March 17, 1954.

33. Baltimore *Afro-American,* March 28, 1953.

34. *Sporting News,* April 15-29, 1953.

35. *Sporting News,* May 27, 1953.

36. *Sporting News,* August 5, 1953; Pittsburgh *Courier,* September 19, 1953; Baltimore *Afro-American,* December 19, 1953.

37. *Sporting News,* June 10, 1953; Arkansas *Gazette* cited in Baltimore *Afro-American,* April 25, 1953; *Delta Democrat Times* cited in Pittsburgh *Courier,* April 18, 1953.

38. *Sporting News,* September 24, 1952.

39. *Sporting News,* February 3, 1954.

40. For biography of Nat Peeples, see Pittsburgh *Courier,* April 3, 1954; Baltimore *Afro-American,* April 3, 1954; Whitlow Wyatt in *Sporting News,* March 31, 1954.

41. *Sporting News,* June 12, 1954; Robert Patterson in Perrett, *Dream,* p. 371.

42. Woodward, *Strange Career,* p. 162.

43. *Sporting News,* May 19-June 16, 1956.

44. *Sporting News,* October 24, 1956.

45. *Sporting News,* February 12, 1957; on collapse of Shreveport franchise, see the *Sporting News,* July 3, 1957.

46. *Sporting News,* July 24, 1957.

47. Robert Objoski, *Bush League: A Colorful Factual Account of Minor League Baseball From 1877 to the Present* (New York, 1975), p. 220.

48. Woodward, *Strange Career,* pp. 173-74; Brooks, *Walls,* p. 129.

49. Bob Gibson with Phil Pepe, *From Ghetto to Glory: The Story of Bob Gibson* (New York, 1968), pp. 36-37; on comments on playing in the South, see Curt Flood with Richard Carter, *The Way It Is* (New York, 1971), p. 38; Gibson, *Ghetto,* p. 43; Robinson, *Baseball,* pp. 61, 154.

50. Robinson, *Baseball,* pp. 136-37.

51. Flood, *Way It Is,* p. 38.

52. Frank Robinson with Al Silverman, *My Life is Baseball* (Garden City, N.Y., 1968), p. 61; Robinson, *Baseball,* p. 154; Flood, *Way It Is,* p. 43.

53. Flood, *Way It Is,* p. 43; Robinson, *My Life,* p. 62; Flood, *Way It Is,* p. 43.

54. Henry Aaron with Furman Bisher, *Aaron, r.f.* (Cleveland, 1968), pp. 35-6.

55. Interview with Piper Davis.

56. Interview with Chuck Harmon.

57. Aaron, *Aaron,* p. 36; Robinson, *My Life,* p. 62.

58. Interview with Chuck Harmon; on Carlos Bonilla, interview with Bob Thurman.

59. Interview with Chuck Harmon.

60. Robinson, *My Life*, p. 62; Flood, *Way It Is*, p. 43; interview with Chuck Harmon.

61. Hank Aaron in Robinson, *Baseball*, pp. 123-24; Robinson, *My Life*, p. 68; *Sporting News*, June 20, 1968.

62. Flood, *Way It Is*, p. 38; Robinson, *My Life*, p. 69; Aaron, *Aaron*, p. 30.

63. Flood, *Way It Is*, p. 38.

64. Interview with Chuck Harmon; Earl Battey in Robinson, *Baseball*, p. 184.

65. Interview with Church Harmon; interview with Piper Davis.

66. Aaron, *Aaron*, pp. 31-32; Frank Robinson in Robinson, *Baseball*, p. 154; interview with Bill White.

67. Flood, *Way It Is*, p. 38; Leon Wagner in Robinson, *Baseball*, p. 195; Bill White in Robinson, *Baseball*, p. 136.

68. Stan Baldwin and Jerry Jenkins, *Bad Henry* (Radnor, 1974), p. 137.

69. Bill White in Robinson, *Baseball*, p. 136; interview with Chuck Harmon.

CHAPTER 15. WITH ALL DELIBERATE SPEED

1. Cited in Richard Kluger, *Simple Justice: The History of Brown v. Board of Education and Black America's Struggle for Equality* (New York, 1977), p. 686.

2. Frick, *Games*, p. 99.

3. *Sporting News*, December 10, 1952; Pittsburgh *Courier*, May 24, 1952; interview with Fred Saigh by Bill Marshall, Chandler Papers; Pittsburgh *Courier*, March 1, 1952; Wendell Smith in the Pittsburgh *Courier*, July 25, 1950.

4. *Sporting News*, November 21, 1951.

5. *Sporting News*, November 14, 1951.

6. Bill DeWitt in an undated clipping, Baseball Hall of Fame.

7. Art Ehlers in the Pittsburgh *Courier*, March 7, 1953; Clark Griffith in the *Sporting News*, July 4, 1951; George Weiss in the *Sporting News*, October 7, 1953.

8. Frick, *Games*, p. 99; Burt Shotton in the Pittsburgh *Courier*, May 21, 1949: on Earl Wilson, see the Boston *Globe*, July 22, 1979; on Elston Howard, see the *Sporting News*, October 28, 1953.

9. Pittsburgh *Courier*, February 28, 1953.

10. Willie Mays and Charles Einstein, *Willie Mays: My Life In and Out of Baseball* (New York, 1972), pp. 27-31.

11. *Sporting News*, June 27, 1951.

12. Charles Einstein, *Willie's Time: A Memoir of Another America* (New York, 1980), p. 72; interview with Monte Irvin; Dan Daniel in the New York *World Telegram*, August 18, 1951.

13. Grantland Rice in the *Sporting News*, August 15, 1951; Mays, *Willie Mays*, p. 25; Pittsburgh *Courier*, June 2, 1951; Leo Durocher in the *Sporting News*, August 15, 1951.

14. Interview with Lee MacPhail.

15. Al Hirschberg, *What's the Matter With the Red Sox?* (New York, 1973), pp. 145-46.

16. Ibid., pp. 149-50.

17. Boston *Globe*, July 21, 1979.

18. Undated clipping, Baseball Hall of Fame.

19. Clark Griffith in the *Sporting News*, July 4, 1951; Pittsburgh *Courier*, May 17, 1952, August 29, 1953; the Philadelphia mayor in the *Sporting News*, July 16, 1952.

20. Clark Griffith in the New York *World Telegram*, April 17, 1953; George Weiss in the New York *World Telegram*, July 18, 1952.

21. On Judy Johnson, see *Sporting News*, February 7, 1950; on Bob Trice, see *Sporting News*, September 23, 1953.

22. Baltimore *Afro-American*, March 28, 1953; Pittsburgh *Courier*, August 22, 1953.

23. Pittsburgh *Courier*, August 29, 1953.

24. Pittsburgh *Courier*, April 4, 1953.

25. Gaines, *Jane Pittman*, p. 203.

26. Kahn, *Boys*, p. 160; Bill McCorry in Maury Allen, *You Could Look It Up: The Life of Casey Stengel* (New York, 1979), pp. 172, 174 and Baltimore *Afro-American*, October 24, 1953; Wendell Smith in the Pittsburgh *Courier*, October 17, 1953.

27. Dan Topping in the *Sporting News*, August 19, 1953; George Weiss in an undated clipping, Baseball Hall of Fame.

28. Interview with Bob Thurman.

29. Undated clipping, Baseball Hall of Fame.

30. *Sporting News*, October 12, 1952.

31. Pittsburgh *Courier*, September 5, 1953.

32. *Sporting News*, September 5, 1953.

33. Dan Topping in an undated clipping, Baseball Hall of Fame; Dan Daniel in an undated clipping Baseball Hall of Fame; Baltimore *Afro-American*, March 20, 1954.

34. Pittsburgh *Courier*, September 5, 1953.

35. Vic Power in an undated clipping, Baseball Hall of Fame; interview with Lee MacPhail; Vic Power in an undated clipping, Baseball Hall of Fame; Wendell Smith in the Pittsburgh *Courier*, September 5, 1953.

36. New York *World Telegram*, December 17, 1953.

37. Baltimore *Afro-American*, October 28, 1953.

38. George Weiss in the New York *World Telegram*, December 17, 1953; Sam Lacy in the Baltimore *Afro-American*, March 20, 1954.

39. On Howard at spring training, see the Baltimore *Afro-American*, March 20-April 17, 1954.

40. Chicago *Defender*, April 17, 1954; *Sporting News*, May 19, August 4, 1954.

41. Interview with Lee MacPhail.

42. Undated clipping, Robinson Scrapbooks; Harold Rosenthal in the *Sporting News*, October 28, 1953.

43. Undated clipping, Baseball Hall of Fame.

44. Jack Saunders in the Pittsburgh *Courier*, September 14, 1948; Alvin Moses in the Pittsburgh *Courier*, January 14, 1948; Branch Rickey in the Pittsburgh *Courier*, February 3, 1951.

45. Aaron, *Aaron, r.f.*, p. 10.

46. J. B. Martin in the Baltimore *Afro-American*, May 31, 1952; *Sporting News*, December 10, 1952; Pittsburgh *Courier*, February 13, 1954.

47. On the Cleveland Buckeyes, see Young, *Baseball Stars*, pp. 122-23; on Toni Stone, see Peterson, *Only the Ball*, p. 204.

48. Pittsburgh *Courier*, September 18, 1948; on the Indianapolis Clowns, see Pittsburgh *Courier*, December 16, 1950; interview with Quincy Trouppe.

49. Pittsburgh *Courier*, December 16, 1950; Chicago *Defender*, September 4, 1948.

50. Young, *Baseball Stars*, pp. 123, 126.

51. Negro League Folder, Baseball Hall of Fame; on sale of the Monarchs, see the *Sporting News*, February 1, 19, 1956.

52. *Sporting News*, August 7, 1958, April 9, 1958; on the Dodgers and the Negro Leagues, see the Pittsburgh *Courier*, May 14, 1959 and New York *Times*, July 31, 1960; on Indianapolis Clowns, see the *Sporting News*, April 17, 1965.

53. Einstein, *Willie's Time*, p. 71; Wendell Smith in the Pittsburgh *Courier*, September 18, 1948; "Doc" Young in the *Sporting News*, August 7, 1957.

CHAPTER 16. THEY'VE JUST GOT TO FORGET THEY'RE BLACK

1. New York *Times*, September 8, 1964.

2. Flood, *Way It Is*, p. 18.

3. Interview with Bob Thurman.

4. Thompson, "Wrecked My Life," p. 96; Rowan, *Next Year*, pp. 218-19.

5. Interview with Chuck Harmon; interview with Bob Thurman.

6. Thompson, "Wrecked My Life," p. 96; interview with Brooks Lawrence.

7. Wendell Smith in the Pittsburgh *Courier*, August 9, 1947; Casey Stengel in Allen, *Look It Up*, p. 172.

8. Interview with Sam Jethroe; Rudy York quoted in Whitey Ford, Mickey Mantle, and Joe Durso, *Whitey and Mickey* (New York, 1977), pp. 87-88.

9. Elston Howard in Allen, *Look It Up*, p. 172; Willie Mays in Einstein, *Willie's Time*, p. 210; Aaron in Robinson, *Baseball*, p. 127.

10. Pittsburgh *Courier*, June 4, 1949; Luke Easter in the *Sporting News*, June 22, 1949; Willie Mays in the *Sporting News*, July 19, 1950.

11. Einstein, *Willie's Time*, pp. 58-59.

12. *Sporting News*, December 21, 1949; Branch Rickey in the text of an uncited speech, Mann Papers.

13. *Sporting News*, January 21, 1954.

14. Billy Cox in Kahn, *Boys*, p. 167; *Sporting News*, April 1, 1953.

15. Milton Gross in the New York *Post*, March 23, 1953; Kahn, *Boys*, p. 168; Preacher Roe in the New York *Post*, March 23, 1953; Jackie Robinson in the *Sporting News*, April 1, 1953.

16. Undated clipping, Robinson Scrapbooks; New York *World, Telegram and Sun*, April 26, 1954.

17. Pittsburgh *Courier*, September 12, 1953.

18. Thompson, "Wrecked My Life," p. 96; Kahn, *Boys*, p. 151.

19. Pittsburgh *Courier*, August 21, 1952; Kahn, *Boys*, pp. 133-35; Fred Saigh in the New York *World Telegram*, June 1, 1952.

20. Interview with Monte Irvin; Thompson, "Wrecked My Life," p. 96.

21. Baltimore *Afro-American*, August 23, 1952; Rowan, *Next Year*, p. 239; Roger Kahn in New York *Herald Tribune*, August 29, 1954.

22. Baltimore *Afro-American*, May 10, 1952; *Sporting News*, June 27, 1951; *Sporting News*, June 1, 1955.

23. *Sporting News*, July 21, 1955; Robinson, *My Life*, p. 91; interview with Ernie Banks.

24. Kahn, *Boys*, pp. 334-35.

25. Larry Doby in Robinson, *Baseball*, p. 63; *Sporting News*, July 12, 1950, June 3, 1953; Shirley Povich in the *Sporting News*, June 6, 1957.

26. Sam Jethroe in the Boston *Globe*, July 22, 1979; interview with Bob Thurman.

27. Interview with Brooks Lawrence.

28. Kahn, *Boys*, p. 109; interview with Bob Thurman; interview with Brooks Lawrence; Pittsburgh *Courier*, September 12, 1953.

29. Interview with Brooks Lawrence.

30. *Sporting News*, July 4, 1970.

31. Don Newcombe in ibid.; Bill Veeck in Baltimore *Afro-American*, March 28, 1953.

32. Robinson, *Baseball*, p. 57.

33. Interview with Carl Erskine by Bill Marshall, Chandler Papers.

34. Pittsburgh *Courier*, May 8, 1954.

35. Interviews with Bob Thurman and Chuck Harmon; Hank Aaron in Robinson, *Baseball*, p. 126.

36. Chicago *Defender*, October 10, 1953; on Elston Howard, see *Sporting News*, June 8, 1955, and Allen, *Look It Up*, p. 173.

37. *Sporting News*, November 22, 1950; Dan Daniel in the *Sporting News*, August 3, 1955; Howard and Skowron in Japan in an interview with Bob Fishel.

38. Gibson, *Ghetto*, pp. 41-42.

39. Flood, *Way It Is*, p. 35; interview with Chuck Harmon; Jackie Robinson in the *Sporting News*, June 6, 1955.

40. Interview with Bob Thurman; Aaron, *Aaron*, p. 131.

41. Roseboro, *Glory Days*, pp. 114-15.

42. *Sporting News*, March 23, 1955; interview with Brooks Lawrence.

43. Interview with Brooks Lawrence; Philadelphia *Daily News*, September 11, 1964.

44. Robinson, *Baseball*, pp. 169-70.

45. Ibid., p. 141.

46. Roseboro, *Glory Days*, p. 111.

47. Baltimore *Afro-American*, April 10, 1948; on Gifford, see Roseboro, *Glory Days*, p. 111.

48. Baltimore *Afro-American*, April 10, 1948.

49. Interview with Don Newcombe; Robinson, *Baseball*, pp. 74-75.

50. Roseboro, *Glory Days*, p. 114.

51. Ibid.

52. Baltimore *Afro-American*, April 2, 1949; *Sporting News*, April 19, 1950.

53. Rachel Robinson in Rust, *Off the Field*, p. 79; Sam Lacy in the Baltimore *Afro-American*, April 2, 1949.

54. Baltimore *Afro-American*, April 16, 1949; Kahn, *Boys*, p. 112.

55. Interview with Monte Irvin; interview with Chuck Harmon.

56. *Sporting News*, June 6, 1956.

57. Aaron, *Aaron*, pp. 40-41; New York *World Telegram and Sun*, February 28, 1961; Robinson, *Baseball*, p. 128.

58. Robinson, *Baseball*, p. 207.

59. Kahn, *Boys*, p. 358.

60. Myrdal, *American Dilemma*, p. 734.

61. Ed Charles in Joe Durso, *Amazing: The Miracle of the Mets* (New York, 1970), pp. 18-19.

62. John Head, "Great Grandaddy vs. Jackie Robinson," *Southern Exposure* 7 (Fall, 1979): 14.

63. Ibid.; *Sporting News*, September 26, 1951.

64. Bill Corum in the New York *Journal-American*, July 5, 1951; Rowan, *Next Year*, pp. 216-17.

65. *Ebony*, June, 1948; *Sporting News*, September 11, 1948.

66. Rowan, *Next Year*, p. 199.

67. *Sporting News*, March 23, 1949.

68. Jocko Conlan and Robert Creamer, *Jocko* (Philadelphia, 1967); Jackie Robinson in Young, *Baseball Stars*, p. 111.

69. Dick Young in the *Sporting News*, October 12, 1949; Ed McAuley in the *Sporting News*, December 17, 1952; *Sporting News* editorials on Robinson appeared in the following issues: March 23, November 11, 1949, January 11, 1950, May 2, June 13, 1951; December 10, 1952; and June 18, 1954.

70. Pittsburgh *Courier*, May 12, 19, 1951.

71. Interview with Carl Erskine, Chandler Papers; Jackie Robinson in Young, *Baseball Stars*, p. 111; Roger Kahn in New York *Herald Tribune*, August 29, 1954.

72. Robinson, *Had It Made*, p. 83; *Look*, January, 1955.

73. Dick Young in Robinson, *Had It Made*, pp. 138-39; Jackie Robinson in the New York *World Telegram and Sun*, January 9, 1957; John Hanlon in Rowan, *Next Year*, p. 286.

74. *Sporting News*, September 17, 1952; Rowan, *Next Year*, p. 247.

75. *Sporting News*, September 17, 1952.

76. New York *Post*, March 29, 1957; interview with Red Smith, Chandler Papers.

77. Wendell Smith in the Pittsburgh *Courier*, March 19, 1949; Milton Gross cited in Rowan, *Next Year*, p. 252.

78. Joe Williams in the *Sporting News*, May 23, 1954; death threat in the Chicago *Defender*, September 26, 1953 and Baltimore *Afro-American*, September 26, 1953; Roger Kahn in the New York *Herald Tribune*, August 29, 1954.

79. *Sporting News*, March 23, 1949, May 2, 1951, and June 18, 1954.

80. *Sporting News*, February 2, 1955; Roy Campanella in the New York *Daily News*, January 26, 1957.

81. Robinson, *Had It Made*, p. 119; Harold Weissman in Rowan, *Next Year*, p. 288.

82. Los Angeles *Examiner*, September 24, 1949; Rowan, *Next Year*, pp. 297, 339.

83. Robinson, *Baseball*, p. 71; New York *Post*, March 29, 1957.

84. Roscoe McGowen in the *Sporting News*, February 6, 1957; Dick Young and Jackie Robinson in Rowan, *Next Year*, pp. 296-97.

CHAPTER 17. BASEBALL HAS DONE IT

1. Robinson, *Baseball,* p. 11.
2. Robinson, *Had It Made,* p. 256.
3. *Sporting News,* February 13, 1957.
4. *Sporting News,* April 17, 1957.
5. *Sporting News,* May 7, 1958.
6. Chicago *Defender,* January 31, 1959; *Sporting News,* May 28, 1958.
7. Sam Lacy in the Baltimore *Afro-American,* April 25, 1947; Jackie Robinson in the Chicago *Defender,* January 31, 1959; Joe Cronin in the Baltimore *Afro-American,* February 7, 1959.
8. Hirschberg, *What's the Matter,* pp. 149-52.
9. *Sporting News,* April 10, 1957.
10. Interview with Pumpsie Green.
11. Ibid.; Chicago *Defender,* March 7, 1959; Pumpsie Green in the Pittsburgh *Courier,* March 7, 1959.
12. *Sporting News,* March 4, 1959; Pittsburgh *Courier,* March 7, 1959.
13. Interview with Pumpsie Green; *Sporting News,* April 8, 1959.
14. Interview with Pumpsie Green; Bucky Harris in the Baltimore *Afro-American,* April 25, 1959; Chicago *Defender,* May 2, 1959.
15. Mike Higgins in Hirschberg, *Whta's the Matter,* p. 143; interview with Pumpsie Green; *Sporting News,* August 19, 1959.
16. Sam Lacy in the Baltimore *Afro-American,* April 25, 1959; Harold Kaese in the Chicago *Defender,* April 18, 1959; on the placards, see the Baltimore *Afro-American,* April 25, 1959; on the calls for investigation, see the Chicago *Defender,* April 25, 1959 and *Sporting News,* April 22, 1959.
17. Baltimore *Afro-American,* April 25, 1959; Chicago *Defender,* April 25, 1959.
18. Baltimore *Afro-American,* April 25, May 30, 1959.
19. Interview with Pumpsie Green; *Sporting News,* July 1, 1959.
20. Orville Faubus in Woodward, *Strange Career,* p. 167; Paul Douglas in Carl Brauer, *John F. Kennedy and the Second Reconstruction* (New York, 1977), p. 111; on Clyde Kennard, see Perrett, *Dream,* pp. 683-84.
21. Robert Ruark in the New York *World Telegram and Sun,* October 13, 1958; *Sporting News,* October 2, 1957; Ernie Harwell in the *Sporting News,* April 13, 1955.
22. New York *World Telegram and Sun,* October 13, 1958; Robinson, *Baseball,* p. 16; Dodson, "Integration of Negroes," p. 73.
23. *Sporting News,* August 19, September 16, 1956.
24. On Robinson and Robeson, see Ron A. Smith, "The Paul Robeson-Jackie Robinson Saga and A Political Collision," *Journal of Sport History* 6 (Summer, 1979): 5-27 and Rowan, *Next Year,* pp. 208-10.
25. Robinson, *Had It Made,* p. 87.
26. *Sporting News,* July 16, 23, 1952.
27. On blacks in other sports see, Orr, *The Black Athlete.*
28. Baltimore *Afro-American,* August 8, 1959.
29. New York *World Telegram and Sun,* July 25, 1949.
30. Honig, *Man in Dugout,* p. 10; interview with Lee MacPhail.

31. Robert Lipsyte in the New York *Times*, February 11, 1971; Allan P. Barron in an undated clipping, Baseball Hall of Fame.

32. Frank Robinson, Earl Battey and Hank Aaron in Robinson, *Baseball,* pp. 158-59, 186, 128.

33. Anthony Pascal and Leonard A. Rapping, "The Economics of Racial Discrimination in Organized Baseball," in Anthony Pascal, ed., *Racial Discrimination in Economic Life* (New York, 1972), pp. 134-36.

34. Ibid.; Gerald Scully, "Discrimination: The Case of Baseball," in *Government and the Sports Business* (Washington, D.C., 1974), p. 261.

35. Aaron Rosenblatt, "Negroes in Baseball: The Failure of Success," *Transaction* 4 (September, 1967): 51-53; Scully, "Discrimination," p. 263; San Francisco *Examiner*, June 23, 1982.

36. Pascal and Rapping, "Economics," p. 147; Scully, "Discrimination," pp. 241, 246; Rosenblatt, "Negroes in Baseball," p. 52.

37. Robinson, *Baseball,* pp. 64-65; on black managers in the minor leagues, see *Sporting News,* March 28, 1951, March 19, 1952, and July 10, 1959.

38. Undated clipping, Baseball Hall of Fame.

39. On blacks in baseball in 1982, see San Francisco *Examiner,* June 22-26, 1982.

40. On Jackie Robinson's business experiences, see Robinson, *Had It Made,* Chs. 10, 17.

41. Ibid., pp. 128-29, 157-68.

42. Ibid., pp. 203, 242.

43. Frommer, *Rickey and Robinson,* p. 202.

44. Baldwin and Jenkins, *Bad Henry,* p. 14; Aaron, *Aaron,* p. 216.

45. San Francisco *Chronicle,* August 2, 1982.

46. Jackie Robinson in *Reader's Digest,* October, 1961; Sandy Amoros and Joe Black in New York *Daily News,* July 20, 1972.

47. Branch Rickey in Robinson, *Baseball,* p. 65; *Sporting News,* December 24, 1952; interview with Don Newcombe.

48. Myrdal, *American Dilemma,* p. 48; Kahn, *Boys,* p. xvi.

49. Undated clipping, *Sporting News,* 1972.

Bibliography

ARCHIVAL RESOURCES:

A.B. "Happy" Chandler Papers, University of Kentucky, Lexington.
Gene Benson Scrapbooks, Philadelphia, Pennsylvania.
Arthur Mann Papers, Library of Congress, Washington, D.C.
Negro League Collection, National Baseball Library, Cooperstown, New York.
Player Clipping Files, National Baseball Library, Cooperstown, New York.
Jackie Robinson Scrapbooks, Jackie Robinson Foundation, Brooklyn, New York.

GOVERNMENT DOCUMENTS:

U.S. Congress. House of Representatives. *Hearings before the Subcommittee on the Study of Monopoly Power of the Committee of the Judiciary*, 82nd Cong., 1st sess. (1951), Pt. 6: *Organized Baseball*.

INTERVIEWS:

Walter Alston
Ernie Banks
Gene Benson
Joe Black
Joe Bostic
Stanley "Frenchy" Bordagaray
Bobby Bragan
Roy Campanella
Al Campanis
Lorenzo "Piper" Davis
Charles Feeney
Robert Fishel
Elijah "Pumpsie" Green
Chuck Harmon
Elston Howard

John "Spider" Jorgenson
Sam Lacy
Brooks Lawrence
Lee MacPhail
Don Newcombe
Harold "Pee Wee" Reese
Rachel Robinson
Albert "Red" Schoendienst
Dick Sisler
Clyde Sukeforth
Tom Tatum
Bob Thurman
Quincy Trouppe
Bill Veeck
John Welaj

Monte Irvin
Sam Jethroe
Connie Johnson

Artie Wilson
Bill White

NEWSPAPERS:

Atlanta *Constitution*
Baltimore *Afro-American*
Baltimore *Sun*
Boston *Daily Record*
Boston *Globe*
Brooklyn *Eagle*
Buffalo *Evening News*
Chicago *Daily News*
Chicago *Defender*
Cincinnati *Enquirer*
Cleveland *News*
Cleveland *Plain Dealer*
Cleveland *Press*
Daily Worker
Daytona Beach *Evening News*
Deland *Sun News*
Florida *Times-Union*
Long Island *Newsday*
Louisville *Courier-Journal*
Louisville *Times*
Miami *Herald*
Montreal *Daily Star*
Montreal *Gazette*

Montreal *Herald*
Newark *Star Ledger*
New York *Age*
New York *Daily News*
New York *Herald Tribune*
New York *Journal-American*
New York *Mirror*
New York *Post*
New York *Times*
New York *World Telegram (and Sun)*
People's Voice
Philadelphia *Afro-American*
Philadelphia *Daily News*
Philadelphia *Tribune*
Pittsburgh *Courier*
Pittsburgh *Post-Gazette*
San Francisco *Examiner*
St. Louis *Gazette-Democrat*
St. Louis *Post Dispatch*
Syracuse *Herald*
The Sporting News
Washington *Star and News*

BOOKS:

Aaron, Henry, as told to Furman Bisher. *Aaron, r.f.* (Cleveland World Publishing, 1968).

Allen, Lee. *The Giants and the Dodgers* (New York: G.P. Putnam's Sons, 1964).

Allen, Maury. *You Could Look It Up: The Life of Casey Stengel* (New York: Times Books, 1979).

Astor, Gerald. ". . . And a Credit to His Race"; The Hard Life and Times of Joseph Louis Barrow, a.k.a. Joe Louis* (New York: E.P. Dutton, 1974).

Baldwin, Stan and Jerry Jenkins in collaboration with Hank Aaron. *Bad Henry* (Radnor, Pa.: Chilton Book Co., 1974).

Barber, Red with Robert Creamer. *Rhubarb in the Catbird Seat* (Garden City: Doubleday, 1968).

Bernstein, Barton, ed. *Politics and Policies of the Truman Administration* (Chicago: Quadrangle, 1970).

Bledstein, Barton. *The Culture of Professionalism: The Middle Class and the Development of Higher Education in America* (New York: Norton, 1976).

Boudreau, Lou with Ed Fitzgerald. *Player-Manager* (Boston: Little, Brown and Co., 1952).

Brashler, William. *Josh Gibson: A Life in the Negro Leagues* (New York: Harper and Row, 1978).

Brauer, Carl. *John F. Kennedy and the Second Reconstruction* (New York: Columbia University Press, 1977).

Brooks, Thomas. *Walls Come Tumbling Down: A History of the Civil Rights Movement, 1940-1970* (Englewood Cliffs: Prentice-Hall, 1974).

Campanella, Roy. *It's Good To Be Alive* (New York: Signet, 1974).

Chalmers, David M. *Hooded Americanism: The History of the Ku Klux Klan* (New York: New Viewpoints, 1981).

Conlan, Jocko and Robert Creamer. *Jocko* (Philadelphia: Lippincott, 1967).

Crepeau, Richard C. *Baseball's Diamond Mind* (Orlando: University Presses of Florida, 1980).

Durocher, Leo with Ed Linn. *Nice Guys Finish Last* (New York: Pocket Books, 1976).

Durso, Joe. *Amazing: The Miracle of the Mets* (Boston: Houghton Mifflin, 1970).

Edmonds, A.O. *Joe Louis* (Grand Rapids: William B. Eerdman's, 1973).

Einstein, Charles. *Willie's Time: A Memoir of Another America* (New York: Berkley Books, 1980).

Ellison, Ralph. *Invisible Man* (New York: Vintage Books, 1952).

Flood, Curt with Richard Carter. *The Way It Is* (New York: Trident Press, 1970).

Ford, Whitey, Mickey Mantle, and Joseph Durso. *Whitey and Mickey* (New York: Viking Press, 1977).

Frick, Ford C. *Games, Asterisks and People: Memoirs of a Lucky Fan* (New York, Crown Publishers, 1973).

Frommer, Harvey. *New York City Baseball: The Last Golden Age, 1947-1957* (New York: Macmillan, 1980).

Frommer, Harvey. *Rickey and Robinson: The Men Who Broke Baseball's Color Barrier* (New York: Macmillan Publishing Co., 1982).

Gaines, Ernest. *The Autobiography of Miss Jane Pittman* (New York: Bantam Books, 1972).

Gibson, Bob. *From Ghetto to Glory: The Story of Bob Gibson* (New York: Popular Library, 1968).

Goldman, Eric. *The Crucial Decade—and After* (New York: Vintage Books, 1960).

Goldstein, Richard. *Spartan Seasons: How Baseball Survived the Second World War* (New York: Macmillan Publishing, 1980).

Higbe, Kirby. *The High Hard One* (New York: Viking Press, 1967).

Hirschberg, Al. *What's the Matter With the Red Sox* (New York: Dodd, Mead 1973).

Holway, John. *Voices From the Great Negro Baseball Leagues* (New York: Dodd Mead, 1975).

Honig, Donald. *Baseball: Between the Lines* (New York: Coward, McCann and Geoghegan, 1976).

Honig, Donald. *Baseball: When the Grass Was Real* (New York: Coward, McCann and Geoghegan, 1975).

Honig, Donald. *The Man in the Dugout: Fifteen Big League Managers Speak Their Mind* (Chicago: Follett Publishing, 1977).

Jenkins, Ferguson as told to George Vass. *Like Nobody Else: The Fergie Jenkins Story* (Chicago: H. Regnery Co., 1973).

Kahn, Roger. *The Boys of Summer* (New York: Signet Books, 1973).

Kluger, Richard. *Simple Justice: The History of Brown v. Board of Education and Black America's Struggle for Equality* (New York: Vintage Books, 1977).

Leuchtenberg, William. *A Troubled Feast: American Society Since 1945* (Boston: Little, Brown, 1979).

Lieb, Fred. *Baseball As I Have Known It* (New York: Coward, McCann and Geoghegan, 1977).

Lipman, David. *Mr. Baseball: The Story of Branch Rickey* (New York: G.P. Putnam's Sons, 1966).

Lowenfish, Lee and Tony Lupien. *The Imperfect Diamond: The Story of Baseball's Reserve System and the Men Who Fought to Change It* (New York: Stein and Day, 1980).

Manley, Effa and Leon Hardwick. *Negro Baseball . . . Before Integration* (Chicago, 1976).

Mann, Arthur. *Branch Rickey: American in Action* (Boston: Houghton Mifflin, 1957).

Mann, Arthur. *The Jackie Robinson Story* (New York: Grosset and Dunlap, 1951).

Mays, Willie and Charles Einstein. *Willie Mays: My Life In and Out of Baseball* (New York: E.P. Dutton, 1972).

Mead, William. *Even the Browns: The Zany, True Story of Baseball in the Early Forties* (Chicago: Contemporary Books, 1978).

Myrdal, Gunnar. *An American Dilemma: The Negro Problem and Modern Democracy* (New York: Harper and Row, 1962).

Obojski, Robert. *Bush League: A Colorful, Factual Account of Minor League Baseball From 1877 to the Present* (New York: Macmillan, 1975).

Orem, Preston D. *Baseball: 1845-1881* (Altadena: Preston D. Orem, 1961).

Orr, Jack. *The Black Athlete: His Story in American History* (New York: Pyramid Books, 1970).

Paige, Leroy "Satchel" and David Lipman. *Maybe I'll Pitch Forever* (New York: Doubleday, 1962).

Parrott, Harold. *The Lords of Baseball* (New York: Praeger, 1976).

Perrett, Geoffrey. *A Dream of Greatness: The American People, 1945-1963* (New York: Coward, McCann and Geoghegan, 1979).

Peterson, Robert. *Only The Ball Was White* (Englewood Cliffs: Prentice Hall, 1970).

Robinson, Frank with Al Silverman. *My Life is Baseball* (Garden City: Doubleday, 1968).

Robinson, Jackie. *Baseball Has Done It* (New York: Lippincott, 1964).

Robinson, Jackie and Alfred Duckett. *Breakthrough to the Big Leagues* (New York: Harper and Row, 1965).

Robinson, Jackie and Alfred Duckett. *I Never Had It Made* (New York: Fawcett, Crest, 1974).

Robinson, Jackie and Wendell Smith. *Jackie Robinson: My Own Story* (New York: Greenberg, 1948).

Roeder, Bill. *Jackie Robinson* (New York: A.S. Barnes, 1950).

Roseboro, John with Bill Libby. *Glory Days With the Dodgers and Other Days With Others* (New York: Atheneum, 1978).

Rowan, Carl T. with Jackie Robinson. . . . *Wait Till Next Year* (New York: Random House, 1960).

Rust, Art, Jr. *"Get That Nigger Off the Field"* (New York: Delacorte, 1976).

Seymour, Harold. *Baseball: The Early Years* (New York: Oxford University Press, 1960).

Seymour, Harold. *Baseball: The Golden Years* (New York: Oxford University Press, 1971).

Shapiro, Milton J. *Jackie Robinson of the Brooklyn Dodgers* (New York: Julian Messner, 1957).

Sitkoff, Harvard. *A New Deal for Blacks: The Emergence of Civil Rights as a National Issue* (New York: Oxford, 1978).

Sitkoff, Harvard. *The Struggle for Black Equality, 1954-1980* (New York: Hill and Wang, 1981).

Tannenbaum, Frank. *Slave and Citizen: The Negro in the Americas* (New York: Vintage Books, 1963).

Trouppe, Quincy. *20 Years Too Soon* (Los Angeles: Sands Enterprises, 1977).

Veeck, Bill. *Veeck—As in Wreck: The Autobiography of Bill Veeck* (New York: G.P. Putnam's Sons, 1962).

Voigt, David Quentin. *American Baseball* (2 vols., Norman: University of Oklahoma, 1966, 1970).

Voigt, David Quentin. *America Through Baseball* (Chicago: Nelson-Hall, 1976).

Wills, Maury and Steve Gardner. *It Pays to Steal* (Englewood Cliffs: Prentice Hall, 1963).

Winks, Robin. *The Blacks in Canada: A History* (New Haven: Yale University Press, 1971).

Woodward, C. Vann. *The Strange Career of Jim Crow* (3rd ed., New York: Oxford University Press, 1974).

Young, Andrew S. "Doc". *Great Negro Baseball Stars and How They Made the Major Leagues* (New York: A.S. Barnes, 1953).

ARTICLES:

Broom, Leonard and Philip Selznick, "The Jackie Robinson Case," in John T. Talamini and Charles H. Page, eds., *Sports and Society: An Anthology* (Boston: Little Brown, 1973).

Cohane, Tim. "A Branch Grows in Brooklyn," *Look* (March 19, 1946).

Dodson, Dan W. "The Integration of Negroes in Baseball," *The Journal of Educational Sociology* (October, 1954).

"Family Man, Jackie Robinson," *Ebony* (September, 1947).

Frio, Daniel C. and Marc Onigman. "Good Field, No Hit: The Image of Latin American Baseball Players in the American Press, 1871-1946," *Revista/Review Interamericana* (Summer, 1979).

"The Future of Negroes in the Big Leagues," *Ebony* (May, 1949).

Gross, Milton. "The Truth About Happy Chandler," *Sport* (April, 1949).

Head, John. "Great Grandaddy vs. Jackie Robinson," *Southern Exposure* (Fall, 1979).

Leggett, William. "The Tortured Road to 715," *Sports Illustrated* (May 28, 1973).

Lowenfish, Lee. "Sport, Race, and the Baseball Business," *Arena Review* (Spring, 1978).

Loy, John W. and Joseph McElvogue. "Racial Segregation in American Sport," *International Review of Sport Sociology* (1970).

Manley, Effa. "What's Right With the Negro Leagues," *Our World* (August, 1948).

Meany, Tom. "Does Jackie Robinson Belong in the Hall of Fame?" *Sport* (November, 1957).

Murray, Arch. "Brooklyn Spells Hustle," in *Street and Smith's Pictorial Baseball Yearbook* (1947).

Oursler, Fulton. "Rookie of the Year," *Reader's Digest* (February, 1948).

Pascal, Anthony and Leonard A. Rapping. "The Economics of Racial Discrimination in Organized Baseball," in Anthony H. Pascal, ed., *Discrimination in Economic Life* (New York: Heath, 1972).

"Rap with Jackie Robinson on racism in sports, 'progress' and the Black athlete," *Black Sports* (March, 1972).

Rice, Robert, "Thoughts on Baseball," *New Yorker* (May 26, June 2, 1950).

Robinson, Jackie. "The Most Unforgettable Character I've Met," *Reader's Digest* (October, 1961).

Robinson, Jackie. "What's Wrong With the Negro Leagues," *Ebony* (May, 1948).

Rosenblatt, Aaron. "Negroes in Baseball: The Failure of Success," *Transaction* (September, 1967).

Rosengarten, Theodore. "Reading the Hops: Recollections of Lorenzo 'Piper' Davis and the Negro Baseball League," *Southern Exposure* (1977).

Scully, Gerald. "Discrimination: The Case of Baseball," in *Government and the Sports Business* (Washington, D.C.: The Brookings Institute, 1974).

Smith, Ron A. "The Paul Robeson-Jackie Robinson Saga and A Political Collision," *Journal of Sport History* (Summer, 1979).

Thompson, Hank with Arnold Hano. "How I Wrecked My Life—and How I Hope to Save It," *Sport* (December, 1965).

Weaver, Bill L. "The Black Press and the Assault on Professional Baseball's Color Line, October, 1945-April, 1947," *Phylon* (Winter, 1979).

Young, A.S. "Doc". "The Jackie Robinson Era," *Ebony* (November, 1955).

Young, A.S. "Doc". "How Sports Helped Break the Color Line," *Ebony* (September, 1963).

UNPUBLISHED ARTICLES:

Crepeau, Richard. "The Jake Powell Incident and the Press: A Study in Black and White. Paper presented at the meetings of the North American Society for Sport History, Banff (May, 1980).

Mann, Arthur. "The Negro and Baseball: The National Game Faces A Racial Challenge Long Ignored," Mann Papers, Library of Congress, Washington, D.C.

Onigman, Marc. "The Integration of Major League Baseball, 1900-1947." Paper presented at the meetings of the Organization of American Historians, San Francisco (April, 1980).

Tygiel, Jules. "The Court-Martial of Jackie Robinson," forthcoming, *American Heritage*.

Index

388   INDEX

Doby, Larry (*Cont.*)
    ground, 212–13; joins Cleveland In-
    dians, 212–19; as manager, 339; 1948
    season, 232–40, 243
Dodgertown, 316–17
Dodson, Dan, 54, 57–58, 67, 162, 177,
    195, 201, 333
Doubleday, Abner, 10
Douglas, Paul, 333
Doyle, Jimmy, 93
Drebinger, John, 200
Dressen, Chuck, 305, 307, 322
Dudley, Bruce, 140–41
Duffy, Hugh, 44
Dufresne, Marcel, 153
Dunbar, Lee, 74, 90
Duncan, Frank, 220
Durocher, Leo, 31, 79, 190; as Dodger
    manager, 166–67, 170, 173–74, 241;
    as Giant manager, 263–64, 289–90,
    322; suspension of, 176–77, 181, 198
Durrett, Red, 5, 7, 120
Dyer, Eddie, 186
Dykes, Jimmy, 39

Easter, Luscious "Luke," 246–48, 250–
    52, 259–60, 286, 288, 305, 309
Eastern Colored League, 22
Eastern Interstate League, 15
Eastern League, 79, 242, 244, 251, 255,
    262, 330
East-West All-Star game, 24, 72, 302
Edwards, Bruce, 175, 204
Egan, Dave, 44, 177, 329
Ehlers, Art, 258, 287
Einstein, Charles, 289–90, 302
El Centro Imperials, 224
Ellis, Frank, 131
Ellison, Ralph, 252–53
Emancipation Proclamation, 75
Erskine, Carl, 312, 322
Escalera, Nino, 281, 293, 304
Ethridge, Mark, 265
Evangeline League, 273, 277

Fair Employment Practices Commission,
    43, 239
Fallgren, Jack, 149
fan boycotts, 122, 265–67, 278–79, 329
fans, black, 3, 222, 224, 230, 247–48,
    290; and Jackie Robinson, 83, 107,
    114–15, 130–31, 141, 178, 266–68,
    320–21; in South, 266–74, 278, 316–
    18
fans; Brooklyn, 170, 178, 181, 197, 202;
    Canadian, 83, 125–26, 143–45, 153;
    Cuban, 165–66; in North, 5, 128, 196,
    205, 212, 215, 233, 237, 290, 303–4;

    Panamanian, 173; in West, 246–48,
    252–54; white southern, 107, 114,
    122, 141–42, 262, 267–74, 282, 317–
    18, 342. *See also* attendance; baseball
    players, black; harassment by fans;
    fans, black
Faubus, Orville, 332–33
Federal Bureau of Investigation, 256
Feeney, Charles "Chub," 264
Felder, Ben, 273
Feller, Bob, 27, 76, 160, 202–3, 243
Ferguson, Elmer, 74
Fernandez, Chico, 328
Fetchit, Stepin, 19, 27, 305
fights, interracial, 255–56, 297, 309–10;
    fears of, 39, 66, 114
Finch, Bob, 105, 145–46
Finch, Frank, 247
Fishel, Bob, 229, 232, 313
Fitzgerald, Tommy, 142–43
Flaherty, Vincent X., 60, 194
Fleming, Les, 215
Flood, Curt, 280, 282–84, 303, 314, 319,
    324
Florida International League, 273
Florida State League, 91
football, 60–62, 73, 83, 91, 212, 270,
    294, 334–35
Forbes, Frank, 53
Ford, Whitey, 296, 305
Foster, Bill, 28
Foster, Rube, 18, 22
Fowler, Bud, 10–16
Foxx, Jimmy, 336
Frankfurter, Felix, 285
Franklin, Bernice, 197
Franks, Herman, 125, 135
Frederick Douglass Non-Partisan Civic
    League, 131
Freeman, Herschel, 303–4
French Canadians, 123–24, 140, 143,
    152–53, 156
Frick, Ford, 31–32, 41, 80, 186–88, 285,
    287, 302, 324
Furillo, Carl, 171, 191, 309

Gaines, Ernest J., 196, 294
Gallipeau, Gus, 255
Gandhi, Mohandas K. (Mahatma), 49
Garagiola, Joe, 183, 204
Gardner, J. Alvin, 270
Garrett, Lula Jones, 132
Gaven, Mike, 175
Gavreau, Romeo, 71
Gee, Sammy, 224
Geraghty, Ben, 283
Germinio, Hugo, 75
Gibbon, Frank, 234